BOARD OF EDITORS
RICHARD J. CONVISER
Professor of Law, IIT/Kent
MICHAEL R. ASIMOW
Professor of Law, U.C.L.A.
JOHN A. BAUMAN
Professor of Law, U.C.L.A.
PAUL D. CARRINGTON
Dean and Professor of Law, Duke University
JESSE H. CHOPER
Professor of Law, U.C. Berkeley
GEORGE E. DIX
Professor of Law, University of Texas
JESSE DUKEMINIER
Professor of Law, U.C.L.A.
MELVIN A. EISENBERG
Professor of Law, U.C. Berkeley
WILLIAM A. FLETCHER
Professor of Law, U.C. Berkeley
MARC A. FRANKLIN
Professor of Law, Stanford University
EDWARD C. HALBACH, JR.
Professor of Law, U.C. Berkeley
GEOFFREY C. HAZARD, JR.
Professor of Law, University of Pennsylvania
STANLEY M. JOHANSON
Professor of Law, University of Texas
THOMAS M. JORDE
Professor of Law, U.C. Berkeley
HERMA HILL KAY
Dean and Professor of Law, U.C. Berkeley
JOHN H. McCORD
Professor of Law, University of Illinois
PAUL MARCUS
Professor of Law, College of William and Mary
RICHARD L. MARCUS
Professor of Law, U.C. Hastings
ROBERT H. MNOOKIN
Professor of Law, Harvard University
THOMAS D. MORGAN
Professor of Law, George Washington University
JARRET C. OELTJEN
Professor of Law, Florida State University
JAMES C. OLDHAM
Professor of Law, Georgetown University
WILLIAM A. REPPY, JR.
Professor of Law, Duke University
THOMAS D. ROWE, JR.
Professor of Law, Duke University
JON R. WALTZ
Professor of Law, Northwestern University
DOUGLAS J. WHALEY
Professor of Law, Ohio State University
CHARLES H. WHITEBREAD
Professor of Law, U.S.C.
KENNETH H. YORK
Professor of Law, Pepperdine University

MW01703516

gilbert
LAW SUMMARIES

CRIMINAL LAW

Fifteenth Edition

George E. Dix
Professor of Law
University of Texas

THE barbri GROUP

A COMPLETE PUBLICATIONS CATALOG IS FEATURED AT THE BACK OF THIS BOOK.

HARCOURT BRACE LEGAL AND PROFESSIONAL PUBLICATIONS, INC.
EDITORIAL OFFICES: 176 W. Adams, Suite 2100, Chicago, IL 60603
gilbert LAW SUMMARIES
REGIONAL OFFICES: New York, Chicago, Los Angeles, Washington, D.C.
Distributed by: **Harcourt Brace & Company** 6277 Sea Harbor Drive, Orlando, FL 32887 (800)787-8717

PROJECT EDITOR
Elizabeth L. Snyder, B.A., J.D.
Attorney At Law

QUALITY CONTROL EDITOR
Blythe C. Smith, B.A.

Copyright © 1997 by Harcourt Brace Legal and Professional Publications, Inc. All rights reserved. No part of this publication may be reproduced or transmitted in any form or by any means, electronic or mechanical, including photocopy, recording, or any information storage and retrieval system, without permission in writing from the publisher. Printed in the United States of America.

gilbert
LAW SUMMARIES

Titles Available

Administrative Law
Agency & Partnership
Antitrust
Bankruptcy
Basic Accounting for Lawyers
Business Law
California Bar Performance Test Skills
Civil Procedure
Commercial Paper & Payment Law
Community Property
Conflict of Laws
Constitutional Law
Contracts
Corporations
Criminal Law
Criminal Procedure
Dictionary of Legal Terms
Estate & Gift Tax
Evidence
Family Law
Federal Courts
First Year Questions & Answers
Future Interests
Income Tax I (Individual)
Income Tax II (Corporate)
Labor Law
Legal Ethics (Prof. Responsibility)
Legal Research, Writing, & Analysis
Multistate Bar Exam
Personal Property
Property
Remedies
Sales & Lease of Goods
Securities Regulation
Secured Transactions
Torts
Trusts
Wills

Also Available:

First Year Program
Pocket Size Law Dictionary
The Eight Secrets Of Top Exam Performance In Law School

All Titles Available at Your Law School Bookstore, or Call to Order: 1-800-787-8717

Harcourt Brace Legal and Professional Publications, Inc.
176 West Adams, Suite 2100
Chicago, IL 60603

There are two things BAR/BRI will do for you:

1 Get you through LAW SCHOOL

2 Get you through the BAR EXAM

[O.K. we'll throw in a highlighter*]

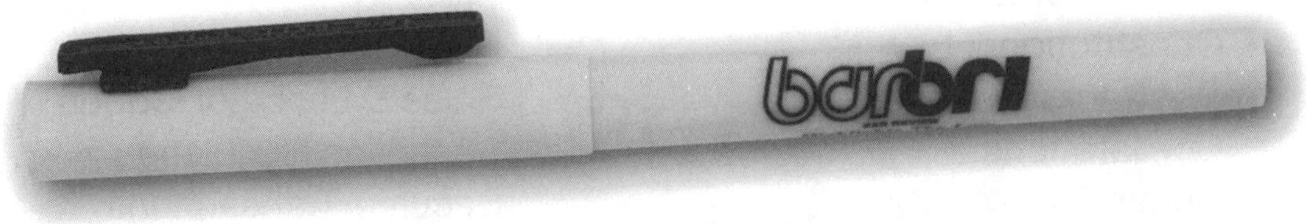

*Available at your local BAR/BRI office.

gilbert
LAW SUMMARIES

Over 4 Million Copies Sold!

- Gilbert Law Summaries
- Legalines
- Law School Legends Audio Tapes
- Employment Guides
- Casebriefs Interactive Software

barbri
BAR REVIEW

Relied On By Over 600,000 Students!

- Lectures, Outlines & Mini Review
- Innovative Computer Software
- Multistate, Essay & Performance Workshops
- Complete MPRE Preparation
- First Year Review Program

THE **barbri** GROUP

Our Only Mission Is Test Preparation

BAR/BRI Bar Review 1-888-3BARBRI
GILBERT LAW SUMMARIES 1-800-787-8717

SUMMARY OF CONTENTS

Page

gilbert

capsule summary

criminal law

Text Section

I. INTRODUCTION

A. CRIME DEFINED

A crime is an act or omission prohibited by law for the protection of the public, the violation of which is prosecuted by the state and punishable by fine, incarceration, and/or other restriction of liberty . . . . [1]

B. SOURCES OF CRIMINAL LAW

The definition of the basic crimes and defenses are taken from the English common law. Criminal matters are now largely governed by statute, but the interpretation of statutes often refers to the common law cases . . . . [2]

C. CLASSIFICATIONS OF CRIMES

1. **Felonies and Misdemeanors:** Except for treason, crimes traditionally have been classified as felonies or misdemeanors. At common law, felonies are those offenses punishable by forfeiture of property. Statutory felonies are generally those offenses punishable by death or incarceration in a prison for more than one year. Misdemeanors are those offenses that are not classified as felonies . . [5]
2. **Malum in Se and Malum Prohibitum:** Malum in se crimes are ***inherently*** dangerous, bad, or immoral (*e.g.*, the common law felonies). Malum prohibitum offenses are not prohibited because of any basic immorality but out of ***necessity*** to regulate the general welfare (*e.g.*, prohibition against driving on the wrong side of the road) . . . . [10]

D. BURDEN OF PROOF AND RELATED MATTERS

1. **Proof Beyond a Reasonable Doubt:** Due process and the defendant's Sixth Amendment right to a jury trial require that the prosecution prove ***each element beyond a reasonable doubt*** before a jury; *i.e.*, an element may not be withdrawn from jury consideration and decided as a matter of law by the court . . . . [14]
2. **Defensive Matters:** Due process permits placing the burden on the defendant to prove most defenses . . . . [16]
3. **Presumptions and Inferences:** Presumptions and permissive inferences may so interfere with the prosecution's burden of proof as to violate due process (*e.g.*, presumptions regarding elements of crime, such as intent) . . . . [19]
   a. **Permissive inferences:** Due process is not violated if a jury is instructed that it may, but need not, infer one fact from another if the ultimate fact to be inferred more likely than not flows from the fact . . . . [21]
4. **Homicide Prosecutions—Allocating Burdens**
   a. **Burden of proof on provocation by presuming malice:** If the jury in a murder prosecution is permitted to presume malice aforethought from the killing itself, thus requiring the defendant to prove a sudden provocation in order to reduce the crime to voluntary manslaughter, due process is violated . . . . [22]
   b. **Burden of proof on extreme emotional disturbance:** When intent to kill is an element, the defendant's due process rights are ***not*** violated by

Copyright © 1997 Harcourt Brace Legal and Professional Publications, Inc.

requiring him to prove that he acted under extreme emotional disturbance which would reduce the killing to manslaughter .... [24]

II. THE CRIMINALIZATION DECISION

A. JUSTIFICATIONS FOR PUNISHMENT

1. **Specific Prevention:** Punishment may prevent an offender from committing future crimes through ***deterrence*** or ***incapacitation*** (restraint) of the offender, and by affording her the opportunity for ***treatment and possible rehabilitation*** .... [26]
2. **General Prevention:** Penalizing offenders may also prevent others from committing crimes by ***generally deterring*** them through anticipation of similar punishment, by ***educating*** the public as to the ***moral*** wrong of crime, by ***creating social solidarity***, and by ***keeping others from taking the law into their own hands*** .... [30]
3. **Retribution:** The fact that defendant committed a crime is ***itself*** reason to punish her .... [35]

B. COSTS VS. BENEFITS

The benefits to be gained from making conduct criminal turn on the extent to which the social interests justifying criminalization will be furthered. But any benefits must be weighed against the direct costs of criminalization (*e.g.*, costs of law enforcement, etc.), the incidental costs (*e.g.*, improper searches and seizures), and the impact on society .... [37]

III. BASIC LEGAL LIMITS UPON CRIMINAL LAW

A. CONSTITUTIONAL RIGHT OF PRIVACY

Although the Constitution does not expressly protect the right of privacy, the Supreme Court has found such a right implied in several constitutional provisions. A person may not be convicted for engaging in conduct falling within the scope of this federal right (*e.g.*, the use of contraceptives and the private possession of obscenity) .... [39]

B. DUE PROCESS PROHIBITION AGAINST VAGUENESS

1. **General Rule—Criminal Statute Must Be Precise:** The Due Process Clauses of the Fifth and Fourteenth Amendments require that criminal statutes must be precise so as to give ***notice*** as to what conduct is criminal and to ***discourage arbitrary enforcement*** .... [44]
2. **Criteria for Evaluating Vagueness:** A criminal statute is unconstitutionally vague if it fails to define the offense with sufficient definiteness so that ordinary people can understand what is prohibited and so as to discourage arbitrary enforcement of the statute .... [45]
3. **Curing Vagueness by "Scienter":** A statute that would otherwise be unconstitutionally vague may be upheld if it requires that the offense be committed with "scienter" or intent .... [49]

C. CRUEL AND UNUSUAL PUNISHMENT

The Eighth Amendment prohibition against cruel and unusual punishment is binding on the states via the Fourteenth Amendment and imposes a number of different limits on criminal law .... [50]

1. **Inherently Impermissible Punishments:** ***Inherently*** barbaric or degrading punishment is prohibited. Torture, death by painful or lingering methods, and expatriation are probably also prohibited .... [51]
2. **Disproportionate Penalties:** Penalties that are so ***grossly and outrageously disproportionate*** to the defendant's conduct are also prohibited .... [52]

3. **Death Penalty:** The death penalty is constitutionally permissible if it is imposed under a procedure that adequately assures evenhanded determinations as to whether the penalty is appropriate in a particular case .... [54]

D. MULTIPLE LIABILITY FOR IDENTICAL OR RELATED CRIMINAL ACTS

1. **In General—Overlapping Criminal Liability:** Overlapping liability may be incurred when the ***same act constitutes several crimes*** (*e.g.*, murder and battery) and when acts constituting ***different offenses are committed closely together*** and for ***related reasons*** (*e.g.*, burglary as a means to commit a larceny). Such overlapping criminal liability is sometimes criticized as resulting in disproportionately severe punishment .... [61]
2. **Common Law Doctrine of Merger:** If the same act was both a felony and a misdemeanor, the misdemeanor merged into the felony and there could be ***no conviction*** for the misdemeanor. The doctrine did ***not*** apply if ***both*** crimes were misdemeanors or felonies .... [63]
   a. **Modern law:** Today there is ***no*** common law merger in the United States . [64]
3. **Fifth Amendment Prohibition Against Double Jeopardy:** The constitutional prohibition against double jeopardy primarily applies to repeated prosecutions for the same or perhaps related crimes .... [65]
   a. **Multiple convictions in one proceeding:** If a legislature makes the same conduct two crimes, a defendant ***may*** be convicted in ***one proceeding*** of both offenses as long as this was the ***legislative intent*** .... [66]
   b. **Determining legislative intent—*Blockburger* rule:** In federal cases, Congress is presumed to have intended to prohibit punishing a defendant for two crimes arising from the same conduct unless ***each crime*** requires proof of an ***additional fact*** that the other does not .... [68]
      (1) **Caveat:** The *Blockburger* rule is a means of determining intent. If there is ***direct*** evidence that Congress did intend double punishment, *Blockburger* does not apply .... [69]
4. **State Double Jeopardy Prohibitions:** Many state constitutions contain prohibitions against double jeopardy similar to the federal provisions. State courts may construe these provisions more stringently, thus giving defendants broader protection than the federal provision .... [70]
   a. **Multiple interests approach:** State double jeopardy provisions may bar punishment for related crimes unless those crimes are designed to protect different social interests .... [71]
5. **Statutory Bars to Multiple Conviction or Punishment:** State statutes often prohibit multiple convictions for a ***single act***. Some courts have interpreted "single act" to include several crimes related in their commission and committed pursuant to a ***single and primary objective*** .... [72]
6. **Modern Merger of Offenses as Matter of Legislative Intent:** Courts sometimes hold that a defendant cannot be convicted of related crimes because one offense "merges" into another. However, this is ***not*** the application of the common law merger rule but rather a determination of legislative intent barring convictions for both crimes. Courts often apply the ***Blockburger rule*** *(supra)* in determining the existence of such intent .... [75]
7. **Exception—Multiple Victims:** Where there are multiple victims, a defendant can be convicted of an offense committed on each victim, even if there was only one criminal act .... [77]

IV. ELEMENTS OF CRIMES

A. CRIMINAL ACTS—ACTUS REUS

1. **In General:** An ***affirmative act***, or occasionally a ***failure to act***, is necessary for the commission of a crime. Mere thoughts are not enough .... [78]

a. **Constitutional limitation:** A ***status*** (*e.g.*, being an alcoholic) may not be made a criminal offense. However, there is no constitutional bar to making acts related to a status criminal (*e.g.*, public drunkenness) . . . . [80]

2. **"Acts" Sufficient for Criminal Liability—Affirmative vs. Negative "Acts":** Acts that will support a conviction vary with the crime itself; an act may be an affirmative act or a failure to act (an omission). Some crimes are defined specifically in terms of what acts are required. Other crimes do not particularize the requisite acts, and thus any act or omission that meets the general concepts of a criminal act is sufficient . . . . [82]
   a. **Affirmative acts (acts of commission):** An affirmative act will suffice for criminal liability if it involves some ***conscious*** and ***volitional movement*** . . [83]
      (1) **Exceptions:** A defendant may be held liable if she ***caused her unconsciousness*** or had ***knowledge of pending unconsciousness*** . [87]
   b. **Negative acts (acts of omission):** A defendant's failure to act may support criminal liability where she was under a ***legal duty to act***, had the requisite ***knowledge***, ***and*** it was ***possible*** for her to act . . . . [89]
      (1) **Situations giving rise to legal duties:** A legal duty to act may arise from a relationship between the parties (*e.g.*, parent-child), a particular statute, a contract, the voluntary undertaking of a task, or from creating a situation of peril. Also, if the defendant has a duty to control the conduct of others (*e.g.*, as an employer), she may be obliged to act. Note that a ***moral obligation*** is ***not*** enough . . . . [90]
      (2) **Knowledge required for liability:** In omission cases, a probable majority of courts hold that a defendant must be ***aware of the facts*** giving rise to a legal duty to act. Some jurisdictions require in addition that a defendant be ***aware of the law*** that creates a duty (although in some circumstances, knowledge of this sort is required by due process) . . . . [100]
      (3) **Act must be capable of performance:** For criminal liability to attach, it must have been ***possible*** for the defendant to have done the act. There is no liability where the omission was due to the fact that she lacked the means or ability to perform . . . . [105]

B. ATTENDANT CIRCUMSTANCES

In addition to the requisite elements, many crimes require proof that certain circumstances existed at the time of the act in question. Without a showing of these facts, the defendant's actions are not criminal . . . . [107]

C. CRIMINAL STATE OF MIND—MENS REA

1. **In General:** The element of mens rea establishes what the defendant must have been thinking at the time the act was committed for criminal liability to attach. There is no single "criminal intent"; the intent required for each crime ordinarily is part of the definition of that crime and may vary with regard to the different elements of the crime . . . . [110]
   a. **Compare—motive:** Motive refers to the ***reason*** for acting and generally is ***not*** essential for criminal liability . . . . [113]
2. **Traditional Mens Rea Analysis:** Traditionally, the requisite mens rea is either one of "general intent," "specific intent," or "criminal negligence" . . . . [115]
   a. **General intent:** General intent means only that the defendant must have ***intended to commit the act*** constituting the crime. This is the mental element of any crime not requiring a specific intent or which cannot be established by criminal negligence (*e.g.*, rape is a general intent crime) . . [116]
      (1) **Proof of general intent:** General intent may be ***inferred*** from the commission of the prohibited act . . . . [118]
   b. **Specific intent:** Specific intent is generally an intent to do some ***further act or cause some additional consequences*** beyond that required to

complete the actus reus (*e.g.*, larceny and burglary are specific intent crimes) . . . . [120]

(1) **Proof of specific intent:** Unlike general intent, specific intent must be ***specifically proven*** . . . . [121]

c. **Criminal negligence:** Liability for certain crimes (*e.g.*, manslaughter, battery) may be based on a showing of criminal negligence. In such cases, the defendant acted with ***gross lack of care***. But note that the negligence must involve a ***higher probability of harm*** and a ***greater degree of unreasonableness*** than is necessary for civil liability purposes . . . . [122]

d. **Malice:** Some crimes require malice, which is usually construed as requiring the commission of a volitional act ***without legal excuse or justification***. Ill will or hatred need ***not*** be shown . . . . [124]

(1) **Compare:** Malice may be given a different meaning in relation to certain crimes (*e.g.*, malice aforethought for murder) . . . . [125]

e. **"Willfully," "deliberately," "feloniously":** These terms, as used in criminal statutes, are usually equated with general intent (*supra*) . . . . [126]

f. **Knowledge of law:** Some crimes require that the defendant be aware of the law and that his conduct violated it (*e.g.*, federal tax crimes) . . . . [127]

g. **Proof of intent—federal constitutional requirements:** The prosecution must prove the element of intent beyond a reasonable doubt. A presumption relieving the prosecution of this burden violates the defendant's right to due process . . . . [128]

3. **Strict Liability Crimes:** A few crimes dispense entirely with a mens rea requirement in regard to some or all of the elements . . . . [131]

a. **Identifying strict liability crimes:** Whether a crime imposes strict liability is a matter of ***legislative intent***. Such intent will most likely be found if (i) the crime is a "new" statutory offense; (ii) the crime does not infringe on other person's rights; (iii) the crime is part of a ***regulatory scheme***; (iv) the crime imposes a relatively ***light penalty***; and (v) it appears that requiring proof of mens rea would ***impede*** giving effect to legislative purpose . . . . [134]

(1) **Examples:** ***Public welfare offenses*** are likely to be strict liability crimes. ***Bigamy*** and ***statutory rape*** are common law crimes that have been traditionally regarded as serious strict liability crimes . . . . [139]

b. **Constitutional limitations:** Due process prohibits strict liability in some situations, particularly if a serious penalty is involved and the crime resembles a traditional common law offense for which mens rea has usually been required . . . . [145]

4. **Modern Classifications of State of Mind:** The modern trend is for statutes to adopt the Model Penal Code approach which distinguishes four levels of state of mind . . . . [147]

a. **Different states of mind**

(1) **Purpose:** A ***desire*** to engage in certain conduct or cause a certain result . . . . [149]

(2) **Knowledge:** An ***awareness*** that something will occur or does exist . [150]

(3) **Recklessness:** An ***awareness*** of a ***substantial and unjustifiable risk*** that something will occur or does exist . . . . [152]

(4) **Negligence:** A situation in which a person ***should have been aware*** of a substantial and unjustifiable risk that a certain result would occur or that a certain circumstance would exist . . . . [155]

(a) **Compare:** Recklessness requires a ***conscious awareness*** of the risk involved. Negligence involves circumstances in which a ***reasonable person would have been aware*** of the risk . . . . . [157]

b. **General requirement—at least recklessness:** Unless specifically provided otherwise, a showing of at least recklessness is required as to ***all elements*** of the offense . . . . [158]

5. **"Transferred Intent"—Responsibility for Unintended Results:** Ordinarily, for criminal liability to attach, a defendant must have ***intended the actual harm done***. However, if the defendant intends to harm one person or item of property and does ***similar harm*** to another person or item, she will be treated as if she had, in fact, intended the result that occurred (the intent is transferred) and criminal liability will attach . . . . . [167]

D. CONCURRENCE OF ACTUS REUS AND MENS REA

The defendant's act and intent must concur; *i.e.*, the result must be ***attributable*** to the culpable state of mind . . . . . [170]

1. **Concurrence Between Mens Rea and Act:** Generally, the defendant must have had the requisite intent ***at the moment*** he performed the act . . . . . [171]
2. **Concurrence Between Mens Rea and Result:** If proof of a result is required, the occurrence of the result must be ***attributable*** to the mens rea. However, it is ***not*** essential that the intent and result concur in point of time . . . . . [172]
3. **Special Problem—Mistake of Death Cases:** Special problems arise where the defendant mistakenly believes he has caused death and then, without intent to kill, takes other action which actually does cause death. Jurisdictions are split, with some refusing to find liability because there is no intent, and others finding liability because defendant's behavior was all part of a single scheme . . . . . [174]

E. CAUSATION

If a crime is one that requires proof of a result, the defendant's conduct must be shown to have been the ***legal cause*** of that result. Two kinds of causation must exist . . . . . [175]

1. **Factual Causation:** The prosecution must show that ***"but for"*** the defendant's actions, the result would not have occurred ***when and as it did*** . . . . . [178]
   a. **Speeding up result:** Where the defendant has simply speeded up an ***inevitable result***, most courts find factual causation . . . . . [180]
   b. **Concurrent sufficient cause:** An exception to the general "but for" requirement applies when two factors acting concurrently cause a result and either alone would have been sufficient to cause that result. ***Both*** factors will be considered as factual causes . . . . . [182]
2. **Proximate Causation:** In addition to factual causation, there must be proof that the defendant is the proximate cause of a result. Generally, proximate cause is present when the result occurs as a ***natural and probable consequence*** of defendant's act ***and*** there is ***no intervening factor*** sufficient to break the chain of causation (*i.e.*, a superceding factor) . . . . . [184]
   a. **Intervening factor:** An intervening factor is one set in motion ***after*** the defendant's act. Therefore, a preexisting condition will not break the chain of causation . . . . . [190]
   b. **Unforeseeable:** The intervening factor must have been ***unforeseeable*** by defendant at the time of the act . . . . . [191]
   c. **Sole direct cause:** The intervening factor must also be the ***sole major cause*** of the result . . . . . [196]

V. SCOPE OF CRIMINAL LIABILITY

A. COMPLICITY IN THE CRIME

Complicity rules define those participants in the crime who may be held guilty of the crime itself. Generally, liability extends not only to the actual perpetrator, but also to anyone who has ***encouraged or assisted*** the commission of the crime or, at common law, ***hindered apprehension*** of the perpetrator . . . . . [202]

1. **Common Law Classification of Participants—Party Rules**

a. **Parties to felonies:** These persons are classified according to their role in the perpetration of the crime and whether they were present at its commission . . . . [204]

(1) **Principal in the first degree:** This is the person who ***actually perpetrates*** the crime by his own acts, by the acts of an innocent person, or by means of an inanimate agency . . . . [205]

(2) **Principal in the second degree:** This classification includes a person who ***incites or abets*** the commission of a crime and who is ***actually or constructively present*** at its commission (*e.g.*, a lookout) . [206]

(3) **Accessory before the fact:** This is a person who ***incites or abets*** the principal but who is ***not actually or constructively present*** at the commission of the crime . . . . [208]

(4) **Accessory after the fact:** This is one who receives or assists another, ***knowing*** that the other has committed a felony, in order to ***hinder*** the arrest, prosecution, or conviction of the perpetrator. Note that a ***wife*** could ***not*** be an accessory after the fact at common law . [210]

b. **Significance of party rules:** At common law, a person charged as an accessory could ***not*** be convicted as a principal, and vice versa. An accessory could ***not*** be convicted ***unless the principal was convicted***, nor could an accessory be convicted of a ***higher offense*** than the principal . . . . [212]

c. **Misdemeanors and treason:** No distinction is made among parties to these offenses; all parties are liable as ***principals***. Note that there is ***no*** liability for aiding a person after the commission of a misdemeanor . . . . . [217]

2. **Classification of Participants Under Modern Statutes:** Modern statutes tend to abandon the categories of participants and simply make ***all who aid and abet*** the commission of a crime ***guilty of that crime*** . . . . [219]

a. **Inciters and abettors—Model Penal Code position:** A person is guilty as an ***accomplice*** if she is ***legally accountable*** by her own conduct ***or*** for the conduct of the accused . . . . [221]

b. **Accessory after the fact:** One who would be an accessory after the fact at common law is generally now punished for the commission of a ***separate and distinct offense***; no liability is incurred for the crime of the principal . . . . [222]

c. **Effect of modern changes:** Procedural limitations accompanying the common law party rules no longer exist under most statutory schemes. Thus, the procedural aspects of the law of complicity have been substantially simplified . . . . [223]

(1) **No constitutional bar:** Neither double jeopardy nor due process prohibits the trial and conviction of an aider and abettor after the acquittal of the principal . . . . [226]

3. **Accomplice Liability:** Accomplice liability attaches to those who aid or encourage the commission of a crime . . . . [227]

a. **Requirements for liability:** The defendant must have incited or abetted the perpetration of the crime ***with the requisite mens rea***, and the person incited or abetted must ***actually have committed the offense*** . . . . . [228]

(1) **Abetting:** One abets the commission of a crime if he provides assistance in ***any significant way*** . . . . [230]

(2) **Inciting:** One incites the commission of a crime if he ***encourages*** (*i.e.*, provides any inducement to) another to commit it. However, the ***perpetrator must be aware*** of the encouragement . . . . [235]

(3) **Mens rea requirement:** Authorities agree that an accomplice ***must have the mens rea required for the crime***. However, courts are ***divided*** as to whether an accomplice must ***intend*** that his efforts effectively assist or encourage the successful commission of the crime ***or*** whether awareness that the offense will be committed by the

person aided or encouraged will suffice. (The modern trend is to require that the accomplice act with ***purpose***) .... [238]

(4) **Perpetrator must have committed crime:** The person encouraged or aided must have committed the offense (although conviction of the perpetrator is ***not*** necessary). Jurisdictions are ***split*** on whether an accomplice can assert the ***perpetrator's defenses*** .... [245]

b. **Scope of liability:** The scope of accomplice liability is a controversial subject. The ***traditional rule*** holds accomplices liable for ***all probable consequences*** of their conduct, *i.e.*, crimes incited or abetted ***and*** all crimes committed by the perpetrator that were ***reasonably foreseeable results*** of the contemplated crime. A ***minority view*** limits accomplice liability only to those crimes of the perpetrator that the accomplice ***anticipated and intended*** .... [252]

c. **Possible defenses to accomplice liability**

(1) **Withdrawal:** One who incites or abets another can avoid accomplice liability by ***effective and timely*** withdrawal before the crime is committed. If defendant is an ***inciter***, he need only ***communicate a renunciation*** to the perpetrator; however, if defendant is an ***abettor***, he must also ***deprive*** the given aid of its ***effectiveness*** (*e.g.*, retrieve gun) .... [255]

(2) **Accomplice liability inapplicable:** If the participant is (i) within a special ***class of persons intended to be protected*** by the statute (*e.g.*, a prostitute in a Mann Act prosecution), (ii) a ***victim*** of an offense, or (iii) a person ***inherently necessary*** to commission of the crime (*e.g.*, buyer of cocaine), she is not liable as an accomplice ... [260]

(3) **Compare—accomplice unable to commit crime as perpetrator:** The fact that an accomplice cannot commit a crime by his own actions does not preclude liability as an accomplice to that crime (*e.g.*, a husband can incur liability as an accomplice to the rape of his wife) .... [265]

4. **Liability of Post-Crime Aiders (Accessories After the Fact):** At common law, a defendant is liable as an accessory after the fact if she ***knew*** the person assisted committed a ***felony***, and aid was given for the purpose of ***impeding enforcement*** of the law. However, ***modern statutes*** either retain the category of accessory after the fact but make it a ***separate offense*** with a penalty unrelated to the perpetrator's penalty, or else establish an entirely ***new offense*** (*e.g.*, hindering prosecution) .... [266]

B. VICARIOUS LIABILITY

1. **Definition—Liability for Acts of Others:** Vicarious liability exists when one person is held guilty of a crime committed by another simply ***because of the relationship*** between the two persons. No affirmative participation is required . [277]

2. **When Vicarious Liability Is Imposed—Legislative Intent:** In practice, vicarious liability is usually limited to ***employer-employee*** relationships. However, in all cases, legislative intent determines whether to apply vicarious liability. Absent an expressed intent, the courts look for the existence of certain circumstances (*e.g.*, a business activity, light penalties, no personal fault requirement) .... [280]

a. **Application:** There is a split of authority on the propriety of imposing vicarious liability where a crime was committed in ***disregard of the defendant's (usually employer's) instructions.*** Some courts have ***compromised*** by allowing defendant to ***prove lack of fault*** .... [284]

3. **Constitutional Limits on Vicarious Liability:** Vicarious liability may violate Fourteenth Amendment due process or the Eighth Amendment prohibition against cruel and unusual punishment if the defendant had ***no ability to control*** the actual perpetrator or if conviction would impose a ***severe penalty*** ... [289]

C. CRIMINAL LIABILITY OF CORPORATIONS AND ASSOCIATIONS

1. **Background:** At ***common law***, corporations and associations could ***not*** be convicted of a criminal offense. The ***modern rule*** is to impose ***corporate liability***, although certain ***policy considerations*** continue to cause controversy . . . . [294]
2. **Requirements for Corporate Liability:** Liability is now often imposed on corporations for the acts and omissions of corporate employees if consistent with the ***legislative intent*** and dependent on the nature of the crime involved (*i.e.*, severity of the crime). If the crime is a ***minor*** one, a corporation is usually held liable merely upon proof that the employee was acting in the ***course of his employment***. If the crime is serious, there is disagreement concerning the requirements: Some courts require only that the offense have been committed by an ***employee in the course of the employment***. Others adopt the Model Penal Code approach, which permits conviction only if the perpetration of the offense was ***authorized***, ***performed***, or at least ***recklessly tolerated*** by the board of directors or a high managerial agent. Other jurisdictions require proof that the corporation gave the actual perpetrator ***enough authority to act for it*** in the specific activities related to the criminal conduct . . . . [299]
3. **No Effect on Individual Liability:** Corporate liability has ***no*** effect on the actual perpetrator's criminal responsibility . . . . [307]
4. **Liability of Unincorporated Associations:** Generally, partnerships and other unincorporated associations are ***not*** subjected to criminal conviction for crimes of their individual partners or employees. However, some jurisdictions recognize the ***entity theory*** of partnerships under which partnerships can sue and be sued in their own name. This may lead to criminal prosecutions of such associations in the future . . . . [309]

VI. DEFENSES

A. INFANCY

1. **Common Law:** At common law, a child ***under age seven*** cannot be guilty of a crime. Between the ***ages of seven and fourteen*** a child is ***rebuttably*** presumed incapable of forming criminal intent. Children aged ***fourteen and older*** are treated as adults . . . . [313]
2. **Modern Statutes:** Under both common law and modern statutes, the ***chronological age at the time of the crime controls***. However, modern statutes vary in their treatment of the infancy defense and may depart from the common law rules . . . . [318]
3. **Compare—Juvenile Court Jurisdiction:** All jurisdictions have juvenile court legislation under which children are "adjudicated delinquent" (rather than "convicted") in a juvenile court proceeding. Under some statutes, however, certain children may be tried as adults . . . . [321]

B. INSANITY

1. **In General:** A defendant is entitled to acquittal if he was ***so impaired by mental illness or retardation at the time of the crime*** as to be "insane" within the meaning of the law . . . . [322]
   a. **Compare—incompetency to stand trial:** This concerns the defendant's state of mind ***at the time of the trial*** and is ***not*** a defense; it may, however, postpone the proceedings . . . . [323]
   b. **Compare—diminished capacity:** The diminished capacity rule allows proof of mental illness or retardation to show that the defendant ***lacked the required mens rea*** . . . . [324]
2. **Condition Giving Rise to Insanity:** Although all insanity tests require the defendant to have some sort of mental impairment, not all impairments give rise to insanity . . . . [326]

abolition or limitation of the insanity defense are: difficulty of the courts in making determinations, the time involved with this defense, jury confusion, its bias in favor of wealthier defendants, and inadequate treatment programs. Arguments favoring the retention and broadening of the defense include the fact that certain impaired persons are not ethically blameworthy, individual responsibility is reinforced, and the process could divert proper persons into the mental health system . . . . [356]

5. **Burden of Proof on Insanity:** Before the Hinckley acquittal, most jurisdictions provided that once the defendant raised the defense, the prosecution bore the burden of proving beyond a reasonable doubt that defendant was sane. However, a ***recent trend*** places on the defendant the burden of proving insanity . . . . [359]
6. **Jury Instructions:** Most jurisdictions do not instruct the jury on the consequences of insanity acquittal, although others consider such instructions to be necessary . . . . [362]
7. **Procedure Following Acquittal by Reason of Insanity:** All jurisdictions have commitment procedures for the possible hospitalization of defendants found not guilty by reason of insanity ("NGRI"). Typically, the defendant is automatically committed; then a prompt hearing is held to afford the defendant an opportunity to show that she is no longer dangerous. This procedure is constitutionally adequate, and there is ***no*** constitutional right to release from hospitalization on expiration of the maximum prison term the defendant could have received if convicted . . . . [363]
8. **Guilty But Mentally Ill:** Several states allow a verdict of guilty but mentally ill as an alternative to an insanity acquittal if the jury finds that when the defendant committed the offense, she was mentally ill but not legally insane. Defendant is sentenced under the regular sentencing provisions. If imprisonment is imposed, she must undergo treatment . . . . [368]

C. DIMINISHED CAPACITY

In some states, evidence of mental illness that does not establish insanity may be introduced to prove that the defendant did not have or could not have formed the requisite mens rea for the crime charged. This is known as the ***Wells-Gorshen or diminished capacity rule*** . . . . [371]

1. **Majority Approach Distinguished—Evidence Inadmissible:** A probable majority of courts ***reject*** the rule, reasoning that the insanity defense is the vehicle for relating mental illness to criminal liability and that it should not be circumvented by manipulation of the mens rea requirement . . . . [374]
2. **Application—Limited to Specific Intent Crimes:** Even where recognized, the rule is applied only to specific intent crimes . . . . [375]
3. **Compare—English Diminished Responsibility Rule:** Under the English diminished responsibility rule, a defendant charged with murder will be convicted only of manslaughter if mental illness "substantially impaired his mental responsibility" for the killing . . . . [378]

D. INTOXICATION

1. **Source of Intoxication:** In addition to the ingestion of liquor, the rules apply to the effect of other intoxicating substances, (*e.g.*, drugs and medicine) . . . . . [380]
2. **Involuntary Intoxication:** Involuntary intoxication is a ***complete defense*** if it rendered the defendant insane within the meaning of the jurisdiction's insanity test . . . . [381]
   a. **"Involuntary" defined:** "Involuntary" means the defendant either ***did not know*** the substance ingested was intoxicating or consumed it under ***direct and immediate duress*** even though she knew it was intoxicating . . [382]
   b. **Pathological intoxication:** The Model Penal Code regards intoxication as involuntary if it is grossly excessive in proportion to the amount of the

Text Section

substance consumed and the defendant did not know of her unusual susceptibility . . . [383]

c. **Permanent insanity:** A permanent (or "settled") impairment (*e.g.*, organic brain damage) caused by the defendant's long-term and voluntary use of intoxicants can, under the majority view, sustain an insanity defense . . . . [384]

3. **Voluntary Intoxication:** This is a defense only if it shows that the defendant lacked a ***specific intent*** for the crime charged . . . [385]

   a. **Minority views:** A few jurisdictions entirely ***disregard*** evidence of voluntary intoxication even if it demonstrates lack of specific intent, and a few states permit evidence of voluntary intoxication to be used to negate ***any*** required mental state, not just specific intent . . . [389]

   b. **Application—convincing trier of fact that intoxication negated mens rea:** If a jurisdiction's rule permits evidence of voluntary intoxication to negate the culpable mental state, the defendant must show, at a minimum, that her intoxication raises a reasonable doubt that the prosecution has proved the required mens rea . . . [393]

4. **Compare—Crimes Requiring Proof of Intoxication:** Where intoxication is an element of the crime charged (*e.g.*, public drunkenness), courts have not applied the above rules. Arguably, however, involuntary intoxication should be a defense . . . [394]

E. IGNORANCE OR MISTAKE OF FACT

1. **In General:** Ignorance or mistake of fact is a defense if it shows the defendant ***lacked a mental state*** essential to the crime charged . . . [395]

   a. **"Fact" and "law" distinction:** The Model Penal Code and some states do not distinguish between mistakes of fact and law, simply requiring acquittal if the mistake negates the requisite mens rea . . . [396]

2. **Requirement of "Reasonableness":** Traditionally, the mistake must be reasonable, but many courts depart from this rule where the mistake is offered to disprove ***specific intent*** . . . [399]

   a. **Constitutional issues:** The requirement of reasonableness may violate the defendant's ***due process*** right to have the prosecution prove all elements of the crime and also her ***Sixth Amendment right*** to have a jury determination of guilt or innocence . . . [400]

3. **Requirement that Conduct Have Been Morally and Legally Permissible Had Facts Been as Defendant Believed:** A few decisions have suggested that the mistake must have been such that if the situation had been as the defendant believed it to be, her actions would have been both legally and morally permissible. However, since this would impose strict liability for serious offenses, it is doubtful whether these early cases would be followed today . . . . . [403]

4. **Prosecutions for Strict Liability Offenses:** Ignorance or mistake of fact is ordinarily ***no defense*** to a strict liability crime. However, a number of courts have implied an intent requirement where the defendant offers evidence of a reasonable mistake. Furthermore, some courts unwilling to find a mens rea requirement have still sustained a ***defense of reasonable mistake*** . . . [405]

F. IGNORANCE OR MISTAKE OF LAW

Ignorance or mistake of law arises in two situations: (i) where the defendant lacked the requisite mental state, and (ii) where the defendant had the requisite mental state but believed his conduct was not proscribed by law . . . [408]

1. **Ignorance or Mistake Showing Lack of Mens Rea:** Where a crime requires a particular belief concerning a legal matter, defendant's mistake as to that matter may show she lacked the requisite mental state. If this is the case, the defendant may rely on the mistake to negate the mens rea element of the crime . . [410]

   a. **Reasonableness not required:** The ignorance or mistake need not be reasonable since such a requirement would raise serious doubts regarding the defendant's Sixth Amendment right to have a jury determine guilt or innocence . . . . [411]

2. **Mistaken Belief that Law Will Not Be Violated:** Generally, it is ***no defense*** that the defendant was passively unaware her acts were prohibited by the criminal law or that she affirmatively but mistakenly believed the acts were not prohibited. However, in limited situations, the defendant may base a defense on an ***affirmative decision***, after consideration of the matter, that the law did not make the conduct a crime . . . . [415]
   a. **Constitutional considerations:** Some courts have reasoned that under certain limited circumstances, convictions based on mistaken beliefs that conduct is not criminal violates due process . . . . [419]
   b. **Requirements for defense:** To the extent this defense is recognized, it is limited by two requirements: (i) defendant's belief that her conduct is not prohibited by law ***must be reasonable***, and (ii) defendant must have formed her belief ***based on certain grounds*** that provide assurance that the mistake was made and that it was objectively reasonable . . . . [421]
      (1) **Reliance on statute later held unconstitutional:** If the defendant acted in good faith reliance upon a statute making her conduct permissible, she can assert a defense even though the statute is later held invalid. A similar reliance on a reasonable ***judicial decision*** precludes a conviction . . . . [424]
      (2) **Reliance on official interpretations:** In some jurisdictions, a defense is also established by reasonable reliance upon an interpretation of the law by an official with responsibility for interpreting that law. However, reliance upon ***advice of private counsel*** will ***never*** support a mistake of law defense . . . . [426]

G. NECESSITY OR JUSTIFICATION

Defendant has a defense where he ***reasonably believed*** his actions were necessary to avoid an ***imminent*** and ***greater harm*** than would be caused by commission of the crime. A necessity defense can arise only from situations created by ***physical force of nature***; if duress caused by other persons is involved, the necessity defense is inapplicable . . . . [429]

1. **Requirements**
   a. **Reasonable belief:** The necessity defense requires that the defendant reasonably believe the threatened harm is greater than that resulting from the crime; some courts require that, ***in actual fact***, the threatened harm be greater. In any case, the defense is unavailable if the ***legislature*** has determined that the harm is not greater than that involved in the crime . . . . [431]
   b. **Other requirements—limits on defense:** Some courts require that the defendant show that the threatened harm was ***imminent***, while other decisions require that the defendant ***must not have been at fault***. The necessity defense usually applies only if there were ***no less harmful alternatives*** available . . . . [434]
2. **Economic Necessity Sufficient?** Various decisions have indicated that economic necessity alone will ***not*** justify the commission of a crime . . . . [437]
3. **Defense to Prison Escape?** Courts are especially reluctant to accept the necessity defense when it is offered in a prosecution for escape from prison. To limit the defense in this situation, some courts require that the defendant surrender as soon as the necessity has lost its coercive force . . . . [438]

H. DURESS

It is a defense to all but the most serious crimes (*i.e.*, intentional murder) that the defendant committed the crime under duress . . . . [439]

1. **Requirements:** Traditionally, there is sufficient duress only where the conduct of another causes the defendant to ***reasonably believe*** that unless he perpetrated

Text Section

the crime, he or some third person would suffer ***imminent death or serious bodily harm***. There must ***in actual fact*** have been a sufficient threat made . . [440]

a. **Submission must be reasonable:** The defendant's submission to the coercion and demand that he commit the crime must be reasonable . . . [444]

2. **Limitation—Not Applicable to Intentional Killings:** Although duress is not applicable to intentional murder, it is unclear whether it can be asserted in defense to ***felony murder*** (since it provides a defense to the underlying felony). In a prosecution for first degree murder, however, duress may show a ***lack of premeditation***, which reduces the offense to second degree murder . . . . [446]

3. **Compare—Coercion of Wife by Husband:** At common law, a wife is not responsible for crimes she commits under her husband's coercion. If she perpetrated the offense in his ***presence***, it is rebuttably ***presumed*** that he coerced her. ***Most jurisdictions have now abandoned*** this common law rule, and today, duress must be proven under the generally applicable standards . . . . . . [451]

I. ENTRAPMENT

1. **In General:** An entrapment defense rests upon enticement by a law enforcement officer or one acting as an agent of an officer . . . . [454]

a. **Not a constitutional rule:** No specific formulation of the entrapment defense need be adopted as a matter of due process . . . . [455]

2. **Substantive Limitations:** Entrapment is ***limited to nonserious crimes*** and cannot be asserted in defense to crimes involving serious injury (*e.g.*, rape, murder). Furthermore, ***only law enforcement officers and agents can entrap***; the defense is inapplicable to acts by purely private individuals . . . . [457]

3. **Procedural Limitation—Defendant Cannot Deny Act:** In some jurisdictions, a defendant cannot both deny commission of the act constituting the crime and claim entrapment. However, the Supreme Court has held that under ***federal criminal law***, a defendant ***can*** deny guilt and alternatively claim entrapment . [459]

4. **Entrapment Criteria:** There are several views concerning what must be shown to establish entrapment . . . . [461]

a. **Traditional (subjective) standard:** Entrapment exists only if a law enforcement officer (or agent) ***creates the intent*** to commit the crime in the mind of a person ***not otherwise predisposed*** to commit crimes of this sort . . . . [462]

(1) **Predisposition:** The accused's predisposition to commit the crime is the ***crucial issue*** and is decided by the jury. Under federal law, it must be shown that the defendant was ***predisposed prior to first being approached*** by government agents . . . . [463]

(2) **Burden of proof:** The traditional approach requires the defendant to establish that officers ***induced*** him to commit the crime. Thereafter the prosecution bears the burden of proving beyond a reasonable doubt that the ***defendant was predisposed***. . . . . [466]

(3) **Procedural disadvantages:** Because predisposition is at issue, the prosecution can introduce much evidence that would otherwise be inadmissible (*e.g.*, evidence of prior crimes and reputation) . . . . . . [467]

b. **Modern (objective) standard:** Entrapment exists if the offense was committed ***in response to law enforcement activity*** that was reasonably likely to cause a ***reasonable*** (but unpredisposed) ***person*** to commit a crime. The ***focus is on the nature of the police activity*** and its likelihood to induce commission of the crime; the defendant's own predisposition is irrelevant . . . . [468]

(1) **Fewer procedural disadvantages:** Entrapment under this approach is a matter for the court to decide (rather than the jury) and evidence of predisposition is ***not*** admissible . . . . [473]

c. **Other police misconduct as entrapment:** In a few jurisdictions, entrapment may be found if a law enforcement officer ***provides materials*** for the commission of the offense or approaches a subject ***without probable cause*** (or at least a reasonable suspicion) to believe the suspect is predisposed to commit crimes of the sort involved. At least one court found entrapment where the police conduct, for any reason, was so offensive as to shake public confidence in law enforcement . . . . [474]

J. CONSENT AND RELATED MATTERS

To constitute a defense, the consent must be ***legally effective*** . . . . [478]

1. **Consent as Negating Element of Crime:** Consent prevents liability for a crime requiring that the act be perpetrated without the victim's consent (*e.g.*, rape) . [479]
2. **Consent as Defense to Assault or Battery:** As to all other crimes, consent is ordinarily ***no bar to conviction***. However, it may be a defense to minor assault or battery if ***no serious bodily injury*** was involved, if there is ***widespread acceptance of the risk*** (*e.g.*, football game), and if there is a ***distinct beneficial effect*** attending the defendant's conduct (*e.g.*, medical surgery) . . . . [480]
3. **Legal Effectiveness of Consent:** In all cases, the consent must be legally effective. It must have been: (i) ***given voluntarily***; (ii) by a person with ***legal capacity*** to consent; and (iii) the consent must be ***free of fraud or mistake*** concerning the very nature of the conduct at issue . . . . [482]
4. **Compare—Condonation No Defense:** Ordinarily, the victim's ***forgiveness*** after the commission of a crime is ***no*** defense unless it is a statutorily authorized compromise . . . . [486]
5. **Compare—Negligence or Criminality of Victim No Defense:** The victim's negligence or criminal activity is not a defense because crimes involve wrongs against the public . . . . [488]

K. SELF-DEFENSE

A person is privileged to use such force as ***reasonably*** appears necessary to defend herself against an apparent threat of ***unlawful*** and ***immediate*** violence from another . . . . [490]

1. **General Requirements for Self-Defense:** Whether or not deadly force is used, self-defense requires that the defendant have a ***reasonable belief*** that she was ***threatened with imminent physical harm*** and that ***force was necessary to prevent the harm*** . . . . [491]
2. **Additional Requirements Where Deadly Force Used:** Deadly force may be used in self-defense ***only*** if the defendant ***reasonably believes*** the other person would inflict ***death or great bodily harm*** upon her and the use of deadly force is ***necessary*** to prevent this . . . . [497]
   a. **Compare:** If the defendant is threatened with ***nondeadly harm*** that can be prevented only with deadly force in self-defense, the law expects the defendant to submit to the nondeadly injury . . . . [498]
   b. **Duty to retreat:** Most jurisdictions ***no longer require the defendant to retreat*** before using deadly force, even if safe retreat is possible. And, in jurisdictions where the duty to retreat is the rule, there is ***no obligation to retreat*** when it is ***unsafe*** or when ***the defendant is attacked in her own home*** . . . . [500]
3. **Special Problem—Battered Victim:** Assertion of self-defense arising from a long history of abuse creates problems involving the issues of ***imminence and unreasonableness***. Some courts have held that reasonableness of a defendant's actions must be evaluated in light of her physical and psychological characteristics, her specific experiences, and perhaps the disadvantaged position of women in society . . . . [507]
4. **Limitation—Right of Aggressor to Self-Defense:** One who was the ***initial aggressor cannot*** use force in self-defense ***unless*** (i) the victim has responded with ***excessive force***, ***or*** (ii) the ***aggressor first withdraws*** from the affray (usually by notifying the adversary of his desire to desist) . . . . [513]

Text Section

5. **Resisting Unlawful Arrest:** Traditionally, force can be used to resist an ***unlawful*** arrest. However, there is an increasing trend away from this rule. Some jurisdictions reject it entirely and others allow use of force to resist only when the unlawful arrest is ***accomplished by excessive force*** . . . . [518]
6. **Compare—"Imperfect" Self-Defense:** If ***the defendant causes death*** while acting in what he honestly but ***unreasonably believes*** to be self-defense, he cannot escape conviction. However, some jurisdictions will reduce the crime from murder to manslaughter (*see infra*) . . . . [522]

L. DEFENSE OF OTHERS

Reasonable force may also be used to defend another person against unlawful harm . . . . [523]

1. **Relationship with Party Defended:** In some jurisdictions, the defendant has a defense only if he stands in a familial or employment relationship to the person aided. The ***modern view***, however, requires ***no special relationship***, and reasonable force may be used to defend ***any third person*** . . . . [524]
2. **Right of Party Defended to Act in Self-Defense:** Some courts uphold the defendant's use of ***reasonable*** force in defense of another ***only*** if the person aided has a right to defend himself (*i.e.*, defendant stands in the place of the person assisted). However, the better rule sustains the defense so long as the defendant ***reasonably believed*** the person assisted had the legal right to act in self-defense . . . . [527]
3. **Compare—Force to Prevent Criminal Offense:** The circumstances under which the defendant claims to have acted in defense of others may also support the defense of crime prevention (*see infra*) . . . . [531]

M. PROTECTION OF PROPERTY

1. **In General:** The right of use force in protection of property is much ***more limited*** than the use of force in protecting persons . . . . [532]
   a. **Deadly force not allowed:** Deadly force ordinarily can ***never*** be used merely to defend one's property. However, deadly force may be justified when defendant's reasonable use of force in protection of property is met with an attack threatening imminent serious bodily harm or, in some cases, in defense of one's ***dwelling*** . . . . [533]
2. **Reasonable Nondeadly Force:** Nondeadly force ***may be used*** where it reasonably appears necessary to prevent or terminate an unlawful intrusion onto, or interference with, property in defendant's possession. Usually a ***request to desist*** must be made ***before*** using any force unless it would be futile or dangerous to do so . . . . [536]
3. **Property in Possession of Another:** Traditionally, the property defended must be in the defender's ***lawful possession***. However, the Model Penal Code permits the use of nondeadly force when the property is in the possession of defendant or another for whose protection defendant acts . . . . [538]
4. **Use of Force to Regain or Reenter Property:** Nondeadly force may be used if action is taken ***immediately after the wrongful intrusion*** or in ***hot pursuit*** of the dispossessor . . . . [540]
5. **"Spring Guns" and Similar Devices:** Traditionally, injuries inflicted by mechanical devices are justifiable only if the person who set the device would have been justified in inflicting the same harm had he been present . . . . [543]

N. PROTECTION OF DWELLING

Jurisdictions greatly differ regarding a defendant's right to use force in defense of his dwelling . . . . [547]

1. **Common Law View—Deadly Force in Defense of Dwelling:** Early common law permitted use of deadly force if the defendant reasonably believed it was

necessary to prevent a forcible entry and a warning to desist had first been given to the intruder. There was ***no duty to retreat*** . . . . [548]

2. **Modern View—Limited Right to Use Deadly Force:** Modern courts ***limit*** the right to use deadly force to situations where the defendant reasonably believed the intruder intended to ***commit a felony or harm someone*** in the dwelling . . [550]
   a. **Intruder already inside dwelling:** Courts are split regarding use of deadly force when the intruder has already entered. Some courts rationalize that once an intruder has gained entry, the defense of dwelling right no longer is applicable; use of force is governed by other rules such as self-defense . [552]
   b. **Statutory provisions:** Several jurisdictions have legislated extreme provisions permitting use of force to defend one's dwelling (*e.g.*, Colorado's "Make My Day" statute authorizing use of ***any degree of force*** if certain minimal requirements are met) . . . . [553]

O. USE OF FORCE TO EFFECTUATE ARREST

1. **Right of Police Officers:** A police officer may use whatever ***nondeadly*** force reasonably appears necessary to make an arrest for a felony ***or*** misdemeanor. The use of ***deadly force*** has ***traditionally*** been limited to situations where an officer suspects commission of a ***felony*** . . . . [555]
   a. **Modern view:** Deadly force is limited to arrests of ***dangerous defendants*** or those ***reasonably*** believed to have committed a ***dangerous felony*** . . [557]
      (1) **Fourth Amendment requirement:** An arrest is unconstitutionally unreasonable if the arresting officer used deadly force while not reasonably believing the arrestee posed a significant threat of death or serious bodily injury. Such an arrest gives rise to a ***civil cause of action*** for damages . . . . [559]
   b. **Reasonable appearance controls:** The defense is available so long as the officer reasonably believes the suspect is guilty, even if the suspect is actually innocent . . . . [560]
   c. **Compare:** An officer who is met with resistance in attempting an arrest may have the right to use force (including deadly force). Note that this would be ***self-defense*** . . . . [561]
2. **Right of Private Persons:** A private person also has the right to use force to make an arrest, but unlike police officers, it is ***not enough that he had a reasonable belief*** that grounds for use of force existed. If he causes ***death***, a defense exists ***only if a felony was in fact committed*** and the ***person killed in fact committed it***. The law is less clear where death is ***not*** caused . . . . [562]
   a. **Compare:** Where a private person is called on to ***assist a police officer*** in making an arrest, he has the ***same privilege*** as the officer . . . . [566]
3. **Use of Force to Prevent Escape from Custody:** Force may be used to thwart a custodial escape ***if*** that force would have been allowed to effectuate the arrest in the first place . . . . [567]

P. CRIME PREVENTION

Sometimes force may be used to ***prevent*** commission of a crime but this must be distinguished from the use of force to effectuate an arrest . . . . [568]

1. **Common Law Position:** ***Reasonable "nondeadly" force*** can be used to prevent or terminate the commission of a felony or a misdemeanor amounting to a breach of the peace. However, ***deadly force*** can be used only to prevent perpetration of a ***felony*** . . . . [569]
2. **Modern View:** Deadly force is limited to the termination of felonies that create a risk of ***death or serious bodily harm*** to others . . . . [570]

Q. PUBLIC AUTHORITY

A public officer may use ***reasonable force*** to carry out duties pursuant to a valid statute or court order. Under the better view, it is only necessary that the official reasonably believe the actions are valid . . . . [572]

R. DOMESTIC AUTHORITY

Parents and schoolteachers may use ***reasonable nondeadly force*** to control and discipline their ***minor*** charges. Similar authority is extended to wardens of institutions, captains of ships and aircraft, etc. . . . . [574]

VII. PRELIMINARY OR INCHOATE CRIMES

A. SOLICITATION

1. **Common Law:** One who intentionally ***counsels, incites, or induces another*** to commit an offense is guilty of the common law misdemeanor of solicitation. The crime is ***complete*** upon the act of counseling, inciting, or inducing, no matter what the response is of the person solicited . . . . [578]
2. **Modern Statutes:** The modern trend is to limit the crime of solicitation to the incitement of ***serious*** offenses (*e.g.*, murder, rape) and to provide a lesser penalty than that imposed for the crime itself . . . . [581]
3. **Special Problems in Solicitation**
   a. **Uncommunicated solicitation:** An uncommunicated solicitation (*e.g.*, an intermediary fails to deliver a message) is generally a crime, although some jurisdictions limit the charge to attempted solicitation . . . . [583]
   b. **Renunciation:** It is unclear whether a solicitor can escape liability by withdrawing before the solicited offense is committed . . . . [584]
4. **Relationship to Other Crimes**
   a. **Accomplice liability distinguished:** If the person solicited commits the target crime, the solicitor is ***liable as a party*** to that crime ***in addition*** to his liability for solicitation . . . . [586]
   b. **Conspiracy distinguished:** Conspiracy may follow a solicitation; however, an agreement is ***not*** required for solicitation . . . . [587]
   c. **Attempt distinguished:** If the solicitor ***goes beyond*** mere incitement, he may incur liability for attempt . . . . [588]
   d. **Merger of solicitation with attempt or conspiracy:** Solicitation is a ***lesser included offense*** of attempt or conspiracy, and thus, a solicitor ***cannot*** be convicted of ***both*** . . . . [589]

B. CONSPIRACY

1. **In General**
   a. **Common law:** At common law, conspiracy (a misdemeanor) is an agreement between two or more persons to accomplish ***an unlawful purpose*** or a ***lawful purpose by unlawful methods*** . . . . [591]
   b. **Modern statutes:** Modern statutes often limit the offense to agreements to commit a ***crime*** or specify the proscribed unlawful objectives . . . . [592]
2. **Requirements for Liability for Conspiracy**
   a. **Mens rea:** The conspirators must ***intend to agree*** with each other ***and*** each person must have the ***intent to accomplish the objective***. Intent is often shown by the defendant's expectation of financial benefit—*i.e.*, a stake in the venture. In some circumstances, the conspirators' awareness that the target offense will be committed is sufficient . . . . [594]
      (1) **Providing goods or services:** If the objective is ***not a serious crime***, the defendant probably must have affirmatively ***desired the accomplishment*** of an unlawful purpose; mere knowledge that the goods would be used for an unlawful purpose is generally insufficient. However, the ***more serious the crime***, the more likely the defendant will be found a conspirator merely upon proof he was ***aware*** of an unlawful purpose . . . . [598]

(2) **Requirement of a "corrupt motive":** Some courts hold that each party must have known that the objective was illegal (*i.e.*, corrupt motive) . . . . [601]

b. **Actus reus:** The conspirators must ***actually enter into an agreement***. The agreement need not be express; it can be ***implied*** from the cooperative action of the parties . . . . [602]

(1) **Nexus to agreement:** If the existence of a conspiracy is clearly shown, relatively slight evidence will be sufficient to connect a party to it . . . . [604]

(2) **Overt act:** The common law crime is complete when the agreement is reached. However, some modern statutes impose the additional requirement of an overt act—*i.e.*, ***any*** single act by ***any*** member in pursuit of the unlawful objective . . . . [605]

(3) **Number and characteristics of agreements:** Complex situations involving many parties and several schemes may result in one large agreement among all participants or several small agreements with some overlap of members . . . . [609]

(a) **Multiple unlawful purposes:** If many crimes are plotted in a single agreement, there is only ***one*** conspiracy . . . . [610]

(b) **"Chain" situation:** If the parties to a series of transactions each have a general interest in the success of the ***overall series*** of transactions, there is one large conspiracy involving all participants (*e.g.*, sale and resale of narcotics) . . . . [611]

(c) **"Wheel" and "spoke" situation:** If one person enters into many different transactions with various other persons who are concerned only with their own transaction, there are ***several*** conspiracies . . . . [613]

(4) **"Unknown" conspirators:** The conspiracy includes all persons ***known by other members to be involved***, even if each member does not know the identity of all the others or how many are involved . . . . [615]

(5) **Husband-wife conspiracies:** At common law, husband-wife conspiracies could not be formed (spouses regarded as "one"); however, modern courts reject this concept . . . . [616]

(6) **Corporate conspiracy:** A corporation can be a party to a conspiracy, but there is ***no*** conspiracy where the only members are a corporation and one of its agents or two corporations and one person acting as agent for both since only one human actor is involved . . . . [617]

c. **Objective of agreement:** The common law did not require commission of a crime to be the objective. ***Modern statutes***, however, differ. Some require an objective to ***commit a crime*** while others designate specific unlawful purposes (*e.g.*, to pervert or obstruct justice). As a result, some conspiracy statutes raise constitutional ***vagueness*** problems . . . . [618]

3. **Punishment:** Modern statutes also depart from the common law (which made conspiracy a misdemeanor) by imposing penalties related to, but less than, those for the crime the parties agreed to commit or by imposing the same punishment as that provided for the most serious offense the parties conspired to commit . . . . [622]

4. **Conviction for Conspiracy and Completed Crime:** Contrary to the common law rule, if the target crime has been completed, the conspirators can be convicted of ***both*** the conspiracy and the crime. There is ***no merger*** . . . . [623]

5. **Special Problems Applying Conspiracy Law**

a. **"Plurality" requirement:** The requirement that a conspiracy involve an agreement between ***two or more persons*** means that no conviction may be obtained if ***all other members*** of the alleged conspiracy (other than the defendant) have been ***acquitted*** or are shown to have been ***feigning involvement*** . . . . [626]

b. **Conspiracy to commit concerted action crimes: *Wharton's Rule*** precludes a conspiracy conviction where the parties are charged with conspiring to commit an offense that by its definition requires a preliminary agreement among the participants, and where the agreement charged is no larger than is inherently necessary for the crime charged (*e.g.*, conspiracy between two persons to commit adultery or bigamy) . . . . [632]

(1) **Exceptions:** Many courts do not apply this rule if the number of conspirators ***exceeds*** the essential number of participants. Further, some courts apply the rule only where the parties have ***achieved their objective***. Thus, the rule, in effect, only ***bars*** conviction for ***both*** conspiracy and the completed crime . . . . [634]

c. **Defenses**

(1) **Impossibility:** Most courts take the view that impossibility is ***no*** defense to a conspiracy. However, a few decisions have suggested that "legal," but not "factual," impossibility may be a defense . . . . [638]

(2) **Withdrawal:** Generally, withdrawal is ***no*** defense to a charge of conspiracy. However, the Model Penal Code would allow a co-conspirator to defend on the ground that he "thwarted the success of the conspiracy under circumstances manifesting a ***complete and voluntary renunciation*** of his criminal purpose" . . . . [639]

(a) **Compare:** Withdrawal ***may*** be a defense to ***crimes*** committed by conspirators in furtherance of the conspiracy . . . . [642]

6. **Liability for Crimes of Co-Conspirators: *All*** conspirators are guilty of those crimes committed by their co-conspirators that were ***reasonably foreseeable results*** of the conspiracy and done ***in furtherance*** of it. Note that this ***differs from accomplice liability*** in that co-conspirators may be liable for crimes of others even though they would not be liable as accomplices . . . . [643]

a. **Crimes prior to joining:** Some opinions suggest that a conspirator can also be held liable for crimes committed by other members prior to his joining; however, there are ***no*** apparent convictions for such pre-joinder crimes . . . . [649]

b. **Withdrawal preventing liability:** A defendant is ***not*** liable for crimes of other conspirators committed ***after*** his ***effective withdrawal***. A withdrawal is effective if ***communicated to all*** other members (unless perhaps this is an unmanageable task) and according to some courts, is also ***timely***. Most courts, however, do ***not*** require the defendant to prevent the former co-conspirators from completing their plans . . . . [650]

7. **Duration of the Conspiracy:** Determination as to when a conspiracy ends affects liability for co-conspirators' crimes and procedural matters (*i.e.*, statute of limitations). A conspiracy ordinarily ends once ***all objectives*** of the agreement have been successfully completed . . . . [654]

a. **Efforts to conceal the offense:** The Supreme Court has required direct evidence of a specific agreement to conceal the crime in order to find that such behavior extended the conspiracy beyond the completion of the crime . . . . [656]

8. **Tactical Advantage for Prosecution:** Charging a criminal conspiracy provides the prosecution with many tactical advantages (*e.g.*, broad choice of venue, use of hearsay, etc.) and therefore, may materially aid the chances of a conviction . . . . [657]

C. ATTEMPT

Taking a ***sufficient step*** toward the completion of a crime, if done with the requisite intent, may be a crime itself . . . . [658]

1. **Elements of Attempt:** Attempt consists of a ***specific intent*** to commit a crime and an ***act in furtherance*** of that intent which sufficiently approaches completion of the crime . . . . [660]

a. **Mens rea:** The mens rea of attempt has two components: (i) the intent to commit the acts or cause the results constituting the target crime; and (ii) the intent necessary for the target crime (*e.g.*, attempted murder requires intent to cause death). Note that intent is sometimes a necessary element of attempts to commit a ***strict liability*** crime . . . . [661]

b. **Actus reus:** The actus reus of attempt is an act that progresses sufficiently toward commission of the attempted offense. A number of criteria have been used or suggested to determine whether the defendant's act is sufficient: . . . . [664]

(1) ***Act must go beyond mere "preparation"*** and into the zone of "perpetration."

(2) ***Defendant must have committed the last proximate act*** before commission of the offense.

(3) ***Defendant must have obtained control over all factors indispensable*** to the commission of the crime—*i.e.*, nothing must be left undone.

(4) ***Defendant's conduct must be physically proximate*** to the intended crime.

(5) ***Defendant must have gone so far*** that in the ordinary course of events (without interference) the crime would be completed ***(probable desistance test)***.

(6) ***The act itself must show unequivocally that defendant intended*** to complete the crime ***("equivocality" or "res ipsa loquitur" test)***.

(7) ***The Model Penal Code*** would require that the ***conduct constitute a substantial step strongly corroborative of defendant's intent*** to complete the crime. This approach is gaining increasing acceptance.

3. **Defenses**

a. **Impossibility:** It is generally agreed that ***factual impossibility***—the inability of defendant to carry out her intention because of factors unknown to her—does ***not*** prevent liability for attempt. However, traditionally it is a defense that the defendant's intended activity would not constitute a crime, *i.e.*, ***legal*** impossibility . . . . [674]

(1) **"Inherent" or "obvious" impossibility:** Apparently, there is no criminal attempt if it is blatantly obvious that the defendant's chosen methods could not result in the attempted crime (*e.g.*, attempt to kill by voodoo) . . . . [682]

b. **"Withdrawal" or abandonment:** Traditionally, once an attempt is complete, the defendant cannot avoid liability by abandoning her plan. The Model Penal Code and modern statutes would establish a defense of ***complete and fully voluntary*** abandonment. Note that even if not a defense, evidence of abandonment may be used to show that the defendant ***lacked the requisite intent*** . . . . [684]

4. **Punishment:** Attempts are usually punishable by a ***lesser*** penalty than that for the completed crime. Attempt is a lesser included offense of the completed crime, ***precluding defendants conviction for both*** . . . . [689]

a. **"Attempt-like" crimes:** Some authorities urge that attempts to commit "attempt-like" crimes (*e.g.*, burglary, assault) should not be punished. However, convictions of this type have been upheld . . . . [691]

b. **Solicitation as attempt:** Although there is conflicting authority, the better view is that ***mere*** solicitation, without more, is ***not*** an attempt . . . . [692]

VIII. HOMICIDE CRIMES

A. DEFINITION AND CLASSIFICATION

1. **Definition:** A homicide is the killing of one human being by another human being. . . . . [693]

Text Section

2. **Common Law Classifications:** At common law, homicides are categorized as ***justified*** (those authorized by law), ***excusable*** (those in which the killer is not necessarily without fault but circumstances do not justify infliction of normal punishment), and ***criminal homicide*** (murder or manslaughter). At common law, murder is not divided into degrees .... [694]
3. **Classification Under Modern Law:** Since excusable homicides are no longer punished, the justifiable-excusable distinction is unnecessary. Modern statutes, however, often divide murder into two degrees and sometimes create a ***negligent homicide*** offense. Recently, many states have distinguished murder from "capital murder," a separate offense for which the death penalty may be imposed .... [695]

B. MURDER

1. **Murder Defined:** Murder is the unlawful killing of another human being with ***malice aforethought*** .... [696]
2. **"Malice Aforethought":** Malice aforethought refers to ***any*** of several different mental states (below) plus the ***absence*** of factors sufficient to reduce a killing to voluntary manslaughter. No ill will or hatred of the victim is necessary ...... [697]
   a. **Sufficient mental states**
      (1) **Intent to kill:** If the defendant intended to cause the death, the killing is with malice aforethought. In most cases, the intent may be ***inferred*** from the defendant's conduct, *e.g.*, where defendant intentionally uses a deadly weapon on another ***(deadly weapon doctrine)*** ..... [699]
      (2) **Intent to inflict great bodily injury:** Proof that the defendant intended to inflict serious bodily injury, even though there was no conscious desire to cause death, will support a murder conviction ..... [701]
      (3) **Intent to commit a felony:** If a death occurred while the defendant was in the process of committing a felony *(infra)*, malice aforethought is present .... [702]
      (4) **Intent to resist lawful arrest:** Such conduct established malice aforethought under the older cases. However, today such a killing is murder only if it satisfies one of the other tests of malice aforethought (*e.g.*, felony murder) .... [703]
      (5) **Awareness of a high risk of death—"depraved mind" or "abandoned and malignant heart":** Traditionally, this was called the "abandoned and malignant heart" test. The better view requires that the defendant be ***subjectively*** aware of the risk involved .... [704]
   b. **Proof of malice aforethought:** Malice aforethought can be proved by circumstantial evidence and can be inferred from the act of killing itself ..... [710]
3. **Degrees of Murder:** There are no degrees under common law. However, modern statutes often divide murder into first and second degree .... [711]
   a. **First degree murder**
      (1) **Premeditated killings:** These are killings in which the intent to kill is formed ***with some reflection, deliberation, reasoning, or weighing,*** rather than on sudden impulse. Many courts require only that the defendant have had an ***opportunity*** to premeditate. Some demand an ***appreciable period***; others hold that premeditation can occur ***instantaneously***. Note that some courts require a further showing that defendant did in fact premeditate during this opportunity ...... [713]
      (2) **Killing during enumerated felonies:** First degree murder includes killings committed during the perpetration of ***certain enumerated felonies*** (*i.e.*, arson, rape, robbery, burglary, kidnapping, and sexual molestation of a child) and killings by ***poison, bomb, lying in wait, or torture*** .... [718]
   b. **Second degree murder:** Under statutes that divide murder into degrees, all killings committed ***with malice aforethought*** and that are ***not specifically***

raised to first degree murder are typically classified as second degree murder . . . . [721]

4. **Capital Murder:** This is a ***separate offense*** from murder and usually requires proof of at least one ***statutory aggravated factor or "special circumstances."*** A conviction subjects the defendant to the possibility of a death sentence . . . . [722]

C. FELONY MURDER

1. **Felony Murder Rule:** A killing will be a felony murder if it was caused ***with the intent to commit a felony. All co-felons are liable*** if one of them accidentally causes a death, even when a ***co-felon is killed***, although courts many times will find an exception in the latter situation . . . . [723]
2. **Limitations on Felony Murder:** Several limitations have emerged, perhaps as a result of the increasing discontent with the rule . . . . [726]
   a. **Death of another must be "foreseeable":** Some courts require that the death have been a foreseeable consequence of the felony (although the death usually is found foreseeable) . . . . [727]
   b. **"Dangerous" felony:** A number of states limit application of the rule to ***dangerous*** felonies. Some states require the felony to be ***inherently dangerous***; others require only that the felony ***as committed*** involved a special or significant risk to human life . . . . [728]
   c. **"Independent" felony:** Some courts require that the felony be ***independent of the killing***. If the predicate felony was the very means by which the victim's death was caused, the felony ***"merges"*** into the killing and no felony murder exists . . . . [731]
   d. **One of the felons must "directly" cause death:** The modern trend holds that the felony murder rule does ***not*** apply when a victim is killed by a resisting victim or pursuing police officer rather than by the defendant or one of the co-felons. However, the killing may ***still*** be murder under the ***awareness of a high risk*** rule . . . . [733]
   e. **Death caused in perpetration of felony:** The killing must be caused ***during the perpetration*** or attempted perpetration of the felony. However, in some states, a death caused ***after*** the technical completion of the felony may still be felony murder. The preferable position applies the felony murder rule to killings occurring during commission of the felony or ***in immediate flight*** from the crimes (*i.e.*, stops upon reaching temporary safety) . [739]
3. **Future of Felony Murder:** Several courts have wholly or in part ***abandoned*** the felony murder rule. The effect of abandonment may be minimal since many situations will also support murder charges under the "depraved mind" doctrine . [741]

D. VOLUNTARY MANSLAUGHTER

1. **Voluntary Manslaughter Defined:** A killing that would ***otherwise be murder*** but that was committed in response to ***adequate provocation*** is voluntary manslaughter . . . . [746]
2. **Elements of Provocation Reducing Murder to Manslaughter:** The common law requires ***all*** four of the following elements: (i) reasonable provocation; (ii) the defendant was actually provoked; (iii) absence of adequate cooling period; and (iv) no actual cooling off. Modern statutes also usually require ***all or most of these requirements*** . . . . [748]
   a. **Reasonable provocation:** The provocation must have been ***reasonable*** as judged by an ***objective*** standard. Generally, it must have been such as might render ordinary persons of average disposition liable to act rashly, without deliberation, and from passion rather than judgment . . . . [749]
      (1) **"Reasonable person":** In deciding whether particular provocation would provoke a reasonable person, courts differ over the extent to which the reasonable person should be attributed with the defendant's peculiar characteristics . . . . [750]

(2) **Particular situations**

(a) **Words alone:** Traditionally, mere words are ***not*** adequate provocation. However, a minority view accepts that at least sometimes mere words can be reasonable provocation, especially if the words are informational words (*i.e.*, words that convey information of a fact which if witnessed would be adequate provocation) . . . . [755]

(b) **Other situations: *Violent and painful blows*** (unless the defendant was at fault), ***aggravated assault***, and ***witnessing one's spouse commit adultery*** all constitute adequate provocation. Some courts will consider an ***illegal arrest*** to be adequate provocation . . . . [757]

(c) **Mutual combat:** A killing caused during a fight in which both participants voluntarily entered is reduced to manslaughter . . . . [762]

(3) **Mistake concerning provocation:** The better view would reduce a killing to manslaughter as long as the defendant ***reasonably believed*** she was responding to adequate provocation . . . . [763]

(4) **Provocation by someone other than victim:** If the victim was not the provoking party, a killing will be manslaughter if the defendant ***intended to kill the actual provocator*** but accidentally killed a third party . . . . [764]

(5) **Injury to persons other than defendant:** The subject of the provocation generally must be the defendant or a close relative. Some courts indicate that if the subject is only a friend or distant relative, the provocation will not be adequate . . . . [767]

b. **Actual provocation:** The provocation must ***actually*** have caused the killing; *i.e.*, the provocation must have been such that a reasonable person would lose control ***and*** defendant ***in fact*** acted due to passion rather than reason (a subjective test) . . . . [768]

c. **Absence of reasonable cooling period:** The majority of courts hold that homicide is not reduced to manslaughter if sufficient time elapsed between the provocation and the killing to permit the ***passions of a reasonable person*** to cool (an objective test) . . . . [769]

(1) **"Reinflaming" occurrences:** Under the better view, if an intervening event reminds the defendant of the provocation and "reinflames" the passion, the cooling period begins to run again . . . . [773]

d. **No actual cooling off:** The defendant's passion must not in fact have subsided during the interval (a subjective test) . . . . [774]

3. **Model Penal Code Position—"Extreme Disturbance":** The Code would reduce murder to manslaughter if the killing was committed "under the influence of ***extreme mental or emotional disturbance*** for which there is a ***reasonable explanation or excuse.***" This is somewhat similar to the adequate provocation standard but encourages submission of the case to the jury . . . . [775]

4. **"Imperfect" Defense Situations as Voluntary Manslaughter:** Some courts reduce a killing if the evidence tends to establish a defense but falls short of doing so because the defendant's conduct was unreasonable (*e.g.*, he overreacted) . . . . [777]

E. INVOLUNTARY MANSLAUGHTER

1. **Involuntary Manslaughter Defined:** An ***unintended*** killing is involuntary manslaughter if it is the result of ***criminal negligence*** or caused during the commission of an ***unlawful act not amounting to a felony*** or that for some other reason is insufficient to trigger the felony murder rule . . . . [778]

2. **Killing by Criminal Negligence:** An unintentional killing caused by the commission of ***any*** act in a criminally negligent manner is involuntary manslaughter . [779]

a. **Negligence required:** A greater degree of unreasonableness is required for criminal negligence than would otherwise suffice for imposition of civil liability. It is possible that the defendant actually have been ***aware of the high and unreasonable risk*** of death, although this is unclear . . . . [780]

3. **Commission of Unlawful Act ("Misdemeanor Manslaughter"):** Unintentional killings caused during the commission of an unlawful act are involuntary manslaughter (unless the unlawful act supports application of the felony murder rule). The act must be ***unlawful*** but need not be criminal (*e.g.*, killing caused during a defendant's attempted suicide) . . . . [782]
   a. **Limitations:** Some states hold that the unlawful act must be ***malum in se*** (inherently wrong). Others require that the unlawful act be perpetrated in a criminally ***negligent*** manner. And a number of courts require that ***death be caused by the unlawful aspect*** of the defendant's conduct . . . . [784]

F. **MODERN STATUTORY DISTINCTIONS**

1. **Modern Penal Code Scheme:** Modern statutes tend to redefine homicide offenses by grading them according to the different states of mind defined by the Model Penal Code . . . . [788]
   a. **Murder:** The Code defines murder as a killing committed ***purposely, knowingly, or recklessly*** under circumstances manifesting ***extreme indifference*** to the value of human life . . . . [789]
   b. **Manslaughter:** The Code establishes a single manslaughter offense which is a killing committed ***recklessly or*** under the influence of ***extreme mental or emotional disturbance*** for which there is reasonable explanation or excuse . . . . [790]
   c. **Negligent homicide:** The Code creates a new homicide offense of negligent homicide, *i.e.*, a killing committed negligently . . . . [791]
2. **Homicide Caused During Operation of a Motor Vehicle:** Other modern statutes often contain a separate offense for death caused in the negligent operation of a motor vehicle or by operating a vehicle in an unlawful manner . . . . [792]

G. **GENERAL PROBLEMS RELATING TO HOMICIDE LIABILITY**

1. **Victim Must Be a Living Human Being—Killing of Fetus:** A fetus is not a human being until fully brought forth from the mother and having an independent circulation . . . . [793]
   a. **Statutory changes:** Some states have broadened their homicide statutes to include a fetus, contrary to common law . . . . [794]
2. **When Does Death Occur:** Under the ***traditional*** rule, death does not occur until ***heartbeat and respiration stop***. However, some courts now hold that death occurs when the ***brain ceases to function*** . . . . [797]
3. **Death Must Occur Within a Year and a Day:** Death must occur within a year and a day from the time the cause of death was administered. However, some courts have ***abandoned*** this time limitation while others have ***extended*** the time . . . . [800]
4. **Aiding or Causing Suicide:** At common law, suicide is murder. The modern view holds that suicide is ***not*** an offense; thus, the aider cannot be guilty as a party. Some statutes, however, make aiding suicide a ***separate offense*** . . . . . [802]
   a. **Compare:** Generally, one who ***actively*** takes the life of another, even if at the other person's specific request, is guilty of murder . . . . [805]

IX. **OTHER CRIMES AGAINST THE PERSON**

A. **ASSAULT AND BATTERY**

1. **Battery:** Battery is the unlawful application of force to the person of another . . [807]
   a. **Actus reus:** The mere application of force is sufficient under traditional law; ***no injury*** or marks on the victim are required. Modern statutes, however, often require either some injury or that the touching (application of

force) be offensive. Under either approach, the application of force may be ***indirect*** (*e.g.*, administering poison) . . . . [808]

b. **Mens rea:** The application of force need not be intentional; ***negligence*** is usually ***sufficient***. Some courts do not even require negligence where the defendant was engaged in ***unlawful*** behavior . . . . [814]

c. **Effect of consent:** There is no battery if the victim ***effectively*** consented . [817]

d. **Punishment:** At common law, battery is a misdemeanor, as is today's classification of simple battery. However, certain aggravated batteries are felonies . . . . [818]

2. **Assault:** Two different activities may constitute a criminal assault, but not all states punish both types . . . . [819]

a. **Attempted battery as assault:** An attempted battery is always an assault . . . . [820]

(1) **Mens rea:** Generally, the defendant must have ***intended the application of force*** to the victim. An intent to frighten is ***not*** sufficient for this type of assault . . . . [821]

(2) **Actus reus:** The defendant must have come ***reasonably close to successfully completing*** the battery. Some statutes require that the defendant have had the ***present ability to succeed*** . . . . [824]

(3) **Conditional assault:** Representations by the defendant that she will not commit a battery if the victim complies with certain demands do not preclude an assault conviction . . . . [826]

b. **Intentional placing in fear as assault:** In a probable majority of the states, it is also assault to intentionally place another in fear of immediate bodily harm. This kind of assault requires that the defendant ***intend*** to cause apprehension of harm, the victim must ***in fact be apprehensive*** (*i.e.*, aware of assault), and defendant's ***conduct must be sufficient to create reasonable apprehension. Mere words*** are ***not*** enough . . . . [827]

c. **Model Penal Code:** The Code's definition differs in that the victim need not have actual fear, and the attempt must be to put the victim in fear of ***serious*** bodily harm . . . . [831]

B. MAYHEM

Mayhem (a felony) consists of maliciously depriving another of the use of one of his members ***(disablement)*** or injuring the victim so as to permanently change his appearance ***(disfigurement)*** . . . . [833]

1. **Actus Reus:** The defendant must have caused the victim bodily injury that ***permanently*** disfigures or disables her . . . . [835]
2. **Mens Rea:** Generally, the defendant must have ***intended to injure*** the victim . . [839]

C. RAPE AND RELATED OFFENSES

Rape is unlawful sexual intercourse with a female without her consent. Modern statutes often designate the crime as sexual assault and classify it as a crime against the person . . . . [841]

1. **Forcible (or Common Law) Rape:** The defendant must have completed an act of sexual intercourse with a woman ***other than his wife*** and against her will. The slightest penetration of the female sexual organ is sufficient . . . . [842]

a. **Husband cannot rape wife:** Traditionally, a husband cannot rape is wife, but he may be convicted as a ***party*** to the rape of his wife by someone else. *But note:* Modern statutes in many states now allow forcible rape convictions for a husband's forcible rape of his wife . . . . [844]

b. **Against her will:** Intercourse is against the will of the victim in several types of situations all of which involve the lack of ***effective*** consent by the victim . . . . [848]

(1) **Intercourse accomplished by force:** Intercourse accomplished by force is against the victim's will. However, no rape occurs if the victim

resisted at first but consented before the actual act of intercourse . . [849]

(2) **Intercourse accomplished by threats:** Consent obtained by threats of serious and immediate bodily harm is ***ineffective*** . . . . [850]

(3) **Incapacity to give effective consent:** Consent given by a victim lacking capacity due to intoxication, mental deficiency, or insanity is also invalid . . . . [851]

(4) **Consent obtained by fraud:** Consent obtained by deceiving the victim as to the ***nature of the act*** (*i.e.*, as to whether the act is intercourse) is invalid. Some courts also hold consent ineffective if obtained by deceiving the victim into ***believing she is married*** to the defendant. Other types of fraud will not invalidate consent . . . . . [852]

c. **Mens rea:** The mens rea requirement for rape is not clearly defined. It is unclear whether the defendant must actually know the victim is not consenting. Some courts hold that it is enough that the defendant ***should*** have been aware of the lack of consent. A few courts do not focus on the mens rea required but rather recognize a defense consisting of proof that the defendant ***reasonably*** believed that the victim consented . . . . [857]

d. **Special problems**

(1) **Corroboration:** In some jurisdictions a rape conviction cannot be based on the victim's uncorroborated testimony . . . . [861]

(2) **Victim's resistance:** Some courts also require proof that the victim ***resisted to the utmost*** unless resistance would have been futile or was prevented by the defendant's threats . . . . [862]

(3) **Victim's promiscuity:** There is no formal requirement that the victim have been previously chaste although evidence of past sexual conduct is sometimes admitted on the issue of consent. However, the ***modern trend*** would ***limit*** the use of such evidence . . . . [863]

e. **Special age defense:** A defendant under the age of 14 is presumed incapable of rape. Although ***conclusive at common law***, under some ***modern statutes***, this presumption ***can be rebutted*** by proof beyond a reasonable doubt of the defendant's ability to have intercourse. Many jurisdictions no longer apply the special age rule . . . . [864]

2. **Statutory Rape:** In most jurisdictions, intercourse with a female who is too young to give legally effective consent is rape. The ***age of consent*** is set by statute . [867]

a. **Awareness of victim's age:** Statutory rape is a ***strict liability crime***. The defendant's awareness of the victim's age (or his reasonable mistaken belief that she was older) is irrelevant under the general rule. However, some states permit a defense on the basis that there was only a ***small difference*** between ***defendant's age and the age of the victim*** . [869]

3. **Equal Protection Issues Regarding Sex Offenses:** Since sex crime statutes penalize mostly males, it has been argued that they violate equal protection. However, these statutes will be upheld if the distinction made realistically reflects a difference in the actual situation of the sexes (*e.g.*, statutory rape laws are aimed at preventing teenage pregnancies) . . . . [872]

4. **Modern Trend—"Sex Neutral" Offense of Sexual Assault:** Some jurisdictions have replaced rape with a more sexually neutral offense (*e.g.*, crime of "sexual assault"). Under such statutes, sexually motivated assaults other than vaginal penetration are punished, as are assaults on males . . . . [873]

5. **Intercourse "By Forcible Compulsion":** Several states have statutorily eliminated the concept of consent from the rape definition. These jurisdictions instead focus on the use of force in sexual intercourse . . . . [876]

D. FALSE IMPRISONMENT

False imprisonment is the intentional unlawful confinement of another person . . . . [877]

1. **Actus Reus—Confinement:** The victim must have been compelled by the defendant's use of force ***or*** threats to remain somewhere or go somewhere

against his desire. There is ***no*** confinement where the victim is simply ***prevented from proceeding*** in a certain direction . . . . [878]

2. **Mens Rea:** Traditionally, the defendant must have ***intended to confine*** the victim. The Model Penal Code requires only that the restraint be ***knowingly*** accomplished . . . . [881]
3. **Unlawful:** The confinement must have been done ***without legal authority*** . . [882]
4. **Punishment:** Generally, under both common law and modern statutes, false imprisonment is a ***misdemeanor*** . . . . [883]

E. KIDNAPPING

1. **Common Law:** At common law, kidnapping is the forcible abduction or stealing away of a person from his own country and sending him into another country . [885]
2. **Modern Statutes:** Today, kidnapping has been extended to mean a form of ***aggravated false imprisonment*** . . . . [886]
   a. **Examples:** Various statutes include the following conduct as kidnapping: . [887]
      (1) ***Confinement and movement (asportation)*** of the victim;
      (2) ***Confinement*** of the victim ***in a secret place***;
      (3) ***Confinement accomplished by deadly force***;
      (4) ***Confinement for ransom or sexual abuse.***
3. **Confinement—How Accomplished:** Statutes vary as to the methods of accomplishing confinement. Some proscribe use of ***deception*** as well as ***force or threats*** . . . . [895]
4. **Mens Rea:** Generally, ***actual intent*** to confine or move the victim is required . [900]
5. **Relationship of Kidnapping to Other Crimes:** Where kidnapping is defined simply as the forcible movement of the victim, it may often take place ***incidental to*** the commission of another crime (*e.g.*, robbery or rape). In such cases, some courts find a kidnapping only if the compelled movement ***substantially increased the risk*** to the victim . . . . [902]
6. **Punishment:** Kidnapping is usually punished as a ***felony***, although some statutes provide a more ***severe penalty*** for certain ***aggravated kidnappings***. Other statutes authorize a ***reduced penalty*** where the defendant releases the victim in a ***safe condition*** . . . . [905]

X. CRIMES AGAINST THE HABITATION

A. BURGLARY

1. **Common Law:** Common law burglary is the breaking and entering of the dwelling house of another in the nighttime with the intent to commit a felony . . . . . . [908]
   a. **Entry:** There must be ***actual or constructive*** (*e.g.*, defendant sends an ***innocent*** agent into the structure) entry. Note that the slightest intrusion by the defendant will suffice. The ***insertion of an instrument*** into the structure is an entry ***only*** if the purpose is to ***commit the intended felony*** . . . . [909]
   b. **Breaking:** Entry must be accomplished by the ***use of force to create a trespassory opening*** of the structure where none previously existed . . . [915]
      (1) **Force:** Use of force includes not only physical force, but also ***fraud, threats, or collusion*** with someone already inside (*e.g.*, a servant) . . [916]
      (2) **Breaking to leave:** If the defendant uses force only to leave the structure, most courts hold that this is ***not*** burglary . . . . [919]
      (3) **Consent to enter:** Since the breaking must be trespassory, one who enters with consent is not a burglar. However, the defendant must have had authority to be in the ***particular area*** of the premises at ***the relevant time*** . . . . [920]
      (4) **Causal relationship:** The breaking must be the means by which the entry is accomplished . . . . [922]
   c. **Dwelling house:** A place regularly used to ***sleep*** in is a dwelling, even if it is ***also*** used for business or ***other purposes***. Buildings within the ***curtilage***

(*e.g.*, barns, garages) are also included, as are structures from which the inhabitants are ***temporarily absent*** (*e.g.*, summer cottage) . . . . [923]

d. **Of another:** A person cannot burglarize her own dwelling. However, the right of ***habitation***, rather than ownership, is determinative . . . . [929]

e. **In the nighttime:** Nighttime is the period when the countenance of a person cannot be discerned by natural sunlight. Although the breaking and entering must occur during this period, the two acts can occur on ***different nights*** . . . . [933]

f. **With the intent to commit a felony:** At the ***time of entry***, the defendant must intend to commit a ***felony*** within the structure . . . . [936]

(1) **Completion of intent:** Burglary is complete at the moment of entry with the requisite intent. Thus, ***abandonment*** of the plan once entry is accomplished will ***not*** preclude a burglary conviction . . . . [938]

(2) **"Within" the structure:** Traditionally, the situs of the intended felony must be "in" the structure entered. However, a close connection between the place of entry and the situs of the felonious scheme may be enough . . . . [940]

2. **Modern Statutes:** Modern statutes have significantly modified common law burglary . . . . [941]

a. **Breaking not required:** ***Any entry***, however accomplished, is sufficient, but statutes generally require that the entry be "unlawful" or at least without consent . . . . [942]

b. **Dwellings:** The structure entered need ***not*** be a dwelling. Some statutes include ***any*** building or a ***motor vehicle*** . . . . [945]

c. **Time irrelevant:** Entry need not be in the nighttime, although nighttime burglary is often made a more serious offense than daytime burglary . . . . [947]

d. **Intent to commit misdemeanor:** The intent element is frequently broadened to include intent to commit a felony or ***any theft*** . . . . [950]

e. **Punishment:** Burglary is a felony but many statutes divide the crime into ***degrees***, penalizing certain ***aggravated burglaries*** (*i.e.*, burglary of an inhabited dwelling or with a deadly weapon) more severely . . . . [951]

(1) **Conviction for both crimes:** If the defendant successfully completes the intended crime, she can be convicted for both the burglary ***and*** the target crime . . . . [953]

B. ARSON

1. **Common Law:** Arson is the malicious burning of the ***dwelling house of another***. The burglary definitions of "dwelling" and "of another" also apply to arson . . . . [954]

a. **Compare—"houseburning":** At common law, one who intentionally burns his own dwelling commits the ***misdemeanor*** of houseburning if a risk of burning other houses exists . . . . [957]

b. **Burning:** Some part of the structure itself ***must be physically damaged*** by fire. Although the slightest ***charring*** will suffice, mere discoloration by heat (scorching) is ***not*** enough . . . . [958]

c. **Mens rea—malice:** The defendant must ***intend*** the burning, ***know*** that it will occur, or intentionally and without justification or excuse create an ***obvious fire hazard*** to the structure. Simple ***negligence*** is ***not*** enough . [963]

2. **Modern Statutes:** Arson is commonly broadened in scope under modern laws . . . . [967]

a. **Structures other than dwellings:** The burning of many structures other than dwellings is often punishable arson (*e.g.*, any structure, forest land, or property) . . . . [968]

b. **Ownership and occupancy:** Some statutes consider these limitations irrelevant. Thus, an offense can be committed by a defendant burning a structure that she owns and occupies. Note that the defendant probably must be ***aware*** of a creation of a risk to others to satisfy the intent requirement . . . . [969]

c. **Burning:** Some states simply require that the defendant ***set a fire*** with intent to burn. Numerous arson statutes also cover ***explosions*** . . . . [971]

d. **Intent to defraud insurer:** An intentional burning for purposes of collecting insurance may be a separate offense of "arson with intent to defraud an insurer" . . . . [974]

3. **Punishment:** Arson is a felony . . . . [975]

XI. CRIMES AGAINST PROPERTY—ACQUISITION OFFENSES

A. INTRODUCTION

The basic crimes against property are those involving a wrongful acquisition of property. At common law, these crimes have differing and detailed technical requirements, but the modern trend is to consolidate the common law crimes into a single crime of theft . . . . [976]

B. LARCENY

1. **Elements:** Larceny is a crime against another's ***possessory*** interest in property and requires a ***trespassory taking and asportation of the personal property of another with the intent to permanently deprive*** the owner thereof . . . . [978]

2. **Subject Matter of Larceny—Personal Property:** Only ***tangible personal property*** can be the subject of larceny. Realty, fixtures, base and wild animals, services, and intangibles are generally outside the scope of larceny at common law . . . . [979]

a. **Exception:** ***Severed*** fixtures, crops, or minerals, and ***wild*** animals may be the subject of larceny ***if*** they remain on the victim's property long enough to come into his possession before they are taken by the defendant . . . . [981]

b. **Modern statutes:** Today there is a trend to broaden the scope of property subject to larceny, and statutes often cover the wrongful appropriation of realty, intangible property, services, computer programs, etc. . . . . [989]

3. **Asportation:** The property must be ***carried away***. However, the ***slightest movement*** in a ***carrying away motion*** is enough. (Modern statutes often require only a "taking" or "exercising of control" over property) . . . . [998]

4. **Taking:** The defendant must have acquired ***dominion and control*** over the property. Note that larceny can be committed by causing possession to be taken by an innocent agent . . . . [1001]

5. **Requirement of a "Trespass":** The taking must be wrongful, *i.e.*, ***without effective consent*** of the victim . . . . [1005]

a. **Larceny by trick:** Consent induced by deception is ineffective and the defendant may be guilty of larceny by trick. (However, if the defendant defrauds the victim into parting with ***title*** as well as possession, the crime is only false pretenses, *infra*) . . . . [1007]

6. **"Of Another":** The property must have been taken from the ***possession*** of someone who had a right to possession ***superior*** to defendant's right . . . . . . [1016]

a. **"Possession" vs. "custody":** If the defendant has ***possession*** at the time of misappropriation, she has ***not*** taken the property from another's possession and thus is not guilty of larceny (*but see* embezzlement, *infra*). If the defendant has only ***custody***, her misappropriation is from the possession of another and ***may be larceny*** . . . . [1018]

(1) **Determinative factors:** The distinction between possession and custody generally turns on the nature of control vested in the defendant—*i.e.*, the more limited the defendant's authority, the more likely she has only custody. (*But see* the special rules for delivery of property to employees, *infra*) . . . . [1019]

b. **Joint owners:** Since joint owners each have a right to possession, one joint owner cannot commit larceny of the jointly owned property . . . . [1021]

c. **Larceny from spouse:** At common law, spouses are considered as "one," and thus cannot commit larceny of the other's property . . . . [1022]

7. **Mens Rea—"Intent To Permanently Deprive":** Generally, the defendant must intend to ***permanently*** deprive the victim of the property. It is not necessary that the victim be permanently deprived; rather the controlling factor is defendant's intent at the time of taking . . . . [1023]

a. **Effect of intent:** Intent ***to keep,*** of course, is sufficient for larceny. Therefore, an intent to ***borrow and return*** the same item does ***not*** constitute larceny. But if the defendant takes property with the intent of dealing with it in a manner that would create ***a substantial risk of permanent loss***, this suffices for larceny . . . . [1024]

b. **Intent to sell to owner:** An intent to sell back to the owner or an intent to pledge the property will support a larceny conviction on the theory that the action involves a sufficient risk of permanent loss . . . . [1028]

c. **Intent to pay:** A taking with the intent to pay the owner may or may not be larceny ***depending on the circumstances*** (*e.g.*, whether property was for sale) . . . . [1029]

d. **Intent to return equivalent property:** There is ***no*** larceny where the defendant acted with intent to return the ***identical*** property. However, if the defendant intended to return equivalent property, the result usually turns on the nature of the item (*e.g.*, is it an adequate substitute?) . . . . [1030]

e. **Intent to collect debt:** Cases are split where the defendant takes property in satisfaction of a debt but knows the property is not specifically owed her under the terms of the debt. However, there is ***no*** larceny when the defendant takes the ***specific money*** she reasonably believed was owed her . . . . [1031]

f. **Modern statutes:** Theft statutes generally retain the essence of the common law requirement of intent to permanently deprive . . . . [1033]

8. **Taking and Intent Must Coincide:** Generally, the defendant must have the requisite intent ***at the time of the initial taking*** of the property. An ***exception*** to this requirement applies where the defendant ***wrongfully*** obtains the property and ***afterwards*** forms the intent to steal it. This constitutes a ***continuing trespass*** and is larceny . . . . [1037]

9. **Special Problem Areas**

a. **Property acquired by finding**

(1) **Abandoned property:** Abandoned property ***cannot*** be the subject of larceny because it is not the property of another . . . . [1042]

(2) **Lost or mislaid goods:** Lost or mislaid property ***may*** be the subject of larceny. The taking of such items is ***larceny only if*** (i) defendant has the intent to steal when she first finds and takes possession of the property, and (ii) defendant has some clue as to the ownership . [1043]

b. **Misappropriations by employee**

(1) **Delivery to employee by third party:** A servant who takes delivery of goods for his employer receives ***possession*** and thus does ***not*** commit larceny by misappropriating those items, although he may be guilty of embezzlement. However, if the employee ***first*** deposits the goods in a ***receptacle*** designated by the employer for such goods, the employer has possession and the employee who takes the goods has committed larceny . . . . [1049]

(2) **Delivery by employer:** Ordinarily, a servant who has been entrusted with property by her employer receives only ***custody***, and misappropriation from the employer's possession is larceny. If the employee has been delegated ***considerable responsibility***, she may have possession and in that case there can be ***no*** larceny . . . . [1052]

Text Section

C. EMBEZZLEMENT

1. **Statutory Crime:** Generally, embezzlement involves the ***fraudulent conversion of the property of another by one who is already in lawful possession***. Embezzlement is a crime against ***ownership*** .... [1055]
2. **Elements of the Crime**
   a. **Conversion:** Conversion requires a ***serious act of interference*** with the owner's rights. Mere movement is not enough .... [1058]
   b. **Property:** Property that can be embezzled is often defined more broadly than it is in larceny statutes (*e.g.*, real property may be the subject of embezzlement) .... [1059]
   c. **Of another:** This requirement has created some complex issues (*e.g.*, involving advance payments, commissions, partnership property). Often the critical question is whether the property was transferred to the defendant and thus was his property or whether it remained the property of the victim .... [1060]
   d. **Lawful possession:** The primary distinguishing characteristic of embezzlement is that the defendant must be in lawful possession at the time of conversion .... [1062]
   e. **Fraudulent intent:** The conversion must be accompanied by the defendant's intent to defraud the victim. Thus, conversion under ***claim of right*** or with the ***intent to return*** the ***identical*** property is ***not*** embezzlement . [1063]
3. **Demand for Return:** Although ***not a formal element*** of embezzlement, a demand for return of the property facilitates proof of conversion .... [1069]

D. FALSE PRETENSES

1. **Statutory Crime:** In general, false pretenses is ***obtaining title*** to the property ***by means of a material false representation with intent to defraud*** the victim .... [1070]
2. **Elements of the Crime**
   a. **Obtaining title:** The defendant must obtain ***title*** to the property by means of the misrepresentation. Note that if only possession is obtained, the crime is not false pretenses but may be larceny by trick. Whether the defendant has acquired title or simply possession usually depends on what the victim intends to convey .... [1075]
   b. **Property:** Broader in scope than larceny, such property includes title to real property, securities, and sometimes services, credit, etc. .... [1078]
   c. **False representation:** There are several traditional restrictions regarding the false representation that will suffice .... [1079]
      (1) **Nature of false representation:** The misrepresentation must be of a ***past or existing fact***. Traditionally, a false promise (even if made with no intent to perform) is ***not*** sufficient, ***nor*** is the failure to correct a false impression harbored by the victim. However, false promises are sufficient under some modern statutes .... [1080]
      (2) **Materiality:** The misrepresentation must concern a ***material fact***. In other words, it must be a controlling inducement (although it need not be the sole inducing reason) for the victim's decision to part with the property. Additionally, the victim ***must in fact have been deceived*** and acted on that deceit .... [1085]
   d. **Mens rea:** The mens rea element is twofold: The defendant must (i) ***know*** the representation is false, and (ii) ***intend to defraud*** the victim .... [1088]
3. **Special Evidentiary Requirement:** Some jurisdictions require additional evidentiary proof (*e.g.*, corroboration, witness to misrepresentation) .... [1093]

E. ROBBERY

Robbery is ***larceny*** (*supra*) in which the property is ***taken from the victim's person or presence*** by means of ***violence or intimidation*** .... [1094]

1. **Taking from Victim's Person or Presence:** Property is within the ***presence*** of the victim if it is close to him and ***within his control*** in the sense that he could have prevented its taking had it not been for defendant's use of violence or threats . . . . [1095]
2. **Taking by Violence or Intimidation**
   a. **Violence:** If violence is used, ***any force*** applied to obtain the property or to overcome the victim's immediate resistance is sufficient. But a ***pickpocket*** does ***not*** commit robbery because no force is involved. Similarly, ***snatching*** property from a person's grasp is not robbery where the defendant acts so suddenly that the victim offers no resistance . . . . [1098]
   b. **Intimidation:** If ***threats*** are used, the subject of the threats must be the victim herself, a member of her family, or someone in her presence. Traditionally, the threatened harm must place the victim ***in reasonable fear*** of ***immediate*** death, bodily injury, or destruction of the dwelling house . . [1104]
      (1) **Model Penal Code:** Modern statutes do not require fear on the part of the victim if the threat is of serious bodily injury. Also, if the defendant purposely put the victim in fear, victim's response does not have to be reasonable . . . . [1106]
   c. **Violence or intimidation used to take property:** The force or intimidation must occur ***before or during the taking*** of the property . . . . [1113]
4. **Punishment:** Robbery is a common law felony ***regardless of the value*** of the property taken. It is often classified as ***aggravated robbery*** if serious bodily harm results and then it is subject to greater penalties . . . . [1119]

F. EXTORTION (OR BLACKMAIL)

1. **Common Law:** Extortion is corrupt collection of an unlawful fee by a public officer under color of office. It is a misdemeanor . . . . [1120]
2. **Modern Statutes:** Statutory revisions have broadened the crime of extortion, generally defining it either as ***obtaining property*** by means of certain ***threats or*** as the making of certain threats with the ***intent to thereby obtain property*** . . . . [1121]
   a. **Nature of threats:** The proscribed threats vary among jurisdictions but typically include threats to injure a person or property, accuse a person of a crime, or expose a secret affecting another . . . . [1126]
   b. **Limitation:** Under statutes requiring that property actually be acquired, it is necessary to show a ***causal connection*** between the threats and the surrender of property . . . . [1128]
   c. **Claim of right defense:** Some jurisdictions permit as a defense a good faith belief by defendant that he was legally entitled to the money or property . . . . [1129]
   d. **Punishment:** Today, extortion is generally punished as a ***felony*** . . . . . . [1131]

G. RECEIVING STOLEN PROPERTY

1. **Historical Background:** At early common law, there was no criminal liability for receiving stolen property . . . . [1132]
2. **Elements Under Modern Statutes:** The statutory offense consists of ***receiving stolen*** property ***knowing*** it to be stolen with the ***intent to deprive*** the owner thereof . . . . [1133]
   a. **Stolen property:** The property must in fact have been stolen at the time the defendant receives it. Property obtained by robbery or burglary suffices. However, some statutes do not cover property obtained by embezzlement or false pretenses . . . . [1134]
      (1) **Property recovered:** If the owner (or police) recovers the property, it is no longer "stolen," and the defendant is ***not*** guilty of receiving it but may be liable for an ***attempt*** to receive stolen property, although some courts find that this involves legal impossibility . . . . [1136]

Text Section

b. **Receiving:** The defendant need ***not*** take physical possession of the property as long as she ***exercises control*** over it . . . . [1138]

c. **Knowing goods are stolen:** The defendant's knowledge can be inferred from circumstances (*e.g.*, disproportionately low purchase price) . . . . [1139]

3. **Conviction of Thief for Receiving Stolen Property:** Although one who actually stole the property ***cannot*** be convicted of receiving it, other participants in the theft can be convicted of receiving ***from the actual thief***. However, they may ***not***, under the better view, be convicted of both offenses . . . . [1145]

H. CONSOLIDATION OF ACQUISITION OFFENSES—THEFT

The modern trend is to consolidate many of the acquisition offenses into a new crime of theft consisting of exercising control over the property of another unlawfully and with the intent to permanently deprive that person of property . . . . [1149]

1. **Statutory Patterns:** Different jurisdictions reflect several approaches toward the crime of theft. Some statutes consolidate the traditional offenses—particularly larceny, false pretenses, and embezzlement—into a ***single crime***. Others create ***multiple theft crimes*** that correspond to the traditional common law crimes . . . . [1150]
2. **Punishment:** Theft is typically divided into degrees: grand theft (a felony) and petty theft (a misdemeanor). Grand theft often includes theft of property (or services) above a given value, theft of certain enumerated items (*e.g.*, farm animals), and theft from the person of another . . . . [1154]

XII. OFFENSES AGAINST GOVERNMENT

A. TREASON

1. **Ancient Definition:** Under early English law, treason was neither a felony nor misdemeanor, but a crime in a separate class by itself. There was high treason (crimes against the king), and petit treason (*e.g.*, killing of spouse, clergyman, master) . . . . [1155]
2. **Modern Formulations of the Crime:** Under modern statutes, treason consists of levying war against the United States (or, under state codes, against the individual states), adhering to their enemies, or giving their enemies aid and comfort. Treason is the only crime proscribed by the Constitution . . . . [1156]
3. **Requirements:** Treason can be committed only by one who owes ***allegiance*** to the prosecuting government, and acts with ***intent to betray*** that government. Disloyal thoughts alone are not enough; some ***overt act*** of aid is necessary . . . . [1159]

   a. **Special evidentiary requirement:** Conviction of treason requires either ***two witnesses*** or the defendant's ***confession in open court*** . . . . [1162]
4. **Misprision of Treason:** This offense consists of the ***concealment*** of the known treason of another . . . . [1163]

B. TREASON-LIKE CRIMES

1. **Rebellion:** It is a federal offense to incite or engage in any rebellion against the United States . . . . [1165]
2. **Advocating Overthrow of Government:** It is a federal crime knowingly or willfully to advocate the overthrow or destruction of the government of the United States or any state . . . . [1166]

XIII. OFFENSES AGAINST THE ADMINISTRATION OF JUSTICE

A. HINDERING APPREHENSION OR PROSECUTION OF FELON

Modern statutes often make it an independent crime to aid or warn another with the intent to hinder that person's apprehension, conviction, or punishment. This crime is sometimes called "accessory after the fact," but unlike the common law parties rule of that name it does not create liability for the crime committed by the person aided or warned . . . . [1167]

B. MISPRISION OF FELONY

At common law, misprision of felony is the failure to report or prosecute one known to have committed a felony. Today, federal law requires some ***affirmative act*** to conceal a felon . . . . [1170]

C. COMPOUNDING A CRIME

1. **Common Law:** One who agrees for consideration not to prosecute another person for a felony is guilty of the misdemeanor of compounding a crime . . . . [1173]
2. **Modern Statutes:** Modern codes often extend the offense to agreements to forgo prosecution of ***any*** offense, felony or misdemeanor. There must be an ***agreement*** and ***valuable consideration*** . . . . [1174]
3. **"Settlement" of Crimes:** It is unclear whether compounding is committed by a victim of a crime who agrees not to press charges in return for restitution from the offender . . . . [1178]

D. PERJURY

1. **Common Law:** Perjury is the willful giving of a false statement under oath in a judicial proceeding . . . . [1179]
2. **Modern Statutes:** Modern statutes may extend the crime of perjury to ***any proceeding*** in which the law authorizes the ***administration of an oath***. Some statutes require that the false testimony be ***material*** to the proceeding (*i.e.*, likely to influence the outcome) . . . . [1180]
3. **Special Evidentiary Requirements:** Testimony of ***two witnesses*** is generally required for conviction . . . . [1183]
4. **Effect of Retraction:** Many jurisdictions provide a defense where the defendant retracts false testimony in the same proceeding . . . . [1184]
5. **Subornation of Perjury:** Subornation of perjury consists of intentionally causing another person to commit perjury. The crime is essentially the same under common law and modern statutes: The defendant must have ***known*** the testimony to be given by the witness would be false ***and*** the perjured testimony must actually have been given . . . . [1185]

TEXT CORRELATION CHART

Gilbert Law Summary Criminal Law	Boyce, Perkins **Criminal Law and Procedure Cases and Materials** 1989 (7th ed.)	Dix, Sharlot **Criminal Law Cases and Materials** 1996 (4th ed.)	Johnson **Criminal Law Cases, Materials and Text** 1995 (5th ed.)	Kadish, Schulhofer **Criminal Law and Its Processes Cases and Materials** 1995 (6th ed.)	La Fave **Modern Criminal Law** 1988 (2nd ed.)	Moenssens, Imbau, Bacigal **Criminal Law Cases and Comments** 1992 (5th ed.)	Weinreb **Criminal Law Cases, Comment, Questions** 1993 (5th ed.)
I. INTRODUCTION							
A. Crime Defined	5-9			1, 171, 297		159, 268-274	836-859
B. Sources of Criminal Law		2, 6-13	1-81		42-71	156-216	436-520
C. Classifications of Crimes	9-30	13-23		297-298	881		
D. Burden of Proof and Related Matters	45-58	39-58	523-540	38-59		119-155	54-69
II. THE CRIMINALIZATION DECISION							
A. Justifications for Punishment	1-5	59-76	120-123	97-153	23-42		392-401
B. Costs Versus Benefits	4						392-401
III. BASIC LEGAL LIMITS UPON CRIMINAL LAW							
A. Constitutional Right of Privacy	298-301			155-167, 253-254, 881-892	82-95	305-366	819-859
B. Due Process Prohibition Against Vagueness	6-9, 303-304	108-122	82-104	298-314	42-44, 71-82, 584-600, 636-637	275-304	807-809
C. Cruel and Unusual Punishment	10-21	77-108, 119-122	105-146	282-294, 509-545, 1011-1022	94-95, 334-353, 422	366-437	401-409, 804-807
D. Multiple Liability for Identical or Related Criminal Acts	942-988	241-265			225-237, 649-650		
IV. ELEMENTS OF CRIMES							
A. Criminal Acts—Actus Reus	313-319, 353-370	123-124, 129-180	49-81, 322-333	171-203, 998-999, 1011-1034	96, 187-225, 419-438	17-32, 1041-1049	349-370, 809-819
B. Attendant Circumstances		125, 545-546		210, 234-235			
C. Criminal State of Mind—Mens Rea							
1. General Requirement of Mens Rea	474-486, 556-563, 572-582	267-274	1	204-212	96-97, 105		
2. Traditional Mens Rea Analysis	487-536	270-271, 280-313	1-35	205-210, 213-214, 218-225	98-150	33-47, 68, 139-146	72-73, 153-169, 170-177, 220-221, 313-323, 340, 704-707, 714, 726-727
3. Strict Liability Crimes	537-556	313-331	35-49	235-257, 1034-1037	150-165	53-83, 86-102	724-732
4. Modern Classifications of State of Mind	487-497, 517-536	271-313	62-81	209-213, 214-218, 219-225	46-47, 127-132, 140-143, 816, 824	47-49	322, 399-400, 714
5. Mens Rea Requirements and "Defenses"	477-478, 486, 675-676	331-332	9-30, 77-81	226			

TEXT CORRELATION CHART—continued

Gilbert Law Summary **Criminal Law**	Boyce, Perkins **Criminal Law and Procedure Cases and Materials** 1989 (7th ed.)	Dix, Sharlot **Criminal Law Cases and Materials** 1996 (4th ed.)	Johnson **Criminal Law Cases, Materials and Text** 1995 (5th ed.)	Kadish, Schulhofer **Criminal Law and Its Processes Cases and Materials** 1995 (6th ed.)	La Fave **Modern Criminal Law** 1988 (2nd ed.)	Moenssens, Imbau, Bacigal **Criminal Law Cases and Comments** 1992 (5th ed.)	Weinreb **Criminal Law Cases, Comment, Questions** 1993 (5th ed.)
6. "Transferred Intent"—Responsibility for Unintended Results	564-572		1-4	560-561	108	49-53	115-116
D. Concurrence of Actus Reus and Mens Rea	582-588		1, 62		330-334		
E. Causation	424-473	514-544	259-273	547-581	315-334	102-118	370-391
V. SCOPE OF CRIMINAL LIABILITY							
A. Complicity in the Crime	408-424	673-722	621-659	641-683	704-762	898-925	757-760
B. Vicarious Liability	397-401, 422, 552-556	49, 723-733	635, 637-638	244-247	762-775	55-60, 68-81	725-727
C. Criminal Liability of Corporations and Associations	401-407	732-733	637-638	683-719	775-793	925-933	
VI. DEFENSES							
A. Infancy	589-617		300		455-459, 844	1020-1027	699-703
B. Insanity							
1. In General	617-621	822-824	275-282	929-932	354-372	1092-1093	594
2. Condition Giving Rise to Insanity	617-650	843-848	294-302, 322-333	973-983, 994-999	384-385, 391-393, 412-413, 447-454	1039-1040, 1049-1057	648-650, 653-655
3. Tests for "Insanity"							
a. Basic distinction—"cognitive" and "volitional" impairment	619-620, 645-647	848-867	294-302	949-959		1093	617-622, 624-628
b. Basic issue—should loss of control constitute a defense?	619-620	826-828	294-302	948, 953-955		1071, 1093	
c. *M'Naghten* rule	620-623, 629-637	825-826	283-310	932-945, 950	372-375, 389-393	1058-1070, 1083-1091	595-628
d. Loss of control tests	624-637, 649-650	826-832	289, 291-292, 294-295	945-948	375-376, 839	1070-1071, 1076-1083	622-624, 626, 637-645
e. Broader tests	626-629, 635	832-834	289-291, 295	944-945, 948, 999-1010	376-387	1072-1083	629-637
f. Revised cognitive tests	629-633, 638-640, 649-650	828-832	295-299, 337-339	953-959	387	1081-1083	644
g. "Mens rea" approach alternative	621	834-836	299-300, 334-337, 339-344, 347-352		445-448	1093-1094	
4. Proposal to Abolish Insanity Defense			298-299	966-973	387-389	1093-1110	645-648
5. Burden of Proof on Insanity	627, 638-640, 645-649	837-839	302, 319-323, 338, 344-347	935-937, 988	400-401	124, 1061-1063, 1083, 1092-1093	651-653
6. Jury Instructions on Consequences of Insanity Acquittal		842-843		935-936	403-405		

TEXT CORRELATION CHART—continued

Gilbert Law Summary **Criminal Law**	Boyce, Perkins **Criminal Law and Procedure Cases and Materials** 1989 (7th ed.)	Dix, Sharlot **Criminal Law Cases and Materials** 1996 (4th ed.)	Johnson **Criminal Law Cases, Materials and Text** 1995 (5th ed.)	Kadish, Schulhofer **Criminal Law and Its Processes Cases and Materials** 1995 (6th ed.)	La Fave **Modern Criminal Law** 1988 (2nd ed.)	Moenssens, Imbau, Bacigal **Criminal Law Cases and Comments** 1992 (5th ed.)	Weinreb **Criminal Law Cases, Comment, Questions** 1993 (5th ed.)
7. Procedure Following Acquittal by Reason of Insanity	618, 621, 629, 644, 647	839-842	296-297, 310-313, 315-318	983-991	405-408		668-698
8. Guilty But Mentally Ill Alternative	640-644	836-837	293, 313-322	991-994		1093-1110	645
C. Diminished Capacity	621-623	879-884	334-352	999-1011	408-418, 839	1031-1039	128-150, 650-651
D. Intoxication	313-314, 650-670	369-386	66, 70, 322-333, 347-352	913-929	419-454	1027-1031	703-710
E. Ignorance or Mistake of Fact	696-712	331-339, 582-590	14-20, 65-66, 69	225-235	165-175, 826	53-55, 86-91, 94-102	710-715
F. Ignorance or Mistake of Law	674-696	294-303, 331-334, 339-369, 785-786	19-30, 70, 77-81	257-282	175-186, 826	40-47, 81-83, 86-94	715-724
G. Necessity or Justification	712-724	735-758	356-364, 370-379	131-136, 860-880, 903-905	519-520, 527-533, 831	992-1019	221-222, 297-298, 306-310, 410-433
H. Duress	670-673, 713-714	735-739, 741-758	353-370	896-913	514-526, 829-830	988-992	297-307
I. Entrapment	841-854	801-821	441-459	617-621, 673-675, 1046-1047	491-493, 831	934-987	
J. Consent and Related Matters	724-737, 740-749		437-440	329, 333-339	533-539, 830		349
K. Self-Defense							
1. In General	779	759	413	801-846	460-463	540, 547	223-258
2. General Requirements for Self-Defense	779-780, 818	782-786	379-387, 423	801-814, 833-835	462-468, 832	540, 547	230-234
3. Additional Requirements Where Deadly Force Used	780-782, 787-815, 818-819	759-774	387-388, 407-413, 422-423	801-814, 835-836, 838-842	462-481, 832-833	540-559	223-229, 230-233
4. Special Problem—Battered Victim Claiming Killing in Self-Defense	798-799	759-773	379-402	814-835	474-480	559-561	244-258
5. Limitation—Right of Aggressor to Self-Defense	781, 815-817	776-780	422-423	842-846	462-469, 831-832	547-548	223-233, 235-244
6. Resisting Unlawful Arrest as Self-Defense	1029-1030	781-783, 785	417-422, 424-425	1145	504-509		234-235
7. Compare—"Imperfect" Self-Defense in Homicide Prosecution	782, 799-802	737-738	402-406	812-814, 827	462-468	536-559	233-234
L. Defense of Others	819-831	786-792	407-413, 423-424	836-837	481-484, 833-834	561-565	259-268
M. Protection of Property	834-841	792-800	426-430	846-852	484-491	574	268-273
N. Protection of Dwelling	831-834	775-776, 796-799	414-417	849-852	466-467, 469-470, 484-488, 833-834	565-574	273-274
O. Use of Force to Effectuate Arrest	1042-1044		430-437	852-860	495-504, 834-835	574-591	276-285
P. Crime Prevention	767-779		434-437	846-852	470-471, 491-493, 503-504, 835-836	574-591	218-221, 274-276
Q. Public Authority	750-760				493-503, 836		

TEXT CORRELATION CHART—continued

Gilbert Law Summary Criminal Law	Boyce, Perkins **Criminal Law and Procedure Cases and Materials** 1989 (7th ed.)	Dix, Sharlot **Criminal Law Cases and Materials** 1996 (4th ed.)	Johnson **Criminal Law Cases, Materials and Text** 1995 (5th ed.)	Kadish, Schulhofer **Criminal Law and Its Processes Cases and Materials** 1995 (6th ed.)	La Fave **Modern Criminal Law** 1988 (2nd ed.)	Moenssens, Imbau, Bacigal **Criminal Law Cases and Comments** 1992 (5th ed.)	Weinreb **Criminal Law Cases, Comment, Questions** 1993 (5th ed.)
R. Domestic Authority and Similar Special Relationships	761-767				509-515, 837-838		
VII. PRELIMINARY OR INCHOATE CRIMES							
A. Solicitation	326, 347-348, 352-353	625-628	574-576	617-623	696-703	826-831	756, 799-800
B. Conspiracy							
1. In General	371	592-594, 628-633	577-581	720	596-598, 682-683	832-834	756-757, 799-800
2. Requirements	379-381, 384-386, 390-395	633-672	568-573, 577-581, 597-621, 659-678	692-696, 743-774, 781-799	598-640, 645-660, 682-696, 846-847	833-834, 882-893	760-781, 784, 785, 788-792, 794-802
3. Punishment	352-353, 371	671-672	576-577, 661-662	720, 731-733	676-678, 847	833-834, 882-893	781-784, 793-794
4. Conviction for Conspiracy and Completed Crime	381-384	629, 703-705	650-659	729-743	676-677, 732-737	834, 882-889	781-784, 793-794
5. Special Problems Applying Conspiracy Law	350, 372-379, 383, 387-390	568-572, 645-660, 721-722	634-637, 650-659	727-729, 774-780	604-610, 640-645, 668-682	868-882, 894-898	788-789, 792-794, 800-801
6. Liability for Crimes of Co-Conspirators	381-386	703-722	603-607, 611-615, 621-659	727-729, 734-743, 798-799	668-670, 732-737	892-893, 901-904	781-783, 788-789
7. Duration of the Conspiracy		671	626-631	727-729	661-668	889-892	784-789
8. Tactical Advantages for the Prosecution		628-633, 636-638	611-621	720-727	596-598		783-784
C. Attempt	319-353, 506-507	592-625	555-574, 581-597	581-617, 623-640	540-595	794-826	732-756
VIII. HOMICIDE CRIMES							
A. Definition and Classification	9-10, 59-61, 82, 121-122	387-390	163-170	385-393	238-245, 334-335	447, 455-458	117-118
B. Murder	31-36, 39-46, 52-58, 62-70, 81-86, 89-93, 444-445, 471-472	398-429	147-195, 269-273	385-405, 456-468	264-290	438-476	72-73, 117-178
C. Felony Murder	70-81, 437-440, 446-462	457-509	206-232	468-509	296-313, 737-740	476-524	178-217
D. Voluntary Manslaughter	36-39, 52-59, 81-84, 87-106, 118-121, 430-436, 441-442, 462-466	429-449	49-52, 140-163, 183-195	405-437	238-264	524-536	72-116
E. Involuntary Manslaughter	59-62, 106-117, 425-429, 443-444, 466-467	449-457, 509-513	195-206, 249-251	437-468	290-296, 313-315, 728-730	17-22, 591-599	310-370
F. Modern Statutory Distinctions	106-108, 121-124, 368-369	390-397	52-59, 163-170, 183-195, 259-269	388-393, 1171-1173	860-861	455-460	117-152, 313-323

TEXT CORRELATION CHART—continued

Gilbert Law Summary Criminal Law	Boyce, Perkins **Criminal Law and Procedure Cases and Materials** 1989 (7th ed.)	Dix, Sharlot **Criminal Law Cases and Materials** 1996 (4th ed.)	Johnson **Criminal Law Cases, Materials and Text** 1995 (5th ed.)	Kadish, Schulhofer **Criminal Law and Its Processes Cases and Materials** 1995 (6th ed.)	La Fave **Modern Criminal Law** 1988 (2nd ed.)	Moenssens, Imbau, Bacigal **Criminal Law Cases and Comments** 1992 (5th ed.)	Weinreb **Criminal Law Cases, Comment, Questions** 1993 (5th ed.)
G. General Problems Relating to Homicide Liability	47-52, 111-114, 122, 363-365, 467-470, 557-558	391, 394-397	233-249, 251-259	167-168, 197-203, 298-303, 561-569, 880-892	47-60, 262-264, 315-334, 536	118-119, 217-258, 466-471	1-21, 52-54, 429-431
IX. OTHER CRIMES AGAINST THE PERSON							
A. Assault and Battery	124-137, 344-346, 562-563, 566-569, 725, 774-778	3, 237-241, 252-253, 270-274	9-14, 74-76, 347-352, 438-440, 584-586, 590-594, 597-603	234-235, 489-490, 495, 603-606, 679-680, 918-922, 1175	113-116, 439-445, 590-593, 864	262-267, 532	
B. Mayhem	150-151, 513-515	3			101	259-262	
C. Rape and Related Offenses	144-148, 340-342, 592-596, 702-712, 733-737	81-95, 253, 546-590	14-20, 438-440	315-384	165-175, 534, 866-868	32, 86-91, 94-102, 600-678	521-591
D. False Imprisonment	148, 752-753	4		1176	865		
E. Kidnapping	137-138, 148-150, 782-786, 911-916	4, 238, 255-265	13, 353-356	281-282, 873-875, 1176	864-865	501-503	
X. CRIMES AGAINST THE HABITATION							
A. Burglary	152-182, 476, 498, 505-507, 564, 651, 771-773	4, 226-237, 250, 288-289	13, 69, 222, 226-228, 334-337, 339-344, 555-559, 626-631	213, 490-491, 493-494, 602-603, 671-674, 1181	109-113, 593-595, 870-871	760-775	
B. Arson	182-185, 512-513, 582-583	4, 226	1-4, 59-60, 226-228, 246-249	207-208, 468-470, 551-552, 593-594, 1180	869		
XI. CRIMES AGAINST PROPERTY—ACQUISITION OFFENSES							
A. Introduction			698-700				
B. Larceny	186-244	5, 181-187, 247-249	681-700	1041-1048, 1051-1058, 1064-1075, 1100-1101, 1114-1125	161-165	679-715	436-450, 454-458, 460-462, 472-473, 478-485, 489-499, 506-510, 514
C. Embezzlement	202, 250-254	5, 187-196, 304, 309-313	681-700, 713-716	1049-1053, 1059-1064, 1121-1122		716-718	445-450, 462
D. False Pretenses	255-272	5, 196-201, 304	738-757	1064-1079, 1090-1092		719-731	451-452, 459-462, 503-505

TEXT CORRELATION CHART—continued

Gilbert Law Summary Criminal Law	Boyce, Perkins **Criminal Law and Procedure Cases and Materials** 1989 (7th ed.)	Dix, Sharlot **Criminal Law Cases and Materials** 1996 (4th ed.)	Johnson **Criminal Law Cases, Materials and Text** 1995 (5th ed.)	Kadish, Schulhofer **Criminal Law and Its Processes Cases and Materials** 1995 (6th ed.)	La Fave **Modern Criminal Law** 1988 (2nd ed.)	Moenssens, Imbau, Bacigal **Criminal Law Cases and Comments** 1992 (5th ed.)	Weinreb **Criminal Law Cases, Comment, Questions** 1993 (5th ed.)
E. Robbery	245-254	4, 205-217, 249-250, 257-265, 304-309	719-721	595-596, 610-615, 1048-1049, 1123-1125, 1182	871	750-759	510-511
F. Extortion (or Blackmail)	293, 295, 304	5, 217-226	721-738	1079-1088		201-209, 744-750	512-513
G. Receiving Stolen Property	289, 296, 330-335		594-596, 702-709	623-625, 1099-1100		732-744	751-753
H. Consolidation of Acquisition Offenses—Theft	273-289, 293-297	4, 201-208, 303-304	712-713, 716-718, 743-745	1062-1064, 1088-1090, 1182-1186	60, 164, 301-302, 871-875	722-731	466-485, 489-499, 510-511, 515-520
XII. OFFENSES AGAINST GOVERNMENT							
A. Treason	9, 304, 714, 856	6					
B. Treason-Like Crimes							
XIII. OFFENSES AGAINST THE ADMINISTRATION OF JUSTICE							
A. Hindering Apprehension or Prosecution of Felon	305-306	674-676			793-802		
B. Misprision of Felony	306			181-184, 186-187	802-807	718, 919-925	
C. Compounding a Crime	307			219-220		718, 925	
D. Perjury	304	6		74-89	883-884		

approach to exams

The ultimate issue in a Criminal Law examination question is whether the accused's conduct creates criminal liability. This involves consideration of: (i) whether the conduct, on its face, constitutes a crime; (ii) if so, whether there are any defenses which may be asserted; and (iii) whether there are any constitutional bars to conviction and punishment. Sometimes a statute will be presented in the question that will define the crime (or crimes), and often there will be statutes relating to possible defenses. However, these statutes may explicitly or implicitly incorporate common law rules and therefore even these questions require you to have a thorough understanding of the common law crimes and defenses.

With this in mind, approach Criminal Law questions using the following basic analytical framework. And don't forget to review the more detailed approaches to specific topics in the chapter approach sections at the beginning of each chapter.

A. IS DEFENDANT'S CONDUCT, ON ITS FACE, A VIOLATION OF THE CRIMINAL LAW?

Where the defendant is the ***actual perpetrator*** of the crime, ask:

1. Did his conduct constitute the requisite ***"act"***? Did it meet the general requirements for an "act" (§82), ***and*** did it satisfy the specific requirements of the statute creating or defining the crime? (Keep in mind that the criminal "act" may consist of a failure to act when under a legal duty to do so; §89.)

    a. If the defendant apparently intended to commit the act constituting the crime but did not actually succeed, consider possible liability for the inchoate crimes—*i.e.*, ***solicitation, attempt,*** and ***conspiracy*** (§§578 *et seq.*).

2. If the crime requires proof of ***certain circumstances*** that must have existed at the time of the defendant's act, can they be shown? (For example, if the defendant is charged with common law rape, it must be established that the victim was not his wife.)

3. Did the defendant, at the time of the act, have the ***mens rea*** or state of mind required by the crime? Ordinarily, at least ***"general intent"*** (§116) is required; however, certain crimes also require proof of ***"specific intent"*** (§120).

    a. Consider the possibility that the crime imposes ***"strict liability"*** and thus does not even require full general intent (§131).

4. Does the definition of the crime require a ***concurrence of the act and mens rea***, and if so, was there such a concurrence?

5. If the crime as defined requires proof of a result, did such result occur and was it ***"caused"*** by the defendant's act? Consider possible problems of ***factual causation*** (§178), ***proximate causation*** (§184), and any special causation requirements that may be imposed (as in the case of felony murder, §§723 *et seq.*).

B. IS DEFENDANT LIABLE FOR A CRIME COMMITTED BY THE ACTIONS OF ANOTHER PERSON?

If a crime was in fact perpetrated by another person, consider whether the defendant may incur liability therefor under one of the following theories:

1. Can the defendant be held liable because of his participation in the events ***before*** the commission of the crime?

    a. Under the law of complicity, did the defendant render the sort of assistance or encouragement that would make him, in common law terms, a ***principal in the second degree*** (§206) or an ***accessory before the fact*** (§208)?

    b. Is he liable as a ***co-conspirator*** for the crime of another conspirator (§644)?

    c. If the defendant's guilt is sought to be based on one of the above two theories, consider the possibility that he made a legally effective ***withdrawal*** before the crime was actually perpetrated (§§255, 650).

2. Is there a basis for imposing ***vicarious liability***? (Usually limited to employer-employee cases; §§276 *et seq.*)

3. Can liability be imposed based on the defendant's participation in the events ***after*** the commission of the crime? Did he act to hinder a felon's apprehension or prosecution and thus qualify as an ***accessory after the fact*** (§210)?

    a. In addition, consider whether the defendant's post-crime involvement with the actual perpetrator might render him liable for the separate crimes of ***misprision of felony*** (§1170) or ***compounding a crime*** (§1173).

C. IF DEFENDANT'S CONDUCT, ON ITS FACE, DOES CONSTITUTE A CRIME, ARE THERE ANY DEFENSES?

1. Do the facts show that the defendant ***lacked the mens rea*** required for the crime? Consider mistake of fact (§395), mistake of law (§408), intoxication (§379), or a mental defect short of insanity that negates intent under the diminished capacity rule (§371).

2. Do the facts show additional matters that prevent conviction? Consider problems of infancy (§313), insanity (§322), and other defenses such as self-defense, defense of others, entrapment, duress, necessity, etc.

D. ARE THERE ANY CONSTITUTIONAL BARS TO CONVICTION?

Specifically, you should consider:

1. Does holding the defendant liable violate ***privacy rights***?

2. Is the statute creating the crime ***unconstitutionally vague***?

3. Is the penalty imposed so disproportionate to the conduct involved as to violate the Eighth Amendment ***prohibition against cruel and unusual punishment***?

4. Is there an applicable prohibition against convicting and punishing defendant for ***several crimes arising out of one act***?

I. INTRODUCTION

chapter approach

The ultimate issue in your Criminal Law examination question is whether the accused's conduct creates criminal liability. Criminal liability is to be distinguished from other forms of liability: It is liability arising from the commission of a "crime." Although at common law crimes were defined by case law, today criminal law is almost entirely a statutory matter. Your decision as to whether the accused's conduct creates criminal liability necessarily involves consideration of the definition of the crime according to a given statute and/or with reference to the common law. The prosecution has the burden of proof on all elements of the crime as so defined, and to convict the accused the prosecution must prove those elements beyond a reasonable doubt.

A. CRIME DEFINED [§1]

A crime is an act or omission prohibited by law for the protection of the public, the violation of which is prosecuted by the state in its own name, and punishable by fine, incarceration, other restrictions upon liberty, or some combination of these. [Model Penal Code §1.04(1)]

B. SOURCES OF CRIMINAL LAW

1. **English Common Law:** [§2] The English common law is a major source of modern criminal law. Definitions of the basic crimes and defenses were developed in the decisions of the English courts and became part of the common law adopted in early America. Even where criminal law matters are now covered by statute, the meaning given these statutes is often determined by reference to the common law cases.

2. **Statutory Codes:** [§3] Criminal law matters are now largely governed by statute. Many jurisdictions have comprehensive criminal codes that define general principles of liability, specific crimes, and defenses. Even jurisdictions lacking such codes generally define criminal offenses by statute.

3. **Model Penal Code:** [§4] The Model Penal Code is a proposed penal code developed and approved by the American Law Institute. Final approval to the Model Penal Code was given in 1962. Although the Code does not itself constitute "law," since the Institute has no authority to promulgate law, the Code has served as the basis for almost all post-1962 revision of criminal statutes, and its provisions are often followed in state criminal statutory provisions.

C. CLASSIFICATIONS OF CRIMES [§5]

There are several methods of classifying crimes, which may be useful for different purposes.

1. **Felonies and Misdemeanors:** [§6] Traditionally, crimes were divided into felonies and misdemeanors; treason was categorized separately.

a. **Misdemeanors:** [§7] At common law, misdemeanors were those offenses not classified as felonies. This distinction is often retained by modern statutes.

b. **Common law felonies:** [§8] At common law, felonies are those offenses punishable by total forfeiture of land, goods, or both. Common law felonies include murder, manslaughter, rape, sodomy, mayhem, robbery, arson, burglary, and larceny.

c. **Statutory felonies:** [§9] Under modern statutes, felonies are those offenses for which a defendant may be sentenced to ***death or imprisonment for a certain period*** [Model Penal Code §1.04(2)—offense punishable by imprisonment for more than one year is felony] or by imprisonment in a ***state prison*** rather than a local jail [Cal. Penal Code §17].

2. **Malum in Se and Malum Prohibitum:** [§10] Crimes may also be classified as "malum in se" or "malum prohibitum."

a. **Malum in se:** [§11] Crimes that are ***inherently*** dangerous, bad, or immoral in themselves are regarded as malum in se. The common law felonies, for example, are all malum in se because they involve acts inherently immoral.

b. **Malum prohibitum:** [§12] Other acts are made criminal not because they are inherently wrong but because their prohibition is ***necessary*** to regulate the general welfare. For example, the prohibition against driving a motor vehicle on the left side of the road is not based upon the inherent wrongfulness of such conduct but rather upon the practical need for persons to agree on which side of the road to use.

D. BURDEN OF PROOF AND RELATED MATTERS [§13]

The prosecution has the burden of proof in a criminal proceeding. This has a number of implications, some of them constitutional in nature.

1. **Due Process Requirement—Proof Beyond a Reasonable Doubt:** [§14] As a general matter, the prosecution has the burden of proof and must prove ***all elements*** of a crime ***beyond a reasonable doubt***. This requirement is so important to reducing the risk that an innocent person will be convicted that it has been incorporated into the principle of due process of law and thus is a federal constitutional requirement. [*In re* Winship, 397 U.S. 358 (1970)]

2. **Element of Crime Cannot Be Treated as "Matter of Law":** [§15] The due process requirement is closely related to a criminal defendant's Sixth Amendment right to jury trial, and together the two rights require the prosecution to prove to the satisfaction of the jury all elements of the crime beyond a reasonable doubt. [Sullivan v. Louisiana, 113 S. Ct. 2078 (1993)] Thus, treating an element of the crime as a matter of law and withdrawing it from jury consideration violates the defendant's rights to due process and to a jury trial. [United States v. Gaudin, 115 S. Ct. 2310 (1995)]

a. **Example:** In a perjury trial requiring the prosecution to prove that a material false statement was made under oath, the trial judge told the jury that the materiality of the statement was a matter of law for decision by the court (not the jury) and that the statement at issue was material. This violated the defendant's federal constitutional rights. [United States v. Gaudin, *supra*]

3. **Defensive Matters—Burdens May Be Imposed on Defendant:** [§16] If a matter is not an element of the crime but rather relates to a defense, federal constitutional requirements are considerably more flexible.

   a. **Burden of going forward with evidence:** [§17] The burden of going forward with evidence on a defensive matter may be placed on the defendant. Under this approach, the defendant must produce evidence supporting the defense before the jury will be instructed on the defensive matter. [Simopoulos v. Virginia, 462 U.S. 506 (1983)]

   b. **Burden of proof or persuasion:** [§18] With regard to some and perhaps all traditional defenses, due process permits placement of the burden of proving the defense on the defendant, even if that burden is a quite high one. [Martin v. Ohio, 480 U.S. 228 (1987)—in murder prosecution, burden of proof on self-defense can be placed on defendant; Leland v. Oregon, 343 U.S. 790 (1952)—burden of proof beyond a reasonable doubt on insanity can be placed on defendant]

4. **Presumptions and Inferences Modifying Burden of Proof:** [§19] Procedural devices such as presumptions and even permissive inferences may so interfere with the prosecution's burden of proof as to violate due process.

   a. **Presumptions—shifting of burden of proof:** [§20] A presumption concerning elements of the charged crime is likely to be regarded as having the practical effect of relieving the prosecution of its burden of proof and thus violating due process. [Sandstrom v. Montana, 442 U.S. 510 (1979)]

      (1) **Example:** At D's trial for "deliberate homicide," the jury was told that "the law presumes that a person intends the ordinary consequences of his voluntary acts." This was likely to be understood by the jury as requiring the prosecution to prove only that D voluntarily did the act that caused death as an ordinary consequence and thus relieving the prosecution of its burden of proving criminal intent. It also shifts the burden to D to prove that he did not intend the death caused by his voluntary acts. Due process was violated. [Sandstrom v. Montana, *supra*]

      (2) **Example:** At D's trial for theft by fraud, the jury was told that intent to commit theft by fraud is presumed if one who rents property fails to return it within 20 days after expiration of the rental contract and after demand for return by the owner. This violated the due process mandate that the prosecution prove the required intent to defraud. [Carella v. California, 491 U.S. 263 (1989)]

   b. **Permissive inferences—ultimate fact must "more likely than not" flow from proved fact:** [§21] A "permissive inference" rather than a presumption is used if a jury is told that it may, but need not, infer one fact from another. A permissive inference does not violate due process if the ultimate fact (the fact to be inferred) more likely than not flows from the fact the prosecution proved. [County Court of Ulster County v. Allen, 442 U.S. 140 (1979)]

(1) **Example:** At D's trial for possession of a firearm, the jury was told that it could—but need not—infer from the presence of the firearm in a car occupied by D that D possessed the firearm. This was only a permissible inference rather than a presumption, and it did not violate due process because the ultimate fact—D's possession of the firearm—was more likely than not to flow from the proved fact—the presence of the firearm in a car occupied by D. [County Court of Ulster County v. Allen, *supra*]

5. **Homicide Prosecutions—Allocating Burdens Regarding Provocation or Its Equivalent:** [§22] In two confusing cases, the Supreme Court has addressed constitutional limits on the characterization of and burdens regarding provocation, which traditionally distinguishes voluntary manslaughter from murder.

a. **Burden of proof on provocation if malice is "presumed":** [§23] Due process is denied in a murder prosecution if the jury is told that the malice aforethought required for murder is "presumed" from the killing of the victim by the defendant, and that the defendant must prove that he acted in the heat of passion on sudden provocation so as to reduce the crime from murder to voluntary manslaughter. [Mullaney v. Wilbur, 421 U.S. 684 (1975)]

b. **Burden of proof on "extreme emotional disturbance" under modern statutory scheme:** [§24] Where murder requires the prosecution to prove beyond a reasonable doubt intent to kill, due process is ***not*** violated by placing on the defendant the burden of proving by a preponderance of the evidence that he killed under the influence of an extreme emotional disturbance for which there was reasonable explanation or excuse, which would reduce the killing from murder to manslaughter. [Patterson v. New York, 432 U.S. 197 (1977)]

(1) **Rationale:** If murder requires proof of a meaningful mens rea, as in *Patterson*, the additional facts—heat of passion/provocation or extreme emotional disturbance—distinguishing murder from manslaughter are in a meaningful sense "defensive facts" on which the burden of proof can fairly be placed on the defendant. In *Mullaney*, however, the mens rea required for murder was "presumed," and the facts distinguishing manslaughter from murder were not really defensive because the prosecution was not required to first make any meaningful showing.

II. THE CRIMINALIZATION DECISION

chapter approach

Exam questions occasionally call for a discussion of the policy considerations of making certain conduct criminal. While you should have no problem justifying the criminalization of murder or robbery, the wisdom of criminalizing less serious crimes (*e.g.*, possession of marijuana) may not be as clear. In addressing general examination questions concerning the wisdom of criminalizing conduct, you should ask the following questions:

1. ***What social interests*** might be furthered by criminalizing the conduct, and also, how might those interests be furthered?
2. ***What are the "costs"*** of criminalizing conduct that must be weighed against those benefits, and what would be the probable result of a ***balancing*** of those costs and benefits?

A. JUSTIFICATIONS FOR PUNISHMENT [§25]

Clearly, when specific conduct is made a crime, criminal punishment can be imposed upon those who engage in the proscribed behavior. But what are the justifications for subjecting those who violate the criminal law to punishment?

1. **Specific Prevention:** [§26] One theory often advanced is that of "specific" prevention—*i.e.,* punishment may prevent the offender from committing future crimes. [114 U. Pa. L. Rev. 949] This concept may work in several ways:

   a. **"Specific" deterrence:** [§27] Imposing punishment upon the offender may cause her to fear the penalty for future crimes and thus deter her from committing them.

   b. **Incapacitation:** [§28] Further, punishment often involves restraints on the offender's liberty, thus making it virtually impossible for her to engage in criminal behavior during the period of restraint.

   c. **Treatment:** [§29] Moreover, punishment in the form of restraints enables authorities to treat and perhaps rehabilitate the offender. (Note that treatment differs from specific deterrence in that treatment is designed to alter the offender's basic motivations, rather than frighten her into forgoing the commission of crimes that she may still desire to commit.)

2. **General Prevention:** [§30] Penalizing offenders may also prevent the commission of crimes by others—so-called "general" prevention. [114 U. Pa. L. Rev. 949] For instance:

   a. **"General" deterrence:** [§31] Punishing the offender can have a "general deterrent" effect, by indirectly warning others to anticipate similar punishment should they violate the criminal law.

b. **"Moralizing" effect:** [§32] In addition, punishment may serve an educational function, convincing others that the violation of criminal statutes is morally wrong. Accordingly, quite apart from the fear of punishment, such persons might abstain from criminal conduct because of their unwillingness to engage in morally reprehensible behavior.

c. **"Social solidarity" effect:** [§33] Some argue that social order requires a widespread consensus that criminal behavior is wrong and that subjecting offenders to punishment will maintain this consensus. Otherwise, it is felt, the "social solidarity" encouraged by criminal punishment will dissolve and people will regard themselves as free to violate other criminal laws. [*See* P. Devlin, The Enforcement of Morals (1965)]

d. **Channeling resentment:** [§34] Moreover, there are those who feel so strongly that persons who violate criminal statutes should be punished that they will inflict punishment themselves if the law does not. Therefore, it is urged that punishment pursuant to law is necessary to prevent others from committing additional criminal offenses by taking the law into their own hands.

3. **Retribution:** [§35] Finally, there are those who believe that punishing an offender is justified simply because she has committed a wrongful act. This is the notion of retribution—the commission of the past offense itself justifies punishment. [*See* P. Brett, An Inquiry Into Criminal Guilt (1963)]

a. **Compare—"social solidarity" effect:** [§36] Note that unlike the social solidarity theory, which urges punishment of what the community regards as morally wrong as a means of maintaining general order and thus preventing future criminal conduct, the retribution notion rests solely on the premise that what the offender did was "wrong."

B. COSTS VERSUS BENEFITS

1. **Benefits:** [§37] The benefits to be gained from making conduct criminal turn on the extent to which the social interests justifying criminalization will be furthered. As discussed above, the interests that might be furthered are those in prevention of crime and retribution.

a. **Prevention:** Will criminalization prevent offenders and others from engaging in future criminal acts through general or specific prevention? This may depend on whether the conduct involved is of a type likely to be deterred or whether the offender herself is likely to be rehabilitated during imprisonment.

b. **Retribution:** Is the conduct sufficiently "wrong" that the retributive notion is of significant value?

2. **Costs:** [§38] Obviously there are direct costs of criminalization (*e.g.,* costs of law enforcement, prosecution, imprisonment, etc.). Besides direct costs, the costs of criminalization are reflected to a large extent in terms of the impact upon those who commit the acts. For instance, criminalization may not only subject offenders to physical discomfort but may also stigmatize them in such a way as to produce a long-term disability.

a. **Incidental costs:** In addition, enforcement of criminal sanctions can also involve incidental costs, such as improper searches and seizures.

b. **Impact on society:** Quite apart from the impact upon the offenders themselves, criminalization of a widespread activity may tend to bring the law into disrespect among a significant portion of the population. In such cases, the crucial, albeit philosophical, question becomes whether the benefits are worth the sacrifices.

III. BASIC LEGAL LIMITS UPON CRIMINAL LAW

chapter approach

On your exam you may encounter a defendant who appears to be guilty of a crime under the definition of the crime charged and who is without any specific defense available to him. Don't give up on the defendant just yet because there may be a basic prohibition against convicting or punishing him. Most of these prohibitions are ***constitutional rules***, and most bar any form of criminal conviction or punishment. Sometimes, however, only particular penalties are prohibited. And the last doctrine discussed in this chapter considers a bar to conviction (or perhaps only punishment) for multiple offenses that may be based on statutes or case law.

On your exam, remember, before concluding that defendant can be convicted and a particular penalty imposed, always consider whether any of the following bars to conviction or punishment exist:

1. Would holding defendant liable violate his constitutional ***right of privacy***?

2. Is the statute creating the crime ***unconstitutionally vague*** and therefore in violation of due process?

3. Is the penalty to be imposed inherently impermissible or so disproportionate to the conduct as to violate the Eighth Amendment prohibition against ***cruel and unusual punishment***?

4. If by one act or course of conduct defendant may have committed what are technically several crimes, is ***conviction and punishment for several crimes*** permissible? Is there evidence of legislative intent to allow multiple liability for identical or related criminal acts? Are there statutory or constitutional bars to multiple liability?

A. CONSTITUTIONAL RIGHT OF PRIVACY

1. **In General—Right of Privacy:** [§39] No right of privacy is expressly mentioned in the United States Constitution, although some state constitutions provide for such a right. Nevertheless, the Supreme Court has found in various provisions of the Constitution a federal right of privacy. Certain conduct is protected by the right of privacy, and a person may not be convicted of a crime for engaging in such protected conduct. [Griswold v. Connecticut, 381 U.S. 479 (1965); *and see* detailed discussion in Constitutional Law Summary]

2. **Application:** [§40] The following examples illustrate the impact of the right of privacy on substantive criminal law:

   a. **Contraceptive information:** [§41] A state statute making it a criminal offense to use or assist others in using any drug or medical instrument to prevent conception has been held to violate married couples' right of privacy. [Griswold v. Connecticut, *supra*]

b. **Private possession of obscenity:** [§42] Although obscenity does not enjoy First Amendment protection, a person's right of privacy means that one cannot be convicted of a crime for possession of obscene materials in one's own home. [Stanley v. Georgia, 394 U.S. 557 (1969)]

c. **Possession of marijuana:** [§43] A few courts have held that the right of privacy bars convicting a person for possessing small amounts of marijuana in the person's own home for personal use. [*See, e.g.,* Ravin v. State, 537 P.2d 494 (Alaska 1975)—protection under state constitution] The weight of authority, however, is that neither state nor federal constitutional privacy rights afford such protection. [*See, e.g.,* State v. Murphy, 570 P.2d 1070 (Ariz. 1977)]

B. DUE PROCESS PROHIBITION AGAINST VAGUENESS

1. **General Rule—Criminal Statute Must Be Precise:** [§44] The Due Process Clauses of the Fifth and Fourteenth Amendments prohibit enforcement of statutes defining crimes if those statutes are impermissibly vague. [Winters v. New York, 333 U.S. 507 (1948)]

a. **Rationale:** The due process rule serves in part to assure that persons can tell, by examining the statutes, whether the conduct anticipated will be criminal; thus, it assures ***notice***. It also and perhaps more importantly requires that statutes be sufficiently precise to ***discourage arbitrary enforcement***.

2. **Criteria for Evaluating Vagueness:** [§45] A criminal statute is unconstitutionally vague if it fails to define the offense with sufficient definiteness:

(i) So that ordinary people can understand what conduct is prohibited; or

(ii) So as to discourage arbitrary and discriminatory application.

[Kolender v. Lawson, 461 U.S. 352 (1983)]

a. **Example—no notice:** [§46] A statute provided that "any person not engaged in any lawful occupation, who is known to be a member of any gang consisting of two or more persons, is guilty of a crime." The statute is unenforceable because the meaning of "gang" is so unclear that it is virtually impossible to determine in advance whether a contemplated course of conduct is forbidden by law. [Lanzetta v. New Jersey, 306 U.S. 451 (1939)]

b. **Example—opportunity for arbitrary and discriminatory enforcement:** [§47] A statute defined disorderly conduct as including loitering or wandering about the streets or from place to place without apparent reason or business, and refusing to produce credible and reliable identification and to account for one's presence when requested to do so by a law enforcement officer. The statute is vague because the phrase "credible and reliable identification" is so unclear that police officers have virtually complete discretion in determining whether persons have committed the offense. The grant of such unfettered discretion creates the opportunity for arbitrary and discriminatory enforcement. [Kolender v. Lawson, *supra*]

3. **Vagueness Evaluated "As Applied":** [§48] Generally, a defendant can challenge only whether a criminal statute is vague ***as applied to the facts of the***

defendant's case. Such a defendant cannot argue that a statute would deny notice to some other hypothetical defendant. If a criminal statute covers a considerable amount of constitutionally protected conduct, however, the courts will evaluate its vagueness "on its face" rather than as applied. [Posters 'N' Things, Ltd. v. United States, 114 S. Ct. 1747 (1994)]

4. **Curing Vagueness by "Scienter":** [§49] A statute that would otherwise be unconstitutionally vague may be upheld if it requires that the prohibited act be committed with "scienter" or intent. The rationale often urged for this is that some scienter elements are met only if the vagueness did not affect the particular defendants; if the defendants were uncertain as to whether the statute applied in their situation, they could not have the culpable mental state necessary for the scienter requirement. Thus, any persons denied actual notice by the statute's imprecision—any persons left uncertain about whether the statute applied to their situation—could not be convicted and thus were not harmed by the statute's vagueness. [Screws v. United States, 325 U.S. 91 (1945)] In a close case, a scienter requirement may mitigate a statute's imprecision enough to save it. [Posters 'N' Things, Ltd. v. United States, *supra*]

   a. **Example:** A statute makes it a crime to "willfully" deprive a person of federal rights while acting under state law. The phrase "federal rights" may be vague. But the requirement of willfulness permits conviction only if the defendant understood that his conduct violated what he knew was a federal right of the victim. Any accused harmed by the vagueness (and thus uncertain as to whether the victim's federal rights were violated) could not be convicted. [Screws v. United States, *supra*]

C. CRUEL AND UNUSUAL PUNISHMENT

1. **In General:** [§50] The Eighth Amendment prohibition against cruel and unusual punishment, binding on the states by virtue of the Fourteenth Amendment, imposes a number of different limits upon criminal law. Some of these limits are discussed below, *and see infra,* §80, considering whether a status can be made a crime.

2. **Inherently Impermissible Punishments:** [§51] The Eighth Amendment "draw[s] its meaning from the evolving standards of decency that mark the progress of a maturing society." Under this standard, some punishments are so ***inherently*** barbaric or degrading—and therefore disproportionate to defendants' culpability—as to preclude them from ever being used. It is likely that this doctrine bars the use of torture, death by painful and lingering methods, or expatriation (*i.e.,* forfeiture of citizenship). [Wilkerson v. Utah, 99 U.S. 130 (1878); Trop v. Dulles, 356 U.S. 86 (1958)]

3. **Disproportionate Penalties:** [§52] Some penalties that are not inherently cruel and unusual are nevertheless prohibited in particular cases because they are so ***grossly and outrageously disproportionate*** to the defendant's conduct. [Weems v. United States, 217 U.S. 349 (1910)]

   a. **Example:** D was convicted of falsifying entries in a public record. A sentence of 15 years' imprisonment at hard labor carrying chains and perpetual disqualification from political rights was so excessive in comparison to the offense as to violate the Eighth Amendment. [Weems v. United States, *supra*]

b. **Disproportionately long prison terms:** [§53] In certain exceptional situations, a prison term may be so excessive as to violate the prohibition against cruel and unusual punishment. [Solem v. Helm, 463 U.S. 277 (1983)] *But note:* Because of the absence of any objective standards for judging excessiveness, however, this will seldom be the case. [Rummel v. Estelle, 445 U.S. 263 (1980)]

(1) **Relevant considerations:** In deciding whether a penalty is unconstitutionally disproportionate, the courts should consider: (i) the gravity of the offense committed and the harshness of the penalty imposed; (ii) sentences imposed on other offenders in the same jurisdiction; and (iii) sentences imposed upon others committing the same offense in other jurisdictions. [Solem v. Helm, *supra*] Such an analysis is necessary, however, only in rare cases where a threshold comparison of the crime and the sentence suggests gross disproportionality. [Harmelin v. Michigan, 501 U.S. 957 (1991)]

(2) **Examples:** A sentence of life imprisonment without the possibility of parole imposed upon an accused under a recidivist statute for several minor offenses violated the Eighth Amendment, where no such penalty could be imposed for the crime in 48 of the 50 states. [Solem v. Helm, *supra*] But no violation occurred when a defendant convicted of a minor property crime (theft of $120) was sentenced to life imprisonment because of his two prior convictions for similar offenses, but was eligible for parole after serving 12 years. [Rummel v. Estelle, *supra*] Nor was there a violation when a defendant convicted of possessing 672 grams of cocaine was sentenced to life imprisonment without parole. [Harmelin v. Michigan, *supra*]

4. **Death Penalty**

a. **General rule—death penalty not prohibited:** [§54] The death penalty is not inherently excessive and therefore may, pursuant to a proper procedure, be imposed on a defendant and carried out. The procedure, however, must be adequate to assure evenhanded determinations as to whether the penalty is appropriate in each case. [Gregg v. Georgia, 428 U.S. 153 (1976); Tuilaepa v. California, 114 S. Ct. 2630 (1994)]

b. **Death penalty sometimes disproportionate:** [§55] In some categories of cases, however, the Supreme Court has held that the penalty of death would be so disproportionate to the offense as to violate the Eighth Amendment. [Coker v. Georgia, 433 U.S. 584 (1977); Enmund v. Florida, 458 U.S. 782 (1982)]

(1) **Rape of adult woman:** [§56] If the defendant has been convicted of the rape of an adult woman, the penalty of death is unconstitutionally disproportionate. [Coker v. Georgia, *supra*] This is the case even if serious physical harm was caused to the victim. [Eberheart v. Georgia, 433 U.S. 917 (1977)]

(2) **"Nontriggerperson" in murder:** [§57] Under complicity rules (*see infra,* §§202 *et seq.*) and the co-conspirator rule (*see infra,* §§590 *et seq.*), a person may be criminally responsible for a murder directly committed

by someone else. However, the Eighth Amendment somewhat limits the imposition of the death penalty upon such "nontriggerpersons." Death is a constitutionally permissible penalty only if the person's participation in the offense was "major" and the person participated either with the intention to cause death or with "reckless disregard" for whether death would result from the venture. [Tison v. Arizona, 481 U.S. 137 (1987)]

(3) **Young murderers:** [§58] A murderer who was under 16 years of age at the time of the crime cannot be executed for that crime as a matter of Eighth Amendment law. [Thompson v. Oklahoma, 487 U.S. 815 (1988)] The amendment does, however, permit execution of murderers who were 16 or 17 at the time of their crimes. [Stanford v. Kentucky, 492 U.S. 361 (1989)]

c. **"Insane" prisoner cannot be executed:** [§59] If a condemned prisoner has become "insane," the Eighth Amendment bars the prisoner's execution. In this context, a prisoner is probably "insane" if the prisoner does not realize the fact of impending execution or the reason for it. [Ford v. Wainwright, 477 U.S. 399 (1986)]

d. **Statutory standards must not be vague:** [§60] Statutory standards for determining which convicted defendants are eligible for the death penalty and which will be sentenced to death violate the Eighth Amendment if those standards are not sufficiently precise. [Maynard v. Cartwright, 486 U.S. 356 (1988)]

(1) **Example:** A statute permitting the sentencing jury to consider whether murder was "especially heinous, atrocious, or cruel" was so vague as to violate the Eighth Amendment. [Maynard v. Cartwright, *supra*]

D. MULTIPLE LIABILITY FOR IDENTICAL OR RELATED CRIMINAL ACTS

1. **In General—Overlapping Criminal Liability:** [§61] Defendants may incur overlapping liability in two ways: (i) The same act may constitute several crimes (*e.g.*, a murder is often accomplished by activity that also constitutes a battery). (ii) In addition, different acts constituting different crimes are often committed closely together and for related reasons (*e.g.*, a burglary is often committed as a means of accomplishing a larceny or theft inside the entered premises, although the act constituting the burglary—the entry—is different from the act constituting the larceny—the taking and asportation of the property).

a. **Policy concerns with overlapping liability:** [§62] Those who object to convicting and punishing defendants for all offenses technically committed argue that this permits imposition of liability and punishment disproportionate to defendants' actual blameworthiness. A thief who steals after entering a dwelling to find the item, for example, may not be twice as blameworthy as another thief who steals a similar item he finds in a public place. Yet the first thief is subject to conviction for two crimes and to twice as long a prison term. Some courts, as a result of these concerns, have sought ways to limit criminal liability for one act or related acts.

2. **Common Law Doctrine of Merger:** [§63] At common law, if the same act constituted both a felony and a misdemeanor, the misdemeanor was regarded as "merging" into the felony and there could be no conviction for the misdemeanor.

However, this doctrine did not apply if ***both*** crimes were felonies or misdemeanors. Nor did it apply if the two crimes were based upon ***different conduct*** or acts. [Graff v. People, 70 N.E. 299 (Ill. 1904)]

a. **Examples:** If the defendants conspired to commit a felony and did in fact commit it, the misdemeanor of conspiracy merged into the committed felony. If a defendant committed a battery on a victim and the victim died, rendering the defendant guilty of murder, the misdemeanor of battery merged into the murder.

b. **Modern law—no common law merger:** [§64] The doctrine of merger as it was known and applied at common law is no longer applied in American jurisdictions. [J. Miller, Criminal Law 51 (1943)—afterwards cited as "Miller"]

3. **Fifth Amendment Prohibition Against Double Jeopardy:** [§65] The Fifth Amendment bar against double jeopardy applies primarily to repeated prosecutions for the same or perhaps related crimes. It may, therefore, sometimes bar a second prosecution (and, of course, a conviction) for a crime where the defendant has already been tried and convicted of a related offense. [Harris v. Oklahoma, 433 U.S. 682 (1977); *and see* detailed discussion in Criminal Procedure Summary]

a. **No absolute double jeopardy bar to multiple convictions in one proceeding:** [§66] If a legislature makes the same conduct two crimes, a defendant can be convicted ***in one proceeding*** of both offenses and punished by consecutive prison terms as long as this was the ***legislative intent.*** [Missouri v. Hunter, 459 U.S. 359 (1983)]

(1) **Example:** D robbed V using a pistol. D was convicted of robbery and, in addition, of the separate crime of using a dangerous weapon in the commission of a crime. Consecutive prison terms were imposed for the crimes. Since the legislature intended to permit conviction for both crimes on the basis of the same conduct (using a gun to obtain property from another), no double jeopardy as prohibited by the federal Constitution occurred. [Missouri v. Hunter, *supra*]

(2) **Rationale:** Why does double jeopardy impose no more rigorous limits on multiple convictions? In part, this is probably because there are no objective standards for determining when multiple convictions result in constitutionally offensive disproportionality. Further, legislatures could circumvent any constitutional limits by manipulating penalty provisions, as by providing that robbery is punishable by X years but if a gun was used it is punishable by 2X years.

b. **Multiple conviction not legislatively intended:** [§67] If a defendant in federal court is convicted of and punished for multiple offenses in violation of congressional intent, the punishment violates both the separation of powers doctrine and double jeopardy. Conviction of a defendant in a state court for several related crimes in a manner not intended by the state legislature would most likely violate federal double jeopardy law, although this is not entirely clear. [Whalen v. United States, 445 U.S. 684 (1980)]

(1) **Determining legislative intent—*Blockburger* rule:** [§68] In applying this aspect of federal constitutional law, the *Blockburger* rule is used in

ascertaining legislative intent. Congress is presumed to have intended to prohibit punishing a defendant for two crimes stemming from the same activity ***unless each crime*** requires proof of an ***additional fact*** that the other does not. [Blockburger v. United States, 284 U.S. 299 (1932)]

(a) **Example:** D was convicted in federal court of rape and of felony murder on the basis of the victim's death caused during the rape. Consecutive sentences were imposed. Under the *Blockburger* test, it is assumed that Congress intended no double punishment. Although felony murder requires proof of a fact—the victim's death—that rape does not, proof of the rape does not require proof of any fact that the felony murder does not. In the absence of any evidence that Congress intended a different result, these convictions violated congressional intent and thus D's federal constitutional rights. [Whalen v. United States, *supra*]

(2) **Caveat:** [§69] Remember that the *Blockburger* rule is only a means of determining legislative intent. If there is ***direct evidence of congressional intent*** to permit conviction and punishment for several offenses, this is constitutionally permissible even if each crime does not require proof of at least one fact that the other does not.

4. **State Double Jeopardy Prohibitions:** [§70] Many state constitutions contain prohibitions against double jeopardy similar in terminology to the Fifth Amendment to the United States Constitution. These provisions are sometimes construed by state courts as giving defendants broader protection against multiple prosecution than is afforded by the federal Constitution.

a. **"Multiple interests" approach—Alaska Constitution:** [§71] The Alaska constitutional prohibition against double jeopardy has been construed as barring multiple punishment for several crimes arising out of the same criminal event or episode unless the different crimes were designed to protect different social interests. [Whitton v. State, 479 P.2d 302 (Alaska 1970)]

(1) **Example:** D was convicted of and sentenced for robbery and the different crime of using a firearm during a robbery. Both crimes were designed to protect the same social interest, *i.e.,* the security of citizens. Therefore, punishing the defendant for violating both criminal statutes offended the Alaska Constitution's prohibition against double jeopardy. [Whitton v. State, *supra*]

5. **Statutory Bars to Multiple Conviction or Punishment:** [§72] In some jurisdictions, statutes prohibit defendants from being convicted or punished for more than one crime arising out of a single act. [Cal. Penal Code §654—when "[a]n act" is punishable by different provisions of the Penal Code, it may be punished only under one provision] Consideration of whether only a single act is involved has resulted in widely differing views.

a. **Separable actions approach:** [§73] Some courts find such statutes inapplicable if each crime consists of actions that can be mechanically distinguished.

(1) **Example:** D, intending to steal V's wallet, enters V's house and takes the wallet. Under this approach, D can be convicted of both burglary and

larceny, because the burglary is committed by the act of entering and the larceny by the distinguishable act of taking and asporting the wallet.

b. **"Single objective" standard:** [§74] Some courts have defined a "single act" to include crimes related in their commission that were committed pursuant to a single and primary objective. [People v. Miller, 18 Cal. 3d 873 (1977)—construing Cal. Penal Code §654, *supra*]

(1) **Example:** D, intending to steal V's wallet, enters V's house and takes the wallet. Under the "single objective" approach, D cannot be convicted of both burglary and larceny, because both crimes were committed pursuant to the primary objective of the taking of the wallet.

6. **Modern Merger of Offenses as Matter of Legislative Intent:** [§75] Courts sometimes hold that defendants cannot be convicted of related crimes because one offense "merges" into another. This is not, however, an application of the old common law merger rule (*see supra,* §63). Instead, it represents a construction of legislative intent that convictions for both crimes should not be permitted. [State v. Burroughs, 636 A.2d 1009 (Md. 1994)]

a. ***Blockburger* rule as guide to intent:** [§76] Courts often apply the *Blockburger* test (*supra*) as a guide to legislative intent. Legislatures are regarded as having intended to merge two crimes and to bar conviction for both unless each crime requires proof of facts that the other does not. This means that usually there can be no conviction for both a greater offense and a lesser included one. [Commonwealth v. Jones, 416 N.E.2d 502 (Mass. 1981)]

(1) **Example:** D takes property from V by means of force, with the intent of keeping the property. D has committed both larceny and robbery by the same act of taking the property. Conviction for robbery requires proof of a fact that larceny does not—use of force—but larceny does not require proof of anything the robbery does not; *i.e.,* the robbery requires proof of the entire larceny plus something else. This makes the larceny a lesser included offense of the robbery. Generally, as a matter of legislative intent, the larceny will be regarded as having "merged" into the robbery and there can be no conviction for both. [People v. Nelson, 79 App. Div. 2d 171 (1981)]

7. **Exception—Multiple Victims:** [§77] Where there are multiple victims of a defendant's action, the defendant can almost always be convicted of an offense committed on each victim, even though there was only one criminal "act." Even under the Alaska constitutional approach discussed *supra,* the prohibition against multiple convictions for crimes protecting the same social interests contains an exception permitting multiple convictions where multiple victims were involved. [State v. Dunlop, 721 P.2d 604 (Alaska 1986)]

IV. ELEMENTS OF CRIMES

chapter approach

Most examination questions ask you to discuss the potential criminal liability of a defendant (or defendants) in a particular fact situation. In responding to such questions, it is important to address whether the prosecution can prove all elements of the crime charged. This requires that you first identify the elements of the crime. If your exam provides you with a statute defining the crime under which the defendant is charged, you should, of course, focus on that statute in identifying the elements. But in any case—for statutory or common law crimes—you can identify the elements by asking yourself:

1. ***What "acts"*** must the defendant have performed to be guilty? (This is the actus reus element.)

2. ***What attendant circumstances*** must have existed (usually at the time of the conduct) for the acts to constitute the crime?

3. ***What state of mind*** must the defendant have had to be guilty? (This is the mens rea element.)

4. ***Must there have been concurrence of the actus reus and the mens rea?*** (Must the act have been attributable to the state of mind required?)

5. ***Is there any particular result*** that must be shown, *i.e.,* something that must have occurred as a result of the defendant's acts?

Of course, not all crimes involve all of these five elements, but all do contain an actus reus requirement, and most will contain a mens rea element.

In addition to the specific requirements imposed by the statute or other definition of the particular crime involved, you should consider certain general issues. For example, in regard to acts constituting the actus reus, you must consider both the specific requirements of the crime (*i.e.,* an act constituting an "entry" in burglary) and the more general requirements of the actus reus element considered in this chapter (*e.g.,* whether the conduct constituting entry was "volitional").

A. CRIMINAL ACTS—ACTUS REUS

1. **In General:** [§78] To be convicted of a crime, the defendant must have committed a criminal act; the law does not punish mere criminal thoughts (*see infra*). Generally, liability is based upon an ***affirmative physical act*** by the defendant; however, under some circumstances, liability can rest upon a total ***failure to act*** at all—*i.e.,* an omission. A crime's required act is commonly referred to as the "actus reus" of the crime.

   a. **Requirement of an Act:** [§79] Whether the criminal conduct is an act or a failure to act, the authorities are in general agreement that basic principles of jurisprudence demand that crimes be defined in terms of acts. Indeed, this requirement is to some extent embodied in the federal Constitution.

(1) **Rationale:** If no act is required, punishment would be imposed on the basis of mere intent. However, thoughts are often not converted into action, and thus intent alone poses an insufficient danger to society to justify criminal liability. Hence, no legitimate function is served by subjecting persons to criminal liability solely for harboring an evil intent. Moreover, the requirement of an act also serves a notice function by defining precisely what it is that the law proscribes.

(2) **Constitutional limitation:** [§80] Defining a crime in terms of a ***"status,"*** rather than a particular activity, violates the Eighth Amendment prohibition against cruel and unusual punishment. [Robinson v. California, 370 U.S. 660 (1962)]

(a) **Example:** Conviction of a person for a crime consisting of "being addicted to narcotics" violates the Eighth Amendment. [Robinson v. California, *supra*]

(b) **Rationale:** It does not necessarily follow from the fact that a person has a certain status that he will commit serious antisocial acts; hence, conviction for status alone would amount to punishing for "propensity" or "intent." Moreover, the definition of a given "status" is often so vague that prospective defendants are denied adequate notice of the nature of the criminal offense (*e.g.,* what amounts to being an "addict" and how does one stop being an "addict"?). [Powell v. Texas, 392 U.S. 514 (1968)]

(c) **Compare—acts related to status:** [§81] The rationale for prohibiting status crimes does not apply to crimes consisting of conduct merely related to the offender's status. Thus, a person can be convicted of a crime requiring a particular act, even if that act is closely related to the person's status.

1) **Examples:** Although "being an alcoholic" cannot constitute a crime, an alcoholic can be convicted of appearing in public while drunk even though that appearance is related to his status as an alcoholic. [Powell v. Texas, *supra*] And although being a homeless person cannot be made a crime, homeless people can probably be convicted of crimes consisting of camping or storing personal property in public. [Tobe v. City of Santa Ana, 9 Cal. 4th 1069 (1995)]

2. **"Acts" Sufficient for Criminal Liability—Affirmative versus Negative "Acts":** [§82] The act required to support conviction of a given crime varies with the crime itself; it may be one of commission (affirmatively doing something) or omission (failing to do something). Some crimes are specifically defined in terms of the acts the defendant must have committed. With such crimes, proof of these acts is essential to a finding of guilt (*e.g.,* burglary requires a "breaking" and "entering," rape requires "intercourse," and embezzlement requires a "conversion").

However, other crimes—such as the homicide offenses—do not particularize the requisite acts and thus a conviction must be based upon the general concepts of what constitutes a criminal "act." In any case, regardless of the extent to which the requisite act is described in the crime itself, all "acts" for criminal law purposes must meet certain fundamental requirements.

a. **Affirmative acts (acts of commission):** [§83] Where criminal liability is based upon the defendant's affirmative act (as is the usual case), there must be a showing that the defendant made some ***conscious*** and ***volitional movement.***

(1) **Movement:** [§84] Ordinarily, the "act" is a physical movement of the defendant's body, such as pulling the trigger of a gun or stabbing the victim with a knife. (The consequences of that activity—*e.g.,* the firing of the gun, the killing of another—are best considered to be the "results" of the act rather than part of the "act.")

(2) **Act must be "volitional":** [§85] The physical movement constituting the act must be a ***conscious*** and ***volitional*** one. [State v. Mercer, 165 S.E.2d 328 (N.C. 1969); People v. Newton, 8 Cal. App. 3d 359 (1970)] Thus, reflexes, convulsions, movements during sleep, and conduct during hypnosis or resulting from hypnosis are not sufficient "acts" because they are not volitional. Similarly, criminal liability cannot ordinarily be based on movements made while the defendant was ***unconscious.*** [Model Penal Code §2.01(2)(b)]

(a) **Example:** D, while arguing with a police officer, was shot in the stomach. Although D lost consciousness, he engaged in a struggle with the officer. During the struggle, the officer's gun discharged, killing the officer instantly. Since D's acts were committed while unconscious, they will not support a conviction for criminal homicide. [People v. Newton, *supra*]

1) **But note:** If D is found to be at fault in causing the altercation, his state of unconsciousness will be no bar to liability (*see infra,* §87).

(b) **Compare—altered consciousness arising from certain causes:** [§86] If the defendant's loss of consciousness is caused by a factor covered by a specific defense, its effect on liability should be determined by that defense. Thus, if the defendant was mentally ill, criminal liability turns on the law of insanity (*see infra,* §§322 *et seq.*), and if he was rendered unconscious by reason of intoxication, the law of intoxication controls (*see infra,* §§379 *et seq.*). [People v. Cox, 67 Cal. App. 2d 166 (1944)]

(c) **Exception—defendant caused unconsciousness:** [§87] A state of unconsciousness will ***not*** preclude a finding of criminal liability where the defendant was at fault in causing his unconsciousness. In such a case, there is a sufficient "act."

1) **Example:** After starting a fight with V, D was struck on the head and rendered unconscious. During this period of unconsciousness, D killed V. Since D was at fault in starting the fight

and therefore in causing his own unconsciousness, he has committed an "act" for purposes of criminal homicide. [Watkins v. People, 408 P.2d 425 (Colo. 1965)]

2) **Comment:** This exception uncritically equates the volitional conduct that causes unconsciousness with the act committed while unconscious. Arguably, such a person's criminal liability would most appropriately be limited to the initial wrongful act, *i.e.,* to the crime involved in starting the fight.

(d) **Exception—knowledge of pending unconsciousness:** [§88] A person may incur criminal liability by engaging in a course of conduct ***knowing*** he will or might become unconscious and do harm.

1) **Example:** D, knowing that he is subject to epileptic seizures that render him unconscious, nevertheless decides to drive his car. While driving, he has a seizure, and during the period of unconsciousness the car runs over and kills V. By placing himself in a position where his anticipated unconsciousness would cause harm, D may be held criminally responsible for the homicide. [People v. Decina, 2 N.Y.2d 133 (1956)]

2) **Rationale:** Under this rule, liability is not imposed for the act committed while unconscious (running over V) but rather for the earlier act committed while fully conscious (driving with knowledge that a seizure may occur).

b. **Negative acts (acts of omission):** [§89] Under certain circumstances, liability may be based upon a defendant's ***failure to act.*** This issue most typically arises in homicide cases where the defendant's conviction is sought on the ground that he failed to take steps to save the victim's life. However, regardless of his intent or motives, the defendant's omission will support a finding of criminal liability only where it is shown that:

(i) Defendant was under a ***legal duty*** to act;

(ii) Defendant had the necessary ***knowledge; and***

(iii) It would have been ***possible*** for defendant to act.

[Jones v. United States, 308 F.2d 307 (D.C. Cir. 1962); People v. Chapman, 28 N.W. 896 (Mich. 1886)—husband who failed to protect wife from rapist held guilty of her rape] *Note:* The requirement of a ***legal duty*** is probably the most significant one.

(1) **Rationale for legal duty requirement:** Requiring that an actionable omission be traced to a legal duty to act is apparently based primarily on the need to set ***reasonable and discernible limits*** on liability for omissions. Otherwise, it is at least arguable that persons would not have sufficient advance notice of when they would have to act to avoid liability. [People v. Heitzman, 9 Cal. 4th 189 (1994)—crime consisting of permitting infliction of pain on elderly person would deny notice to defendants unless construed as limited to those with special relationship to victim]

(a) **Compare—"common decency" approach:** It has also been urged that, absent the legal duty limitation, liability could reasonably be imposed whenever "the failure to take action constitutes a substantial deviation from common decency." This would arguably be no more objectionable than imposing liability for negligent affirmative acts. [G. Dix and M. Sharlot, Criminal Law, Cases and Materials 179 (4th ed. 1995)]

(2) **Situations giving rise to legal duties:** [§90] The legal duty that will suffice to make an omission an "act" may arise from a number of different sources.

(a) **Duties based upon relationship of parties:** [§91] The common law imposes certain affirmative duties on persons standing in a particular relationship to others. For example, parents have a duty to prevent physical harm to their children and a husband has a duty similarly to protect his wife. [Commonwealth v. Breth, 198 S.E. 309 (Pa. 1915)—violation of parent's duty to provide medical care to child; State v. Smith, 65 Me. 257 (1876)—violation of husband's duty to provide shelter and clothing for insane wife]

(b) **Statutory duties:** [§92] In addition, a variety of specific duties are prescribed by statute—*e.g.,* the statutory obligation to file tax returns and report automobile accidents. And some duties based upon the relationship of the parties (above) are now embodied in statutes in many jurisdictions. [*See, e.g.,* Cal. Penal Code §270a—duty of one spouse to support and provide other spouse with necessary food, clothing, shelter, and medical care]

1) **Constitutional limitation:** [§93] Recall the constitutional due process limitation that criminal statutes be sufficiently specific and precise so as to give fair warning of the required conduct. (*See supra,* §§44 *et seq.*)

(c) **Duties arising from contract:** [§94] Failure to perform a duty created by contract will, at least in some situations, be sufficient to create criminal liability. This will clearly be the case if the defendant was under a contractual duty to ***protect or care for others***. [State v. Harrison, 152 A. 867 (N.J. 1931)]

1) **Example:** A defendant who contracted to provide shelter and food to an elderly person who was an invalid but who failed to provide food as required by the contract could be convicted of murder, where the elderly person died from starvation. [Commonwealth v. Pestinikas, 617 A.2d 1339 (Pa. 1992)]

2) **Compare—contracts unrelated to safety:** Court may well be reluctant and perhaps completely unwilling to impose criminal liability for breach of a contractual duty if the contract has nothing to do with the safety of others.

(d) **Duties arising from voluntarily undertaking task:** [§95] One who is not otherwise legally obligated to render aid to another (*e.g.,* because there is no preexisting familial or contractual relationship, *supra*) but who voluntarily undertakes to render such aid has a duty to use reasonable care in so doing. Indeed, refusal to continue a voluntary assumption of care may constitute a criminal "act," at least where abandoning one's efforts would leave the imperiled person in a worse condition. [Cornell v. State, 32 So. 2d 610 (Fla. 1947)—grandmother who took care of grandchild violated duty of reasonable care when she got so drunk that she let the child smother; held guilty of manslaughter]

(e) **Duties based on creation of peril:** [§96] Moreover, one who wrongfully places another in a position of danger comes under a duty to aid that person. Failure to render assistance will give rise to criminal liability. [People v. Fowler, 178 Cal. 657 (1918)—D who committed battery on victim violated duty to rescue by leaving victim unconscious on side of road, where victim later was run over by a car; D held guilty of murder]

1) **Compare:** The result is less clear, however, where the defendant has ***accidentally*** created the perilous situation—although some authorities would hold that a similar duty exists; *i.e.,* even those who innocently create the danger have a duty to act to prevent harm. [*See* Commonwealth v. Cali, 141 N.E. 510 (Mass. 1923)—D accidentally set fire to house but intentionally let it burn down to collect insurance; held guilty of arson]

(f) **Duties to control conduct of others:** [§97] A particular relationship between two persons may create a legal duty on the part of one person to prevent criminal conduct by the other. Thus, for example, an employer may have a duty to prevent employees from committing crimes while the employees are performing the employer's work. [Moreland v. State, 139 S.E. 77 (Ga. 1927)—owner of car had duty to prevent chauffeur from speeding]

(g) **Trend—creation of new duties:** [§98] In addition, the trend of the law has been toward the recognition of new duties and the expansion of duties well settled under the criminal law. For instance, a landowner may have an affirmative duty to provide for the safety of persons invited onto his land. [Commonwealth v. Welansky, 55 N.E.2d 902 (Mass. 1944)—patrons of nightclub killed as result of owner's failure to supply proper fire escapes; owner held guilty of manslaughter]

(h) **Compare—moral duty alone not enough:** [§99] However, despite the increased flexibility toward finding a legal duty, the law still does not impose criminal liability for an omission simply because the defendant had a ***moral*** obligation to act. In other words, the need of one person and the opportunity of another to be of assistance are ***not*** enough to create a legal duty to take affirmative action. Thus, absent one of the special circumstances discussed above, a person can, with impunity, stand idly by as others suffer imminent peril—and this is true even though that person can render assistance with little danger or inconvenience to himself! [People v. Beardsley, 113 N.W. 1128 (Mich. 1907); Connaughty v. State, 1 Wis. 159 (1853)—bystander not guilty of murder even though committed in his presence and he made no effort to prevent it]

(3) **Knowledge required for liability:** [§100] Omission cases raise two questions on the issue of knowledge: (i) whether the defendant must be aware of the facts giving rise to a legal duty; and (ii) whether she must have knowledge of the law creating the duty.

(a) **Knowledge of facts creating duty:** [§101] While the courts split on the issue, the probable majority view is that, although one may be under a duty to act, an omission will render the defendant criminally liable only if she has knowledge of the facts creating the duty. *Rationale:* A person does not have a fair opportunity to perform her duty unless and until she is at least aware of the circumstances prompting the duty. [People v. Henry, 23 Cal. App. 2d 155 (1937)—conviction for violation of hit-and-run statute requires proof that defendant was aware that accident had occurred]

1) **Compare—duty to know the facts:** [§102] However, in some situations the law may impose an ***obligation to know the facts*** creating a legal duty. In such cases, it need not be shown that the defendant was aware of the facts; *i.e.,* criminal liability may be imposed for failure to exercise reasonable care in learning the facts. [Cornell v. State, *supra,* §95]

(b) **Knowledge of law creating duty:** [§103] Courts seldom require that the defendant have knowledge that the law imposes the duty to act, the general rule being that "ignorance of the law is no excuse" (*see infra,* §416). However, if a statute requires a "willful" failure to act, courts may require knowledge of the law creating the duty on the theory that ignorance of the existence or scope of the duty negates the requisite mental state. [United States v. Murdock, 290 U.S. 389 (1933)—failure to file tax return not criminal unless defendant was aware of legal duty to file return]

1) **Constitutional due process limitation:** [§104] Moreover, imposing criminal liability for an omission, without proof that the defendant had knowledge of the law creating the duty to act, may violate due process—especially if the circumstances are such that persons in the defendant's position are generally unlikely to be aware of the duty. [Lambert v. California, 355 U.S. 225 (1957)—due process violated by conviction for failure to register with police as sex offender, where knowledge of duty not element of offense and circumstances moving persons to inquire as to existence of duty are lacking]

(4) **Act must be capable of performance:** [§105] Regardless of the facts giving rise to a duty to act and the defendant's knowledge thereof, the omission must have been one that the defendant could have avoided; *i.e.,* it must have been ***possible*** for her to have done what she failed to do.

Thus, there is no criminal "act" where the defendant's omission was due to the fact that she lacked the means or ability to perform. [*See, e.g.*, Model Penal Code §2.01(1)—criminal liability imposed for "the omission to perform an act of which [a person] is physically capable"]

(a) **Compare—mere inconvenience or need to solicit assistance:** [§106] Mere inconvenience will not excuse a failure to perform a duty. Also, a defendant even physically incapable of performing herself cannot escape criminal liability if it was reasonably possible to obtain the help of others. [Stehr v. State, 139 N.W. 676 (Neb. 1913)—failure to provide food and shelter for children would not be criminal if parent unable to obtain such necessaries, but failure to seek help at available welfare agency would be a breach of duty]

B. ATTENDANT CIRCUMSTANCES

1. **In General:** [§107] In addition to the elements ordinarily common to most crimes (actus reus, mens rea, etc.), many crimes require proof of certain circumstances that must have existed at the time of the act in question. Absent a showing of these extrinsic facts, the conduct of the accused will not constitute a crime.

   a. **Example:** A statute provides: "It is an offense to injure a federal officer while that officer is performing his duties." Thus, in addition to the element of an injury to a person caused by the defendant, two attendant circumstances are required: (i) that the victim was a federal officer, and (ii) that the officer was engaging in his official duties at the time of the injury. Both factors are crucial elements of the offense and, absent a showing of their existence when the defendant acted, the crime cannot be established.

2. **Compare—Results:** [§108] Attendant circumstances differ from the result required by a crime in that circumstances need not have been caused by the defendant's conduct. (In the example above, the fact that the victim was a federal officer or was performing his official duties is not attributable to an act of the defendant.)

3. **Mens Rea Issues:** [§109] Attendant circumstances elements often raise questions as to whether the defendant must have been ***aware*** of the existence of the circumstances. These issues involve application of the mens rea requirement, discussed below.

C. CRIMINAL STATE OF MIND—MENS REA

1. **General Requirement of Mens Rea:** [§110] "Mens rea" is traditionally defined as the "nonphysical element" of a crime. This usually addresses what the defendant must have been thinking at the time she committed the actus reus, although for some crimes, a showing of something less—criminal negligence—will suffice (*see infra,* §122). Most crimes require a mens rea. Some—"strict liability" offenses—do not, or require only a limited mens rea, although there is clearly a constitutional limit on the extent to which conduct may be made criminal without requiring a criminal intent.

   a. **Rationale:** There are at least two basic reasons for the mental element, or mens rea, aspect of crimes:

(1) **Demonstrates moral culpability:** Since conviction imposes a stigma of moral condemnation, it is important that crimes be defined so as to encompass only morally reprehensible behavior. Generally, however, only that conduct that is engaged in "intentionally" is regarded as morally wrong. Therefore, the requirement of mens rea tends to assure that only the morally blameworthy will be convicted of crimes.

(2) **Filters out those dangerous to society:** In addition, the requirement of mens rea tends to identify those most dangerous to society. Arguably, one who "unintentionally" engages in conduct or causes a result is less inclined to engage in future dangerous conduct than one who "intentionally" does the same thing. Accordingly, a requirement of mens rea narrows the focus to those who pose a serious danger to others and helps to assure that society will be protected from those most likely to do it harm.

b. **No single mens rea:** [§111] There is no single state of mind, or mens rea, that will suffice for purposes of imposing criminal liability. Rather, the requisite state of mind is defined separately for each specific crime. [Regina v. Tolson, 23 Q.B.D. 168 (1889)]

c. **State of mind dimensions:** [§112] There are two dimensions to criminal state of mind requirements:

(1) **Object dimension:** On the one hand, the mens rea element embraces the ***subject*** of the state of mind—*i.e.,* what the state of mind must be concerned about. For example, a crime might require a particular state of mind concerning a possible consequence of conduct (such as the death of another person) or concerning certain attendant circumstances (such as the victim's lack of consent to the intercourse in rape).

(2) **Quality dimension:** But the mens rea element also concerns the ***quality*** of the state of mind required. For example, in the case of murder, the mental element might be satisfied only by a showing that the defendant desired the victim's death. Or it might be defined so as to be satisfied by a showing that she was aware that a risk of death existed at the time that she acted. (*See infra,* §§698 *et seq.*)

d. **Compare—motive:** [§113] "Motive" refers to the defendant's ***reason*** for perpetrating the crime in question (*e.g.,* hatred, revenge, jealousy, etc.). Although a showing of motive may constitute reliable evidence that the defendant did in fact commit the crime, generally it is ***not essential*** to proof of criminal liability.

(1) **Example:** While failure to establish the requisite mens rea will result in the accused's acquittal of the crime charged, failure to prove any motive—or even proof of a good motive—will not prevent a conviction. [People v. Roberts, 178 N.W. 690 (Mich. 1920)—D who killed his wife to put her out of her misery from incurable and painful disease convicted of first degree murder]

(2) **And note:** The motive that prompts an act, however bad it may be, will not make the act a crime if the act in itself is not a crime. [State v. Asher,

8 S.W. 177 (Ark. 1888)—no criminal liability where, with intent to defraud, D obtained goods by representations he thought were false but which turned out to be true]

e. **Awareness of law not required:** [§114] Mens rea generally requires awareness of ***factual matters***, and thus does not usually require that the defendant be aware that the law makes the conduct involved a criminal offense.

2. **Traditional Mens Rea Analysis:** [§115] The mens rea required for the various crimes traditionally falls into one of three categories: ***general intent***, ***specific intent***, or ***criminal negligence***. In addition, some crimes, either by statute or by judicial construction, may require "malice," "willfulness," etc., but these terms have often not been carefully defined.

a. **General intent—volitional doing of prohibited act:** [§116] General intent consists of the volitional doing of a prohibited act. Accordingly, the only state of mind required is an ***intent to commit the act*** constituting the crime; the defendant need not have intended to violate the law, nor need he have been aware that the law made his act criminal.

(1) **Applicable where no other requirement:** [§117] Under traditional analysis, general intent is the mental element of any crime that does not by its terms require a specific intent and for which a showing of criminal negligence is not sufficient. Among the crimes for which general intent is sufficient are rape and mayhem.

(2) **Proof of general intent:** [§118] General intent need not be specifically proven but can be inferred from the fact that the defendant engaged in the proscribed conduct. In other words, one who voluntarily does an act is presumed to have intended that act. [State v. Carlson, 93 N.W.2d 354 (Wis. 1958)]

(3) **Additional knowledge requirements for some crimes:** [§119] Along with general intent, some crimes require that the defendant have had "knowledge" (or "scienter") of certain facts which the prosecution must prove to establish the crime.

(a) **Example:** The crime of passing a forged instrument requires proof that the instrument was in fact forged and also that the defendant had ***knowledge*** that it was forged.

b. **Specific intent—intent to do something further:** [§120] Certain crimes require—in addition to general intent—an ***intent to do some further act or cause some additional consequence*** beyond that which must have been committed or caused in order to complete the crime. These are so-called specific intent crimes, and the additional mens rea required is referred to as a "specific intent."

(1) **Rationale—punish preparatory conduct:** Specific intent crimes tend to consist of activity in preparation for the commission of a more serious

offense. By making such "preparatory" conduct criminal, the law can intervene before the more serious crime is perpetrated. Thus, a specific intent is required to provide assurance that the defendant would indeed, if not stopped, engage in the more serious activity.

(2) **Examples:** Among the specific intent crimes are burglary (which requires an intent to commit a felony in the premises, although actual commission of that felony is not part of the actus reus of burglary; *see infra,* §938) and larceny (which requires an intent permanently to deprive the victim of his property, although the defendant need not actually have caused permanent deprivation to complete the actus reus of larceny; *see infra,* §1023).

(3) **Proof of specific intent:** [§121] Unlike general intent, specific intent ***cannot*** be inferred from the commission of the actus reus of the crime. Rather, specific proof is required, but it may be circumstantial. [Sullateskee v. State, 428 P.2d 736 (Okla. 1967)]

c. **Criminal negligence:** [§122] For some crimes, liability can be based on a showing of criminal negligence, in which event the defendant may be convicted for an act done without awareness of the facts but with a "gross" lack of care. The most frequent examples involve the crimes of manslaughter, battery, and criminal nuisance.

(1) **Definition—greater than ordinary negligence:** [§123] Both civil and criminal negligence involve a breach of the duty owed by a reasonable person under the circumstances. (*See* Torts Summary.) However, civil and criminal negligence differ in the degree of deviation from socially accepted conduct that is required. Thus, criminal negligence is not established simply by the fact that the defendant failed to exercise due care; rather, the negligence must involve a ***higher probability of harm*** and a ***greater degree of unreasonableness*** than is necessary for purposes of imposing civil liability.

d. **Malice:** [§124] As indicated earlier, crimes are sometimes defined in case law or by statute as requiring "malice." Although there is no clear meaning for the term, it is most commonly construed as requiring the commission of a volitional act ***without legal excuse or justification***. Ill will or hatred of the victim need ***not*** be shown. [State v. Lambert, 178 So. 508 (La. 1938)]

(1) **Example:** Criminal libel is generally defined as the malicious publication of durable defamation of another. But the requirement of "malice" is satisfied by a showing of an intentional publication without justification or excuse. No ill will directed toward the victim need have been harbored by the defendant.

(2) **Compare—other meanings:** [§125] However, as will be seen, "malice" has a different meaning in relation to certain other crimes, such as murder (which requires "malice aforethought," *infra,* §697).

e. **"Willfully," "deliberately," "feloniously":** [§126] Various criminal statutes might also use words such as willfully, deliberately, or feloniously to describe the requisite state of mind. Again, these terms have no generally agreed upon meaning but are often equated with general intent (*supra*). Sometimes, however, they will be construed as requiring an unusually significant mental state (*see* §127, below).

f. **Knowledge of law sometimes required:** [§127] Courts will occasionally construe crimes as requiring that the defendant have been aware of the law and aware that his conduct violated it. This usually pertains to crimes where the conduct is not always regarded as illegal and thus persons without actual knowledge of the illegality are likely to unwittingly commit the crime. Courts are especially likely to so interpret a crime if that crime by its terms requires that it be committed "willfully." [Ratzlof v. United States, 114 S. Ct. 655 (1994)] *Examples:*

(1) **Federal tax crimes:** Federal tax crimes that prohibit willfully failing to pay taxes require proof that the defendant knew of and understood his legal duty to pay the tax and nevertheless intentionally failed to do so. [United States v. Pomponio, 429 U.S. 10 (1976)]

(2) **Federal food stamp offenses:** A federal statute prohibits "knowingly" acquiring food stamps "in any manner not authorized by . . . [the food stamp statute or] the regulations" promulgated by the government. "Knowingly," as used in this crime, demands proof by the prosecution that the defendant knew enough about the statute and/or the regulations under it to understand that his particular acquisition of the food stamps at issue was unauthorized by the statute or the regulations. [Liparota v. United States, 471 U.S. 419 (1985)]

(3) **Federal "structuring" statute:** Federal law requires certain financial institutions to report all cash transactions exceeding $10,000. In addition, that law makes it a crime to willfully "structure" a transaction—to break it up into several smaller transactions—for the purpose of avoiding the reporting requirement. But many people may for quite "innocent" reasons seek to avoid having their transactions reported, and thus the crime creates a high risk of convicting persons who did not act in a blameworthy manner. Therefore, in this crime "willfulness" requires that the defendant know that the "structuring" constituting the offense is unlawful; *i.e.,* the defendant must know that federal law prohibits structuring and that breaking up the transaction violated that prohibition. [Ratzlof v. United States, *supra*]

g. **Proof of intent—federal constitutional requirements:** [§128] Where a crime requires proof of intent, the federal constitutional requirement that the prosecution have the burden of proving guilt beyond a reasonable doubt applies and requires that the prosecution's burden also apply to the element of intent. [Sandstrom v. Montana, *supra,* §20]

(1) **"Presumptions" of intent prohibited:** [§129] A "presumption" that has the effect of relieving the prosecution of its burden of proving criminal intent violates the defendant's right to due process. [Sandstrom v. Montana, *supra*]

(a) **Example:** D is tried for "deliberate homicide," which requires proof that D "purposely or knowingly" caused the death of the victim. The trial judge instructs the jury that "the law presumes that a person intends the ordinary consequences of his voluntary acts." This violates D's right to have the prosecution prove intent beyond a reasonable doubt, because the jurors might construe the instruction as requiring that the prosecution prove that D voluntarily did an act that caused death as an "ordinary consequence." [Sandstrom v. Montana, *supra*]

(2) **Distinguish—"permissible inference" of intent:** [§130] It remains possible, however, that the jury can constitutionally be instructed that if it finds that certain results are the natural and ordinary results of a defendant's conduct, it ***may—but need not***—infer from the defendant's conduct that he intended those results. Such rebuttable or permissible inferences of intent are at least sometimes constitutionally permissible. (*See supra,* §21.)

3. **Strict Liability Crimes:** [§131] Criminal liability without a mens rea requirement (or with a limited mens rea requirement) is called "strict liability." It is an exceptional type of criminal liability and constitutional considerations limit the extent to which it can be imposed.

a. **Types of strict liability**

(1) **"Complete" strict liability:** [§132] A few offenses contain no requirement of a mens rea whatsoever; these offenses have traditionally been characterized as "strict liability" crimes. [United States v. Balint, 258 U.S. 250 (1922)]

(2) **"Limited" strict liability:** [§133] Other offenses include no requirement of awareness with regard to ***one or more important aspects*** of the offenses, although some mens rea must be proved. These offenses are sometimes also called strict liability crimes, although they would more accurately be characterized as imposing "limited" strict liability as contrasted with "complete" strict liability.

(a) **Example—National Firearms Act:** The National Firearms Act creates an offense consisting of: (i) possession of a weapon (ii) of certain specified types, such as a machinegun or a grenade (iii) that is not registered under the Act. The Supreme Court has considered separately whether the Act imposes strict liability with regard to the second and third elements (*see infra*). As in many modern cases, however, it was clear that some mens rea was required and the real issues were whether the Act imposed limited strict liability by dispensing with mens rea regarding ***some*** of the elements of the crime.

b. **Identifying strict liability crimes—legislative intent:** [§134] Whether a crime imposes strict liability turns initially at least upon the legislature's intent.

However, as is quite often the case, criminal statutes do not clearly indicate on their face what the legislative intent was, so that courts must look to other factors.

(1) **Burden of establishing strict liability:** [§135] The criminal law's tradition of requiring mens rea for liability and the likelihood that legislatures will follow this approach means that strict liability is disfavored and thus one arguing for strict liability has the burden of establishing that the legislature intended to impose this kind of liability. [Staples v. United States, 114 S. Ct. 1793 (1994)]

(2) **Factors suggesting strict liability:** [§136] Legislative intent to impose strict liability is suggested by the following characteristics:

(i) The crime is a ***"new" statutory offense*** rather than one of the traditional common law offenses;

(ii) It does not involve a ***direct and positive infringement on the rights of other persons***;

(iii) It is part of a ***broad regulatory scheme;***

(iv) It imposes a ***relatively light penalty*** upon conviction; and

(v) Requiring proof of mens rea would ***impede implementation of the legislative purpose.***

Moreover, if most persons charged under the statute would in fact have the mens rea that might otherwise be required, this will encourage a court to find that mens rea need not be proven in each particular case. [Morissette v. United States, 342 U.S. 246 (1952)]

(3) **Factors suggesting no strict liability:** [§137] On the other hand, courts are less likely to conclude that the legislature intended to eliminate mens rea as an essential ingredient if the crime is or closely resembles a traditional common law offense that requires mens rea; if the act constituting the crime involves a direct and serious infringement upon the rights of others; and if a severe penalty is imposed upon conviction. [Morissette v. United States, *supra*] If strict liability would create a serious risk of convicting many entirely "innocent" persons—persons neither aware nor alerted to the possibility that their conduct is criminal—courts are particularly unlikely to find strict liability. [Staples v. United States, *supra*]

(a) **Example:** The National Firearms Act prohibits possession of certain unregistered weapons, such as grenades and machineguns. It imposes limited strict liability because it requires no awareness that the weapons were in fact unregistered; *see supra*. Dispensing with a requirement that a defendant know the nature of a weapon (as, for example, that a rifle would fire automatically and therefore was a "machinegun") would create a significant risk that entirely innocent gun owners would incur criminal liability, and therefore the Act was not construed as imposing strict liability with regard to the nature of the weapon. [Staples v. United States, *supra*]

(4) **Constitutional considerations:** [§138] If strict liability would clearly or likely be unconstitutional (*see infra*), the legislature probably did not intend it. Therefore, a showing that a serious constitutional issue would be presented by strict liability will encourage courts to construe legislative intent as requiring ordinary mens rea.

(5) **"Regulatory" or "public welfare" offenses:** [§139] Applying the above considerations, courts often construe crimes that are part of regulatory schemes designed to further the general welfare as imposing strict liability. These "regulatory" or "public welfare" offenses are particularly likely to impose strict liability if they regulate items that are potentially harmful or injurious. [Staples v. United States, *supra*] *Examples:*

(a) **Housing regulation offenses:** Criminal violations of regulations governing tenement houses were early held by the New York courts to impose strict liability. [Tenement House Department v. McDevitt, 215 N.Y. 160 (1915)]

(b) **Sale of opium:** Selling opium under an early federal statute was held to not require proof that the defendant ***knew*** the item sold was opium. [United States v. Balint, *supra,* §132]

(c) **Unregistered firearms:** Under the National Firearms Act, the offense of possession of certain unregistered firearms does not require proof that defendant knew the firearm was unregistered. [United States v. Freed, 401 U.S. 601 (1971)]

(6) **Traffic offenses:** [§140] Traffic offenses are often construed as imposing strict liability, in large part because requiring proof of mens rea would impede the rapid and efficient enforcement that is necessary to make these crimes an effective incentive for citizens to comply with traffic laws.

(7) **Compare—traditional serious strict liability crimes:** [§141] Despite the general guidelines above, certain common law crimes involving serious penalties have traditionally been regarded as strict liability offenses. *Examples:*

(a) **Bigamy:** Bigamy consists of marrying someone while having another living spouse. Generally, conviction is permitted even if the defendant was unaware that her spouse was alive or that a purported divorce was invalid. Thus, the crime does not require any mens rea in regard to the requirement that a spouse be still living.

(b) **Statutory rape:** Statutory rape has been held not to require an awareness of the female's age—*i.e.*, in regard to the victim's age, it is a strict liability offense. (*See infra*, §869.)

c. **Policy considerations:** [§142] Whether strict criminal liability is desirable as a matter of policy has been hotly debated. [*See* 58 W. Va. L. Rev. 34 (1955)]

(1) **Considerations favoring strict liability:** [§143] Those supporting strict liability argue that if the prosecution were required to prove mens rea in

all cases, convictions would be so difficult to obtain that some crimes would not provide effective deterrents. In turn, important schemes of social regulation would be frustrated. Moreover, courts would be overburdened with frequent and extensive litigation as to whether the requisite mens rea was present.

(a) **And note:** Proponents of strict liability also stress that, regardless of the above considerations, dispensing with the mental element as to certain crimes will not in fact create a risk of convicting many persons who are not morally blameworthy. This argument rests on the premise that strict liability is generally imposed only in situations where those in danger of being charged are operating in a heavily regulated area (*e.g.,* sale of firearms) and therefore either will have the mens rea that would otherwise have been required or would have had it had they used reasonable caution.

(2) **Considerations against strict liability:** [§144] Opponents of strict liability urge that it opens the door for conviction of persons who, because of their ignorance, have not in fact done anything sufficiently "wrong" to justify criminal sanctions. These commentators stress that the requisite mens rea is easily proved in most cases. Only in the few cases where there is some doubt concerning the accused's state of mind will there be extensive litigation, and it is in these few instances that defendants most need an opportunity to contest proof of their blameworthiness. Accordingly, requiring proof of mens rea will not only remove the danger of convicting those who should not be subject to criminal punishment, but it will do so with minimal disruption of the task of enforcing regulatory schemes by criminal prosecution.

d. **Constitutional limitations:** [§145] Aside from the policy considerations affecting the issue of strict liability, there is also a question of whether the mens rea requirement can be ***constitutionally*** eliminated. As will be seen below, at least in some cases, strict liability crimes have been held to violate due process. [Morissette v. United States, *supra;* Speidel v. State, 460 P.2d 77 (Alaska 1969)]

(1) **Rationale:** The due process argument is twofold:

(a) **No notice:** On the one hand, those subjected to conviction under strict liability statutes are arguably denied advance notice of their potential liability. Since they in most cases have violated the law before they have notice of those facts that would otherwise warn them to cease the proscribed conduct, they do not have a fair opportunity to avoid liability.

(b) **Grossly disproportionate punishment:** Further, those strict liability offenses that impose serious criminal penalties may be fundamentally unfair (and hence a due process violation) on the ground that the punishment is grossly disproportionate to the blameworthiness of the conduct involved.

(2) **Example:** A statute made it a felony to fail to return a rented motor vehicle but did not require an intent to deprive the owner of the vehicle or

to injure the owner in any way. Moreover, a serious penalty was authorized for its violation. This was held to violate due process, the court reasoning that to convict a person for a serious offense without requiring a "guilty mind" is "contrary to the general conditions of penal liability" that require a guilty mind in addition to the commission of a prohibited act. [Speidel v. State, *supra*]

(3) **Factors affecting constitutional prohibition:** [§146] It is clear that due process does not always prohibit strict liability. Strict liability crimes are more likely to be held unconstitutional if they are serious and if they are one of the traditional common law crimes for which mens rea has been required (or if they resemble such crimes). Conversely, due process is less likely to bar strict liability if the crime is a "new" statutory offense and imposes only a minor penalty upon conviction.

4. **Modern Classifications of State of Mind:** [§147] Under modern law, there is a trend away from the traditional classification analysis (above). In its place, contemporary criminal codes tend to adopt the Model Penal Code approach, which provides a more structured and carefully defined analysis. These codes distinguish four different levels or qualities of state of mind, and—unless specifically provided otherwise—require at least ***recklessness*** concerning all elements of the offense.

a. **Different states of mind:** [§148] The Model Penal Code distinguishes among ***purpose*** (or intent), ***knowledge, recklessness, and negligence***, reflecting varying quality dimensions (***see supra,*** §112).

(1) **"Purpose"—with desire:** [§149] A person acts purposefully if it is her conscious desire to engage in certain conduct or cause a certain result. She acts purposefully with regard to attendant circumstances if she hopes that they exist, or if she believes or is aware that they exist. [Model Penal Code §2.02(2)(a)]

(2) **"Knowledge"—awareness of a certainty:** [§150] A person acts knowingly with respect to the nature of her conduct if she is aware that her conduct is of that nature or that certain circumstances exist. She acts knowingly in regard to a result of her conduct if she is aware that it is "practically certain" that her conduct will cause the result. [Model Penal Code §2.02(2)(b)]

(a) **Compare—purpose:** [§151] Knowledge differs from purpose in that purpose requires a ***desire to cause a result,*** while knowledge simply requires that the actor be ***aware of a practical certainty*** that the result will occur.

(b) **Example:** D places a bomb in an airplane, setting it to go off when the plane reaches 10,000 feet. Although her sole motive is to destroy the plane's cargo, D is aware that the explosion will kill the crew of the aircraft, and this is in fact what happens.

1) **Analysis:** Since D did not consciously desire to cause the death of the crew members, she has not acted purposely in regard to that result. However, since she acted with awareness

that their death was practically certain to follow from her conduct, she has acted ***knowingly***.

(3) **"Recklessness"—awareness of high risk:** [§152] A person acts recklessly if she is ***aware of a substantial and unjustifiable risk*** that a certain result will occur because of her conduct or that a certain circumstance exists. [Model Penal Code §2.02(2)(c)]

(a) **Risk required:** [§153] The risk must be such that the actor's conduct "involves a gross deviation from the standard of conduct that a law-abiding person would observe." [Model Penal Code §2.02(2)(c)]

(b) **Compare—knowledge:** [§154] Recklessness differs from knowledge in that knowledge requires awareness of a ***certainty*** that a result will occur or that a circumstance will exist. Recklessness, however, simply requires an awareness of a ***risk***, although the risk must be a high one.

(c) **Example:** D places a bomb in an airplane, setting it to go off at 8:30 the next evening. Although she does not know whether the plane will be flying at that time or whether any persons will be in or near it, she does know that the plane is used with some frequency and that a person in the vicinity of the explosion may be severely injured or killed. The bomb goes off when B is loading freight onto the airplane and B is killed.

1) **Analysis:** D has not acted purposefully in regard to B's death, because it was not her conscious desire to cause the death. Nor has she acted knowingly, because she was not aware (and it was not true) that B's death was practically certain to result. However, since the evidence suggests that D was aware of a substantial and unjustifiable ***risk*** that her conduct would result in the death of B or someone like B, D has acted ***recklessly***.

(4) **"Negligence"—existence of high risk:** [§155] A person acts negligently if she ***should have been aware*** of a substantial and unjustifiable risk that a certain result would occur or that a certain circumstance would exist. [Model Penal Code §2.02(2)(d)]

(a) **Risk required:** [§156] The risk must be of the same sort required for recklessness (*supra*).

(b) **Compare—recklessness:** [§157] Negligence differs from recklessness in that recklessness requires a ***conscious awareness*** of the risk involved. Negligence, on the other hand, refers simply to circumstances in which a ***reasonable person would have been aware*** of the risk; the accused herself need not have had actual knowledge of the risk.

(c) **Example:** D places a bomb in an airplane and sets it to go off at 8:30 the next evening, believing that no one will be near the plane at that time. However, the plane is used with such frequency that a reasonable person would have been aware that it might be in use at the time of the scheduled explosion. Moreover, a reasonable person would have been aware that anyone in the vicinity of the explosion might well be killed or injured. The bomb goes off when B is loading freight onto the plane, and B is killed.

1) **Analysis:** Although there was a substantial and unjustifiable risk that B or someone like B would be killed by the explosion, D was not aware of that risk, and so did not act recklessly in regard to B's death. However, since a ***reasonable person*** would have been aware of the risk of B's death, D has acted ***negligently***.

b. **General requirement—at least recklessness regarding all elements:** [§158] The Model Penal Code, and many modern statutes based on it, provide that unless a criminal statute provides to the contrary, such a statute will be interpreted to require that the defendant have acted with ***at least recklessness in regard to each significant element***. [Model Penal Code §2.02(3)]

(1) **Compare—traditional approach:** [§159] This rule is similar to the ***general intent*** requirement of traditional analysis (***see supra,*** §117). It is, however, more carefully structured and makes clearer the state of mind required for particular crimes.

(2) **"Higher" state of mind suffices:** [§160] Where recklessness is required, the prosecution can also prevail upon a showing that the defendant acted knowingly or purposefully. In other words, whenever a lower level of mens rea is required, a higher level will *a fortiori* suffice.

(3) **Negligence may be sufficient:** [§161] A statute may, by specific provision, require only negligence in regard to one or more elements. But because liability for negligence should be the exception rather than the rule, a crime will be so construed only where the legislative intent is clearly indicated in the language of the statute itself.

(4) **Higher state of mind may be required:** [§162] A crime may, of course, be defined as imposing a requirement of knowledge or purpose in regard to one or more elements.

(a) **Example:** The federal crime of treason, which consists of giving aid and comfort to an enemy of the United States, requires that the accused have acted with the ***conscious purpose*** of aiding the enemy. The extremely serious nature of the crime and the penalty require a showing of purpose to assure that only persons with sufficient culpability commit the crime. [United States v. Bailey, 444 U.S. 394 (1980)]

(b) **Example:** The federal crime of escape, which consists of absenting oneself from federal custody without permission, does ***not*** require that the defendant have acted with purpose, *i.e.,* with the conscious objective of leaving such custody and of doing so without permission. The Supreme Court held that there was no basis for concluding that Congress intended this requirement. The Court declined to decide, however, whether the Government must prove knowledge—

that the defendant knew he was leaving custody and that he lacked permission—or whether instead either recklessness or negligence suffices. [United States v. Bailey, *supra*]

(5) **"Specific intent" may be required:** [§163] Under the Model Penal Code approach, crimes may require proof of a state of mind concerning something that is not an element of the offense. This requirement would be in addition to those imposed by the rule discussed here, and would be analogous to the "specific intent" sometimes required under traditional analysis (*see supra,* §120). Model Penal Code analysis, however, would not label such requirements ones of "specific intent."

c. **Analytical example of modern approach:** [§164] Suppose a statute provides: "A person is guilty of arson if he causes an explosion with the purpose of destroying a building." To ascertain the state of mind that will support a conviction under modern codes, the following analysis should be employed:

(1) **What state of mind concerning the nonmental elements of the crime must be proved?** The nonmental elements of this crime are (i) that the defendant did some act (no specific act is designated) and (ii) that there was an explosion. Hence only the state of mind with regard to those elements—some "act" and the occurrence of an "explosion" as a result of the act—need be considered in this step of the analysis.

(a) Does the statute require, in regard to these elements, a state of mind ***higher than recklessness?*** No.

(b) Does the statute provide that ***not even recklessness*** is required, *i.e.,* that negligence is sufficient? No.

(c) Therefore, ***recklessness is adequate***. Accordingly, the prosecution must prove that at the time of his act, the defendant was aware of a substantial and unjustifiable risk that he was engaging in the act and that his conduct would cause an explosion. It need not show, however, that the defendant knew an explosion would occur or that he desired it to occur.

(2) **Does the statute require a state of mind in regard to something that is not an element of the offense?** Yes; the defendant must have acted "with the purpose of destroying a building." The prosecution need not prove that a building was destroyed; "destroying a building" is not an element of the offense. But the prosecution must show that the defendant had a particular state of mind in regard to this result. The requisite state of mind is "***purpose***"; *i.e.*, the defendant must have had the ***conscious desire*** to cause destruction of a building.

(3) **Summary:** In addition to establishing that the defendant acted and caused an explosion, the prosecution must prove:

(a) The defendant was ***aware of a substantial and unjustifiable risk*** that he was engaging in certain conduct and that ***an explosion would occur*** as the result of his conduct; and

(b) The defendant had a ***conscious desire to cause the destruction of a building***.

5. **Mens Rea Requirements and "Defenses":** [§165] Certain so-called defenses are not really defenses in the traditional sense but rather ways by which defendants contest whether the prosecution has really proved the mens rea required by the crime charged. These "defenses," for example, mistake of fact (*see infra,* §§395 *et seq.*), some aspects of mistake of law (*infra,* §§401 *et seq.*), voluntary intoxication (*infra,* §§385 *et seq.*), and "diminished capacity" (*infra,* §§371 *et seq.*), are often described as means by which a defendant can "negate" the mens rea required, but in reality—since the burden of proof is on the prosecution—a defendant is entitled to acquittal if the defense raises a reasonable doubt as to whether the prosecution has proved mens rea.

   a. **Constitutional issues related to mens rea defenses:** [§166] Due process, the Sixth Amendment right to jury trial, or these rights in combination (*supra,* §14) may entitle defendants to an unrestricted opportunity to rely on whatever evidence they choose to negate mens rea. Limitations on the mens rea "defenses" may therefore be unconstitutional; this is considered in more detail in the discussions below of those "defenses."

6. **"Transferred Intent"—Responsibility for Unintended Results**

   a. **General requirement—contemplation of harm actually caused:** [§167] Ordinarily, criminal liability attaches only where the defendant is shown to have contemplated the actual harm that resulted from his conduct. Thus, one who throws a stone at another with the intent to strike that person (*i.e.,* commit a battery), but misses and breaks a window instead, is not guilty of "maliciously causing harm to property." Since he did not contemplate the result required by the crime charged—destruction of the window—he lacked the mens rea required for the crime. It is irrelevant that his intent was to cause a different—albeit criminal—harm. [Regina v. Pembliton, 12 Cox Crim. Cas. 607 (1874); Regina v. Faulkner, 13 Cox Crim. Cas. 550 (1877)]

      (1) **Rationale:** Where the actual result differs from the one intended, there is insufficient indication of the defendant's ability and willingness to act successfully on his criminal intent to justify holding him liable for a crime—and this is so even though the unintended result is harmful.

   b. **Exception—"transferred intent":** [§168] Where the contemplated harm is criminal and there is great ***similarity*** between that harm and the result that actually occurs, the defendant will be legally treated as though he had in fact contemplated the result that occurred. This is often referred to as the doctrine of transferred intent. The defendant's intent will be "transferred" from the intended object or person to the object or person actually injured, and criminal liability will follow.

      (1) **Rationale:** When there is such similarity between the intended and actual results, the defendant is regarded as sufficiently "dangerous" in the eyes of the law to justify subjecting him to criminal sanctions.

      (2) **Example:** D throws a stone at A, intending to injure him. The stone misses A but hits and injures B instead. Although B was an unintended victim, D is nonetheless guilty of battery. His initial intent was criminal

and the harm inflicted was similar to that contemplated; the only difference was that another victim was involved. Accordingly, D's intent is "transferred" from A to B. [People v. Fruci, 188 Misc. 384 (1947)]

(3) **Model Penal Code position:** [§169] The Model Penal Code would impose liability on a transferred intent theory where either of two requirements is met:

(i) The contemplated result and the actual result differ only in that a different person or property is involved or in that the contemplated harm would have been more serious or extended; or

(ii) The contemplated result and the actual result "involve the same kind of injury or harm" and the actual result was not "too remote or accidental . . . to have a [just] bearing" on the defendant's guilt.

[Model Penal Code §2.03]

D. CONCURRENCE OF ACTUS REUS AND MENS REA

1. **In General:** [§170] As indicated at the outset, there must be a concurrence between the mens rea and the act or result required by the crime at issue. This means that the act or result must be ***attributable*** to the culpable state of mind. This principle is sometimes expressed as the requirement of a "union" or "joint operation" between the act and intent. [Thabo Meli v. Regina, 1 W.L.R. 228 (1954)]

2. **Concurrence Between Mens Rea and Act:** [§171] The act constituting the crime must be the result of the intent that constitutes the mens rea. Generally, this means that the defendant must have had the requisite intent ***at the moment he performed the act***.

a. **Example:** D intends to enter B's dwelling for the purpose of stealing certain jewels inside. Subsequently, however, D has a change of heart, and although D does enter B's dwelling, it is simply for the purpose of seeking shelter from the rain. Even assuming D had no consent to enter, D cannot be found guilty of burglary. Burglary requires a trespassory entry with intent to commit a felony in the dwelling (*see infra,* §908), but here the entry was not attributable to the intent to steal. At the time of the entry, the intent to steal had been abandoned; therefore, it cannot be said that the requisite mental state caused the entry. [Jackson v. State, 15 So. 344 (Ala. 1894)]

b. **Example:** Similarly, D could not be convicted of burglary if he entered B's home to seek shelter and ***while inside*** formed the intent to steal B's jewels. Again, the intent to steal did not cause the entry; *i.e.*, there is no liability where the act was performed "innocently" and the mens rea was later formed. (Of course, if D took the jewels, he could be prosecuted for theft.)

3. **Concurrence Between Mens Rea and Result:** [§172] If the crime in question requires proof of a result, there must be concurrence between that result and the requisite intent, which means that the occurrence of the result must be ***attributable*** to the mens rea. Generally, a showing that the defendant had the necessary intent at the time he committed the act that caused the result will suffice.

a. **Example:** D drives his car toward A, intending to injure A. At the final moment, D changes his mind and attempts to stop the vehicle but is unable to do so, and A is injured. Since the harm to A was caused by and is attributable to D's act of driving the car toward A, the requisite concurrence existed. It is irrelevant that at the exact moment of injury, D did not have the necessary intent; having had the proscribed intent at the time he perpetrated the act that caused the harm, D can be convicted of battery. [People v. Claborn, 224 Cal. App. 2d 38 (1964)]

b. **Compare—concurrence in time not essential:** [§173] As the above example makes clear, it is not essential that the intent and result concur in point of time. It need only be shown that the result was ***attributable*** to the intent. [People v. Claborn, *supra*]

4. **Special Problem—Mistake of Death Cases:** [§174] Special problems are posed where the defendant mistakenly believes he has caused death and then—without the intent to kill—performs an act that actually does cause the death of the victim. Some courts find no liability here, on the ground that the result is not attributable to the intent. Others, however, do find liability, often reasoning that the defendant's behavior was all part of a single scheme or constituted part of a single transaction with a single intention.

a. **Example:** D injects V with what D thinks is a fatal dose of poison. V slips into unconsciousness and D, thinking V is dead, cuts off V's head. In fact, the poison was not sufficient to kill V, and it was the act of beheading that caused V's death. Even though D did not intend to kill V when he cut off V's head (having thought he had accomplished this result earlier), many courts would find the necessary concurrence between the intent to kill and V's death, on the theory that D's actions were all part of the original plan that caused the death. [Thabo Meli v. Regina, *supra,* §170]

E. CAUSATION

1. **In General:** [§175] If a crime requires proof of a result, the prosecution must prove that the defendant's conduct was the ***legal cause*** of that result. Problems of causation arise most often in connection with the homicide crimes, where the prosecution must show a causal relationship between the defendant's act and the victim's death. However, the issue can also be encountered in the context of other crimes. The necessary causation is of two types: ***"factual"*** causation and ***"proximate"*** causation. Both must be proved before liability may be imposed. Causation, whether it is factual or proximate, may be "direct" or it may instead cause the particular result by means of other—"intervening"—causes.

a. **Direct causation:** [§176] Causation is direct if the defendant's act causes the result without the involvement of any intervening factor or cause.

b. **Causation through intervening causes:** [§177] Causation may exist even if other factors—such as the actions of other people—intervene and thus contribute to the result. The fact that causation involves such intervening causes does not necessarily mean the defendant's act was not the legal cause of the result. Where intervening causes contribute to the result, however, a defendant has a stronger argument that, under the analyses discussed below, proximate and perhaps even factual causation do not exist.

2. **Factual Causation—"But For" Test:** [§178] The prosecution must first establish that the defendant's acts were the ***"factual cause"*** of the result—*i.e.,* that ***"but for" the defendant's acts, the result would not have happened as and when it did.*** This does not require that the defendant's acts alone caused the result; causation exists even if other actions and circumstances contributed to the bringing about of the result as long as the result would not have happened as and when it did "but for" the defendant's acts. [Perkins and Boyce, Criminal Law 771-772 (3rd ed. 1982) (afterwards cited as "Perkins and Boyce")]

   a. **Substantial factor requirement:** [§179] It is sometimes said that factual causation requires that the defendant's act be a "substantial factor" in bringing about the result. [LaFave and Scott, Criminal Law 280 (2nd ed. 1986) (afterwards cited as "LaFave and Scott")] If the defendant's act did affect the situation sufficiently to be a literal "but for" cause of the result but its impact was ***de minimis***, a court may well find that factual causation was lacking.

      (1) **Example:** D struck V, causing a slight cut. X then shot V, causing a serious wound that bled severely. V lost several drops of blood from the wound inflicted by D and quarts of blood from the wound inflicted by X, and died from loss of blood. Although D's actions arguably were a "but for" cause of V dying how and when he did, those actions were not a "substantial factor" in bringing about the result and therefore may be held not to have factually "caused" it. [Perkins and Boyce, 779]

   b. **Speeding up result:** [§180] Applying the "but for" rule, factual causation will be present even though the defendant's acts simply speeded up the result. A few courts disagree, however, and find causation lacking where the result would otherwise have occurred within a short period of time. [*See* People v. Ah Fat, 48 Cal. 61 (1874)]

      (1) **Example:** While V is lying near death from an independent cause, D shoots V, killing him immediately. D's act is the factual cause of V's death. Even assuming V would have died within the hour anyway, but for D's act, V would not have died when and as he did. That D merely hastened the inevitable is immaterial. [People v. Ah Fat, *supra*]

   c. **Negligence of victim or third party:** [§181] The fact that the victim (*e.g.,* in a homicide case) or a third person was negligent, and this negligence contributed to the causing of the result, does not establish the lack of factual causation. However, in specific cases, such negligence might constitute a ***superseding factor*** (*see infra,* §189), and thus establish the lack of proximate causation. [Commonwealth v. Root, 170 A.2d 310 (Pa. 1961)]

   d. **Exception—concurrent sufficient causes:** [§182] The general requirement of a showing of "but for" causation does not apply where the result is brought about by two factors operating concurrently, either of which would have been sufficient itself to cause the result. In such cases, ***both*** factors will be regarded as "but for" causes, even though the result would have occurred as and when it did if either one of the factors had not come into operation. [Wilson v. State, 24 S.W. 409 (Tex. 1893)]

      (1) **Example:** A and B both shoot C, killing him instantly. Medical testimony establishes that C would have died when and as he did from either

wound alone. Nevertheless, both A's and B's acts are the factual cause of C's death, as they are concurrent sufficient causes. [Wilson v. State, *supra*]

e. **Exception—effect of action comes to rest in position of safety:** [§183] If the direct effect of the defendant's acts comes to rest in a position of apparent safety, matters that occur later—as a result of the defendant's act—will not, according to some authorities, be regarded as having been caused by the defendant's act. [Perkins and Boyce, 780]

(1) **Example:** D rolls a boulder down a hill. The boulder wedges against a tree and stops. A week later, the tree breaks and the boulder continues to roll down the hill, striking and killing V. Although "but for" D's initial actions, V would not have died as and when he did, D's act did not "cause" V's death because the direct effect of that act came to rest in a position of apparent safety when the boulder wedged against the tree. [Perkins and Boyce, 780]

3. **Proximate Causation:** [§184] The existence of factual causation will not alone support a finding of criminal liability. In addition, there must be proof of ***"proximate"*** causation. Proximate causation is a flexible analysis involving a variety of policy considerations and which ultimately asks whether as a matter of policy the defendant should be held responsible for a particular result. [People v. Acosta, 284 Cal. Rptr. 117 (1991)]

a. **Usual problem—result occurs in unexpected manner:** [§185] Proximate causation problems arise primarily when an ***expected result*** occurs in a ***manner not contemplated*** by the defendant. The issue is whether the difference between the anticipated sequence of events and what actually transpired is enough to break the chain of proximate causation.

(1) **Compare—unintended victim:** [§186] If the only difference between the expected result and the actual result is that the actual result involved a ***different victim*** than was contemplated by the defendant, the issue is not one of proximate causation but rather one of transferred intent (*see supra,* §§167-169).

(2) **Compare—"substantial factor" test not met:** [§187] If a defendant's acts were not a sufficiently substantial factor in causing a result (*see supra,* §179), the lack of liability may be explained in terms of no proximate causation rather than no factual causation.

b. **General rule—"all natural and probable consequences":** [§188] As a general rule, the defendant will be regarded as the "proximate cause" if the result occurred as a "natural and probable consequence" of his act ***and*** no intervening factor sufficient to break the chain of causation affected the events, even if the result occurred in a manner different than the defendant expected. [People v. Geiger, 159 N.W.2d 383 (Mich. 1968)] In other words, the defendant will not be relieved of liability simply because the result that he intended materialized by an unanticipated sequence of events.

(1) **Example:** D struck V, aware of a high risk that V might die from the blow. In fact, V was only knocked unconscious. However, while unconscious, V vomited and choked to death. D did not anticipate causing V's death ***in this manner*** (by choking). Nevertheless, V's death was the "natural and probable consequence" of D's action and there were no intervening factors; therefore, D's conduct (striking V) was the proximate cause of V's death. [People v. Geiger, *supra*]

c. **Superseding factors—breaking the chain of causation:** [§189] Proximate causation does not exist if the causal chain between the defendant's act and the result was affected by a ***"superseding factor"***—*i.e.,* an additional act or occurrence that will supersede the defendant's act as the legally significant causal factor. Whether an additional act or occurrence will constitute a superseding cause depends on a number of considerations:

(1) **Must be "intervening":** [§190] An act or occurrence will be a superseding factor only if it is an ***intervening*** one—*i.e.,* one set in motion ***after*** the defendant's act. Therefore, a preexisting condition cannot be a superseding factor and will not break the chain of proximate causation.

(a) **Example:** D stabs V. Ordinarily, the wound would not have been fatal; however, V has hemophilia and bleeds to death from the relatively minor injury. V's preexisting condition does ***not*** break the chain of causation. Accordingly, D's act is the proximate cause of V's death, and D may be held liable for criminal homicide whether he knew of V's condition or not. (Of course, D must be shown to have had the mens rea required for the homicide crime charged, and V's condition may demonstrate that he lacked this. For example, if D is charged with murder and the evidence shows he was unaware of V's hemophilia, the prosecution may not be able to show intent to kill or other sufficient mental state for murder.) [People v. Brown, 62 Cal. App. 96 (1923)]

(2) **Must be unforeseeable:** [§191] Further, the intervening factor must be ***unforeseeable*** (and, of course, not foreseen) by the defendant at the time of his action. [People v. Hebert, 228 Cal. App. 2d 514 (1964)] *Examples:*

(a) **Improper medical treatment:** [§192] D shoots V. Although the wound is not fatal, surgical treatment is required. The surgery is performed, but V dies because of a failure to provide adequate blood transfusions. Since the risks of surgery are foreseeable, the ineffectively administered transfusion is ***not*** a superseding factor. Therefore, D's shot is the proximate cause of V's death.

1) **Compare—grossly negligent treatment:** [§193] Some courts hold that deficient medical care is unforeseeable, and thus may break the chain of causation, if it is ***grossly*** negligent or so poorly administered as to constitute medical malpractice. [State v. Clark, 248 A.2d 559 (N.J. 1968), *aff'd,* 266 A.2d 315 (1970), *cert. denied,* 401 U.S. 958 (1971)]

(b) **Acts of the victim:** [§194] D commits a variety of perverted sexual acts upon V while holding her prisoner. V escapes briefly, takes a poison, and dies. Even though V took her own life, this was a foreseeable consequence of D's actions, since suicide is a normal response to the agonizing situation created by D. Hence, D proximately caused V's death. [Stephenson v. State, 179 N.E. 633 (Ind. 1932)]

(c) **Intervening disease:** [§195] D shoots V and injures her. V is taken to a hospital, where she contracts scarlet fever from her doctor and dies from the disease. Ordinarily, such an occurrence is unforeseeable and hence a superseding factor. Therefore, D will not be found criminally responsible for the death. [Bush v. Commonwealth, 78 Ky. 268 (1880)] The result might well be different, however, if it was generally known that there had been an outbreak of the disease, because then contraction of it by V might be foreseeable.

(3) **Must be sole major cause of result:** [§196] An intervening factor will be a superseding one only if it is the ***sole major cause*** of the result. If it simply combines with the effects of the defendant's conduct, both are concurrent proximate causes and the chain of proximate causation will not be broken. [People v. Lewis, 124 Cal. 551 (1899)]

(a) **Example:** A stabs B and leaves him dying on the ground. C then comes along and also stabs B. B dies from loss of blood caused by both wounds. Although C's act intervened, it is not a superseding factor because it did not become the sole direct cause of B's death. It merely combined with the results of A's act to become a concurrent cause of death. Hence, A (as well as C) is subject to liability for the homicide. [People v. Lewis, *supra*]

(4) **"Independence" of the defendant's action:** [§197] An intervening act is more likely to break the chain of proximate causation the more ***independent it is of the defendant's original action***. In contrast, if the intervening act was committed in response to the defendant's original actions, it is not independent and is less likely to constitute a superseding factor breaking proximate causation.

(a) **Example:** Where the victim of perverted sexual acts by the defendant took her own life (*see* above), her suicidal actions were in response to the defendant's actions and thus were not independent. This further suggests that they would not break the chain of causation. [Stephenson v. State, *supra*]

d. **Special problems—felony murder:** [§198] Felony murder and misdemeanor manslaughter pose special problems of causation because they do not require any mens rea in regard to the death of the victim. (*See infra,* §739.)

4. **Alternative Approaches:** [§199] The complexity, technicality, and uncertain nature of traditional causation analysis has led some to suggest that parts of it—especially proximate causation—be abandoned in favor of alternative approaches.

a. **Model Penal Code approach—not too remote or accidental:** [§200] In situations such as those discussed above where a result occurs in an unanticipated manner, the Model Penal Code provides that the defendant will be treated as causing the result unless the manner in which it occurred is ***too remote or accidental to have a just bearing on the defendant's liability***. [Model Penal Code §2.03]

b. **Result not "highly extraordinary" in light of the circumstances:** [§201] One court has suggested that in these situations, the defendant should be regarded as having caused the result unless the unanticipated way in which the result occurred was ***"highly extraordinary in light of the circumstances."*** [People v. Acosta, *supra,* §184]

(1) **Example:** D drives a stolen car in an effort to elude police and leads officers on a 50-mile high speed chase which creates a high risk that someone will be killed in a vehicle accident. Two police helicopters follow the chase, and during a maneuver to exchange positions one pilot is negligent, the helicopters collide, and the occupants of one are killed. Did D cause the death of the helicopter occupants? The court urged that rather than ask whether the pilot's actions were a superseding cause, it should inquire whether, in the context of a high speed chase dangerous because of the risk of a vehicle accident, the result that actually occurred (the aircraft accident) was so highly extraordinary that D should be regarded as not having caused it. A majority concluded that the helicopter accident was not so highly extraordinary and therefore D did cause it. [People v. Acosta, *supra*]

V. SCOPE OF CRIMINAL LIABILITY

chapter approach

A person may be subject to criminal conviction because, by her own actions, she has engaged in conduct that amounts to a crime. But there are a number of ways in which a person's criminal liability can be based on the commission of a crime by someone else. Therefore, in any examination question, be certain to consider whether a person whose liability is at issue might be subject to conviction for conduct actually committed by another. The following questions focus attention on the main possibilities:

1. Was the defendant involved in the offense in such a way as to be liable under the ***law of parties*** (*e.g.,* principal in the second degree) or under a more ***modern form of liability for offenses committed by others***?

2. Is the situation one giving rise to ***vicarious liability*** for offenses committed by others?

3. Was the offense committed by a person who was a member of a ***criminal conspiracy*** of which the defendant was also a member? (If so, consider the co-conspirator rule discussed in Chapter VII, *infra,* §§643 *et seq.*)

In addition, a corporation or unincorporated association may be criminally liable even though liability is based on crimes actually committed by agents of the corporation or association. Where this is the case, the financial penalty imposed on the corporation or association falls indirectly upon the shareholders or other members, and in a sense, then, they are penalized for offenses actually committed by the corporation or association's agents.

A. COMPLICITY IN THE CRIME

1. **In General:** [§202] Liability for a crime is not limited to the person who actually commits the proscribed act. Rather, liability extends to anyone who has ***encouraged*** (incited) or ***assisted*** (abetted) the perpetration of the crime or—at common law—who has ***hindered apprehension*** of the perpetrator after commission of the offense. All such persons are regarded as "parties" to the crime and can be convicted of the crime as if they themselves had committed the criminal act.

2. **Common Law Classification of Participants—"Party" Rules:** [§203] Under the common law, the parties to a crime are carefully classified. Traditionally, these distinctions were primarily important for procedural purposes, but once the procedural limitations were overcome, all parties were subjected to the same penalty.

    a. **Parties to felonies:** [§204] The parties to a felony are classified according to their role in the perpetration of the crime and whether they were present at its commission.

        (1) **Principal in the first degree:** [§205] Principals in the first degree are those who ***actually perpetrated*** the crime by their own acts, by the acts of ***innocent*** human beings, or by means of an inanimate agency.

(a) **Example:** A causes B, a child, to pass a counterfeit note. B, because of his immaturity, cannot be held liable for his act. A is a principal in the first degree because he accomplished the offense by use of an innocent agent. [Commonwealth v. Hill, 11 Mass. 136 (1841)]

(2) **Principal in the second degree:** [§206] Principals in the second degree are those who either ***incite or abet*** the commission of the crime and who are actually or constructively ***present*** at the time of its commission. [Commonwealth v. Lowrey, 32 N.E. 940 (Mass. 1893)]

(a) **"Constructive" presence:** [§207] A person is "constructively" present when he assists the principal in the first degree at the very time the offense is committed but from such a distance that he is not actually present. [State v. Hamilton, 13 Nev. 386 (1878)]

1) **Example:** Pursuant to a scheme to rob a stagecoach, A is posted as a "lookout," watching for the stage to come. When he sights it, he lights a fire to signal B and C, who then proceed to rob it. Since A was physically absent from the situs of the crime, he was not "actually" present. However, as a lookout, he was constructively present, and thus a principal in the second degree to the robbery. [State v. Hamilton, *supra*]

(3) **Accessory before the fact:** [§208] Those who ***incite or abet*** the commission of a felony by another but are ***not actually or constructively present*** at the commission of the offense are accessories before the fact. Accordingly, this form of liability covers those who provide ***pre-crime*** assistance or encouragement to the actual perpetrators. [Miller, 236]

(a) **Example:** A assisted B in encouraging C to come to a place where B raped C. Since A was not present at the time of the rape but did render pre-crime aid, he is an accessory before the fact to the crime of rape. [State v. Spillman, 468 P.2d 376 (Ariz. 1970)]

(b) **Compare—crime of solicitation:** [§209] One who incites or counsels another to perpetrate a crime commits the misdemeanor of solicitation. However, if the person solicited actually commits the target offense, the inciter will be liable for that crime as a party (*see infra,* §§578 *et seq.*).

(4) **Accessory after the fact:** [§210] Accessories after the fact are those who receive, comfort, or assist another, ***knowing*** that the other has committed a felony, in order to ***hinder*** the perpetrator's arrest, prosecution, or conviction. [Whorley v. State, 33 So. 849 (Fla. 1903)]

(a) **Example:** A, the only witness to B's killing of U, told the sheriff that U had attacked B and that B had killed in self-defense. This was not true; B had acted in cold blood. By fabricating the story, A has in effect hindered the prosecution and conviction of B, and thus is an accessory after the fact to the homicide. [Littles v. State, 14 S.W.2d 853 (Tex. 1929)]

(b) **Exception—wife excluded:** [§211] Under the common law, a wife could not be an accessory after the fact to a crime committed by her husband, because she was considered to be under her husband's control and thus presumed to have acted under his coercion. [State v. Kelly, 38 N.W. 503 (Iowa 1888)]

b. **Significance of party rules:** [§212] The law of parties has considerable procedural significance at common law.

(1) **Variance between pleading and proof:** [§213] Under the common law rules of pleading, a person charged as an accessory could not be convicted upon proof that he was a principal. Similarly, one charged as a principal could not be convicted as an accessory. Thus, whenever there was variance between the pleading and the proof, a party to the crime could potentially escape liability altogether. [Shelton v. Commonwealth, 86 S.W.2d 1054 (Ky. 1935)]

(2) **Conviction of principal necessary:** [§214] At common law, an accessory could not be convicted unless the principal was convicted, although both could be convicted at the same trial if the principal's guilt was determined first. [Bowen v. State, 6 So. 459 (Fla. 1889)]

(3) **Conviction of higher offense than principal:** [§215] Also at common law, an accessory could not be convicted of a higher offense than that for which the principal was convicted. [Tomlin v. State, 233 S.W.2d 303 (Tex. 1950)]

(4) **Not applicable to principals:** [§216] The common law rules do not apply to the two degrees of principals. Therefore, one charged as a principal in the second degree can be convicted despite the acquittal of the principal in the first degree and even if the proof at trial showed him to be a principal in the first degree.

c. **Misdemeanors—no distinction among parties:** [§217] Those who aid or incite the commission of a misdemeanor are, of course, liable for the resulting crime at common law; however, no distinction is made between principals and accessories or between the degrees of principals. [Snead v. State, 8 S.E.2d 735 (Ga. 1940)] Moreover, as will be seen, there is no common law liability at all for aiding a misdemeanant ***after*** the commission of the offense (*see infra,* §268).

d. **Treason—no distinction among parties:** [§218] Similarly, the distinctions among parties do not apply to treason; all participants are liable as principals. [Perkins and Boyce, 735]

3. **Classification of Participants Under Modern Statutes:** [§219] Under modern statutes, most of those who would be "parties" to crimes under the common law are still made guilty of the crimes, but the technical distinctions have largely been abolished. [LaFave and Scott, 574-575]

a. **Inciters and abettors guilty as principals:** [§220] Under many modern statutory schemes, inciters and abettors (*i.e.*, those who under the common law would be principals or accessories before the fact) are made "principals" and guilty of the crime. [*See*, *e.g.*, 18 U.S.C. §2; Cal. Penal Code §31]

b. **Model Penal Code position—inciters and abettors guilty as "accomplices":** [§221] Similarly, the Model Penal Code provides that a person is guilty of an offense if she commits it by her own conduct ***or*** if it is committed by another for whose conduct she is ***legally accountable***. One is "legally accountable" for the conduct of another if she ***causes*** an innocent person to engage in conduct constituting a crime or if she is an ***accomplice*** to the conduct of the other person. An "accomplice" is one who, with the purpose of promoting or facilitating the offense: (i) solicits another to commit it; (ii) aids, agrees to aid, or attempts to aid in planning or committing it; or (iii) having a duty to prevent the offense fails to make proper efforts to do so. [Model Penal Code §2.06(1)-(3)] This has the same effect as the modern statutes discussed above (§220), although different terminology is used.

c. **Accessory after the fact not participant:** [§222] Persons who provide assistance ***after*** the crime (*i.e.,* common law accessories after the fact) are no longer made guilty of the crime committed by the perpetrator. Rather, such persons are usually made guilty of a separate offense that usually carries a lower penalty than the offense committed by the perpetrator (***see infra***, §§273, 1168).

d. **Effect of modern changes:** [§223] The changes made by modern statutes substantially simplify procedural aspects of the law of complicity.

(1) **Fewer pleading and proof problems:** [§224] For instance, it is no longer necessary to specify in the charge whether the defendant is guilty as an accessory or principal; hence, there are no problems of variance between the pleading and the proof. [Johnson v. State, 453 P.2d 390 (Okla. 1969)]

(2) **Conviction of principal may not be necessary:** [§225] Many jurisdictions have abolished the requirement that a principal be convicted before an accessory may be convicted. Thus, one who otherwise would have been an accessory before the fact at common law may be convicted even if the actual perpetrator (the principal in the first degree) has been acquitted. [State v. Spillman, 468 P.2d 376 (Ariz. 1970)]

(a) **No constitutional bar:** [§226] Neither the prohibition against double jeopardy nor the requirement of due process prohibits trial and conviction of an aider and abettor after acquittal of the principal. [Sandefer v. United States, 447 U.S. 10 (1980)]

4. **Accomplice Liability:** [§227] The liability of those who commit crimes by their own actions (*i.e.,* those who would be principals in the first degree under common law terminology) is the subject of this whole Summary. But the liability of those who may be responsible for crimes perpetrated by another because of their involvement in that offense presents special problems. This section considers the issues presented by the liability of those participants in a crime who, at common law, would be principals in the second degree or accessories before the fact. For simplicity, these participants are often collectively called "accomplices."

gilbert LAW SUMMARIES

SUMMARY OF PARTIES TO FELONY

<table>
<tr><th>Parties</th><th>At Common Law</th><th>Liable for Principal Crime?</th><th>Under Modern Statutes</th><th>Liable for Principal Crime?</th></tr>
<tr><td>Principal in First Degree</td><td>actually perpetrates felony</td><td>Yes</td><td>"Principal" (perpetrates felony)</td><td>Yes</td></tr>
<tr><td>Principal in Second Degree</td><td>incites or abets and is present (actually or constructively) at time of crime</td><td>Yes</td><td rowspan="2">"Accomplice" (incites or abets with requisite intent)</td><td rowspan="2">Yes</td></tr>
<tr><td>Accessory Before the Fact</td><td>incites or abets but not present at time of crime (pre-crime aid or encouragement)</td><td>Yes</td></tr>
<tr><td>Accessory After the Fact</td><td>aids in hindering arrest, prosecution, or conviction of person she knows committed felony</td><td>Yes</td><td>Not a party to felony</td><td>No (but may be liable for separate offense)</td></tr>
</table>

a. **Requirements for liability:** [§228] Basically, accomplice liability requires proof that the defendant committed the requisite acts (*i.e.*, incited or abetted), that he had the requisite mens rea, and that the person incited or abetted actually committed the offense. [United States v. Peoni, 100 F.2d 401 (2d Cir. 1938)—aider and abettor must participate in the venture and seek by his actions to make it succeed]

(1) **Requisite acts—"abetting" or "inciting":** [§229] The defendant must have directly or indirectly ***encouraged or facilitated*** the commission of the offense. [People v. Wright, 26 Cal. App. 2d 197 (1938)]

(a) **"Abetting"—any significant assistance:** [§230] One "abets" the commission of an offense if he assists in its commission in any significant way. It need not be shown that without such aid the perpetrator would have been unable to complete the crime. [State *ex rel.* Attorney General v. Talley, 15 So. 722 (Ala. 1894)]

1) **Example:** A desired to kill C, who lived with her young daughter. B took the daughter to another place to keep her from witnessing the killing. A then killed C. By removing the daughter from the scene of the crime, B abetted the commission of the offense, and so became an accessory to the killing. [Middleton v. State, 217 S.W. 1046 (Tex. 1919)]

2) **Perpetrator need not be aware of aid:** [§231] Note that there need not be any communication between the participants, nor need the actual perpetrator be aware that he is benefiting from the accessory's assistance. [State v. Lord, 84 P.2d 80 (N.M. 1938)]

3) **Impact on actual perpetrator necessary:** [§232] Courts often say that the accomplice's actions must have contributed to the commission of the crime, suggesting that some discernible impact upon the actual perpetrator is necessary. [Commonwealth v. Raposo, 595 N.E.2d 773 (Mass. 1992)] However, courts almost always hold that the prosecution has proven a sufficient actual impact upon the actual perpetrator to establish accomplice liability.

a) **Compare—Model Penal Code view:** [§233] Under the Model Penal Code, liability can be based upon an ***attempt to aid*** another in committing a crime. Under this approach, it is not necessary that the defendant successfully provide any actually effective assistance. [Model Penal Code §2.06(3)(a)(ii)]

4) **Omission as abetting:** [§234] Generally, the mere failure to prevent the commission of an offense will not constitute abetting. If one has a legal obligation to intervene, however, the failure to do so becomes an "act" (*see supra,* §89), and the person may be liable as an abettor for his failure to intervene and prevent the offense. [Model Penal Code §2.06(3)(1)(iii)] Some

courts, on the other hand, are reluctant to so expand accomplice liability. [*See* Commonwealth v. Raposo, *supra*—accomplice liability statute requires more than an omission to act]

(b) **"Inciting"—any inducement:** [§235] Quite apart from abetting the commission of an offense, ***encouragement***—even if not accompanied by any physical aid—is sufficient to render one an accomplice. [Hicks v. United States, 150 U.S. 442 (1893)]

1) **Limitation—perpetrator must be aware of encouragement:** [§236] However, encouragement, by definition, cannot exist unless the person sought to be encouraged is ***aware*** of the efforts. Therefore, one who merely attempts to encourage the commission of a crime is not an inciter if the perpetrator had no knowledge thereof. [Hicks v. United States, *supra*]

2) **Presence in readiness to assist:** [§237] Presence at the scene of the crime, without more, does not constitute incitement. However, if by ***prior agreement*** one is present for purposes of rendering aid to the perpetrator should such aid become necessary, this ***is sufficient*** encouragement and is enough to create accomplice liability. Often, the major issue is one of proof—*i.e.,* whether presence and other circumstantial evidence sufficiently demonstrate the existence of a prior agreement between the perpetrator and the accused accomplice so that the accused accomplice's presence is sufficient for liability. [Evans v. State, 643 So. 2d 1204 (Fla. 1994)]

(2) **Mens rea requirement:** [§238] Much confusion exists as to the mental state required for accomplice liability. Basically, the issue is twofold: (i) whether the accomplice must have the ***mens rea required for the crime***, and (ii) whether he must also have ***intended that his actions have the effect of assisting or encouraging*** the successful completion of the crime.

(a) **Mens rea for crime required:** [§239] The authorities are in general accord that an accomplice must have the state of mind necessary to commit the crime by direct action—*i.e.,* the mental state required for the perpetrator. [Wilson v. People, 87 P.2d 5 (Colo. 1939)]

1) **Example:** A pretends that he is willing to help B enter a store and steal certain items inside. B goes with A to the store, helps A enter, and takes the items from A as A hands them out. However, unbeknownst to B, A has notified the police, who arrive before the two leave the area. A is not an accomplice to the burglary and larceny committed by B, because A did not have the specific intent required for those crimes—*i.e.,* he did not intend that the owner be permanently deprived of the goods (required for larceny) or that the larceny be successfully perpetrated (required for burglary). [Wilson v. People, *supra*]

(b) **Mens rea regarding assistance or encouragement:** [§240] There is considerable uncertainty as to the mens rea required in regard to the effect of the accomplice's action, *i.e.*, the assistance or encouragement. All courts agree that one who had no contemplation that his acts would encourage or assist the perpetrator cannot be convicted as an accomplice. [Hicks v. United States, *supra*] Beyond this, however, the result is not so clear: Must the accomplice intend that his conduct have the effect of encouraging or assisting, or is it enough that he acted with knowledge that his conduct would promote or facilitate a crime? Moreover, will an awareness of a substantial risk that his actions would have this effect (*i.e.*, recklessness) suffice?

1) **Example:** A provides B and C with a small amount of his blood. B and C later pour the blood over selective service records, and A is charged as an abettor to the offense of mutilating public records. To convict A, must it be shown that he desired that his blood be used to facilitate the commission of the crime? Is it enough if the prosecution proves that A was aware that his blood would be put to such use? Or, will a showing that A was aware of a high risk or likelihood (but not a certainty) that his blood would be so used suffice? [United States v. Eberhardt, 417 F.2d 1009 (4th Cir. 1969)—supplying blood with knowledge it would be used for unlawful purpose held sufficient for accomplice liability]

2) **Modern position—purpose required:** [§241] The modern trend, adopted in many jurisdictions and embodied in the Model Penal Code, is to require that an aider and abettor act with ***purpose, i.e.,*** with an affirmative desire that his acts have an encouraging or assisting effect. [*See* People v. Beeman, 35 Cal. 3d 547 (1984)—aider or abettor must have intent or purpose of encouraging or facilitating commission of the crime; Model Penal Code §2.06(3)(a)]

a) **Rationale:** Since accomplice liability permits conviction even though the accused did not actually commit the crime himself, special assurance is necessary that the accused is in fact both dangerous and blameworthy enough to justify conviction. This assurance is provided by requiring an exceptionally stringent mens rea, *i.e.*, a showing of purpose. Those who assist another in committing a crime with an affirmative desire that their actions have an encouraging or assisting effect are most assuredly dangerous and blameworthy enough to warrant criminal conviction.

b) **Compare—liability for "facilitating" crime:** [§242] Jurisdictions that require purpose for accomplice liability sometimes provide separately for the liability of one who only ***knowingly*** assists another in committing a crime. This is often done by creating the crime of "criminal facilitation," defined as ***knowingly providing assistance*** to another in committing a crime. [*See* N.Y. Penal Law §§115.00-115.08]

3) **Contrary view—knowledge or recklessness sufficient:** [§243] Some courts disagree, holding that an accomplice will be guilty so long as he ***knew*** his acts would encourage or assist the commission of an offense. [United States v. Ortega, 44 F.3d 505 (7th Cir. 1995)—despite language in decisions, courts in actual practice require only that an accomplice be shown to have known that his actions would assist perpetrator] Furthermore, some decisions have even held recklessness to be sufficient. [*See*, *e.g.*, Backun v. United States, 112 F.2d 635 (4th Cir. 1940)]

a) **Rationale:** Those who act knowing that their conduct will assist in the perpetration of a crime (and those who are aware of a substantial risk that such will occur) have demonstrated that they are both dangerous to society and ethically blameworthy. Consequently, criminal sanctions are justified.

4) **Compromise—nature of crime determinative:** [§244] One court has suggested a compromise between the two views, which would require that purpose be shown unless the crime involved is a ***serious*** one, in which case proof of knowledge alone will suffice. [People v. Lauria, 251 Cal. App. 2d 471 (1967)]

a) **Rationale:** Where the crime is serious (*e.g.,* criminal homicide or burglary), the social need to intervene is significant; hence, a participant should be held liable simply upon proof that he knew his conduct would facilitate perpetration of the offense. But where the crime is less serious (*e.g.,* gambling, unlawful sale of liquor) there is less need for social intervention and, therefore, liability should be limited to those peripheral participants who are most dangerous and blameworthy. [*See* People v. Lauria, *supra*]

(3) **Perpetrator must have committed crime:** [§245] Generally, a person can be convicted as an accomplice only if the crime at issue was actually committed. In other words, the person who was "incited" or "abetted" must be guilty of the offense. [Patton v. State, 136 S.W. 459 (Tex. 1911)]

(a) **Conviction of perpetrator unnecessary:** [§246] Under modern statutes, it is not necessary that the actual perpetrator be convicted. However, the prosecution must ***always prove the perpetrator's guilt*** as part of its case in chief at the trial of the accomplice. [Miller v. People, 55 P.2d 320 (Colo. 1936)]

(b) **Availability of perpetrator's defenses to accomplice:** [§247] It is unclear whether an accomplice may rely on a defense that would be available to the perpetrator. For example, may one charged as an accomplice defend on the theory that the perpetrator was insane or had been entrapped into committing the crime? If a conviction of the principal is not a prerequisite to conviction of the accomplice, there would appear to be no reason to permit the accomplice to assert defenses available to the perpetrator. But if the purpose of the defense is to discourage improper police conduct (as is arguably true in regard to entrapment; *see infra*, §468), perhaps it would be sound policy to allow the accomplice as well as the perpetrator to rely on it. [*But see* United States v. Azadian, 436 F.2d 81 (9th Cir. 1971)—accomplice could not defend on basis of entrapment of perpetrator]

(c) **Compare—other theories of liability:** [§248] If the crime at issue was not completed—so that neither the perpetrator nor the accomplice can be convicted—there may be other offenses for which the aider or inciter may be liable.

1) **Attempt:** [§249] If the perpetrator progressed far enough toward the commission of the crime to be guilty of attempt (*see infra,* §§658 *et seq.*), the accomplice's actions may make him an accomplice to that attempt. [People v. Berger, 131 Cal. App. 2d 127 (1955)]

2) **Conspiracy:** [§250] If there was a ***preliminary agreement*** between the participants, all may be guilty of conspiracy. (*See* discussion *infra,* §§590 *et seq.*)

b. **Scope of accomplice liability:** [§251] There is some question as to the actual scope of liability of an accomplice and a substantially greater question as to what the scope of liability ought to be.

(1) **Traditional rule—accomplice liable for all probable consequences:** [§252] Traditionally, an accomplice is held liable for all probable (*i.e.,* foreseeable) consequences of his conduct. Thus, liability may be imposed not only for the offense incited or abetted but also for ***all other crimes*** committed by the perpetrator that were a ***reasonably foreseeable result*** of the contemplated crime. In effect, then, the accomplice is liable for those crimes that, in the exercise of reasonable care, he should have foreseen; this is something akin to a negligence theory. [People v. Croy, 41 Cal. 3d 1 (1985)—aider and abettor's intent to encourage or facilitate primary crime sufficient to impose liability for other reasonably foreseeable crimes committed by perpetrator] On the other hand, accomplice liability does not extend to those crimes that were not reasonably foreseeable, as where the perpetrator has engaged in a "personal frolic" of his own.

(a) **Example:** Suppose X assists Y in planning a robbery of Z, and Y thereafter carries out the plan. However, in the course of the robbery, Z resists and Y kills Z. X is an accomplice to both the murder and the robbery, because, even though not contemplated, the killing was a reasonably foreseeable consequence of the robbery. [State v. Barrett, 41 N.W. 463 (Minn. 1889)]

(b) **Compare:** Suppose X joins in a scheme to enter a building and steal a safe inside. Y, another member of the group, is left alone with the night watchman and decides to rob him. X is not an accomplice to the robbery because this was a personal frolic of Y's, not reasonably foreseeable by X. [State v. Lucas, 7 N.W. 583 (Iowa 1880)]

(2) **Minority rule—liability limited to contemplated crimes:** [§253] Some courts and commentators have argued that the traditional rule is unjust and inconsistent with well-accepted notions of criminal liability. They contend that such a broad rule exposes an accomplice to liability without requiring a culpable state of mind and therefore is inconsistent with mens rea principles and the policy upon which they are based. Accordingly, a minority of courts follow the Model Penal Code position, which rejects the traditional rule. Under this approach, an accomplice is liable only for those crimes of the perpetrator that he ***actually anticipated*** and therefore intentionally incited or abetted. [LaFave and Scott, 587-591; Model Penal Code §2.06; State v. Bacon, 658 A.2d 54 (Vt. 1995)—liability for all crimes that are the "natural and probable consequence" of the intended offense violates the basic principle that criminal liability requires a culpable mental state]

(a) **Example:** A joined B in the crime of falsifying corporate books. B also filed a false tax return, using the falsified corporate records. Recognizing the criticisms to the traditional rule of accomplice liability, the court held A not an accomplice to the false tax return offense. Even though it was arguably a foreseeable result of falsification of the books, there was no evidence that A had actually contemplated the latter crime. [People v. Weiss, 256 A.D. 162, *aff'd,* 280 N.Y. 718 (1939)]

c. **Possible defenses to accomplice liability:** [§254] There are several possible defenses that might apply when accomplice liability is at issue.

(1) **Withdrawal:** [§255] One who has encouraged or assisted the commission of a crime may escape liability as an accomplice by making an ***effective and timely withdrawal.*** The requirements for a legally effective withdrawal differ somewhat with the nature of the accomplice's initial action.

(a) **Withdrawal must be timely:** [§256] In all cases, the withdrawal must be timely, which means it must take place before the chain of events leading to the crime has progressed so far as to become unstoppable. [People v. Brown, 186 N.E.2d 321 (Ill. 1962)]

(b) **Inciter—communication of renunciation sufficient:** [§257] If the initial action consisted only of ***inciting*** (*i.e.,* encouraging or soliciting commission of the offense), a legally effective withdrawal may be accomplished by ***communicating a renunciation*** of the crime to the perpetrator. [Galan v. State, 184 N.E. 40 (Ohio 1932)]

(c) **Abettor—must countermand prior aid:** [§258] If the initial action consisted of ***abetting*** (*i.e.,* physically assisting commission of the crime), renunciation alone is not enough; the abettor must act to render whatever assistance he has given ***ineffective***. [Commonwealth v. Huber, 15 Pa. D.&C.2d 726 (1958)]

1) **Example:** A gave his gun to B for use in a robbery. When B asked A to come along on the robbery, A responded that he did not wish to get involved. B committed the robbery and A was held liable as an accessory. Having provided B with the gun, A became an abettor. Therefore, A could not effectively withdraw by renouncing the robbery; rather, A should have retrieved the gun from B prior to perpetration of the offense. [Commonwealth v. Huber, *supra*]

(d) **Model Penal Code provisions:** [§259] Under the Model Penal Code, an accomplice may withdraw and thus avoid liability for the crime by any of the following methods:

(i) ***Wholly depriving*** his prior assistance of its ***effectiveness***;

(ii) ***Providing timely warning*** of the perpetrator's plan to law enforcement authorities; or

(iii) Making proper ***effort to prevent commission*** of the offense by the perpetrator.

[Model Penal Code §2.06(6)(c)]

(2) **Situations where accomplice liability inapplicable:** [§260] Generally, accomplice liability applies regardless of the offense involved. There are several exceptional situations, however, in which liability for participation as an accomplice is not available.

(a) **Members of protected class:** [§261] If a crime is defined so as to protect persons in a particular category, persons within that category are not guilty of the crime despite their participation. [Gebardi v. United States, 287 U.S. 112 (1932)]

1) **Rationale:** Since the legislature enacted the statute to protect persons like the inciter or abettor, it must not have intended to subject such persons to the severity of a criminal conviction in the event the statute failed to prevent the crime. [Regina v. Tyrell, 17 Cox Crim. Cas. 716 (1893)]

2) **Example:** A prostitute who willingly joins a scheme to transport her across state lines cannot be held liable as an accomplice to a violation of the Mann Act (which prohibits transporting a woman over state lines for an immoral purpose). Since the statute was intended to protect women, it would be contrary to the legislative purpose to impose accomplice liability upon the "victim" (*i.e.,* the woman transported). [Gebardi v. United States, *supra*]

(b) **Victims of offense:** [§262] Similarly, the ***victim of an offense*** is not liable even if the victim participated in it. Again, this is because the legislature could not have intended to criminalize both victimizing such persons and being victimized. [United States v. Southard, 700 F.2d 1 (1st Cir. 1983)]

1) **Example:** By paying D's blackmail demand, V obviously assists D in completing the crime of extortion. Nevertheless, V is not guilty of extortion as an accomplice to D's commission of the offense.

(c) **Participants necessary to commission of offense:** [§263] If a crime inherently and necessarily involves several types of participants but explicitly provides for the guilt of only one or some of those participants, the other participants are not liable for participation of a sort that would usually create accomplice liability. This is because the legislature obviously knew that such persons would be involved in the crimes and by failing to provide for their liability evinced an intention to exclude them from liability. [United States v. Southard, *supra*]

1) **Example:** D sells cocaine to X. X participated in the crime of ***sale*** of narcotics. That crime inherently involves ***both*** sellers and buyers. Since the legislature knew that buyers would be involved and made no provision for their liability, it must have intended that buyers be immune from prosecution despite their involvement.

(d) **Accomplice liability inconsistent with legislative purpose:** [§264] In some situations, accomplice liability may be inconsistent with the legislative purpose in creating the crime and thus, such liability does not exist since the legislature must have so intended. [United States v. Hill, 55 F.3d 1197 (6th Cir. 1995)]

1) **Example:** The federal "drug kingpin" statute provides for liability of certain drug offenders with five or more employees. An employee of a "kingpin" cannot be prosecuted as an accomplice to his employer's crime, because this would be inconsistent with Congress's intention to limit liability to those in a controlling position of such organizations. [United States v. Hill, *supra*]

(e) **Compare—accomplice unable to commit crime as perpetrator:** [§265] Some crimes require that the actual perpetrator have certain characteristics, and thus limit those persons who can commit the crimes as actual perpetrators. However, such limitations do not apply to those who simply encourage or abet commission of the offense. Hence, one who lacks the requisite traits, although he would not be liable had he been the actual perpetrator, ***can*** be convicted as an accomplice. [People v. Fraize, 36 Cal. App. 4th 1722 (1995)]

1) **Example:** H, who is married to W, encourages X to force W to submit to sexual intercourse with X. If by definition, a husband cannot commit rape upon his wife—*i.e.,* he cannot incur

liability as a principal in the first degree (*see infra,* §846), by inciting X to commit the offense, H can be punished as an accomplice to X's rape of W. [People v. Chapman, 28 N.W. 896 (Mich. 1886)]

5. **Liability of Post-Crime Aiders (Accessories After the Fact):** [§266] At common law an accessory after the fact is made a party to the crime of the person assisted (*see supra,* §§202, 210). Modern criminal codes, however, have significantly changed the potential liability of those who assist one known to have committed an offense.

   a. **Common law requirements for liability:** [§267] Under the common law, there are three prerequisites to the conviction of a person as an accessory after the fact:

      (1) **Commission of completed felony:** [§268] The person assisted must have actually committed—*i.e.*, ***completed***—a felony offense. Those who render post-crime assistance to known misdemeanants are not subject to criminal prosecution; therefore, a ***felony*** must in fact have been committed. Moreover, the defendant's mistaken belief that a felony had been perpetrated is not enough. [People v. Hardin, 207 Cal. App. 2d 336 (1962)]

      (2) **Knowledge of felony:** [§269] The defendant must have ***known*** that the person assisted committed the felony. [Hearn v. State, 29 So. 433 (Fla. 1901)]

      (3) **Aid to felon:** [§270] Some assistance must have been given ***directly*** to the felon for the ***purpose of impeding enforcement of the law***. [Hearn v. State, *supra*]

   b. **Liability under modern criminal codes:** [§271] Modern statutes vary in their treatment of those who assist the perpetrator after commission of a crime.

      (1) **Retention of common law classification:** [§272] Some jurisdictions have retained the category of accessory after the fact, although it is usually made a separate offense and assigned a penalty unrelated to that provided for the person assisted. [*See* Cal. Penal Code §§32, 33—providing for accessory after the fact but assigning uniform penalty of up to $5,000 fine and five years' imprisonment]

      (2) **New offense—"hindering prosecution":** [§273] Many modern criminal codes create distinct offenses consisting of providing aid to others who may have committed an offense. These offenses are sometimes called "hindering prosecution." [*See* Model Penal Code §242.3] Some typical provisions include the following:

         (a) **Person aided need not have committed offense:** [§274] Under these modern statutes, the prosecution often need not prove that the person whom the defendant sought to aid actually committed a criminal offense. It is enough that the defendant provided aid to another with the purpose of hindering the other's apprehension, prosecution, conviction, or punishment. [Model Penal Code §242.3]

(b) **Exception for family members:** [§275] Modern statutes often contain exceptions providing that no crime is committed by aiding a spouse or close relative, such as a child, parent, or sibling. [*See* N.M. Stat. Ann. §30-22-4]

B. VICARIOUS LIABILITY [§276]

Criminal liability usually must be based upon the defendant's own acts (or sometimes failure to act) that show some participation in the offense. The major exception to this rule covers limited situations in which vicarious liability may be imposed.

1. **Definition—Liability for Acts of Others:** [§277] "Vicarious liability" is liability for the crimes committed by another person imposed simply ***because of the relationship*** between the defendant and the perpetrator. In such situations, the prosecution need not show that the defendant acted in any way or participated in the offense; it need only establish that the crime was committed by another and that the defendant stood in the required relationship to that person.

a. **Compare—accomplice liability:** [§278] Accomplice liability is not vicarious. An accomplice's liability is based upon her ***affirmative participation*** in the offense rather than upon her relationship to the perpetrator (*see supra,* §229).

b. **Compare—strict liability:** [§279] Strict liability and vicarious liability are both forms of liability without "fault," but they dispense with the fault requirement in entirely different ways and hence are two distinct concepts. Strict liability consists of eliminating (or reducing) the ***mens rea*** requirement; vicarious liability consists of eliminating the requirement of an ***act***. Accordingly, even though vicarious liability crimes may often impose strict liability, the two issues should be distinguished and analyzed separately. [State v. Beaudry, 365 N.W.2d 593 (Wis. 1985)] Unfortunately, courts sometimes do not do this and in fact confuse the two issues.

(1) **Example:** In a leading case, the president of a company was charged with violating the Food, Drug and Cosmetic Act, which prohibits the shipment of misbranded or adulterated products in interstate commerce. The prosecution was based on shipment by the company's employees of a defective product in interstate commerce. Proper analysis would require an examination of three issues: (i) whether the statute imposes vicarious liability upon the president for the acts of the company employees; (ii) whether the statute requires that the employees have known that the product shipped was defective (*i.e.*, is strict liability imposed as to this issue); and (iii) assuming that the president can be held vicariously liable for the employees' acts, whether the president must have known that defective products were being shipped (*i.e.*, is strict liability imposed as to this issue). Nonetheless, failing to make a careful analysis, the Supreme Court found an intent to impose strict liability and then summarily concluded that this also meant vicarious liability was to be imposed. [United States v. Dotterweich, 320 U.S. 277 (1943)]

2. **When Vicarious Liability Is Imposed—Legislative Intent:** [§280] In all cases, whether a statute creating a crime imposes vicarious liability depends initially on the ***legislative intent***. As a general rule, courts will assume that vicarious liability was ***not*** intended unless some indication to the contrary appears. In practice, evidence of legislative intent to impose vicarious liability will ordinarily be found only in ***employer-employee situations***, *i.e.*, where an employer is prosecuted for the crimes of her employees.

   a. **Statutes expressly providing for vicarious liability:** [§281] Some statutes expressly impose vicarious liability. For example, if it is made criminal to do an act "by oneself or by one's employee or agent," it is quite clear that the legislature intended to make the employer vicariously liable for the crimes of employees or agents. [*In re* Marley, 29 Cal. 2d 525 (1946)]

   b. **Statutes lacking express provision for vicarious liability:** [§282] Frequently, the legislature does not make its intent clear on the face of the statute. In such cases, courts are likely to interpret the statute as imposing vicarious liability only if vicarious liability seems so necessary to the statute's effectiveness that the legislature must have intended to provide for such liability. [State v. Beaudry, *supra*] This is most likely to be the case if:

      (1) ***The activity*** covered by the statute ***is of the sort likely to be engaged in by employees*** of a business concern;

      (2) ***Prosecution of only the employees*** who actually engage in the prohibited activity appears ***unlikely to accomplish the legislative purpose***;

      (3) ***The statutory penalty imposed is relatively light***; and

      (4) ***There is no language in the statute suggesting that personal fault is required*** for its violation (*e.g.*, a requirement that the crime be committed "willfully" or "knowingly").

   c. **Application—crimes committed by employee beyond scope of employment:** [§283] When an employer is prosecuted for the crimes of her employees, some courts limit the employer's liability to crimes committed by employees ***within the scope*** of their employment. [State v. Beaudry, *supra*] Whether a particular act was beyond the particular employee's scope of employment sometimes poses a difficult issue.

      (1) **Crimes committed in disregard of instructions:** [§284] Courts have split as to whether vicarious liability can be imposed where the actual perpetrator committed the offense in disregard of the defendant's previous instructions. [*Compare* Commonwealth v. Morakis, 220 A.2d 900 (Pa. 1966)—no liability; *with* Overland Cotton Mill Co. v. People, 75 P. 924 (Colo. 1904)—liability]

         (a) **Example:** D, the designated agent of a corporation that owned a tavern, was charged with an after-hours sale of liquor by the bartender. D did not authorize the sale and was not present when it was made. The bartender had been instructed to serve no drinks after closing hour. Nevertheless, the court held that a jury could find that after-hour serving of drinks was "sufficiently similar" to the bartender's authorized activity that it was within the scope of his employment. Thus, vicarious liability could be imposed upon D. [State v. Beaudry, *supra*]

3. **Compromise Position—"Defense" of Lack of Fault:** [§285] Vicarious liability may lead to harsh results. These may be mitigated by construing the applicable statutes as providing a defense that the accused could not have prevented the offense or perhaps that she was for some other reason completely without fault for commission of the offense. [United States v. Park, 421 U.S. 658 (1975)—under Pure Food and Drug Act, corporate agent charged with crimes committed by employees could come forward with evidence that he was powerless to prevent or correct violation and prosecution would then have to prove his power to prevent or correct violation; *see In re* Marley, *supra*—reserving judgment on whether vicarious liability statute would permit employer to avoid liability by showing conspiracy between employee and others to incriminate employer]

4. **Policy Considerations:** [§286] Whether vicarious liability should be imposed as a matter of policy has been vigorously disputed.

   a. **Arguments favoring vicarious liability:** [§287] Those who support vicarious liability argue that it is essential to the effective enforcement of a number of important regulatory schemes, such as pure food regulations and prohibitions against child labor. To encourage employers to prevent violations by their employees, and thus facilitate adherence to the law, employers must be held liable for violations. At the same time, however, employer involvement is for the most part difficult, if not impossible, to prove. Hence, only by imposing vicarious liability can the law deter violations. Moreover, prosecutors can be relied on to invoke vicarious liability statutes only where their application would not do injustice.

   b. **Arguments against vicarious liability:** [§288] It has also been stressed that vicarious liability is inconsistent with a basic principle of American criminal law—that people should be held criminally liable only where they have demonstrated by their ***own*** actions that they are morally blameworthy. Indeed, imposing vicarious liability often allows for the conviction of those who are entirely innocent. Those supporting this position contend that requiring proof of the defendant's participation would not place that difficult a burden on the prosecution and would avoid injustice in many cases. [LaFave and Scott, 255-256]

5. **Constitutional Limits on Vicarious Liability:** [§289] The constitutionality of vicarious liability statutes, or at least their application to particular cases, can reasonably be called into question. This is particularly so in light of the constitutional requirement of an "act" (*see supra*, §§79-81). Vicarious liability, then, may violate the Eighth Amendment prohibition against cruel and unusual punishment. Or, the lack of notice and an opportunity to avoid criminal liability that results from the lack of any requirement that the defendant herself participate in the crime may mean that vicarious liability violates the Fourteenth Amendment requirement of due process. Courts, however, have generally upheld vicarious liability statutes, subject to the following limitations. [*In re* Marley, *supra*]

   a. **Defendant must have had control over perpetrator:** [§290] Due process may well preclude the imposition of vicarious liability for the crimes of persons over whom the defendant had no control. Consequently, and to avoid such constitutional difficulties, statutes imposing vicarious liability are likely to be interpreted as being limited to employer-employee and similar situations. [United States v. Park, *supra*; People v. Forbath, 5 Cal. App. 2d 767 (1935)]

b. **Penalties must not be serious:** [§291] Case law has also restricted the nature of the penalty that can be imposed on those who are held only vicariously liable. Generally, serious penalties will not be upheld. *Rationale:* While there is a social interest in imposing vicarious liability, it is not weighty enough to justify the imposition of serious criminal sanctions. [Commonwealth v. Koczwara, 155 A.2d 825 (Pa. 1959)—punishing tavern owner by imprisonment for bartender's violation of liquor code violated due process]

c. **There must be no less onerous alternatives:** [§292] One court has held that due process is violated by imposing vicarious liability on a store owner for illegal liquor sales by an employee, even if only a fine is imposed, where the important public interests involved could be served by less onerous noncriminal alternatives, such as revocation of liquor license. [Davis v. Peachtree City, 304 S.E.2d 701 (Ga. 1983)]

C. CRIMINAL LIABILITY OF CORPORATIONS AND ASSOCIATIONS

1. **Background:** [§293] Current law governing the criminal liability of organizations, such as corporations, reflects a major modification of traditional notions of criminal responsibility.

a. **Common law rule—no liability:** [§294] At common law, corporations and associations could not be convicted of criminal offenses. This position was, in part, traceable to various conceptual problems in holding corporations liable. Basically, since a corporation is not a person, it could not personally participate in the trial or be imprisoned if convicted. To some extent, however, it is likely that the common law rule was based on policy considerations militating against such liability; *see infra.* [Perkins and Boyce, 718]

b. **Modern rule—corporations may be held liable:** [§295] The common law position is now only of historical significance, the trend away from the rule of no liability having begun with the imposition of corporate liability for acts of nonfeasance—*i.e.,* failure to perform duties owed to the general public (such as keeping railroad bridges in repair). By 1909, the Supreme Court conceded that it was constitutionally permissible to hold a corporation criminally liable for affirmative acts of its employees while acting in the course of their duties. Today, corporate liability for both employee acts and omissions is widely recognized. [New York Central & Hudson River Railroad v. United States, 212 U.S. 481 (1909)]

2. **Policy Considerations:** [§296] Despite the general consensus that criminal liability should extend to corporations at least in certain situations, a number of policy considerations continue to be a subject of much debate.

a. **Arguments favoring corporate liability:** [§297] The basis most often advanced in support of corporate liability rests on the deterrent effect of criminal fines; *i.e.,* the threat of fines provides corporate managers with an incentive to take steps to avoid the commission of criminal offenses by corporate employees in the course of their employment. Moreover, corporate organizations wield such tremendous power in modern society that in many contexts social interests are most efficiently served by providing those organizations with a criminal incentive to minimize the commission of offenses by their agents and employees. In some contexts, this may be the only effective method of enforcing important regulatory schemes. [*See* Model Penal Code §2.07 comment (Tent. Draft No. 4, 1955)]

b. **Arguments against corporate liability:** [§298] The case against criminal liability of corporations rests on the proposition that liability results in ineffective punishment of nonblameworthy persons. A fine is the only penalty that can meaningfully be imposed upon a corporation, yet the burden of a conviction ultimately falls upon the corporation's shareholders, who will usually have no responsibility for commission of the offense. Moreover, the reality of organizational behavior is such that these shareholders are unlikely as a practical matter to be in a position to prevent future crimes of the same sort. In addition, prosecution of the corporation itself tends to detract attention from the corporate employees or managers directly responsible and who should more justly be subjected to criminal sanctions. [Perkins and Boyce, 337]

3. **Requirements for Corporate Liability:** [§299] The requirements for criminal liability depend in part upon an expression of legislative intent and in part upon the nature (and primarily the severity) of the crime involved.

a. **Legislative intent:** [§300] Whether an organization can be convicted of a statutory crime depends on the legislative intent. If a statute creating a crime evidences a legislative intent to limit liability to ***natural persons***, corporations cannot be convicted of the offense. However, if a crime provides for liability of "persons," this may suggest an intention to limit liability to natural persons but it is not determinative. Rather, the ultimate question is whether extending liability to corporations is consistent with the "spirit" of the legislation. [Overland Cotton Mill Co. v. People, *supra,* §284]

b. **Nature of crime**

(1) **Minor offenses—"course of employment":** [§301] Corporations will be held liable for minor offenses (in particular, strict liability offenses) if the crime was committed by a corporate employee ***while acting in the course of employment***. If the offense requires a showing of intent or knowledge, courts generally hold that the intent or knowledge of the ***employee*** suffices. [Standard Oil Co. of Texas v. United States, 307 F.2d 120 (5th Cir. 1962)]

(2) **Major offenses:** [§302] Where a corporation is charged with a serious offense (especially one involving a specific intent), there is disagreement concerning the requirements for liability. Several approaches have been recognized:

(a) **"Respondeat superior" approach:** [§303] Some courts apply the rule applicable to minor offenses (above), often called the "respondeat superior" approach. Hence, these courts simply require that the offense have been committed ***with the requisite intent*** by an employee ***in the course of employment*** and (perhaps) that the employee have had the intention of benefiting the corporation. This is the case even if commission of the crime is contrary to general corporate policy and/or the express instructions of the perpetrating employee's superiors. [United States v. Hilton Hotel Corp., 467 F.2d 1000 (9th Cir. 1972)]

(b) **Model Penal Code approach—authorization by high managerial agent:** [§304] In contrast, the Model Penal Code and statutes based on it permit conviction for such an offense only if its perpetration was ***authorized***, ***performed***, or at least ***recklessly tolerated*** by the board of directors or "a high managerial agent acting in behalf of the corporation within the scope of his office or employment." *Rationale:* The theory is that this approach will most effectively encourage corporate managers to avoid criminal offenses by limiting corporate responsibility to those situations in which persons with authority to prevent major offenses are at least aware of a substantial likelihood that such crimes will be committed. [Model Penal Code §2.07(1)(c)]

(c) **Compromise approach—perpetrator with authority for particular activity:** [§305] Still others have adopted a middle position, requiring proof that the corporation gave the actual perpetrator "***enough authority and responsibility*** to act for the corporation in handling the particular corporate business, operation, or project in which he was engaged at the time he committed the criminal act." This approach does not require commission or approval by a person with overall managerial responsibilities, but focuses upon whether the corporation vested the perpetrator with broad responsibilities concerning the activities related to the criminal conduct. [Commonwealth v. Beneficial Finance Co., 275 N.E.2d 33 (Mass. 1971)]

c. **"Defense" of reasonable effort to avoid offense:** [§306] Under the Model Penal Code, a corporation charged with a crime other than a strict liability offense may successfully defend by establishing that the high managerial agent having supervisory responsibility over the subject matter of the offense employed due diligence to prevent its commission. [Model Penal Code §2.07(5)]

4. **No Effect on Individual Liability:** [§307] The imposition of corporate liability does ***not*** affect the criminal responsibility of the actual perpetrator. Hence, ***both*** the corporation and the guilty employee may be convicted of the offense. [Model Penal Code §2.07(6)(a)]

5. **Liability of Unincorporated Associations:** [§308] In contrast to corporations, unincorporated associations are much less frequently subject to criminal prosecution, conviction, and punishment.

a. **General rule—no liability:** [§309] The law has been more reluctant to extend criminal liability to partnerships and other unincorporated associations. As a general rule, such associations will not be subjected to criminal conviction for the crimes of their individual partners or employees. Indeed, even if vicarious liability is imposed on several partners for the crime of one partner, the partnership ***as an entity*** cannot be convicted, because it is regarded as having no legal existence apart from the individual partners. [People v. Stills, 23 N.E.2d 822 (Ill. 1939)]

(1) **Exception—duty imposed by law:** [§310] However, if a law clearly imposes a duty on the partnership (rather than upon the individual partners) and provides a penalty for failing to perform that duty, the partnership itself may be held liable. [Brown v. State, 111 So. 760 (Ala. 1927), *rev'd on other grounds*—partnership could be fined for failure to obtain license for vehicle]

(2) **Exception—legislative intent to make partnerships liable:** [§311] In addition, a partnership may be prosecuted and convicted where the statute in question expressly or by reasonable interpretation evidences an intent to make the entity liable for the crime. [United States v. A. & P. Trucking Co., 358 U.S. 121 (1958)—partnership could be prosecuted under Motor Carrier Act, which is directed at "any person" but defines "person" to include any firm, partnership, or association]

b. **Compare—implications of entity theory:** [§312] Despite traditional adherence to the general rule of no liability, some jurisdictions recognize an "entity theory" of partnership, under which partnerships can sue and be sued in their own name. In turn, courts that follow this theory may arguably conclude that partnerships have sufficient legal standing to justify subjecting them to criminal liability under the same terms as corporations. [LaFave and Scott, 263]

VI. DEFENSES

chapter approach

If the facts in your exam question indicate that the prosecution can prove the elements of the crime charged, always consider whether there are defenses that may be available to the defendant. There are many recognized defenses to criminal liability, although the defenses available to a particular defendant depend somewhat on the crime charged.

The following is a "checklist" useful in considering what defenses may be available to your defendant. (The specific defenses are discussed in detail in the following chapter.)

1. Is the defendant young? (Consider ***infancy***.)

2. Was the defendant "abnormal" at the time of the conduct? (Consider ***intoxication, insanity,*** or ***diminished capacity***.)

3. Was the defendant mistaken or ignorant in a manner that might show lack of mens rea? (Consider ***mistake of fact*** or ***mistake of law***.)

4. Was the defendant subjected to pressures to commit the offense? (Consider ***necessity, duress,*** or ***entrapment***.)

5. If the crime is an assaultive one (*i.e.,* homicide, assault, battery, etc.), was the attack by the defendant motivated by any conduct of the victim or others that might give rise to a defense? (Consider ***self-defense, defense of others, consent of the victim, protection of property***.)

6. Did the defendant have any public authority or similar right to engage in the conduct?

(Consider ***right to arrest, right to prevent commission of a crime, public authority,*** or ***domestic authority***.)

A. INFANCY

1. **Common Law:** [§313] At common law, some children were regarded as incapable of committing a crime and thus could not be convicted. One of several different presumptions is applied regarding a child's capacity to commit a crime:

   a. **Under age seven:** [§314] A child under age seven is ***conclusively*** presumed unable to form a criminal intent and therefore cannot be convicted of a crime.

   b. **Between ages seven and fourteen:** [§315] A child between seven and 14 years of age is likewise presumed incapable of forming criminal intent. But this presumption is ***rebuttable*** and the prosecution can therefore obtain a conviction by introducing evidence sufficient to establish that the defendant knew what she was doing and that it was wrong. Attempts to conceal the commission of the crime, to bribe witnesses, and to accuse others have often been relied on to rebut the presumption.

(1) **Compare—incapacity to commit rape:** [§316] A male child under age 14 is conclusively presumed incapable of committing rape. (*See infra,* §864.)

c. **Age fourteen and older:** [§317] At ages 14 and older, children are treated as adults, and there is ***no presumption*** of incompetency.

2. **Modern Statutes:** [§318] Modern statutes vary in their treatment of the infancy defense, some codifying the common law rules and others modifying them. Of those jurisdictions that depart from the common law, a few have raised the minimum age for criminal liability; others, however, have made the presumption of incapacity a rebuttable one regardless of the age of the child. [*See, e.g.*, Cal. Penal Code §26—children under age 14 presumed incapable of committing crime, but presumption is rebuttable by evidence child knew wrongfulness of act]

3. **Determining Defendant's Age**

a. **Age at time of crime controls:** [§319] Under both the common law and modern statutes, it is the child's age at the time of commission of the crime—rather than at the time of trial—that controls. [Triplett v. State, 152 So. 881 (Miss. 1934)]

b. **Chronological age controls:** [§320] Similarly, the chronological age—rather than the "mental age"—of the child is determinative. [State v. Dillon, 471 P.2d 553 (Idaho 1970)]

4. **Compare—Juvenile Court Jurisdiction:** [§321] All American jurisdictions have legislation that confers upon juvenile courts jurisdiction over children of certain ages alleged to have committed a crime. In juvenile court proceedings, the child is not "convicted" but is "adjudicated delinquent." Statutes often permit the juvenile court to waive its jurisdiction over a specific child and allow the child to be tried as an adult. [*See, e.g.,* Model Penal Code §4.10—child under 16 to be processed in juvenile court; child 16 or 17 to be so processed unless juvenile court waives jurisdiction]

B. INSANITY

1. **In General:** [§322] A defendant is entitled to an acquittal (usually pursuant to a verdict of "not guilty by reason of insanity" or "NGRI") if, ***at the time of the crime***, he was so impaired by mental illness or retardation as to be "insane" within the meaning of the law. Whether a defendant is not convictable because of insanity, however, does not depend solely upon the severity of the impairment or other medical conclusions. Rather, criminal responsibility turns upon whether as a result of impairment the defendant met the applicable legal standard.

a. **Compare—"incompetency to stand trial":** [§323] Insanity concerns the defendant's state of mind ***at the time of the crime*** and must be distinguished from "incompetency to stand trial," which concerns his condition at the time of trial. Unlike insanity, incompetency to stand trial is ***not a defense***, but requires that the proceedings be postponed until such time as the defendant regains his competency. [Dusky v. United States, 362 U.S. 402 (1960)—defendant is incompetent to stand trial if he lacks sufficient present ability to consult with his lawyer with a reasonable degree of rational understanding or to have a rational as well as factual understanding of proceedings against him]

b. **Compare—"diminished capacity":** [§324] Insanity must also be distinguished from "diminished capacity" (*see infra,* §§371 *et seq.*). The rule of diminished capacity permits a defendant to introduce evidence of mental impairment to show that he ***lacked the mens rea*** required for the crime. Insanity, however, is not invoked to disprove mens rea but rather to prove that the defendant lacked the more basic capacity to engage in morally reprehensible behavior—*i.e.,* to understand what he was doing or (in some jurisdictions) to control his conduct.

c. **Approach to insanity defense analysis:** [§325] In considering whether a defendant is entitled to acquittal on insanity grounds, it is necessary to address two matters: (i) whether at the time of the crime the defendant had a ***sufficient impairment*** to constitute insanity; and (if so) (ii) whether that impairment ***so affected the defendant*** as to meet the legal standard.

2. **Condition Giving Rise to Insanity:** [§326] While the various formulations of the insanity test (*infra*) differ significantly, all require that the defendant have had some sort of ***mental impairment***. However, not all impairments can give rise to insanity.

a. **Mental illness or "disease":** [§327] A traditional mental illness, such as a psychosis, can be a basis for an insanity defense. (This result has been codified in modern statutory provisions providing for a defense based on a "mental disease." [*See* Model Penal Code §4.01]) Recent legislation in some jurisdictions, however, specifically requires that the mental condition be severe. [*See, e.g.,* 18 U.S.C. §20—"severe mental disease or defect" required]

(1) **Compare—"psychopathic personality":** [§328] Many jurisdictions follow the Model Penal Code and provide that the insanity defense cannot be based upon "an abnormality manifested only by repeated criminal or otherwise antisocial conduct." [Model Penal Code §4.01(2)] This is probably intended to mean that so-called psychopaths are not eligible for the insanity defense.

(2) **Compare—multiple personality disorder:** [§329] Multiple personality disorder can serve as the basis for an insanity defense, but jurisdictions are divided on how to evaluate whether such a defendant was in fact insane. [United States v. Denny-Shaffer, 2 F.3d 999 (10th Cir. 1993)—critical question is whether the "host" or "dominant" personality met the insanity standard]

b. **Mental retardation:** [§330] Mental retardation or "feeblemindedness" can, if it satisfies the applicable test, render the defendant legally insane. [State v. Johnson, 290 N.W. 159 (Wis. 1940)] This is codified in many modern statutes as a defense based on a "mental defect." [*See* Model Penal Code §4.01]

c. **Intoxication:** [§331] Involuntary intoxication can support an insanity defense if it produces the required effect on the defendant's mind. [Burrows v. State, 297 P. 1029 (Ariz. 1931)] Similarly, a reasonably settled physical or psychological abnormality caused by repeated use of intoxicants can support the defense. [People v. Griggs, 17 Cal. 2d 621 (1941)]

(1) **Compare—voluntary intoxication:** [§332] Voluntary intoxication does not give rise to insanity, but it is the subject of a specific and different "defense" (*see infra,* §§385 *et seq*).

3. **Tests for Insanity:** [§333] All jurisdictions agree that a mental impairment alone does not constitute grounds for acquittal on insanity grounds. The impairment must have ***created a certain effect*** on the defendant's mental condition at the time of the crime.

a. **Basic analysis—"cognitive" and "volitional" impairment:** [§334] Insanity analysis assumes that impairments may consist of two distinguishable types. "Cognitive" impairments concern the person's intellectual processes and involve impaired ability to ***perceive reality*** and to ***reason*** about it. "Volitional" impairments, in contrast, concern the person's ability to ***control his behavior*** and involve impaired ability to avoid engaging in conduct that the person intellectually—or cognitively—recognizes is wrong.

b. **Basic issue—should loss of control constitute a defense?** [§335] The basic issue that divides jurisdictions is whether the legal standard for insanity should be limited to the defendant's thinking or reasoning abilities (cognitive impairment; *see infra,* §§337-344) or whether the defense should also be permitted based on the defendant's loss of ability to control his conduct (volitional impairment; *see infra,* §§345-348).

(1) **Historical developments:** [§336] Insanity was originally limited to cognitive defects. However, until the early 1980s, the trend was toward expansion of the defense, often by adoption of the Model Penal Code's formulation. However, following the acquittal of John Hinckley on charges arising from his attempt to assassinate President Reagan, many American jurisdictions returned to a restrictive cognitive standard.

c. ***M'Naghten*** **rule:** [§337] The traditional standard for insanity, the *M'Naghten* rule, was formulated by the English House of Lords in 1843. What this standard means, however, depends on how critical terms used in it are defined.

(1) **Statement of rule:** [§338] Under the *M'Naghten* rule, a defendant is to be acquitted by reason of insanity only if, at the time of the crime and as a result of his mental impairment, he either (i) did not know the ***nature and quality of his act***; or (ii) did not know that the act was ***wrong***. [M'Naghten's Case, 8 Eng. Rep. 718 (1843)]

(2) **Definition of "nature and quality of act":** [§339] Most jurisdictions hold that a defendant does not "know the nature and quality of his act" only if, as a result of his mental impairment, he did not understand its ***physical nature and consequences*** (*e.g.,* that holding a flame to a building will cause it to burn). A minority of courts, however, define this as requiring a more basic and accurate understanding of the significance of the action. These courts hold that a defendant should be acquitted if, because of his impairment, he lacked ***"true insight" into the nature of his conduct***. [*See, e.g.,* State v. Esser, 115 N.W.2d 505 (Wis. 1962)]

(3) **Definition of "wrong":** [§340] Authorities have long debated how "wrong" should be defined in *M'Naghten.*

(a) **"Legal wrong" approach:** [§341] English courts define "wrong" to mean ***legally wrong***. [Regina v. Windle, [1952] 2 Q.B. 826] American courts have differed, but most adopt this view. [State v. Crenshaw, 659 P.2d 488 (Wash. 1983)] Thus, a defendant is to be convicted unless his impairment caused him to believe his action was legally permissible.

1) **Compare—"deific decree" rule:** Some jurisdictions that define wrong as legally wrong nevertheless will acquit a defendant who believes his action was ordained by God as a result of a ***direct command from God***, *i.e.*, a "deific decree" to commit the act. [People v. Schmidt, 216 N.Y. 324 (1915)]

2) **Example:** D, because of his severe schizophrenia, believes W, his wife, has been unfaithful. He also believes that God permits and in fact directs one spouse to kill the other if that other spouse has been unfaithful. Nevertheless, he recognizes that if he kills W he may be convicted of a crime. He kills W. *Analysis:* (i) D has a ***sufficient impairment*** to trigger insanity; (ii) D's impairment did not prevent him from knowing the ***nature and quality*** of killing W, as *M'Naghten* is usually interpreted; (iii) D's impairment did not prevent him from knowing that killing W was ***legally*** wrong; (iv) even if the jurisdiction recognizes the "deific decree" rule, D cannot bring himself within it because he has no evidence that he believed his moral view was stimulated by a relatively ***direct message to him from God***. [State v. Crenshaw, *supra*]

(b) **"Moral wrong" approach:** [§342] Some argue that "wrong" should mean ***morally wrong***. Thus, a defendant should be acquitted if, as a result of his impairment, he believed his action was morally acceptable, even if he also recognized that it was (and would be treated by authorities as) legally impermissible. Few if any American jurisdictions take this approach.

(4) **Loss of control irrelevant:** [§343] Under most applications of the *M'Naghten* test, the defendant's ability or inability to control his conduct is not relevant. If the defendant could reason and think about his conduct, he is not entitled to acquittal on the ground that mental impairment deprived him of the ability to avoid committing a crime. [Carnes v. State, 275 S.W. 1002 (Tex. 1925)]

(5) **Criticism of *M'Naghten* test:** [§344] The basic criticism of the *M'Naghten* test is that it is so limited that it permits conviction of some impaired persons who, because of their illnesses, could not have avoided committing crimes and thus are not morally blameworthy despite their actions. Some people experience severe impairments that affect only their ability to exercise control over their conduct, yet the *M'Naghten* test provides them with no defense on this ground. As a result, people

who have not acted in a morally reprehensible manner are improperly convicted of criminal offenses.

d. **Loss of control tests:** [§345] Some formulations of the insanity test permit acquittal if the defendant shows sufficient cognitive impairment (usually as required under *M'Naghten,* above) ***or*** sufficient volitional impairment—*i.e.,* loss of the ability to control behavior. For example, the Model Penal Code proposes that a defendant be acquitted if as a result of mental impairment he lacks substantial capacity ***either*** to (i) "appreciate the criminality [wrongfulness] of his conduct" (thus incorporating a modernly phrased cognitive test based on *M'Naghten*) ***or*** (ii) "conform his conduct to the requirements of law" (thus incorporating a control test).

(1) **Irresistible impulse test:** [§346] Some jurisdictions have long provided that a defendant is entitled to acquittal on insanity grounds if his commission of the crime was caused by an "insane impulse" that ***overcame his will*** to avoid the crime. [Parsons v. State, 2 So. 854 (Ala. 1887)]

(2) **Model Penal Code test—lack of "substantial capacity" to control oneself:** [§347] As stated above, under the Model Penal Code, a defendant is entitled to acquittal if the evidence shows that, because of a mental impairment at the time of the crime, he "lacked substantial capacity to conform his conduct to the requirements of law." [Model Penal Code §4.01(1)] Until the early 1980s, this formulation was widely adopted.

(3) **Criticism of control tests:** [§348] Critics of the loss of control tests argue that few if any persons really are rendered unable to refrain from engaging in conduct they know is criminal. Even if some persons are so affected, even with the help of expert psychiatric testimony, courts simply cannot determine whether particular impaired defendants were rendered unable to avoid committing crimes. Furthermore, testimony on the matter is likely to confuse juries and to cause unjustified acquittals because of jury misunderstanding.

e. **Broader tests:** [§349] Some argue for standards that go beyond the *M'Naghten* or control tests.

(1) ***Durham*** **(or "product") rule:** [§350] The *Durham* rule would require acquittal of a defendant if the evidence shows that the crime was the ***"product of" an impairment*** that the defendant had at the time. [State v. Pike, 49 N.H. 399 (1869)]

(a) **Status of *Durham* rule:** [§351] Although initially formulated by the State of New Hampshire, this test was adopted by the Court of Appeals for the District of Columbia in the famous *Durham* case. [Durham v. United States, 214 F.2d 862 (D.C. Cir. 1954)] It was abandoned in that jurisdiction in 1972. [United States v. Brawner, 471 F.2d 969 (D.C. Cir. 1972)] It remains the law in New Hampshire but no other jurisdiction appears to have adopted or even seriously considered it.

(b) **Criticism of rule:** [§352] Those who criticize the product rule stress that it fails to give juries guidance in determining when a specific crime is the product of a defendant's impairment.

gilbert LAW SUMMARIES

SUMMARY OF INSANITY DEFENSES

Test	Definition	Type
M'Naghten	Because of mental impairment defendant did not ***know nature and quality of act*** or that it was ***wrong***	Cognitive test
Irresistible Impulse	Crime caused by insane impulse that ***overcame defendant's will***	Loss of control test
Model Penal Code	Because of mental impairment, defendant ***lacked substantial capacity*** to ***appreciate criminality*** of conduct or to ***conform it to the law***	Combination of cognitive and loss of control tests
Durham	Crime was a ***product of defendant's impairment***	Causation test
Mens Rea Approach	Because of mental impairment, defendant lacked mens rea required by crime	Mens rea or state of mind test

(2) **"Sense of justice" test:** [§353] A leading federal judge has suggested that the law should not attempt a precise formulation of when impaired defendants should be acquitted, because this is difficult or even impossible. Inevitably, the question is a complex ethical-social one. Therefore, jurors should be told simply to acquit a defendant if they determine that "at the time of his unlawful conduct his mental or emotional processes or behavior controls were impaired to such an extent that he cannot justly be held responsible for his act." [United States v. Brawner, *supra*—Bazelon, C.J., concurring]

f. **Revised cognitive tests:** [§354] After the acquittal of John Hinckley, many American jurisdictions adopted somewhat "modernized" versions of the *M'Naghten* test (*see supra,* §337).

(1) **Example:** Under a California statute adopted by initiative, a defendant is to be found insane only if he was incapable at the time of knowing or understanding the nature and quality of his act and of distinguishing right from wrong at the time of the commission of the offense. [Cal. Penal Code §25(b)]

(2) **Example—broader terminology:** The federal statute, passed in 1984, provides for acquittal if the defendant, as a result of severe mental disease or defect, "was unable to ***appreciate*** the nature and quality or the wrongfulness of his acts." [18 U.S.C. §17] By using the term "appreciate" rather than "know," Congress may have adopted a test broader than the old *M'Naghten* test; a defendant arguably can be less impaired than was required under the old test yet still unable to "appreciate" his situation.

g. **"Mens rea" approach alternative:** [§355] Several jurisdictions have abolished any insanity defense as such (*see infra*) but have substituted an explicit authorization for defendants to use evidence of mental impairment to show that they did not have the mens rea required by the crime charged. [*See* Idaho Stat. Ann. §18-207; Utah Code Ann. §76-2-305] Constitutional challenges to this approach as too limited have been unsuccessful. [State v. Herrera, 895 P.2d 359 (Utah 1995)—whatever due process requires to permit nonblameworthy persons to avoid criminal liability is provided by the mens rea approach]

4. **Proposal to Abolish Insanity Defense:** [§356] Some critics of the insanity defense have urged its total abolition in any form.

a. **Arguments for abolishing or limiting defense:** [§357] The major arguments supporting abolition or limitation of the insanity defense are as follows:

(1) Despite the help of expert testimony, ***courts cannot make the determinations*** necessary to apply insanity standards. Even applying more limited criteria, like the *M'Naghten* test (*supra*) is simply too difficult.

(2) Effort to apply insanity standards are ***time consuming*** and too often so ***confuse juries*** that improper acquittals result.

(3) As applied, the insanity defense ***favors wealthier defendants***, since they are better able to secure the expert witnesses necessary to make a successful defense.

(4) The defense is ***not a useful way of diverting those who need treatment*** into a more treatment-oriented system. Those acquitted are not suffering from the kind of impairments that are better treated in the mental health system than in correctional programs.

(5) Persons acquitted on insanity grounds often spend more time in mental hospitals than they would in prison if convicted, so the defense ***does not really benefit impaired offenders***.

b. **Arguments for retention of defense and broader standards:** [§358] Arguments in favor of retaining the insanity defense and of using a broader standard (such as the control tests, *see supra,* §§345 *et seq.*) include:

(1) Criminal conviction implies that a person has engaged in ethically blameworthy behavior, and many persons suffering from impairments are ***not ethically blameworthy***; it is therefore important to provide a method whereby certain impaired persons can ***avoid the stigma and harsh punishment*** imposed for criminal responsibility.

(2) ***Individual responsibility is reinforced*** by inquiries into whether certain defendants were so impaired as to be nonresponsible; thus, the insanity defense tends to strengthen attitudes of general responsibility that keep people from violating the law.

(3) The process can be made into an ***effective way of diverting proper persons*** into the mental health system. Post-acquittal commitment can be reformed so that only acquitted defendants who are still dangerous are hospitalized, effective treatment not available in prisons is provided, and such persons are released when, but not before, they are no longer dangerous. [A. Goldstein, The Insanity Defense (1967)]

5. **Burden of Proof on Insanity:** [§359] There is a general ***presumption of sanity***. Hence, the defendant has at least the initial burden of going forward with the evidence—*i.e.,* the insanity issue is not raised unless the ***defendant presents some evidence*** tending to show he was insane at the time of the offense. Prior to the post-Hinckley acquittal changes, most jurisdictions provided that once a defendant raised the issue of insanity, the ***prosecution*** was required to prove beyond a reasonable doubt that the defendant was ***sane***.

a. **Recent trend—burden on defendant:** [§360] As part of the reform of insanity law following the Hinckley acquittal, a trend has developed placing on the ***defendant*** the burden of proving ***insanity***. [18 U.S.C. §20(b)—defendant must prove insanity by clear and convincing evidence; Cal. Penal Code §25(b)—defendant must prove insanity by preponderance of evidence]

b. **Constitutionality:** [§361] A state may, consistent with due process, require a defendant to prove his insanity, even beyond a reasonable doubt. [Leland v. Oregon, 343 U.S. 790 (1954)]

6. **Jury Instructions on Consequences of Insanity Acquittal:** [§362] Jurisdictions are split on whether the trial jury should be told the procedural consequences of acquitting the defendant on insanity grounds. Defendants argue that such instructions are necessary to assure that the jury does not mistakenly believe that an acquitted

defendant will be permitted to simply and immediately return to the community, but most jurisdictions do not instruct the jury on the matter. [Shannon v. United States, 114 S. Ct. 2419 (1994)—under federal statute, jury is not told consequences of insanity acquittal]

7. **Procedure Following Acquittal by Reason of Insanity:** [§363] A defendant entitled to acquittal on insanity grounds may nevertheless pose a serious risk of further harm to others. As a result, all jurisdictions have special procedures for processing defendants found not guilty by reason of insanity ("NGRI").

    a. **Verdict of NGRI:** [§364] Although verdicts in criminal cases are usually "general," an exception is made in insanity cases. Juries are instructed that if the defendant is entitled to an acquittal on insanity grounds, the verdict should specify that the defendant is found specifically "not guilty by reason of insanity." [18 U.S.C. §4242(b)]

    b. **Post-acquittal commitment:** [§365] In all jurisdictions, some provision is made for possible hospitalization of defendants found NGRI. Under the federal statute, which is typical of modern statutory schemes, an NGRI defendant is ***automatically committed*** to a hospital for a limited period. This commitment is continued only if, at a hearing held within 40 days, the defendant fails to show that he is no longer dangerous. [18 U.S.C. §4243]

        (1) **Note—hospitalization must rest on defendant's impairment:** [§366] A defendant acquitted on insanity grounds cannot be retained in a custody (without full procedural steps) on the ground that he is dangerous for reasons other than the impairment that caused his acquittal. [Foucha v. Louisiana, 504 U.S. 71 (1992)]

    c. **Constitutionality:** [§367] Although other mentally ill persons cannot be committed unless their dangerousness is affirmatively demonstrated, the Supreme Court has held that defendants found NGRI can constitutionally be committed on that basis. There is no federal constitutional right to be released from hospitalization on the expiration of the maximum time the defendant could have spent in prison had he been convicted. [Jones v. United States, 463 U.S. 354 (1983)]

8. **Guilty But Mentally Ill Alternative:** [§368] Some states give juries the option, when a defendant claims impairment at the time of the offense, of rejecting the defense of insanity but finding the defendant "guilty but mentally ill." This approach is modeled on a Michigan statute. [Mich. Comp. Laws Ann. §768.36]

    a. **Requirements:** [§369] A verdict of guilty but mentally ill is to be returned only if the jury finds that the defendant committed the offense, was not legally insane, but was mentally ill at the time of the crime.

    b. **Effect of finding of "guilty but mentally ill":** [§370] A defendant found guilty but mentally ill is sentenced under regular sentencing provisions. If sentenced to imprisonment, however, the defendant is to be given whatever treatment is indicated. If probation is imposed, treatment may be required as a condition of probation.

C. DIMINISHED CAPACITY

1. **In General:** [§371] In some jurisdictions, evidence of mental illness that does not establish insanity may still be admissible to prove that the defendant did not have, or could not have formed, the specific intent necessary for the crime charged. This position is sometimes referred to as the *"Wells-Gorshen"* rule, after two leading California Supreme Court decisions that adopted it. It is also often called the doctrine of "diminished capacity" because it permits the use of evidence (usually psychiatric testimony) to establish that the defendant's capacity was so ***diminished that she could not have formed the requisite mens rea***. [People v. Wells, 33 Cal. 2d 330 (1949); People v. Gorshen, 51 Cal. 2d 716 (1959)]

   a. **Rationale:** Courts accepting the *Wells-Gorshen* rule generally reason that if mens rea is essential to criminal liability, a defendant should have the right to prove that she lacked the requisite mental state by any evidence that is logically relevant to the issue. In addition, it is felt that the rule provides a reasonable compromise between the extremes of holding a mentally ill person fully liable and completely exonerating her by extending the insanity defense—*i.e.,* even where diminished capacity is established, the accused can ordinarily be found guilty of a less serious offense (*see infra*). [Dix, *Psychological Abnormality as a Factor in Grading Criminal Liability: Diminished Capacity, Diminished Responsibility, and the Like*, 62 J. Crim. L., C. & P.S. 313 (1971)]

   b. **Possible constitutional requirement:** [§372] A defendant's right to due process of law may entitle her to introduce expert testimony that because of her mental impairment, she lacked the mens rea required for the crime charged. [United States v. Skodnek, 896 F. Supp. 60 (D. Mass. 1995)]

   c. **Legislative modification of rule:** [§373] After the *Wells* and *Gorshen* cases, legislation in California modified the rule in that state. Under this legislation, diminished capacity is not a defense in a criminal action. Evidence of mental illness is not admissible to negate a defendant's ***capacity*** to form any mental state. But such evidence may be admitted on the issue of whether the defendant ***actually did form*** a mental state required by the crime charged. However, evidence that the defendant, because of mental illness, lacked the ***ability to control*** his conduct cannot be used to show that the defendant did not form a required mental state. [Cal. Penal Code §§21, 28; People v. Saille, 54 Cal. 3d 1103 (1991)—legislative modification of Wells-Gorshen rule does not violate due process]

2. **Majority Approach—Diminished Capacity Rejected:** [§374] A probable majority of courts reject the *Wells-Gorshen* rule, reasoning that the insanity defense is the vehicle for relating mental illness to criminal liability and that it should not be circumvented by manipulation of the mens rea requirement. It has also been contended that the expert testimony that would be permitted to establish diminished capacity is not reliable, and juries are not equipped to understand it or adequately evaluate it. [State v. Provost, 490 N.W.2d 93 (Minn. 1992); *and see* Fisher v. United States, 149 F.2d 28 (D.C. Cir. 1945), *aff'd,* 328 U.S. 463 (1946); Commonwealth v. Rightnour, 253 A.2d 644 (Pa. 1969)]

3. **Application—Limited to Specific Intent Crimes:** [§375] Even where recognized, the rule is often applied only to specific intent crimes. Therefore, a defendant who successfully asserts it in defense to a major specific intent crime can generally be convicted of a lesser included offense that requires only a general mens rea. [People v. Noah, 5 Cal. 3d 469 (1971)]

a. **Compare—Model Penal Code position:** [§376] The Model Penal Code would admit evidence of mental illness whenever it is relevant to whether the defendant had a state of mind required for the offense. There is no limitation to specific intent offenses or any other category of crimes. [Model Penal Code §4.02(1)]

4. **Tactical Advantage—Advance Notice Not Required:** [§377] Defendants in jurisdictions following the diminished capacity rule may have a tactical advantage in that, unlike with the insanity defense, advance notice of intent to raise the issue may not be required. (Some pretrial notice provisions do cover diminished capacity, however. *See, e.g.,* Federal Rule of Criminal Procedure 12.2(b), requiring pretrial notice of intent to offer evidence that because of mental illness defendant lacked requisite intent.)

5. **Compare—English "Diminished Responsibility" Rule:** [§378] By statute in England, a defendant charged with murder is to be convicted only of manslaughter if he establishes that, at the time of the killing, mental illness "substantially impaired his mental responsibility" for the killing. This does not involve disproof of mens rea. Rather, it permits a defendant to establish that although he was not so disturbed as to be insane, his "responsibility" as addressed by the insanity defense—although not totally lacking—was sufficiently impaired by mental illness to make a murder conviction inappropriate. [Homicide Act, 1957 (5 & 6 Eliz. II, ch. 11, §2)] No American jurisdiction has such legislation, and thus there is no "diminished responsibility" rule in the United States.

D. INTOXICATION

1. **In General:** [§379] The effect of intoxication upon criminal liability depends upon whether the accused was voluntarily or involuntarily intoxicated. While involuntary intoxication may be a complete defense, voluntary intoxication is never a defense—although it may sometimes be used to prove lack of mens rea.

   a. **Source of intoxication irrelevant:** [§380] Although the intoxication defense is most frequently based upon conditions arising from the ingestion of liquor, the rules equally apply to the consumption of other intoxicating substances, such as drugs and medicine. [People v. Penman, 110 N.E. 894 (Ill. 1915)—involuntary intoxication analysis used to determine legal effect of taking cocaine tablets]

2. **Involuntary Intoxication:** [§381] Involuntary intoxication is a ***complete defense*** if it so affected the defendant as to render her insane within the meaning of the insanity test adopted in the jurisdiction. [People v. Penman, *supra*]

   a. **"Involuntary" defined:** [§382] Intoxication is involuntary only if the defendant ***did not know*** the substance ingested was intoxicating, or if she consumed it knowing that it was intoxicating but under ***direct and immediate duress***. Courts require strong evidence of duress to sustain a finding of coerced intoxication. [Burrows v. State, 297 P. 1029 (Ariz. 1931)]

   b. **Pathological intoxication:** [§383] The Model Penal Code also regards intoxication as involuntary if it is "pathological"—*i.e.,* if it is grossly excessive in proportion to the amount of the substance consumed and the defendant did not know that she was unusually susceptible to such intoxication. [Model Penal Code §2.08(4), (5)(c)]

c. **Permanent insanity from use of intoxicants:** [§384] A relatively permanent (or "settled") impairment, such as organic brain damage, caused by the defendant's long-term use of intoxicants can under the majority approach serve as the basis for an insanity defense despite its link to repeated and voluntary intoxication. Some courts, however, question the wisdom of this rule and find limited statutory intoxication defenses as rendering it unavailable. [Bieber v. State, 856 P.2d 811 (Colo. 1993)—comprehensive statute providing for limited voluntary intoxication defense is legislative rejection of "settled condition" rule]

3. **Voluntary Intoxication:** [§385] Voluntary intoxication is never a defense in the sense that it invokes a defensive doctrine (like insanity) unrelated to the elements of the charged offense. At common law, voluntary intoxication apparently had no mitigating or defensive significance whatsoever. Under modern law in most jurisdictions, however, it may be used as evidence to ***"negate" some culpable mental states*** and thus may preclude conviction. But most states limit the culpable mental states that can be so negated.

a. **General rule—voluntary intoxication can "negate" a required specific intent:** [§386] Under the majority approach, a defendant can rely on voluntary intoxication to negate only ***a specific intent*** if one is required by the crime charged. Thus, if the crime in question does not require a specific intent, the defendant's voluntary intoxication has no bearing on liability. [People v. Hood, 1 Cal. 3d 444 (1969)]

(1) **Rationale:** The rationale for this rule is not entirely clear. To some extent, it reflects a desire to minimize the exculpatory effect of intoxication on the grounds that those who commit crimes while intoxicated are undoubtedly dangerous and, to some extent at least, blameworthy by virtue of having become intoxicated. Beyond this, however, the limitation may reflect a perception that intoxication seldom, if ever, prevents persons from forming the relatively simple states of mind required for general intent crimes. Consequently, there is no need to consider it in cases where only a general mens rea is required. [People v. Hood, *supra*; Bieber v. State, *supra*]

(2) **Example:** During an arrest attempt, D strikes one officer with his fist and shoots at another with the officer's own gun. D is tried for assault with a deadly weapon and assault with intent to murder but introduces evidence that he was very intoxicated (voluntarily) at the time. Since assault with a deadly weapon is a ***general intent*** crime, D's intoxication has no impact on his liability for that charge. Assault with intent to murder, however, requires proof of a ***specific intent*** (*i.e.,* the intent to kill). Therefore, if D's intoxication shows he lacked that specific intent, or if it simply raises a reasonable doubt whether he acted with that intent, he cannot be convicted of that offense. [People v. Hood, *supra*]

(3) **Burden of proof:** [§387] Since voluntary intoxication tends to negate mens rea, a matter on which the prosecution has the burden of proof beyond a reasonable doubt, on principle a defendant should be acquitted if the evidence of intoxication simply raises a reasonable doubt as to whether defendant had the required mens rea. Nevertheless, some jurisdictions purport to treat voluntary intoxication as an affirmative defense, putting the burden on the defendant.

(4) **Constitutional issue:** [§388] Defendants have argued that constitutional considerations such as due process permit them to rely on any relevant evidence to challenge whether the prosecution has proved the mens rea required by the crime and that any limitation upon defendants' ability to rely on voluntary intoxication to negate mens rea is unconstitutional. A few courts have accepted this. [*See, e.g.,* Terry v. State, 465 N.E.2d 1085 (Ind. 1984)] However, the United States Supreme Court has held (by a 5-to-4 vote) that federal constitutional requirements permit a state to bar a defendant from using his voluntary intoxication to show he lacked the requisite mens rea. [Montana v. Englhof, 116 S. Ct. 201 (1996)—charged with purposely or knowingly causing the death of another, D wanted to use evidence of his voluntary intoxication to show he acted neither purposely or knowingly]

(a) **Rationale:** A four justice plurality reasoned that the common law view—making voluntary intoxication of no defensive significance at all—has not been so completely rejected as to make it violative of due process, especially since that view is supported by reasonable modern policy considerations, including the views that intoxication does not really "make" a person commit crimes and that juries are too quick to accept misleading testimony that intoxication prevented defendants from forming mens rea. Justice Ginsburg, the fifth member of the majority, reasoned that the state was in effect defining the charged crime as requiring either that defendant have killed knowingly or purposely or that he have killed under circumstances that would show he did so knowingly or purposely except for his voluntary intoxication. State legislatures' right to define the mens rea of state crimes as they wish means that this was a constitutional exercise of their power to define crimes.

(b) **But note:** ***State*** constitutional provisions may still require that defendants be permitted to rely on voluntary intoxication as negating mens rea in some or conceivably even all situations.

b. **Minority rule—voluntary intoxication irrelevant to liability:** [§389] In a few jurisdictions, voluntary intoxication is totally irrelevant to liability, even if it shows the lack of a specific intent required for guilt. [Texas Penal Code §8.04—voluntary intoxication cannot be considered as bearing upon guilt or innocence and may be considered in mitigation of penalty only if it reached the point of "temporary insanity"]

c. **Minority rule—voluntary intoxication can negate any required mental state:** [§390] A few jurisdictions, often motivated by a perception that this is constitutionally required, permit a defendant to rely on evidence of voluntary intoxication to negate ***any*** culpable mental state required by the crime without regard to whether this might be characterized as a "specific intent." [Terry v. State, *supra*]

d. **California rule—negates mens rea but not "capacity":** [§391] Under a California statute, evidence of voluntary intoxication cannot be used to show that the defendant lacked the ***capacity to form*** any mental state required by the crime. However, evidence that the defendant was voluntarily intoxicated at the time of the crime is admissible on whether or not the defendant ***actually did form*** a required mental state. [Cal. Penal Code §22]

e. **Model Penal Code rule—negates mental state higher than recklessness:** [§392] Under modern codes using the state of mind analysis established by the Model Penal Code (*see supra,* §§147-158), evidence of voluntary intoxication can be used to show the absence of certain mental states. The Model Penal Code itself provides that voluntary intoxication can be used to show the absence of the state of mind required for the crime, provided that state of mind requires proof of ***purpose or knowledge***. If, however, recklessness is sufficient for liability and the defendant was unaware of the risk involved because of his voluntary intoxication, that unawareness is immaterial to guilt. [Model Penal Code §2.08(2)] Some statutes are even more restrictive. [*See* Alaska Stat. §11.81.630—intoxication can be used only to show lack of "intent"]

f. **Application—convincing trier of fact that intoxication negated mens rea:** [§393] If a jurisdiction's rule permits a defendant to rely on evidence of voluntary intoxication to negate the culpable mental state required by the charged crime, the defendant will be acquitted only if she can convince the trier of fact that her intoxication at a minimum raises a reasonable doubt that the prosecution has proved the required mens rea. This is often a very difficult task. If despite her intoxication the defendant was able to devise a plan and/or perform actions requiring some physical skill, a jury is likely to find that the intoxication does not negate the mental state required. [Weaver v. State, 643 N.E.2d 342 (Ind. 1994)—despite intoxication from LSD, jury properly found that defendant had intent to kill necessary for attempted murder]

4. **Compare—Crimes Requiring Proof of Intoxication:** [§394] Where intoxication is an element of the crime charged (*e.g.,* public drunkenness), courts have assumed that the above rules do not apply, and consequently intoxication cannot prevent liability. [Shelburne v. State, 446 P.2d 56 (Okla. 1968)—driving under the influence of intoxicating substances] It remains possible, however, that on an adequate showing that intoxication was truly involuntary, a defendant might successfully defend against a charge of this sort.

E. IGNORANCE OR MISTAKE OF FACT

1. **In General:** [§395] Ignorance or mistake as to a matter of fact is ordinarily not a defense in the sense that it invokes a defensive doctrine (like insanity) unrelated to the elements of the charged offense. It will, however, sometimes prevent liability if it shows that the defendant ***lacked a mental state*** essential to the crime charged. [Model Penal Code §2.04(1)]

a. **Rationale:** It is a basic principle of the criminal law that the defendant cannot be convicted where it is shown that he did not have the necessary mental state. Hence, simple ignorance (*i.e.,* defendant never thought about the matter) or affirmative mistake (*i.e.,* defendant thought about the matter but reached a wrong conclusion) that negates an essential mental state is a valid defense.

b. **Distinction between "fact" and "law":** [§396] Mistake or ignorance of "fact" is often treated differently than mistake or ignorance regarding "law."

(*See infra.*) This is somewhat misleading, because ***any*** ignorance or mistake that negates the required mens rea should require acquittal. Hence, the Model Penal Code and statutes based on it draw no such distinction and simply provide that ignorance or mistake "as to a matter of fact or law" requires acquittal if it negatives the mens rea required by the crime charged. [Model Penal Code §2.04(1)]

c. **Burden of proof:** [§397] Since mistake of fact serves only to negate mens rea, which is an element of the crime on which the prosecution has the burden of proof, a defendant's ***due process*** right to have the prosecution prove all elements of the crime bars placement of the burden of proof on the defendant. If the evidence of mistake of fact raises a reasonable doubt as to whether the defendant had the necessary mens rea, the defendant must be acquitted. [Wilson v. Tard, 593 F. Supp. 1091 (D.N.J. 1984)]

d. **Burden of raising the issue:** [§398] The defendant may be given the burden of raising the issue of mistake of fact. This means that the jury need not be given an instruction on mistake of fact unless the defendant comes forward with evidence suggesting that he was mistaken (or ignorant) in a manner raising a doubt as to whether he acted with the required mens rea. If the defendant produces such evidence, the jury will be instructed on mistake.

2. **Requirement of "Reasonableness":** [§399] Traditionally, a mistake of fact must be ***reasonable***, *i.e.,* a reasonable person would have made the same mistake under the circumstances. Many courts, however, have not required a showing of reasonableness where the mistake is offered to negate the existence of a ***specific intent*** required for guilt. [United States v. Short, 4 C.M.A. 437 (1954)—only reasonable mistake as to whether victim consented would prevent liability for rape or assault with intent to commit rape; dissent argued that since assault with intent to commit rape requires proof of specific intent, reasonableness should not be required]

a. **Comment:** The requirement of reasonableness has generally been accepted without critical analysis. Because of the frequent confusion as to what state of mind is required by particular crimes, the distinctions drawn are often confused.

b. **Constitutional issue:** [§400] A requirement that a mistake be reasonable means that in some situations in which the defendant actually lacked the mens rea required by the crime (because of an ***unreasonable*** mistake), the prosecution is relieved of its burden of proving mens rea. Thus, the requirement of reasonableness may violate ***due process*** in that the prosecution is not required to prove all elements of the crime. [State v. Bougneit, 294 N.W.2d 675 (Wis. 1980)] The Supreme Court has indicated in addition that a requirement of objective reasonableness raises a serious question as to whether the accused's ***Sixth Amendment right to have guilt or innocence determined by the jury*** is violated. [Cheek v. United States, 498 U.S. 192 (1991)]

c. **Model Penal Code position:** [§401] Under the Model Penal Code, the mistake of fact need not be reasonable as long as it negates the state of mind required for liability. [Model Penal Code §2.04(1)(a)]

3. **Application:** [§402] D is charged with reckless manslaughter, which requires proof that he caused the death of the victim with recklessness, *i.e.*, awareness of a

substantial and unjustifiable risk of death. D offers evidence that before pulling the trigger on the gun he removed the magazine and believed as a result that the gun would not fire and that pulling the trigger posed no risk of killing the victim. *Analysis:* (i) D's mistake, if he in fact made it, ***tends to negate the mens rea*** required, because if D believed the gun would not fire he was not consciously aware of any risk that his actions would cause death; (ii) D's evidence ***raises the issue of mistake***, and the jury should be instructed on it; (iii) the jury must be told that it must acquit D if, given the evidence of mistake, it has a ***reasonable doubt*** whether D acted recklessly; and (iv) if the jury is told to give weight to D's evidence of mistake only if it finds the mistake was ***objectively reasonable***, D's due process and jury trial rights might well be violated. [Wilson v. Tard, *supra*]

4. **Requirement that Conduct Have Been Morally and Legally Permissible Had Facts Been as Defendant Believed:** [§403] Some decisions apparently require a showing that the defendant's conduct would have been legally permissible (*i.e.,* neither a crime nor a violation of civil duty) and (as suggested by some courts) morally defensible had the facts been as the defendant believed them to be. [Regina v. Prince, L.R. 2 Cr. Cas. Res. 154 (1875)]

   a. **Example:** D was charged with abandonment of his pregnant wife. Proof that he was not aware of his wife's pregnancy was held to be no defense because even if the facts had been as he supposed them to be (*i.e.,* if his wife had not been pregnant), this abandonment would have been a violation of his civil duty to support her. Therefore, he acted "at his peril." [White v. State, 185 N.E. 64 (Ohio 1933)]

   b. **Criticism:** This limitation has been criticized as imposing strict liability for serious offenses, contrary to basic principles of criminal liability. Hence, it is doubtful whether the early decisions imposing this limitation would be followed today.

   c. **Model Penal Code position:** [§404] The Model Penal Code provides that the defense of ignorance or mistake is not available if the defendant would still have been guilty of a ***criminal offense*** had the facts been as he supposed. But it further states that, in such cases, the defendant may be held liable for an offense no more serious than he would have been guilty of had the facts been as he believed them to be. [Model Penal Code §2.04(2)]

5. **Prosecutions for Strict Liability Offenses:** [§405] Since ignorance or mistake of fact is tied to the required mens rea, it applies differently if the crime charged imposes strict liability.

   a. **General rule—mistake irrelevant if offense imposes strict liability:** [§406] If the offense in question does not require mens rea, it logically follows that ignorance or mistake of fact—no matter how reasonable—cannot disprove a required intent. If the offense imposed strict liability with regard to some elements, ignorance or mistake cannot be used to negate mens rea with regard to those elements. Hence, ignorance or mistake of fact is ordinarily ***no defense*** to complete strict liability crimes and may or may not be a defense to those crimes that impose limited strict liability.

b. **"Defense" of reasonable mistake in strict liability situations:** [§407] Some courts are unwilling to hold mens rea required for a particular crime but nevertheless recognize a "defense" of reasonable mistake. [People v. Vogel, 46 Cal. 2d 798 (1956)]

(1) **Example:** D was tried for bigamy (*see supra,* §141) under a statute that did not require proof of the defendant's knowledge that he had a spouse living when he remarried. In his defense, D offered evidence that he reasonably believed he had obtained a valid divorce from his first wife before the second marriage. The court refused to read the element of conscious awareness into the bigamy statute, but it interpreted the statute as inapplicable to a person who marries under a reasonable mistake that he has no living spouse. [People v. Vogel, *supra*]

(2) **Example—statutory rape:** A few states have construed statutory rape as requiring no showing by the prosecution that the defendant was aware of the age of the victim but nevertheless as permitting a defendant to show, as a defense, that he acted under a reasonable, although mistaken, belief that the woman was over the age of consent. [People v. Hernandez, 61 Cal. 2d 529 (1964)]

F. IGNORANCE OR MISTAKE OF LAW

1. **In General:** [§408] Issues concerning the defendant's ignorance or mistake of law arise in two entirely different contexts: (i) those in which, because of ignorance or mistake, the defendant ***lacked the mental state*** required for a conviction; and (ii) those in which the defendant had the requisite mental state but claims was mistaken about the applicable law and consequently ***believed his conduct was not proscribed*** by the criminal law. As will be seen, it is important to distinguish between the two situations, as only rarely will the latter be recognized as a defense.

a. **Ignorance compared to mistake:** [§409] Some aspects of this body of law distinguish between two types of claims by defendants: (i) some defendants claim they were simply and ***passively ignorant*** regarding certain matters of law; (ii) some defendants claim not passive ignorance but rather that they addressed the matter and reached an ***affirmative but mistaken conclusion***.

2. **Ignorance or Mistake Showing Lack of Mens Rea:** [§410] Sometimes a defendant's ignorance or mistake concerning a matter of law tends to negate the mens rea of the crime charged. Where this is the case, the defendant may rely on that ignorance or mistake, and if as a result the trier of fact has a reasonable doubt as to whether the prosecution has proven the required mens rea, the defendant must be acquitted. [Cheek v. United States, *supra,* §400; Model Penal Code §2.04(1)(a)]

a. **Example:** A finds a watch and knows it belongs to B. He advertises his find in the local paper, honestly and reasonably (although mistakenly) believing that he will acquire title to the watch if no one responds to the ad. The ad goes unanswered, and A decides to keep the watch. Even though he at all times knew who the rightful owner was, A is not guilty of larceny: Larceny requires an intent to permanently deprive another of her property (*infra,* §§1023 *et seq.*); however, because of a mistaken belief concerning the law of lost property, A believed the watch was his. He therefore lacked the necessary specific intent to deprive another person of ***her property***. [State v. Sawyer, 110 A. 461 (Conn. 1920)]

b. **Reasonableness not required:** [§411] Under federal criminal law, a defendant's ignorance or mistake must be given its full logical significance, even if that ignorance or mistake was unreasonable—*i.e.*, even if a reasonable person in the defendant's situation would not have made it. [Cheek v. United States, *supra*—error in federal tax prosecution to tell jury to consider defendant's mistake as to the law defining income only if it finds the mistake was reasonable]

(1) **Constitutional issue:** [§412] The Supreme Court has indicated that limiting defendants to reasonable mistakes of law would raise a serious question regarding the defendant's Sixth Amendment jury trial right to have the jury determine guilt or innocence. [Cheek v. United States, *supra*]

c. **Belief in unconstitutionality usually not relevant:** [§413] Under this rule, a defendant's mistaken belief that although the crime applies to his conduct it is unconstitutional, and thus cannot be enforced, usually cannot be relied upon. This is probably because the mens rea of most (and perhaps all) crimes requires no understanding that the law defining the crime is constitutional. [Cheek v. United States, *supra*]

d. **Preliminary issue—content of required mens rea:** [§414] In most cases implicating this rule, the major issue will be the preliminary one as to whether the mens rea of the crime requires awareness of the law about which the defendant claims to have been ignorant or mistaken (*see supra,* §127). Usually, if the crime does require such awareness, application of this rule is fairly obvious.

(1) **Example:** Federal tax laws make it a crime to "willfully" fail to file a return as required by the tax law or to "willfully" evade a tax due under that law. As used in this statute, "willfully" requires that the defendant have known of and understood the legal duty to file the return or pay the tax and nevertheless have intentionally failed to do so (*see supra,* §127). D was prosecuted for failing to file returns and evading tax due on wages received. D testified that he believed that "income" as used in federal tax law did not include wages and that the entire federal tax system was unconstitutional and hence unenforceable. *Analysis:* (i) D's testimony that he believed the law defined "income" as excluding wages tends to negate the required awareness that tax was due on the wages and that because he received wages he was required to file a return; (ii) the jury must be instructed that if D's testimony raises a reasonable doubt whether he acted "willfully," it must acquit D; (iii) the jury is not to be told that it may give effect to D's mistaken perception of the law defining income only if it finds that mistake objectively reasonable; and (iv) D's testimony that he believed the federal tax system unconstitutional is irrelevant to his guilt or innocence. [Cheek v. United States, *supra*]

3. **Mistaken Belief that Law Will Not Be Violated:** [§415] In very limited situations, a defendant who had the mens rea required by the crime charged can nevertheless establish a defense consisting of a mistaken perception of the law that caused her to believe her conduct would not constitute a crime. [*See* Model Penal Code §2.04(3)—defense consisting of a belief that conduct does not legally constitute an offense; Commonwealth v. Twitchell, 617 N.E.2d 609 (Mass. 1993); Ostrosky v. State, 704 P.2d 786 (Alaska 1985)]

a. **Passive ignorance not sufficient:** [§416] This defense must ordinarily be based on more than passive unawareness that the law makes the conduct a crime. Rather, it must be based on evidence that the defendant addressed the matter and ***affirmatively decided****—i.e.,* mistakenly believed—that the law did not make the conduct a crime. Thus, "ignorance of the law is no excuse," even under this rule.

b. **Compare—negating mens rea:** [§417] This rule goes beyond permitting defendants to negate mens rea. Criminal mens rea requires only that the defendant "intended" to do the prohibited act; it does not require that the defendant know the act was illegal and "intended" to violate the law. [State v. Downs, 21 S.E. 689 (N.C. 1895)]

c. **Rationale for limited nature of defense:** [§418] In some sense, those who commit crimes without knowledge that the law prohibits what they are doing are not "blameworthy." But nevertheless the law has traditionally been reluctant to permit defendants to escape conviction because of ignorance or mistake. While this approach is often defended on the theory that "everyone is presumed to know the law," no such presumption can be squared with reality. Perhaps, then, the better justification is that permitting defendants to raise such a defense would open courts up to extensive and often meritless litigation. Moreover, some commentators argue that the rule operates to encourage the public to become aware of legal requirements, thereby avoiding confusion and uncertainty as to what conduct has been made criminal. [LaFave and Scott, 414]

d. **Constitutional considerations**

(1) **In general:** [§419] Some courts have reasoned that under certain limited circumstances, convicting a defendant despite the mistaken belief that her conduct is not criminal would be so unfair as to violate federal constitutional due process requirements. Thus, at least a limited defense of mistake of law may be constitutionally mandated. [Commonwealth v. Twitchell, *supra*; Ostrosky v. State, *supra*]

(2) **Misleading by official:** [§420] If someone in an official capacity misleads a defendant into concluding that her conduct will not be criminal, due process will bar her criminal conviction for this conduct. [Cox v. Louisiana, 379 U.S. 559 (1965)—police official incorrectly told demonstrators that picketing at a particular place would be permissible; Raley v. Ohio, 360 U.S. 423 (1959)]

e. **Requirements for defense:** [§421] To the extent that this defense is recognized, it is limited by two categories of requirements.

(1) **Belief must be reasonable:** [§422] The defendant's belief that the law does not prohibit her conduct must be objectively reasonable—*i.e.,* a belief that a reasonable person would have formed under the circumstances. [Model Penal Code §2.04(3)]

(2) **Reliance must be placed on particular matters:** [§423] The defendant must have formed her belief on the basis of certain limited grounds. This requirement provides special assurance that the defendant's mistake was both actually made and objectively reasonable.

(a) **Statute later held unconstitutional:** [§424] A defendant can successfully defend where she acted in good faith reliance upon a statute making her conduct permissible, even though the statute was subsequently found to be unconstitutional. [Brent v. State, 43 Ala. 297 (1869)—reliance on unconstitutional statute giving defendant right to carry on lottery a defense to prosecution for violation of general lottery statute]

(b) **Judicial decision:** [§425] A defendant can escape conviction where she acted in reasonable reliance on a judicial decision holding that the conduct was not criminal. While some courts hold that the decision must be of the highest state court, most impose no such limitation, although the authority of the court is a factor in determining whether the defendant's reliance is reasonable. [Ostrosky v. State, *supra*—defendant must show by preponderance of the evidence a reasonable reliance upon judicial decision, but this may consist of reliance even on a trial court's decision that is under appeal]

(c) **Official interpretation:** [§426] There is a split of authority as to whether reliance on an interpretation of the law by a person or agency with responsibility for administering or enforcing that law will prevent liability. Arguably, the better view would uphold such a defense if there was no superior source of advice reasonably available. [Model Penal Code §2.04(3)(b)—defense available if defendant reasonably relied on "an administrative order or grant of permission" or "an official interpretation of the public officer or body charged by law with responsibility for the interpretation, administration, or enforcement of the law defining the offense"]

1) **Example:** D was prosecuted for violation of a sign ordinance and argued in defense that the local prosecutor had advised D that the sign would not violate legal requirements. The court rejected the defense, reasoning that otherwise the prosecutor's advice "would become paramount to the law." [Hopkins v. State, 69 A.2d 456 (Md. 1949)] Other courts, however, and perhaps the Model Penal Code would disagree. [Model Penal Code §2.04(3)(b)—requiring an ***official*** interpretation]

2) **Compare—reliance on advice of private counsel:** [§427] All courts agree that good faith reliance on the advice of privately consulted counsel is ***no defense***. *Rationale:* Recognizing such a defense would put a premium on bad legal advice and would create a danger of collusion between a defendant and the lawyer she had (or wished she had) previously consulted. [State v. Downs, 21 S.E. 689 (N.C. 1895)]

3) **Compare—personal interpretation of ambiguous criminal statute:** [§428] One court has held that despite statutory language suggesting the contrary, a defendant cannot base a defense on her own—even "reasonable"—reading of an unclear statute as not covering her conduct. [People v. Marrero, 69

N.Y.2d 382 (1987)—emphasizing strong policy need to discourage mistaken interpretations of the law]

G. NECESSITY OR JUSTIFICATION

1. **In General:** [§429] The defense of "necessity" is available where the accused acted in the ***reasonable belief*** that perpetration of the offense would prevent the occurrence of a ***greater harm*** or evil. [Regina v. Dudley & Stephens, 14 Q.B.D. 273 (1884); United States v. Holmes, 26 F. Cas. 360 (1842); Model Penal Code §3.02—calls defense "justification" rather than "necessity"]

   a. **Examples:** Sailors on a ship who refused to obey the captain's orders were held not guilty of mutiny where their purpose was to force the captain to return the ship to port for necessary repairs. [United States v. Ashton, 24 F. Cas. 873 (1834)] Likewise, the Model Penal Code suggests that the defense is available where a pharmacist dispenses a drug without a prescription to alleviate suffering in an emergency. [Model Penal Code §3.02, comment]

   b. **Compare—duress:** [§430] Necessity is raised only when the pressure to commit the offense is created by the ***physical forces of nature***. If pressure is exerted by other persons, the accused may have the defense of duress (*see infra*), but he cannot escape liability on grounds of necessity. [LaFave and Scott, 443]

2. **Requirements**

   a. **Objectively reasonable belief:** [§431] As is discussed below, several requirements are often imposed for the defense. Authorities are not clear whether all of these must be shown to actually exist or, rather, whether defense requires only that the defendant believe—perhaps "reasonably"—that they exist. On principle, a ***reasonable belief*** on the defendant's part should be sufficient.

   b. **"Greater" harm threatened:** [§432] The defendant must have committed the crime for the purpose of avoiding a harm or evil to himself or someone else. On principle, all that should be required is that the defendant ***reasonably believe*** the threatened harm is greater than that involved in the crime. But courts may require that ***in actual fact*** the threatened harm be greater. [*See* Model Penal Code §3.02(1)(a)—requiring that harm sought to be avoided "is greater" than that sought to be prevented]

      (1) **Exception—legislature has determined greater harm:** [§433] The defense of necessity is not available if the legislature has determined that the harm sought to be avoided by the defendant is not greater than that involved in the crime.

         (a) **Example:** Marijuana laws sometimes contain a provision authorizing physicians to dispense marijuana to patients under limited medical circumstances. Where such a provision exists, a defendant charged with a marijuana offense under circumstances not covered by the provision cannot rely on "medical necessity" based on his desire to avoid pain or symptoms of an illness. By enacting the limited provision, the legislature has determined that in other situations the harm involved in possessing marijuana is greater than that resulting from unalleviated symptoms of illness. [Kauffman v. State, 620 So. 2d 90 (Ala. 1992)]

c. **Threatened harm "imminent":** [§434] Some decisions apparently require a showing that the harm sought to be avoided was imminent. Until the threatened harm becomes imminent, there ordinarily are options available to avoid the harm other than violating the criminal law. Hence, the defendant should wait until there is no longer the possibility of a less drastic alternative.

d. **No less harmful alternatives available:** [§435] The necessity defense normally applies only if there was no less harmful way to avoid the threatened danger. [Bice v. State, 34 S.E. 202 (Ga. 1899)]

e. **Defendant not at fault:** [§436] Some versions of the defense require that the defendant not have been at fault in creating the situation that made it necessary to choose between a crime and a more serious harm. [LaFave and Scott, 449] Under the Model Penal Code, the defense may not be used by a defendant who was reckless or negligent in bringing about the situation if recklessness or negligence is sufficient for the crime charged. [Model Penal Code §3.02(2)]

3. **Economic Necessity Sufficient?** [§437] Some decisions indicate that "economic necessity" alone will ***not*** justify the commission of a criminal act. Thus, one who is unemployed and hungry (but not presently starving) may be convicted of larceny if he steals groceries. However, this result may be explained on the theory that the harm avoided by the crime has not yet become imminent. [State v. Moe, 24 P.2d 638 (Wash. 1933)]

4. **Defense to Prison Escape?** [§438] Persons who are captured after escape from prison have often argued in their defense that escape was necessary to avoid greater evils that awaited them in prison, such as sexual assault. Generally, these claims have been rejected on the ground that there were ***other, noncriminal options available***, such as reporting the danger to authorities. But a few decisions have upheld the defense where the defendant establishes that efforts to secure protection from prison authorities or the courts would have been impossible or useless.

a. **Duty to surrender:** Many courts have indicated that necessity may apply to the crime of escape but that in this context a successful defense would require a showing that once the immediate threat of harm was over, the defendant promptly reported to authorities. [People v. Lovercamp, 43 Cal. App. 3d 823 (1974)]

b. **Example:** Construing the federal law concerning necessity and duress as it applies in a prosecution for the federal crime of escape, the Supreme Court held that both defenses required a showing of a bona fide effort to surrender or return to custody as soon as the claimed duress or necessity lost its coercive force. Vague and "necessarily self-serving" claims of a future intent to surrender or "ambiguous conduct" is not sufficient for such a showing. The Court did not reach the question of what, if any, jail conditions would constitute a serious and immediate enough threat to raise either defense, if an effort to surrender or return after escape was shown. [United States v. Bailey, *supra,* §162]

H. DURESS

1. **In General:** [§439] It is sometimes a defense to a criminal charge that the defendant committed the criminal act under "duress" (or, as it is often called, "coercion" or "compulsion"). Duress is a threat made by another human being to use force against defendant or another unless the defendant commits the offense. [Model Penal Code §2.09]

2. **Requirements**

   a. **Objectively reasonable belief:** [§440] Authorities are not clear on whether the defense requires only that the defendant reasonably believe that he has been sufficiently threatened to meet the following requirements. Many formulations of the defense require that the defendant have actually been "coerced," which suggests that a reasonable belief is not enough and that ***there must in actual fact have been a sufficient threat made***. [LaFave and Scott, 437]

   b. **Threat must be of sufficiently serious harm:** [§441] The common law defense requires that the threat be of ***death or serious bodily injury***. Some modern formulations impose no such limitation and thus permit the defense to be based on threats of lesser bodily harm. [*See* Model Penal Code §2.09(1)—requiring only a threat to use unlawful force against the person]

   c. **Subject of threat:** [§442] It is not necessary that the defendant himself be the subject of the threats. Threats to harm a member of the defendant's family, or even a stranger, are sufficient. [Model Penal Code §2.09(1)—threats of force against the person of the defendant or the person of another]

   d. **Threat must be of "immediate" harm:** [§443] Many formulations of the defense require that the threat be of ***immediate*** harm. Threats to do harm in the future, no matter how serious, will not suffice. [Clark & Marshall, A Treatise on the Law of Crimes, 365-366 (7th ed. 1967)] The Model Penal Code and statutes based on it impose no such requirement, but the immediacy of the threatened harm is clearly relevant to whether the defendant's submission was reasonable (*see* below).

   e. **Defendant's submission must have been "reasonable":** [§444] In all cases, it must be shown that the defendant's submission to the coercion and demand that he commit the crime was ***reasonable***. There must, for example, have been no opportunity to obtain assistance or avoid the harm by some other, non-criminal method.

      (1) **Model Penal Code—person of reasonable firmness unable to resist:** [§445] The Model Code embodies this requirement by stating that the situation must have been such that a person of reasonable firmness in the circumstances would have been unable to resist the demand to commit the crime. [Model Penal Code §2.09(1)]

3. **Limitations**

   a. **Not applicable to some criminal homicides:** [§446] Duress often is ***no defense*** to the ***intentional killing*** of another person. Similarly, it cannot be asserted in defense to a charge of ***attempted*** intentional killing. [Watson v. State, 55 So. 2d 441 (Miss. 1951)]

(1) **Compare—felony murder:** [§447] Courts are split on whether duress can constitute a defense to felony murder. On principle, it should be a defense; felony murders are not intentional killings. Further, if a felony murder defendant has a duress defense to the predicate felony, this will preclude conviction for felony murder because there is no felony on which to base felony murder. Of course, the defense is unavailable if an applicable statute excludes all "murders" from the duress defense. [People v. Patano, 239 N.Y. 416 (1925)]

(2) **Compare—duress as negating premeditation:** [§448] Even if duress is not a defense to a charge of first degree premeditated murder, evidence of duress may be introduced to ***establish a lack of premeditation*** and thereby preclude a conviction for the charged crime. [Rizzolo v. Commonwealth, 17 A. 520 (Pa. 1889)]

(3) **Compare—statutory reduction to manslaughter:** [§449] In some jurisdictions, a showing of duress will reduce a homicide charge that would otherwise be murder to manslaughter. [*See, e.g.*, Wis. Stat. Ann. §939.46]

b. **Not applicable if defendant subjected himself to duress:** [§450] The defense is not available if the defendant intentionally or recklessly placed himself in a position in which he should have foreseen that he would be subject to duress. [Williams v. State, 646 A.2d 1101 (Md. 1994); Model Penal Code §2.09(2)—duress unavailable if accused "recklessly placed himself in a situation in which it was probable that he would be subjected to duress"]

4. **Compare—Coercion of Wife by Husband:** [§451] Claims by a wife that she was coerced by her husband into committing an offense traditionally posed special problems.

a. **Common law—presumption of coercion:** [§452] At common law, a wife is not responsible for a crime committed by her under the coercion of her husband. Although a showing of marriage alone carries no particular evidentiary weight, proof that a wife perpetrated the crime in her husband's ***presence*** raises a rebuttable ***presumption*** that he coerced her. [Rex v. Hughes, 168 Eng. Rep. 1137 (1813)]

b. **Modern rule—no presumption:** [§453] Most courts or legislatures have abandoned the above presumption [People v. Statley, 91 Cal. App. 2d 943 (1949)], and the Model Penal Code expressly provides that a woman claiming coercion by her husband must prove duress under generally applicable standards [Model Penal Code §2.09(3)].

(1) **Rationale:** The common law rule developed at a time when married women were actually much under their husband's control. Today the position of women is quite different—women are so infrequently controlled by their husbands that the presumption no longer has any basis in fact.

I. ENTRAPMENT

1. **In General:** [§454] It is a defense to most crimes that the defendant was "entrapped" into committing the act by a law enforcement officer or one acting as agent of a law enforcement officer.

a. **Not a constitutional rule:** [§455] Despite repeated attempts to elevate the entrapment defense to constitutional status, the Supreme Court has refused to require that the states adopt the modern objective formulation—or any other specific formulation—of the defense as a matter of due process of law. [United States v. Russell, 411 U.S. 423 (1973)]

b. **Compare—due process considerations:** [§456] The Supreme Court has left open the possibility that law enforcement conduct related to the commission of an offense may be so outrageous "that due process principles would absolutely bar the government from invoking judicial processes to obtain a conviction." But such a case has never been brought before the Court, and it is clear that the police action would have to be extremely offensive before a due process violation would be found. [United States v. Russell, *supra*]

2. **Substantive Limitations**

a. **Applicable only to nonserious crimes:** [§457] It is generally agreed that entrapment cannot be claimed as a defense to crimes involving serious injury to others, such as rape or murder. In practice, the defense is most commonly raised in connection with the so-called victimless crimes (*e.g.,* solicitation, sale of drugs). [Model Penal Code §2.13(3)—entrapment not available if crime consists of causing or threatening bodily injury to person other than person perpetrating entrapment]

b. **Only law enforcement officers and agents can "entrap":** [§458] A defense is available only where the entrapment was by a law enforcement officer or a person working in cooperation with law enforcement officers (*e.g.,* informers or "undercover agents" who are paid for their services but who are not formal employees of law enforcement agencies). Accordingly, the act of a purely private individual, although it may have induced another to commit a crime, will not support an entrapment claim. [Henderson v. United States, 237 F.2d 169 (5th Cir. 1956)]

3. **Procedural Limitation—Defendant Cannot Deny Committing Crime:** [§459] Defendants in entrapment cases are prohibited in some jurisdictions from taking inconsistent positions. Thus, a defendant cannot both deny committing the offense and claim entrapment. Some courts even require the defendant to affirmatively ***admit guilt of the crime*** in order to argue entrapment. [State v. Nilsen, 657 P.2d 419 (Ariz. 1983)—defendant must affirmatively admit offense, either by testifying, stipulating as to guilt, or in some similar way]

a. **Rationale:** Prohibiting a defendant from taking inconsistent positions is based upon the desire to encourage defendants claiming entrapment to waive their right not to testify and thus make themselves available for cross-examination by the prosecution. In addition, the rule avoids sanctioning a defendant's perjurious denial that he committed the crime and means that juries will not be confronted with potentially confusing inconsistent positions. It also rests on the premise that absent the commission of a crime there can be no entrapment; hence, it is felt that the accused should not be permitted to take the inconsistent positions that he did not commit the offense, but if he did, he was entrapped. This latter point has been criticized, however, because in other areas of criminal litigation there is no prohibition against a defendant adopting inconsistent positions. [State v. Soule, 811 P.2d 1071 (Ariz. 1991); 56 Iowa L. Rev. 686 (1971)]

b. **Compare—federal criminal law:** [§460] The Supreme Court has held that under federal criminal law a defendant ***can*** deny guilt of the crime and alternatively claim entrapment. *Rationale:* Generally, litigants are not barred from taking inconsistent positions. The awkwardness of this position will discourage most defendants from doing it. Thus, the practical risk that permitting inconsistent positions will encourage perjury by defendants is relatively low. [Mathews v. United States, 485 U.S. 58 (1988)]

4. **Entrapment Criteria—"Subjective" Versus "Objective" Approaches:** [§461] Jurisdictions are split on the criteria for determining whether particular facts show entrapment constituting a defense. This split reflects an underlying difference regarding the conceptual basis and rationale for the defense.

a. **Traditional (subjective) standard:** [§462] Under the traditional approach, entrapment exists only if a law enforcement officer ***created the intent*** to commit the crime in the mind of a person who was ***not predisposed*** to commit crimes of this sort. The test is subjective because a finding of entrapment depends on what subjectively stimulated the defendant to commit the crime—the defendant's predisposition or the officer's inducement. Federal courts apply this standard under a long line of Supreme Court decisions. [Sorrells v. United States, 287 U.S. 435 (1932); Sherman v. United States, 356 U.S. 369 (1958); United States v. Russell, 411 U.S. 423 (1973)]

(1) **Rationale—legislative intent:** The traditional entrapment defense is based on the assumption that the legislature did not intend to include within the crime in question persons who were induced by the police into perpetrating the offense. Consequently, an entrapped person is not guilty of criminal conduct as that conduct was defined by the legislature. [Sorrells v. United States, *supra*]

(2) **Analysis—predisposition is crucial issue:** [§463] Under the traditional subjective standard, the critical question is often whether the accused was ***predisposed*** to commit crimes of the sort involved. If the jury finds that the defendant was predisposed, it must reject the entrapment defense regardless of the nature of police participation in the events.

(a) **Application:** [§464] Under the traditional view, it is not entrapment merely because a law enforcement officer afforded the accused an opportunity to commit the crime (as where undercover agent poses as drug addict and purchases drugs from a dealer). Evidence of repeated requests by the police that the crime be committed and appeals by officers to the defendant's sympathy, however, tends to support the entrapment defense. Conversely, evidence that the defendant responded readily to the opportunity to commit the crime and had previously committed similar offenses indicates a predisposition to commit the crime and thus tends to negate the entrapment defense. [Sherman v. United States, *supra*]

1) **Predisposition prior to first approach:** [§465] In applying the federal entrapment standard, courts are to require proof

that the defendant was predisposed prior to first being approached by government agents. Therefore, if government agents had considerable contact with the suspect before actually providing him with an opportunity to commit the offense, and if the proof shows the suspect was at that time predisposed to commit the offense, the government must also show at trial that this predisposition was not caused by the earlier contact between the government agents and the suspect. [Jacobson v. United States, 503 U.S. 540 (1992)]

(3) **Burden of proof:** [§466] Under the traditional approach, a ***defendant*** claiming entrapment has the burden of establishing that ***he was induced*** by officers to commit the charged crime. Upon proof of such inducement (which raises the entrapment issue), the ***prosecution*** has the burden of proving beyond a reasonable doubt that the ***defendant was predisposed*** so as to preclude entrapment. [Jacobson v. United States, *supra*]

(4) **Procedural disadvantages:** [§467] The subjective entrapment criterion usually results in several procedural disadvantages for defendants who claim entrapment.

(a) **Issue tried to jury:** Since the defense bears on the defendant's guilt or innocence, it must be decided by the jury. Juries may be less receptive to entrapment arguments than are trial judges. [Sorrells v. United States, *supra*]

(b) **Evidence showing predisposition:** Once a defendant raises the entrapment issue, his predisposition becomes relevant, and the prosecution can introduce evidence of prior crimes, reputation, and the like to show this predisposition. Such evidence creates a danger that the jury will reject the entrapment defense and convict the defendant simply on the basis of his "bad character."

b. **Modern (objective) standard:** [§468] Some courts apply an entrapment criterion that ignores the defendant's subjective motivation for committing the crime and instead focuses on the ***propriety of the officers' conduct*** judged by an objective standard. [*See* People v. Barraza, 23 Cal. 3d 675 (1979)]

(1) **Rationale—need to discourage police misconduct:** This formulation of the entrapment defense is not based on a perception of the entrapped defendant as "innocent" of the crime. Rather, the defense is based on the ***need to deter government officials*** from engaging in undesirable conduct. [Sorrells v. United States, *supra*—Roberts, J., concurring]

(2) **Analysis—tendency of police conduct to "create" crime:** [§469] Under the usual version of the objective standard, courts are to find entrapment whenever the offense was committed in response to law enforcement activity that was reasonably likely to cause a ***reasonable person*** (who was not predisposed to commit crimes of the sort at issue) to commit a crime. In contrast to the traditional approach, the test under this formulation is objective. Whether or not entrapment occurred depends solely on the conduct of the law enforcement officers; what effect if any this conduct had on the defendant is irrelevant.

(a) **Model Penal Code:** [§470] The Model Penal Code has adopted this view, and provides that entrapment exists if a law enforcement officer has induced or encouraged the commission of the crime by "employing persuasion or inducement which creates a substantial risk that the offense will be committed by persons other than those who are ready to commit it." [Model Penal Code §2.13(1)(b)]

(b) **Analysis:** [§471] The determinative issue under this approach is whether a reasonable person would have responded to the officer's conduct by committing the crime. Hence, the focus is on the nature of the police activity, and especially the ***vigor*** with which officers urged that the crime be perpetrated and any ***inducements*** they offered the accused.

1) **Note—limited scope of concern:** Under most entrapment standards of this sort, the only characteristics of law enforcement behavior relevant to entrapment are those bearing on the ***likelihood of the police behavior to induce commission of the crime***. Evidence that the police conduct was offensive for other reasons (*e.g.,* unlawful invasion of the defendant's privacy) is not relevant to whether entrapment occurred.

(3) **Burden of proof:** [§472] Jurisdictions adopting the objective approach generally place the burden of proof regarding entrapment on the defendant.

(4) **Procedural advantages of objective approach:** [§473] The procedural implications of the objective approach to entrapment often mean that the procedural disadvantages of the traditional rule are eliminated or reduced.

(a) **Issue tried to court:** Since the "defense" is a rule unrelated to guilt or innocence, the entrapment issue is determined by the judge rather than the jury. [Model Penal Code §2.13(2)]

(b) **Evidence of predisposition not admissible:** Since the defendant's predisposition is not in issue, evidence otherwise inadmissible which only tends to prove predisposition (*e.g.,* the defendant's prior criminal record) is not rendered admissible simply because entrapment has been claimed.

c. **Broader objective standards:** [§474] A few jurisdictions have adopted ***very broad objective standards*** for entrapment that permit the defense to be based on police misconduct that would not satisfy the modern objective standard discussed above.

(1) **Providing materials for offense:** [§475] Some courts have upheld claims of entrapment based on showings that government agents provided the materials for commission of the offenses (such as the drug for an illicit drug sale). [People v. Strong, 172 N.E.2d 765 (Ill. 1961)] The Supreme Court has held, however, that the government's supplying the

material for the commission of an offense, even if that material is contraband, is not entrapment under federal law and does not violate the defendant's constitutional rights. [Hampton v. United States, 425 U.S. 484 (1976)]

(2) **Approach suspect without adequate justification:** [§476] A few courts have suggested that entrapment would occur if a police officer approached a suspect and offered the opportunity to commit an offense without probable cause, or at least reasonable suspicion, to believe the person was predisposed to commit such offenses. [Walker v. State, 262 N.E.2d 641 (Ind. 1970)—probable cause required, *overruled in* Hardin v. State, 358 N.E.2d 134 (Ind. 1976); Childs v. United States, 267 F.2d 619 (D.C. Cir. 1958)—reasonable suspicion required]

(3) **General prohibition against misconduct:** [§477] A few courts have adopted broad rules permitting findings of entrapment on the basis of police conduct found offensive for general policy reasons. [State v. Molnar, 410 A.2d 37 (N.J. 1980)—entrapment occurs if police conduct is so egregious as to impugn the integrity of the court; State v. Sainz, 501 P.2d 1247 (N.M. 1972), *overruled by* State v. Fiechter, 547 P.2d 557 (N.M. 1976)—entrapment occurs whenever the police conduct—for any reason—is "such that if allowed to continue would shake the public's confidence in the fair and honorable administration of justice."]

J. CONSENT AND RELATED MATTERS

1. **In General:** [§478] Consent is a "defense" if it ***negates some element*** of the crime or if the charge is for a ***minor assault or battery***. In either case, however, the consent must be ***legally effective***.

2. **Consent as Negating Element of Crime:** [§479] Some crimes are defined in terms of the victim's lack of consent. For example, rape requires intercourse without the consent of the woman (*see infra*). Clearly then, if lack of consent is an essential element of the crime, proof of consent will be a bar to conviction.

3. **Consent as Defense to Assault or Battery:** [§480] As to all other crimes, consent of the victim is ordinarily ***no defense***. The major exception arises in the case of certain assaults or batteries. Here, courts are more likely to recognize the defense of consent if: (i) the criminal act did ***not involve serious bodily injury*** or the risk of such injury; (ii) there is ***widespread acceptance of the risk*** (*e.g.*, in sporting events); and (iii) there is a ***distinct beneficial effect*** attending the defendant's conduct (as in the case of medical surgery). [People v. Fitzsimmons, 13 Misc. 301 (1895)]

   a. **Example:** D was charged with aggravated assault by reason of his appearance in a sadomasochistic film in which he beat another person with a riding crop. Despite his testimony that the so-called victim had been paid and had acquiesced in the beating, D was convicted of the crime. Because of the severity of the injuries inflicted, consent was no defense. [People v. Samuels, 250 Cal. App. 2d 501 (1967)]

   b. **Model Penal Code position:** [§481] The Model Penal Code adopts a similar approach, providing that consent is a defense to conduct causing or threatening to cause bodily harm if:

(i) The harm involved is ***not serious***; ***or***

(ii) The defendant's conduct and the harm "are ***reasonably foreseeable hazards*** of joint participation in a ***lawful athletic contest or competitive sport*** or other concerted activity not forbidden by law."

[Model Penal Code §2.11(2)]

4. **Legal Effectiveness of Consent:** [§482] Even when consent is recognized as an available defense, a particular consent will be a defense only if the consent is legally effective. For this to be the case, three requirements must be met:

   a. **Voluntarily given:** [§483] The consent must have been given voluntarily—*i.e.,* by a party acting of her own free will without compulsion or duress.

   b. **Consenter must have legal capacity:** [§484] Consent must have been given by a person legally capable of consenting—*i.e.,* someone not disabled by youth, intoxication, or mental abnormality. [Smith v. State, 131 S.E. 163 (Ga. 1925)]

   c. **Free of fraud or mistake:** [§485] Consent given under fraud or mistake as to the very ***nature of the defendant's conduct*** ("fraud in the factum") is ***ineffective***. However, "fraud in the inducement," which involves deception as to some matter ***collateral*** to the nature of the defendant's conduct, will ***not*** vitiate an otherwise effective consent. [People v. Cook, 228 Cal. App. 2d 716 (1964)]

      (1) **Example:** D obtained possession of a motor vehicle in exchange for a bad check and was prosecuted for the statutory crime of taking an automobile without the consent of the owner. D was not guilty, although the owner's acquiescence was falsely induced. The fraud related only to a collateral matter (the consideration given for the consent) and so did not render the consent legally ineffective. [People v. Cook, *supra*]

5. **Compare—Condonation No Defense:** [§486] The victim's ***forgiveness*** after the commission of a crime (*i.e.,* "condonation") is ordinarily no defense, even if that forgiveness follows full restitution by the defendant. [Commonwealth v. Spielel, 82 A.2d 692 (Pa. 1951)]

   a. **Rationale:** The principal injury from the commission of a crime is suffered by the public. The defendant's willingness to settle with the victim does not affect this and therefore should not bar prosecution. [People v. Brimm, 22 Misc. 2d 335 (1960)]

   b. **Exception—compromises authorized by statute:** [§487] Some jurisdictions authorize victims of certain crimes (usually misdemeanors) and offenders to negotiate compromises. In such cases, if the victim acknowledges that she has received satisfaction, the court may dismiss the criminal prosecution. [Cal. Penal Code §§1377-79]

6. **Compare—Negligence or Criminality of Victim No Defense:** [§488] The fact that a specific victim was negligent or engaged in criminal activity at the time of

the crime is not a defense to a crime against that victim. This is because crimes involve wrongs against the public and therefore the unworthiness of a particular victim is not a sufficient basis for barring conviction. [Frazier v. Commonwealth, 165 S.W.2d 33 (Ky. 1942)]

a. **Effect on causation:** [§489] If the crime is one involving a required result, such as criminal homicide, the fact that the victim was negligent after the defendant's behavior may affect proximate causation and thus the defendant's liability for the result. (*See supra*, §§184 *et seq.*)

K. SELF-DEFENSE

1. **In General:** [§490] A defendant charged with an assaultive crime may assert in defense that she reasonably believed her actions were necessary to defend herself against an apparent threat of unlawful and immediate violence from another. The requirements that apply to this defense differ depending upon whether the crime charged involved the use of deadly force. [Perkins and Boyce, 1115]

2. **General Requirements for Self-Defense:** [§491] In all cases where the defendant claims to have acted in self-defense, whether or not deadly force was involved, the following elements must be proved to establish the defense:

a. **Reasonable belief:** [§492] To assert the defense the defendant must ***reasonably*** believe it is necessary to defend herself. However, an honest and reasonable belief is enough; the defense is available even though it turns out that the belief was wrong and there was, in fact, no actual need to use force in self-defense. [Shorter v. People, 2 N.Y. 193 (1849)]

b. **Threatened harm:** [§493] The defendant must have reasonably believed she was threatened with ***physical harm*** at the hands of another.

c. **Imminency of threatened harm:** [§494] The defendant must have reasonably believed the threatened harm was ***imminent—i.e.,*** that the harm ***would be inflicted immediately*** if she did not act in self-defense. In addressing this, the court must consider whether the threatening person was actually present and, if so, whether that person appeared willing and able to injure the defendant. [People v. Williams, 205 N.E.2d 749 (Ill. 1965)]

d. **Unlawfulness of threatened harm:** [§495] The defendant must have reasonably believed the threatened harm would be unlawful. This may raise issues as to whether force can be used to resist an unlawful arrest and whether one who is the initial aggressor in an affray can claim the defense at all (*see infra*).

e. **Force used was necessary to prevent harm:** [§496] The defendant must have reasonably believed that the threatened harm was such as to require the ***defensive force actually used***. There is no defense available to the use of force beyond that which reasonably appeared necessary to prevent the threatened harm. [Model Penal Code §3.04(1)]

3. **Additional Requirements Where Deadly Force Used:** [§497] Although there is no absolute prohibition against the use of deadly force in self-defense, there are some special limits on when it may be used. "Deadly force" is force used with the

intent to cause death or serious bodily injury or which is ***known*** by its user ***to create a substantial risk*** of death or serious bodily injury. [Model Penal Code §3.11(2)]

a. **Perceived threat of death or serious bodily injury:** [§498] All courts agree that deadly force may be used in self-defense ***only if*** the defendant ***reasonably believed*** that the other person was ***about to inflict death or great bodily injury*** upon her. [Beard v. United States, 158 U.S. 550 (1895)]

(1) **Compare:** If a defendant is threatened with ***nondeadly*** harm and she cannot prevent this by using nondeadly force in self-defense, the law expects the defendant to submit to the nondeadly injury rather than resort to the deadly force necessary to prevent that injury. [Perkins and Boyce, 1118]

b. **Deadly force necessary to prevent death or serious bodily injury:** [§499] The defendant will be allowed to use deadly force in self-defense if she ***reasonably*** believed that the deadly force used was ***necessary*** to prevent the death or serious bodily injury with which she was threatened. If she realized—or, in the exercise of reasonable care, would have realized—that nondeadly force would suffice, she has no defense to a crime consisting of the use of deadly force.

c. **Duty to retreat?** [§500] A difficult problem is presented by the question whether a defendant should have a defense to the use of deadly force if she had an opportunity to retreat instead of using deadly force.

(1) **Common law and minority rule—retreat required:** [§501] For a self-defense defense to a crime consisting of deadly force, the common law required that the defendant show she had ***no opportunity*** to retreat or that she unsuccessfully sought to use an available opportunity. Some jurisdictions still follow this approach, which is based on the position that human life should not be jeopardized if reasonable alternatives are available and that retreat—despite its degrading impact—is a reasonable alternative.

(a) **Exception—safe retreat not possible:** [§502] Jurisdictions requiring retreat generally demand such retreat only where it appears available in complete safety. If the defendant reasonably believed that retreat would increase the risk of an attack by deadly force, she may use deadly force herself in self-defense without attempting retreat. [State v. Anderson, 631 A.2d 1149 (Conn. 1993)]

(b) **Exception—attack in the home:** [§503] Jurisdictions requiring retreat generally do not demand it if the defendant is attacked in her own home. Some do not require it if the attack occurs in the defendant's place of business. *Rationale:* Persons in these locations are already in the places of safety to which attacked victims are usually encouraged to retreat; thus to demand more of them would be unreasonable. [People v. Tomlins, 213 N.Y. 240 (1914)]

(c) **Model Penal Code position—retreat required:** [§504] The Model Penal Code is similar to the minority rule, requiring the defendant to retreat, surrender possession of a thing demanded by another asserting a claim of right to it, or comply with a demand that she abstain from any action she has no duty to take, if the defendant knows this can be done with complete safety. [Model Penal Code §3.04(2)(b)(ii)]

(2) **Majority modern rule—retreat not absolutely required:** [§505] Most American jurisdictions have abandoned the common law rule and impose no strict requirement of retreat before the use of deadly force in self-defense. [Beard v. United States, *supra*]

(a) **Compare—opportunity to retreat relevant to reasonableness:** [§506] Under the modern view, any evidence that the defendant could have retreated, the safety of such retreat, and the places to which retreat might be made are relevant to whether the defendant decided that deadly force was ***reasonably necessary***. [State v. Jessen, 633 P.2d 410 (Ariz. 1981)]

4. **Special Problem—Battered Victim Claiming Killing in Self-Defense:** [§507] Application of self-defense law often presents special problems when the defendant relies on a long history of abuse by the victim as a basis for self-defense to the charge of killing that victim. Frequently this situation involves a female defendant whose claim of self-defense relates to a long history of abuse by her husband or another man with whom she had a long personal relationship.

a. **Major problems with defense**

(1) **Imminence of the threatened harm:** [§508] In many such cases, the defendant attacked the victim after a particular episode of abuse had ended. Consequently, any harm she may have feared from the victim arguably was not "imminent" as required by self-defense law. [State v. Norman, 378 S.E.2d 8 (N.C. 1989)—defendant shot abusive husband while he was asleep; thus, evidence did not show she feared imminent harm from him and court found that no issue of self-defense was presented]

(2) **Options to the use of force:** [§509] In some such cases, the absence of any physical barrier to the defendant leaving the relationship suggests options were sufficiently available as to make her use of deadly force objectively unreasonable.

b. **Responses**

(1) **Expert testimony on battered woman syndrome:** [§510] Defendants often produce expert testimony on battered woman syndrome and its effects. Such testimony generally suggests that the effects of a battering relationship are such as to cause the battered person to conclude that leaving the relationship or otherwise preventing further abuse is simply not a practical and available option and thus that further violence is inevitable.

(2) **Need to consider defendant's position:** [§511] At least one court has held that the reasonableness of a battered spouse's actions must be evaluated in light of the spouse's ***physical and psychological characteristics***, the spouse's ***specific experiences*** as a victim of battering, and perhaps

the ***disadvantaged position*** that women have occupied in society. Juries may be so instructed. Under this approach, certain attacks upon battering spouses may be found reasonable in light of these factors to have been reasonable responses to the battering spouses' conduct. [State v. Leidholm, 334 N.W.2d 811 (N.D. 1983)]

(3) **Elimination of requirement of imminent harm:** [§512] Some have urged that at least in these cases the law should no longer impose a requirement that the defendant have reasonably perceived the threatened deadly harm as imminent. Rather, all of the relevant policy concerns would be satisfied if the law required only that the defendant reasonably perceive the use of deadly force in self-defense to be ***necessary***. [State v. Norman, *supra*—Martin, J., dissenting]

5. **Limitation—Right of Aggressor to Self-Defense:** [§513] Generally, a person who was the ***initial aggressor*** in the situation cannot use force to defend herself. By beginning the altercation, she forfeits the right later to assert self-defense. [Rowe v. United States, 164 U.S. 546 (1896)]

a. **Rationale:** The victim, in defending herself against the aggressor, is ordinarily using lawful force, and (as discussed above) the defendant can only use self-defense in response to threats of ***unlawful*** harm.

b. **"Arming oneself" as aggression:** [§514] The defendant's arming herself because of concern regarding a confrontation does not necessarily constitute aggression even if the defendant sought out the victim, if this was to seek a peaceable settlement of their differences. But if the defendant armed herself and returned to the scene of a prior difficulty for further conflict with the other, this is sufficient to render self-defense inapplicable. [Howard v. United States, 656 A.2d 1106 (D.C. 1995)]

c. **Exceptions:** [§515] There are two situations in which a person, although the initial aggressor, regains the right to act in self-defense:

(1) **Nondeadly aggressor met with deadly force:** [§516] If the victim responds to the aggressor's use of ***nondeadly*** force with ***deadly*** force, the aggressor can use whatever force appears reasonably necessary (including deadly force) to repel the attack. *Rationale:* Since nondeadly force cannot be met with deadly force (*supra*), the victim has threatened unlawful harm.

(2) **Withdrawal by aggressor:** [§517] An aggressor regains the right to act in self-defense by ***withdrawing*** from the affray. Ordinarily, the defendant must either physically remove herself from the fight or actually notify her adversary of the desire to desist, but some jurisdictions hold that even unsuccessful efforts to so notify her adversary, if reasonable, will suffice. [State v. Diggs, 592 A.2d 949 (Conn. 1991)—withdrawing from encounter or clearly manifesting an intention to do so will restore right of self-defense]

6. **Resisting Unlawful Arrest as Self-Defense:** [§518] Criminal charges based on force used to resist an ***unlawful*** arrest present a special problem of self-defense law.

a. **Traditional view—force permitted to resist unlawful arrest:** [§519] Traditionally, courts held that a person subjected to an ***unlawful*** arrest—even by a person known to the defendant as a law enforcement officer—may act in self-defense and resist with reasonable force. [Bad Elk v. United States, 177 U.S. 529 (1900)]

b. **Modern rule—no right to resist arrest by officer:** [§520] Many jurisdictions have rejected the traditional rule in part, and hold that force may ***not*** be used to resist even an unlawful arrest if the arrestee ***knows*** that the arresting person is a ***law enforcement officer***. *Rationale:* The legality of an arrest is too complicated an issue to reliably be resolved "in the street." Modern weapons make the cost of so resolving disputes unacceptably high. Moreover, since legal processes are readily available for the release of persons unlawfully arrested, it is not burdensome to require resort to safer and more rational legal methods of resolving the situation. [State v. Koonce, 214 A.2d 428 (N.J. 1965); Model Penal Code §3.04(2)(a)(i)]

(1) **Exception under modern rule—unlawful arrest made with excessive force:** [§521] Some jurisdictions prohibiting the use of force against arrests that are unlawful because they are without adequate grounds nevertheless permit force to be used to resist excessive force being used to make an arrest. *Rationale:* Later resort to legal proceedings to challenge the officer's actions cannot effectively prevent undue physical harm caused by excessive force and thus do not provide an adequate alternative to immediate self-defense. [People v. Curtis, 70 Cal. 2d 347 (1969)]

7. **Compare—"Imperfect" Self-Defense in Homicide Prosecutions:** [§522] Self-defense is usually a "perfect" or complete defense that, if successful, entitles the defendant to acquittal. In murder prosecutions, however, some jurisdictions provide an "imperfect" defense to those unable to establish complete self-defense. Under this approach, a defendant who killed under the ***unreasonable belief*** that this was necessary to defend against an imminent attack or by the use of an ***unreasonable amount of force*** cannot escape conviction on grounds of self-defense but is to be convicted of only manslaughter rather than murder (***see infra,*** §777). [State v. Flory, 276 P. 458 (Wyo. 1929)]

a. **Example:** D instigated a fight with V and in the course of the altercation killed V to protect himself. Even though D had acted to save his own life, D could not claim a complete defense to murder because he was the aggressor. However, under the "imperfect defense" doctrine, the crime was mitigated from murder to manslaughter. [State v. Flory, *supra*]

L. DEFENSE OF OTHERS

1. **In General:** [§523] A defendant charged with an assaultive crime may assert in defense that he reasonably believed his actions were necessary to defend ***another person*** against an apparent threat of unlawful and immediate violence from another. [Regina v. Prince, 2 Cr. Cas. Res. 154 (1875)]

2. **Relationship with Party Defended:** [§524] There is some split of authority on whether the defense is available if the defendant acted in defense of a complete stranger.

a. **Early view—special relationship required:** [§525] Early English case law suggested that force could be used in defense of others only if the defender stood in some special relationship to the imperiled person (*e.g.,* husband-wife, parent-child, or master-servant), and some American statutes still impose such a limitation. [*See, e.g.,* Model Penal Code §3.05, comment (Tent. Draft No. 8, 1958)]

b. **Modern view—no special relationship required:** [§526] Under the modern (and preferable) approach, no prior relationship need be shown between the defendant and the person assisted; thus, as a general rule, reasonable force may be used in defense of ***any third person***, even a stranger. [Foster v. Commonwealth, 412 S.E.2d 198 (Va. 1991); Model Penal Code §3.05(1)] *Rationale:* The only basis for requiring a special relationship—that people will impulsively and hence unwisely and unnecessarily attack others under the mistaken impression that this is necessary to protect strangers—simply has no basis in fact.

3. **Right of Party Defended to Act in Self-Defense:** [§527] Courts differ on whether the defendant has a right to use force in defense of another if the person defended did not in fact have the right to use force in her own defense (as where she was the initial aggressor).

a. **Objective (or "alter ego") rule—defense turns on right of person defended:** [§528] Some courts follow the "alter ego" rule, holding that a defendant who comes to the aid of another ***stands in the place of the person assisted***. Thus, one who intervenes to protect others does so at his peril, and if the person assisted had no right to use force in self-defense (even if it reasonably appeared that such a right existed), the defendant has no privilege. [People v. Young, 11 N.Y.2d 274 (1962)]

(1) **Rationale:** It has been argued that this rule is necessary to "orderly society," because it discourages persons from impulsively—and unnecessarily—attacking others under the mistaken belief that a third person is in danger. It does this by telling persons that they had better be certain that a third person is in danger before they come to the aid of that person because they cannot later rely on reasonable but mistaken beliefs that the person aided was in danger. [People v. Young, *supra*]

b. **Subjective rule—reasonable appearances control:** [§529] Other jurisdictions—and the Model Penal Code—follow what is seemingly a more just rule, under which a defendant has the right to use force in defense of others as long as it ***reasonably appeared*** that the person assisted had the right to use force in self-defense. [State v. Beeley, 653 A.2d 722 (R.I. 1995); Model Penal Code §3.05(1)(b)]

(1) **Example:** D killed her husband in the reasonable belief that he was about to kill their son. In fact, the son knew he was in no danger and so could not himself have killed the father in self-defense. Nevertheless, D was held to have a defense of others defense, since it reasonably appeared to her that her son was entitled to kill in self-defense. [State v. Menilla, 158 N.W. 645 (Iowa 1916)]

(2) **Rationale:** Those supporting this position stress that there is no reason to impose criminal liability upon persons who conducted a reasonable investigation of the circumstances and acted reasonably on their conclusions. Moreover, a contrary rule might well discourage bystanders from rendering aid to those who legitimately and desperately need it. [State v. Fair, 211 A.2d 359 (N.J. 1965)]

4. **Limitation—Force Used Must Be Reasonable:** [§530] As with self-defense, the defendant must not, of course, have used more force than reasonably appeared necessary under the circumstances. Thus, the danger to the person assisted must appear ***immediate,*** and ***only that amount of force reasonably believed necessary*** to eliminate the risk may be exercised. [Model Penal Code §3.05(1)]

5. **Compare—Force to Prevent Criminal Offense:** [§531] The circumstances under which the defendant claims to have acted in defense of others may also support the defense of crime prevention. Thus, as will be seen *infra* (§568), if the defendant reasonably believes that the person assisted is the victim of a criminal offense, he may have a right to use force to prevent or terminate the commission of a crime.

M. PROTECTION OF PROPERTY

1. **In General:** [§532] A defendant charged with an assaultive crime may assert in defense that he reasonably believed his actions were necessary to defend property from wrongful interference. The right to use force in protection of property, however, is much ***more limited*** than the right to use force in protection of persons, and therefore this defense is quite limited.

   a. **Deadly force not allowed:** [§533] A person cannot use deadly force simply to defend his property against unlawful interference even if there is no other way to prevent the threatened harm. This rule is based on the premise that the interest in security of property does not justify jeopardizing the lives of others (*i.e.,* society places a much higher premium on the preservation of human life than on the protection of property). [State v. Metcalfe, 212 N.W. 382 (Iowa 1927)]

   b. **Compare—other privileged use of force:** [§534] Deadly force may be justified where the facts also support another privileged use of force, as where the defendant's reasonable force in protection of his property is met with an attack threatening ***imminent serious bodily harm to the defendant***.

      (1) **Defense of dwelling:** [§535] The right to use force in defense of one's dwelling may sometimes permit the use of deadly force (*see infra,* §§547 *et seq*).

2. **Reasonable Nondeadly Force Permissible:** [§536] Nondeadly force may be used to protect real or personal property in one's lawful possession if the force used reasonably appears necessary to prevent or terminate an unlawful intrusion onto or interference with that property. [People v. Payne, 8 Cal. 341 (1857)]

   a. **Request to desist:** [§537] Some courts hold that force is not reasonable under this rule unless a ***prior request*** has been made for the other to desist from interfering with the property. It is likely, however, that even these courts would hold that no such request need be made where it reasonably appears that doing so would be useless, dangerous, or otherwise not a viable alternative (*e.g.,* where it would permit the other person to do substantial harm to the property before the request is made). [State v. Cessna, 153 N.W. 194 (Iowa 1915)] *Note:* The Model Penal Code adopts this position. [Model Penal Code §3.06(3)(a)—request to desist required unless exception applies]

3. **Property in Possession of Another:** [§538] The traditional rule and many modern rules require that the property defended be in the ***lawful possession*** of the person using the force. Thus, there is generally no right to use force in defense of property in the possession of another (or at least the case law does not clearly establish such a right). [LaFave and Scott, 468]

   a. **Compare—Model Penal Code position:** [§539] The Model Penal Code permits the use of nondeadly force to protect property in the defendant's possession or ***in the possession of another for whose protection the defendant acts***. [Model Penal Code §3.06(1)(a)]

4. **Use of Force to Regain or Reenter Property:** [§540] The right to use force to protect property must generally be used ***at or near the time of the initial wrongful intrusion*** upon the property. Thus one illegally dispossessed of property cannot use force to regain it or, in the case of real property, to reenter it.

   a. **Exception—hot pursuit:** [§541] Nondeadly force can be used to regain property unlawfully taken if the action is taken immediately after the loss of the property or while in "hot pursuit" of the dispossessor. [State v. Dooley, 26 S.W. 558 (Mo. 1894)]

   b. **Model Penal Code position:** [§542] The Model Penal Code would expand the exception, permitting the use of force to retake property when the defendant is in "***hot pursuit***" ***or*** when he reasonably believes the dispossessor has ***no "claim of right" to the property***. However, if real property is involved, the defendant must show that it would have been an "exceptional hardship" to postpone reentry until a court order was obtained. [Model Penal Code §3.06(1)(b)(ii)]

5. **"Spring Guns" and Similar Devices:** [§543] Special problems are posed by the use of mechanical devices in the protection of property.

   a. **Traditional rule:** [§544] Traditionally, an injury or killing caused by means of a mechanical device is justifiable only if the person who set the device would have been justified in inflicting the same harm had he actually been present. Thus, where a trespasser is killed, the use of such devices is tied to the very restricted right to use deadly force in defense of a dwelling (*see* below). [State v. Barr, 39 P. 1080 (Wash. 1895)]

   b. **Model Penal Code position—mechanical devices never permissible:** [§545] The Model Penal Code provides that a mechanical device designed or known to cause death or serious bodily harm is ***never*** permissible. [Model Penal Code §3.06(5)]

   c. **Compromise position—reasonableness:** [§546] One court has rejected the traditional position but has also refused to regard spring guns and similar devices as totally impermissible. Apparently, the test is whether the device was reasonable under the circumstances considering, among other things, that if the defendant were personally present he might decide not to use deadly force even if such force was technically permissible under the law. [People v. Ceballos, 12 Cal. 3d 470 (1974)]

N. PROTECTION OF DWELLING

1. **In General:** [§547] When property defended is the defendant's own dwelling, many authorities recognize a somewhat greater right to use force in defense of that property. Although there is considerable dispute as to the scope of the right to use force in this situation, all of the various formulations of this rule sometimes permit the use of even ***deadly force***.

2. **Common Law View—Deadly Force in Defense of Dwelling:** [§548] Under the early common law view, deadly force could be used in defense of one's dwelling if it reasonably appeared necessary to prevent a forcible entry of the dwelling, and a warning had first been given the intruder to desist and not enter. [State v. Patterson, 45 Vt. 308 (1873)]

    a. **No duty to retreat:** [§549] If a jurisdiction requires retreat before the use of deadly force in self-defense or defense of others, this requirement may be inapplicable if the situation also gives rise to the right to use deadly force against one seeking to enter the habitation. [Law v. State, 318 A.2d 859 (1974)]

3. **Modern Views—Limited Right to Use Deadly Force:** [§550] Modern courts have limited the right to use deadly force in defense of a dwelling. Some hold that deadly force is permissible only if the defendant reasonably believed the intruder intended to ***commit a felony or to harm someone*** in the dwelling. Others adopt a narrower view, recognizing the use of deadly force only against an entry reasonably believed to be for the purpose of committing a felony. [Morrison v. State, 371 S.W.2d 441 (Tenn. 1963)]

    a. **Model Penal Code:** [§551] The Model Penal Code would require that the defendant believe the intruder is attempting to commit a felony ***and*** either (i) that the intruder has used or threatened deadly force, or (ii) the use of non-deadly force would expose someone in the dwelling to substantial danger of bodily harm. [Model Penal Code §3.06(3)(d)(ii)]

    b. **Intruder already inside dwelling:** [§552] Courts are split on whether the right to use deadly force in defense of the dwelling applies only to prevent an entry or whether it can also be used against an intruder who has already accomplished entry. [State v. Brookshire, 353 S.W.2d 681 (Mo. 1962)—once intruder had gained entry, rationale for defense of dwelling no longer applies and use of force is governed by other rules such as self-defense]

    c. **Statutory provisions for protection of dwellings:** [§553] Several jurisdictions have enacted quite extreme provisions permitting force to be used in connection with invasions of the dwelling.

        (1) **Example:** A California statute provides that a defendant is ***presumed*** to have had the reasonable fear of imminent death or serious bodily injury required to trigger self-defense if the defendant: (i) used deadly force

within his residence against another not part of the household; (ii) the other unlawfully and forcibly entered the residence; and (iii) the defendant knew or had reason to believe that an unlawful and forcible entry occurred. [Cal. Penal Code §198.5]

(2) **Example:** The Colorado "Make My Day" statute permits the occupant of a dwelling to use ***any degree of force***, including deadly force, against another if: (i) the other person has made an unlawful entry into the dwelling; (ii) the occupant has reason to believe the other person either has committed a crime in the dwelling or is committing or intends to commit a crime against a person or property in the dwelling; and (iii) the occupant reasonably believes the other person "might use any physical force, no matter how slight, against any occupant." [Colo. Rev. Stat. §18-1-704.5]

O. USE OF FORCE TO EFFECTUATE ARREST

1. **In General:** [§554] Both private citizens and police officers have a right to use force in effecting an arrest and a defense against a criminal prosecution based on force used for this purpose. The scope of the defense may differ depending upon the status in which the defendant acted.

2. **Right of Police Officers:** [§555] Arrests by peace officers are favored over arrests by private parties and thus officers are given the broader defense. Nevertheless, increasing limits have been placed on officers' defense to the use of ***deadly*** force.

a. **Traditional rules:** [§556] Under traditional rules an officer may use whatever ***nondeadly*** force reasonably appears necessary to make an arrest for a felony or misdemeanor. ***Deadly force*** may be used if the officer ***reasonably believes*** that the suspect committed a ***felony***, but it is limited to those situations. [Stinnett v. Virginia, 55 F.2d 644 (4th Cir. 1932)] Thus, if the officer can apprehend a misdemeanor suspect only by using a gun (or other deadly instrument), the officer must forgo the arrest and let the suspect escape. [People v. Klein, 137 N.E. 145 (Ill. 1922)]

b. **Modern view—deadly force limited to "dangerous" felonies:** [§557] Some courts reject the traditional distinction between felonies and misdemeanors and hold that deadly force is only permissible if the officer has reason to believe that the suspect has committed a ***dangerous felony—i.e.***, one involving a risk of physical harm to others, such as murder, manslaughter, kidnapping, rape, or burglary. [Commonwealth v. Chermansky, 242 A.2d 237 (Pa. 1968)]

(1) **Rationale:** There are far more felonies today than there were at common law and many modern felonies are not as "serious" as common law felonies, so the mere fact that a felony is implicated does not establish that the social interest in apprehending a suspect is sufficient to outweigh the potential for harm to innocent parties resulting from the use of deadly force.

(2) **Model Penal Code position:** [§558] The Model Penal Code follows the modern view and would permit the use of deadly force only where

the crime for which the arrest is made involved the use or threatened use of deadly force, or if there was a substantial risk that the subject would cause death or serious bodily injury if the arrest were delayed. [Model Penal Code §3.07(2)(b)]

(3) **Fourth Amendment requirement:** [§559] Under the Fourth Amendment, an arrest is unconstitutionally unreasonable if the arresting officer used deadly force and lacked reason to believe that the arrestee posed a significant threat of death or serious physical injury to the officer or others. Use of deadly force in violation of this rule gives rise to a ***civil cause of action*** for damages. [Tennessee v. Garner, 471 U.S. 1 (1985)] This does not mean that such use of deadly force is a crime; states may absolve the police officer of criminal liability for the use of deadly force if the officer had reason to believe that the suspect committed a felony. Nevertheless, many states have chosen to make it a crime for an officer to use force in violation of this Fourth Amendment rule.

c. **Reasonable appearance controls:** [§560] A police officer is entitled to act on ***reasonable appearances*** in using force to effect an arrest. Thus, as long as the officer reasonably believes the force used is necessary for the arrest, the suspect is guilty of a felony, and—if necessary—that the felony was a dangerous one, the officer has a defense even if his belief turns out to be wrong. Reasonable appearances, not the ultimate truth, control. [Bursack v. Davis, 225 N.W. 738 (Wis. 1929)]

d. **Compare—use of force in self-defense:** [§561] An officer who ***is met with resistance*** in attempting an arrest may well have the right to use force (including deadly force) in his own defense. However, the issue here is one of self-defense and should be carefully distinguished from the right to use force to make an arrest.

3. **Right of Private Persons:** [§562] Arrests by private persons are less favored by the law and hence the defense available for force used to make a "citizen's arrest" is ***more limited*** than that available to a peace officer.

a. **Reasonable appearances not enough:** [§563] A private person's defense, unlike that available to a peace officer, does not depend entirely upon the private person's reasonable belief that grounds for the use of force existed. Authorities are generally in agreement that if a private person causes ***death*** in the making of a "citizen's arrest," he has a defense only if a ***felony was in fact committed*** and the ***person killed in fact committed it***. To some extent, a private person ordinarily acts at his peril in using deadly force to make an arrest. [Commonwealth v. Chermansky, *supra*]

(1) **Model Penal Code position:** [§564] The Model Penal Code takes a somewhat stricter approach regarding deadly force, and would give a private citizen using such deadly force to make an arrest ***no defense*** unless the person believes he is assisting a police officer (*see* below). [Model Penal Code §3.07(2)(b)(ii)]

(2) **Compare—where death not caused:** [§565] Where death is ***not*** caused, the law is less clear. Most likely, courts would protect the citizen (defendant) in his use of force if a felony was in fact committed, the defendant

reasonably believed the arrested person committed it, ***and*** the defendant used no more force than reasonably appeared necessary to effect the arrest.

b. **Compare—private person called to assist officer:** [§566] Where a private person is called upon by a police officer to ***assist*** the officer in making an arrest, the private person has the ***same privilege as the officer***. This is so because those summoned to assist the police in effecting an arrest are required by law to comply. Accordingly, the private person is protected in such cases if it reasonably appeared that the arrest and force were justified; the suspect's actual innocence will not negate the defense. [Commonwealth v. Fields, 183 A. 78 (Pa. 1936)]

4. **Use of Force to Prevent Escape from Custody:** [§567] Once a person has been taken into custody, force may be used to prevent his escape if the force could have been used to effectuate the arrest in the first place. [Model Penal Code §3.07(3)]

P. CRIME PREVENTION

1. **In General:** [§568] A defendant charged with an assaultive crime may assert in defense that the force was used to prevent the commission of a crime. *But note:* Use of force to ***prevent*** the commission of an offense must be distinguished from the use of force to effectuate an arrest (*see supra*).

2. **Common Law Position:** [§569] At common law, one who reasonably believes that a felony or a misdemeanor amounting to a breach of the peace is being committed or is about to be committed in his presence can use reasonable ***nondeadly force*** to terminate or prevent it. ***Deadly force*** can be used only to avert the perpetration of a ***felony***, not to prevent a misdemeanor.

3. **Modern View—Deadly Force Limited to "Dangerous" Felonies:** [§570] Modern authorities hold that the right to use ***deadly*** force is limited to those situations where the felony involved creates a substantial risk of ***death or serious bodily harm*** to others. *Rationale:* Deadly force is too dangerous to be justified in the prevention of certain felonies that pose no direct danger to others. [Storey v. State, 71 Ala. 329 (1882)]

4. **Model Penal Code Position:** [§571] The Model Penal Code would authorize the use of ***nondeadly*** force to prevent crimes involving or threatening bodily harm, damage to or loss of property, or a breach of the peace. But ***deadly*** force would be permissible only if the defendant believed that the subject would cause death or serious bodily injury to another unless the crime were prevented ***and*** the use of deadly force poses ***no substantial risk of injury to third persons***. [Model Penal Code §3.07(5)]

Q. PUBLIC AUTHORITY

1. **In General:** [§572] A public officer is authorized to use force and sometimes to take or damage property in carrying out official duties pursuant to a valid statute or court order. If charged with a crime based upon such actions, the officer may assert as a defense that she acted pursuant to her public authority. But the force employed must be ***reasonable*** and may not exceed what is necessary for the proper performance of the duties. [LaFave and Scott, 450; Model Penal Code §3.03]

a. **Example:** A soldier may kill an enemy during battle. But if a soldier intentionally kills a prisoner of war, this would be murder. The force used is unnecessary to the performance of the soldier's duty. [State v. Gut, 13 Minn. 341 (1868)]

2. **Effect of Mistake as to Validity of Authority:** [§573] While there is authority to the contrary, the better view is that a public officer is protected if she ***reasonably believed*** the statute or process under which she acted was valid. Thus, a showing that the statute or process was in fact invalid will not per se negate the defense. [Model Penal Code §3.03(3)]

R. DOMESTIC AUTHORITY AND SIMILAR SPECIAL RELATIONSHIPS

1. **In General:** [§574] Persons with legally designated authority over others have the right to use ***reasonable nondeadly force*** in the performance of their duties. If they are charged with a crime based upon their use of force, they have a defense to liability. [Model Penal Code §3.08]

2. **Parents of Minor Child:** [§575] Parents may inflict nondeadly force on their minor children for the purpose of achieving discipline and thereby promoting the children's welfare. This right also extends to those "in loco parentis," such as stepparents, guardians, and even a person living with the child's parent out of matrimony. [State v. Alford, 68 N.C. 322 (1873)]

3. **Schoolteachers:** [§576] Teachers have the right to use reasonable and necessary nondeadly force to maintain school discipline and promote the child's education. This right is independent of the parents' right to discipline their children and can be exercised whether or not the parents approve. Moreover, the privilege applies to all pupil misconduct affecting school discipline, even if the behavior takes place off the school grounds. [Annot., 89 A.L.R.2d 396 (1963)]

4. **Other Special Relationships:** [§577] Similar rights have been given to captains of vessels and aircraft, wardens and superintendents of institutions, and other persons with authority over others. [Model Penal Code §3.08(5)-(6)]

VII. PRELIMINARY OR INCHOATE CRIMES

chapter approach

Because of the variety of issues posed by the inchoate crimes, these are favorite topics for examination questions. Be sure to consider solicitation whenever you see someone encouraging another to commit or join in the commission of a crime. When the person in question considers committing a crime but decides not to do so, or where that person makes some effort but fails to complete the crime, think of attempt. And, when there are several participants in a crime or in preparatory discussion or activity, always consider conspiracy issues.

In regard to these possible inchoate crimes, consider first whether the "elements" can be proved, and if so, second, whether the "defenses" unique to each of those crimes might apply.

In reference to ***solicitation***, ask:

1. Did the defendant ***sufficiently encourage*** another person to commit a crime of adequate seriousness?

2. If the defendant ***renounced his desire*** that the crime be committed, should this be a defense?

When you see possible ***attempt*** issues, consider:

1. Can the ***elements*** of attempt be proved?

    a. Did the defendant ***intend*** to commit the object crime ***and*** have the ***intent*** necessary for that crime?

    b. Did the defendant ***proceed*** far enough towards the commission of the crime?

2. Are there any ***defenses*** available?

    a. Is this a ***"legal impossibility"*** situation?

    b. Is this an exceptional jurisdiction where ***voluntary abandonment*** is a defense?

In any situation where the facts involve more than one participant, there are almost certain to be ***conspiracy*** issues. Initially, it is very important to separate and discuss separately the persons' liability for the crime of conspiracy itself and, if raised by the facts, their liability under the co-conspirator rule for crimes committed by others.

To consider ***liability for the conspiracy itself***, ask yourself:

1. Can the ***elements*** be proved?

    a. Was there an ***agreement*** of which the defendant was a member?

    b. Was the ***object*** of the agreement sufficient to make the agreement criminal?

    c. Did the defendant ***intend*** to agree ***and*** to further the object crime?

d. Is an ***overt act*** required, and, if so, was one committed by a party to the agreement?

2. Are there any ***defenses***?

   a. Has it been shown that the other members of the agreement failed to agree so that there is ***no real agreement***?

   b. Is the agreement one that is not a criminal conspiracy under ***Wharton's Rule***?

   c. If the object crime was ***impossible*** to attain, might this be a defense?

   d. Is this an unusual jurisdiction in which ***withdrawal*** is a defense?

As to ***liability for the crimes of co-conspirators***, discuss:

1. Can the ***elements*** of such liability be shown?

   a. Has another member of the conspiracy ***committed the crime*** at issue?

   b. Was the crime committed in ***furtherance of the objectives*** of the conspiracy?

   c. Was the crime a ***foreseeable result*** of the conspiracy?

2. Are there ***defenses*** to such liability?

   a. Had the conspiracy ***terminated*** before the crime was committed?

   b. Did the defendant ***effectively withdraw*** from the conspiracy before the crime was committed?

A. SOLICITATION

1. **Common Law:** [§578] At common law it is a misdemeanor to ***counsel, incite, or induce another*** to commit or to join in the commission of any offense, whether that offense is a felony or a misdemeanor. [Rex v. Higgins, 102 Eng. Rep. 269 (1801)]

   a. **Mens rea:** [§579] The common law crime of solicitation apparently requires a showing that the defendant acted volitionally and with the intent or purpose of ***causing the person solicited to commit the crime***. [Rex v. Higgins, *supra*]

   b. **Actus reus:** [§580] The only act required for the commission of the crime is the ***counseling, inciting, or inducing*** of another to commit the offense. Solicitation is complete upon the performance of this act; it is not necessary that the person solicited respond affirmatively. Nor need the incitement be directed at a specific person; thus, even a general solicitation addressed to an assembled crowd will suffice. [State v. Schleifer, 121 A. 805 (Conn. 1923)]

2. **Modern Statutes:** [§581] Modern statutes tend to limit the crime to the counseling, incitement, etc., of ***serious*** offenses—*e.g.*, murder, rape, kidnapping, robbery—

and to provide a lower penalty for the solicitation than is imposed for the commission of the crime itself, for an attempt to commit it, or perhaps even for a conspiracy to commit it. [*See, e.g.,* N.Y. Penal Law §§100.00 *et seq.*]

a. **Compare—Model Penal Code:** [§582] The Model Code, however, retains the broader common law formulation, making it a crime to solicit the commission of any offense. Moreover, the Code would make solicitation punishable to the same degree as is authorized for the offense solicited. [Model Penal Code §§5.02(1), 5.05(1)]

3. **Special Problems in Solicitation**

a. **Uncommunicated solicitation:** [§583] A solicitation is still criminal even if the defendant fails to effectively communicate it to the intended subject (as where an intermediary fails to pass on the message). *Rationale:* By engaging in the proscribed act with the requisite intent, the solicitor has manifested his dangerousness and should not escape punishment because of a fortuitous event. [Model Penal Code §5.02, comment (Tent. Draft No. 10, 1960)]

(1) **Note:** Some jurisdictions limit the charge in such cases to attempted solicitation. However, the Model Penal Code specifically authorizes a conviction for the crime of solicitation itself. [Model Penal Code §5.02(2)]

b. **Defense of renunciation:** [§584] It is not clear whether a solicitor may escape liability by demonstrating that he later renounced his intention. The matter has not been definitively resolved by the courts.

(1) **Model Penal Code:** [§585] The Model Penal Code would recognize a defense of renunciation. It would require, however, the defendant to show that he persuaded the subject not to commit the crime under circumstances manifesting a "complete and voluntary" renunciation of the criminal purpose. [Model Penal Code §5.02(3)]

4. **Relationship to Other Crimes**

a. **Accomplice liability distinguished:** [§586] If the person solicited actually commits the target crime, the solicitor is clearly an "inciter" and therefore ***liable as a party*** to the crime (*see supra,* §235). However, this is ***in addition*** to his liability for the separate crime of solicitation. Also, as indicated above, the solicitor can be convicted of solicitation even if the subject does not respond to the incitement.

b. **Conspiracy distinguished:** [§587] Unlike conspiracy (below), solicitation does not require that any agreement be reached. Thus, while conspiracy may follow solicitation (*i.e.,* where the person solicited concurs in the criminal scheme), if the subject ***refuses to enter into a conspiracy***, the solicitor is nevertheless liable for the crime of solicitation.

c. **Attempt distinguished:** [§588] Unlike solicitation, attempt requires that the defendant have progressed far enough in his criminal scheme to have gone beyond mere preparation (*see infra,* §§664-673). Generally, then, a person who does the bare minimum that suffices for solicitation will not have done enough to be guilty of attempt. But if a person does more than the bare minimum, this may be attempt. Or if the person solicited progresses towards the commission of the crime, that person will be guilty of attempt and the solicitor will, because of his incitement, incur liability as a party to that attempt. [Gervin v. State, 371 S.W.2d 449 (Tenn. 1963)]

d. **"Merger" of solicitation with attempt or conspiracy:** [§589] One who commits solicitation, and goes on to engage in further conduct constituting attempt or conspiracy as well, ***cannot*** be convicted of ***both*** the solicitation and the attempt or conspiracy. This is because the solicitation becomes a "lesser included offense." (This is not "merger" in the traditional common law sense, since the defendant may be charged and convicted of ***either*** the solicitation or the attempt (or conspiracy); *see supra,* §§63 *et seq.*).

B. CONSPIRACY

1. **In General:** [§590] Like solicitation and attempt, conspiracy is a preliminary or inchoate crime. However, as will be seen, it is of particular significance because: (i) the parties to a conspiracy (unlike those who commit attempt) may be convicted for the object crime ***and*** the conspiracy, if the conspiracy is carried out; and (ii) the parties may, on the basis of the conspiracy, incur liability for crimes committed by other members of the venture.

   a. **Common law:** [§591] At common law, it is a misdemeanor for two or more persons ***to agree*** to accomplish ***an unlawful purpose*** or ***a lawful act by unlawful means*** (*e.g.,* excessive force, extortion, etc.). [Rex v. Jones, 110 Eng. Rep. 485 (1832)]

   b. **Modern statutes:** [§592] Most American jurisdictions now define conspiracy by statute and limit the scope of the crime. For instance, some states require an agreement to commit a ***crime***, while others specify proscribed unlawful objectives somewhat more narrowly than the common law rule (*see infra,* §620).

2. **Requirements for Liability for Conspiracy:** [§593] The crime of conspiracy imposes several requirements for liability:

   a. **Mens rea:** [§594] The mens rea required for conspiracy has several aspects, each requiring separate consideration.

      (1) **Intent to agree:** [§595] The defendant must have actually ***intended to agree*** or combine with others. This requirement arises from the need for an agreement. [LaFave and Scott, 535-536]

      (2) **Intent to accomplish objective:** [§596] The defendant must also have a certain state of mind in regard to the objective of the agreement. Generally, this requirement is stated as one that the defendant must have ***intended to accomplish the objective*** of the conspiracy. [United States v. United States Gypsum Co., 438 U.S. 422 (1978)] If this is applied literally, it is not sufficient that the defendant merely knows he would further that objective; it must be shown that his purpose or desire is that the objective be accomplished. [United States v. Blankenship, 970 F.2d 283 (7th Cir. 1992)] However, there is some question whether courts in fact enforce the requirement of intent to accomplish the objective. Further,

some courts sometimes construe particular kinds of criminal conspiracies as requiring only proof that the defendant had knowledge that he would further the objective.

(a) **Example:** The defendant agreed to let members of a drug ring use his trailer for one day to make drugs, in return for payment of $1,000, to be made after the use of the trailer. This was arguably sufficient to show that he desired the manufacture of the drugs to be made during that day and thus that he was a member of a criminal conspiracy to manufacture those drugs. It was not, however, enough to show that he desired that the members of the drug ring succeed in their overall business, so he was not shown to be a member of a bigger conspiracy including other members of the ring who were not involved in this particular day of work. [United States v. Blankenship, *supra*]

(b) **Example:** The Supreme Court has considered the intent necessary in a prosecution under the Sherman Act, which makes criminal a conspiracy to restrain trade. The Court first rejected the argument that the offense should impose strict liability. It then held that the defendants need not be shown to have acted with a conscious purpose of producing anticompetitive effects; rather, knowledge of the probable anticompetitive effects of their actions would suffice. A requirement of purpose, reasoned the Court, would be burdensome to the government and would be unnecessary to establish that the conduct was blameworthy. [United States v. United States Gypsum Co., *supra*]

(c) **Proof of "intent"—a "stake in the venture":** [§597] A defendant's intent that the objective be achieved is often proved by showing that the defendant stood to benefit financially or otherwise from its successful completion. This is sometimes called showing a stake in the venture. In contrast, evidence that the accused would not gain any benefit should the venture succeed suggests that he lacked the requisite intent. [Direct Sales Co. v. United States, 319 U.S. 703 (1943)]

(d) **Providing goods or services:** [§598] The major problem in this area arises when conviction is sought upon proof that the defendant merely provided goods or services to others, who then used them for an unlawful purpose. If the defendant had ***knowledge*** that the goods or services would be used for an unlawful purpose, is this enough for liability, or must the defendant have affirmatively ***desired*** that the unlawful objective be accomplished? The answer may turn on the nature of the crime that is the objective of the conspiracy:

1) **Objective is not serious crime:** [§599] If the crime is not a serious one, a mere showing that the defendant knew he was furthering an illegal purpose by providing the goods or services is probably not sufficient. [United States v. Falcone, 109 F.2d 579 (2d Cir.), *aff'd,* 311 U.S. 205 (1940)—suppliers of sugar,

yeast, and cans not conspirators to crime of operating illicit stills]

2) **Objective is serious crime:** [§600] At least one court has suggested that ***the more serious the crime, the more likely the defendant-supplier will be found a conspirator*** simply upon proof that he had ***knowledge—i.e.***, that he was aware of the use to which his goods or services would be put. In such cases, a showing of an affirmative desire that the perpetrators achieve their unlawful objective is probably not crucial. [People v. Lauria, 251 Cal. App. 2d 471 (1967)—dictum]

(3) **Requirement of "corrupt motive":** [§601] Some courts have suggested that, besides having the intent to agree and the intent to accomplish the objective, the parties to a criminal conspiracy must also have a "corrupt motive." As the phrase is generally construed, this means that each of the purported conspirators must be shown to have known that the objective of their agreement was ***illegal***. [People v. Powell, 63 N.Y. 88 (1875)] *But note:* Other courts have rejected this approach, reasoning that there is no policy reason to require "awareness of the law" in this one area of criminal liability. [People v. McLaughlin, 111 Cal. App. 2d 781 (1952)]

b. **Actus reus:** [§602] The actus reus of common law conspiracy is the ***entering into of the requisite agreement***. [Williams v. United States, 218 F.2d 276 (4th Cir. 1954)] Modern versions of the crime, however, often imposed an additional requirement of an ***"overt act."***

(1) **"Implied" agreement sufficient:** [§603] The agreement need not be an express or formal one but can be ***implied*** from the cooperative actions of the parties. Thus, one who observes unlawful acts taking place and cooperates in their commission becomes a member of an agreement to carry out those acts, even if the participants never formally exchanged express commitments with each other. [Bender v. State, 253 A.2d 686 (Del. 1969)]

(a) **Example:** An officer, O, approached X and asked X "for a joint." X turned to D and commented that he did not "know" O. D replied, "He looks okay to me." X then sold O some heroin. D could be convicted of conspiring with X to sell heroin. A jury could infer from these facts that D was acting pursuant to an earlier agreement or understanding under which he would later be compensated by X for evaluating O as a "safe" purchaser. [United States v. Brown, 776 F.2d 397 (2d Cir. 1985)]

(2) **Connecting one to existing agreement:** [§604] If the existence of a conspiracy is clearly shown, relatively slight evidence will be sufficient to connect a particular defendant with it. [United States v. Knight, 416 F.2d 1181 (9th Cir. 1969)]

(a) **Example:** In a prosecution for conspiracy to induce aliens to illegally enter the country, the evidence established a scheme by A and

B to lure aliens into the country and charge them for transportation. Once the existence of the conspiracy involving A and B was established, D was found guilty as a co-conspirator simply upon proof that his car was used to transport some of the aliens and that he was present during portions of the unlawful activity. [United States v. Knight, *supra*]

(3) **Overt act requirement:** [§605] At common law, the crime of conspiracy is complete when the agreement is made and no act is required beyond the making of that agreement. Many jurisdictions still adhere to the common law rule, but some modern statutes impose an additional requirement of an "overt act." [*See, e.g.,* Cal. Penal Code §184; 18 U.S.C. §371] The Model Penal Code requires an overt act except for conspiracies to commit more serious offenses. [Model Penal Code §5.03(5)]

(a) **Rationale for overt act requirement:** The overt act requirement serves to assure that the conspiracy is actually "at work, that is, that it is not simply a shared intention of the parties." It also provides an opportunity for those who have agreed on a criminal venture to repent and abandon the venture without incurring criminal liability. [Yates v. United States, 354 U.S. 298 (1957); People v. Olson, 232 Cal. App. 2d 480 (1965)]

(b) **Definition of necessary act:** [§606] The overt act, where required, need only be one that ***effects the object of the conspiracy*** or that has a ***tendency to further*** the objective. It need not be a "substantial step" towards the conspirators' objective as is required for attempt. [State v. Dent, 869 P.2d 392 (Wash. 1994)]

(c) **Discussions as overt acts:** [§607] Conversations among the parties as part of reaching an agreement are probably not sufficient overt acts, since this is simply part of the agreement. [People v. Olson, *supra*] But further conversations among the conspirators after the agreement is reached may qualify as overt acts. [United States v. Armone, 363 F.2d 385 (2d Cir. 1966)]

(d) **One act of one member suffices:** [§608] A single act in pursuit of the unlawful objective by ***any one*** of the members will suffice. When this act is performed, all parties to the agreement become liable for conspiracy. [People *ex rel.* Conte v. Flood, 53 Misc. 2d 104 (1966)]

(4) **Number and characteristics of agreements:** [§609] Traditionally, courts have given considerable attention to the number and characteristics of the agreement alleged by the prosecution. This is sometimes a real difficulty, given the complex situations giving rise to conspiracy prosecutions and the need for the prosecution to plead rather specifically the precise agreement it will prove at trial. Situations often fall into one of several basic patterns:

(a) **One agreement with multiple unlawful purposes:** [§610] If there is only a single agreement, there is only ***one*** criminal conspiracy regardless of how many crimes the conspirators plan to commit. [Doolin v. State, 650 So. 2d 44 (Fla. 1995)]

1) **Example:** Defendants who plotted the illegal manufacture, transportation, and distribution of liquor in violation of a number of internal revenue laws could be punished for only one conspiracy. The plans to commit the various violations were all part of a ***single agreement***, and it is the ***agreement*** that constitutes the conspiracy. [Braverman v. United States, 317 U.S. 49 (1942)]

(b) **"Chain" situation—multiple "links" making up one conspiracy:** [§611] If a series of overlapping transactions is shown (such as sale and resale of narcotics), the situation will often be construed as involving only one overall agreement. Each transaction will be regarded as a "link" in an overall single "chain," if the parties to each link transaction know that other links are involved and have a general interest in the success of the overall series of transactions.

1) **Example:** A smuggler agreed to import heroin and sell it to a "middleman," and the middleman agreed to resell the heroin to a retailer. There was no express communication between the retailer and the smuggler. Nevertheless, this was a single "chain" conspiracy to import, sell, and possess narcotics; each member knew that "the success of that part with which he was immediately concerned was dependent upon the success of the whole." [United States v. Bruno, 105 F.2d 921 (2d Cir.), *rev'd on other grounds,* 308 U.S. 287 (1939)]

2) **Compare—independent links:** [§612] If those involved in each link transaction are unaware that the other transactions are taking place, or know about other transactions but are indifferent as to whether they take place, the situation will be characterized as involving ***multiple*** and ***separate*** conspiracies. The participants in each link transaction are conspirators only with those involved in that particular link transaction. [United States v. Peoni, 100 F.2d 401 (2d Cir. 1938)—no conspiracy between D and Z where D sold counterfeit bills to X who resold to Z who passed them on to innocent purchasers because D was indifferent as to whether X passed the bills himself or sold them to a second passer]

(c) **"Wheel" and "spoke" situation:** [§613] Where one or more persons (the "hub of a wheel") enter into a number of different transactions with various other persons (the "spokes of the wheel") and the persons in each transaction are unconcerned with other transactions entered into by the "hub," the situation will be characterized as involving a number of ***different*** conspiracies. While the hub is a party to each conspiracy, the members of each spoke are regarded as conspiring only with the hub and the other members of that spoke transaction. [Kotteakos v. United States, 328 U.S. 750 (1946)—several companies involved where D made fraudulent loans at different times on behalf of several persons, and each loan was distinct because except for D (the common figure) no conspirator was interested in whether any other's loan went through]

(d) **Modern view—situations analyzed flexibly:** [§614] Some modern courts have abandoned the traditional concern on whether situations show "wheels and spokes" or "chains and links," and look instead to whether the prosecution has proven generally the sort of conspiracy it alleged in the indictment. [United States v. Morris, 46 F.3d 410 (5th Cir. 1995)]

(5) **Conspirator agrees with "unknown" co-conspirators:** [§615] The parties to a conspiracy need not know the identity of each other member, nor need they even be aware of the number of persons involved. Thus, a particular member will be regarded as having conspired with all those he ***must have known were involved*** in the transaction—whether he had specific information about them or not. [Blumenthal v. United States, 332 U.S. 539 (1947)]

(6) **Husband-wife conspiracies:** [§616] At common law, a conspiracy could not be formed between a husband and a wife because they were regarded as one person. Although this principle was accepted by early American courts, the current trend clearly rejects it as premised on an artificial concept of the spousal relationship. [United States v. Dege, 364 U.S. 51 (1960)]

(7) **Conspiracies among corporations:** [§617] A corporation can be a party to a conspiracy—*i.e.*, a corporation can conspire with another corporation or with a natural person. But there is ***no*** criminal conspiracy when the alleged members are only a corporation and one of its agents, or two corporations and one person acting as agent for both. In such situations, only one human actor is involved and so the requisite agreement between two or more persons is lacking. [United States v. Santa Rita Store Co., 113 P. 620 (N.M. 1911)]

c. **Objective of the agreement:** [§618] The law's view on what objectives of agreements justify making those agreements criminal by means of conspiracy law has undergone considerable change from common law.

(1) **Common law:** [§619] At common law, the objective of the parties' agreement need not be the commission of a crime. Indeed, criminal conspiracy covers agreements to do a number of things that would otherwise be lawful if done by a single individual, including grossly immoral acts (*e.g.*, procuring a prostitute), acts injurious to the public welfare, and acts obstructing justice. The theory is that while such acts might not be injurious enough to criminalize when attempted by an individual, when committed by combinations they become sufficiently dangerous to warrant making them crimes. [Rex v. Delaval, 97 Eng. Rep. 913 (1763)]

(2) **Modern statutes:** [§620] All modern statutes depart from the common law position. Some limit criminal conspiracies to agreements to commit ***crimes*** [*see, e.g.,* Model Penal Code §5.03(1)], while others go

beyond this, designating other unlawful purposes that will suffice [*see* Cal. Penal Code §182—criminalizing conspiracies to "commit any act injurious to the public health, to public morals, or to pervert or obstruct justice, or the due administration of the laws"].

(3) **Vagueness problems:** [§621] Certain conspiracy statutes may be objectionable on constitutional grounds. The Supreme Court has recognized that some of the broader formulations of conspiracy law may be unconstitutionally ***vague*** because they do not indicate with the required specificity which agreements are criminal. [Musser v. Utah, 333 U.S. 95 (1948)—remanding for determination whether Utah statute criminalizing any conspiracy "to commit any act injurious to the public health, to public morals, or to trade or commerce, or for the perversion or obstruction of justice or due administration of the laws" is unconstitutionally vague; State v. Musser, 223 P.2d 193 (Utah 1950)—on remand from Supreme Court holding Utah statute unconstitutional]

3. **Punishment:** [§622] At common law, conspiracy is a misdemeanor. Modern statutes, however, vary in the manner punishments provided. Some impose penalties related to, but less than, those provided for the crime the parties agreed to commit. The Model Penal Code would impose the same punishment as is provided for the most serious offense that the parties conspired to commit. [Model Penal Code §5.05(1)]

4. **Conviction for Conspiracy and Completed Crime:** [§623] At common law, a conspiracy followed by a completed crime merges into the completed crime. This has been abandoned today. Accordingly, defendants who conspire to commit a crime and who then commit it can be convicted for ***both*** conspiracy and the crime committed.

   a. **Rationale:** Persons who commit crimes by joint action are more dangerous than those who commit them individually, because the group formed to commit the crime will often continue to commit other offenses. Thus, sound policy dictates that such defendants suffer more severe punishment by conviction for the crime and the conspiracy. [Pinkerton v. United States, 328 U.S. 640 (1946)]

5. **Special Problems Applying Conspiracy Law:** [§624] Application of criminal conspiracy law has given rise to a number of problems. Many of them are a result of taking quite seriously the requirement of an "agreement."

   a. **Acquittal of co-conspirators—no "agreement":** [§625] In some situations, courts traditionally require the acquittal of a defendant charged with conspiracy upon certain showings regarding the status of those the prosecution claims are co-conspirators. A modern "unilateral" approach to conspiracy, however, requests a much different approach.

   (1) **Traditional "plurality" requirement approach:** [§626] Under traditional analysis, a criminal conspiracy requires an actual criminal agreement between ***at least two persons***, *i.e.*, a plurality of participants. If the facts show that all other claimed co-conspirators except the defendant did not enter into an agreement, the defendant must be acquitted because conceptually there could have been no actual agreement. In fact, if one

of the situations below is shown to exist after a defendant's conviction for conspiracy, some courts are willing to overturn that conviction. [Eyman v. Deutsch, 373 P.2d 716 (Ariz. 1962)]

(a) **Acquittal of all other co-conspirators:** [§627] A defendant cannot be convicted of conspiracy under the plurality requirement approach if ***all*** other co-conspirators have been ***acquitted*** of conspiracy charges. Acquittal is not required upon a showing that some but less than all others have been acquitted, because an agreement remains possible as long as there is one other possible guilty co-conspirator. [Eyman v. Deutsch, *supra*]

1) **Compare—acquittals regarded as jury leniency:** [§628] Some courts reject this rule, reasoning that acquittal of the co-conspirators is not necessarily based on a conclusion that there was no agreement but may instead reflect the juries' views that guilty co-conspirators simply deserve a "break." [Commonwealth v. Campbell, 651 A.2d 1096 (Pa. 1994)]

(b) **Dismissal of charges against other conspirators:** [§629] Courts differ as to whether dismissal of charges against all other members of the conspiracy requires dismissal as to the remaining defendant. Some equate dismissals with acquittals and require acquittal of the remaining defendant, while others reject the analogy and proceed with the prosecution against the remaining alleged conspiracy member. [Regle v. State, 264 A.2d 119 (Md. 1970)]

(c) **Showing that all co-conspirators were "feigned accomplices":** [§630] A defendant cannot be held guilty of conspiracy where ***all*** her purported co-conspirators are shown to have only feigned agreement, as for example where all others were actually police officers ***pretending a willingness to undertake the crime***. Some courts even refuse to find a conspiracy where two or more persons enter into an agreement with a police officer who is feigning cooperation and the agreement contemplates that an essential ingredient of the offense is to be performed by the officer. These decisions appear to be based on the theory that since such conspiracies will clearly not be carried out, they do not pose the danger with which the law of conspiracy is concerned. [King v. State, 104 So. 2d 730 (Fla. 1957)]

(2) **Compare—Model Penal Code "unilateral" analysis:** [§631] The Model Penal Code would reach a different result in all the above situations by adopting a "unilateral" approach towards liability for conspiracy. Rather than defining liability in terms of an agreement "between" the parties, the Code simply requires an agreement "***by***" the defendant. Thus, a defendant can be convicted of conspiring with a person who has been acquitted or with a police officer feigning cooperation because the status of the co-conspirator is irrelevant and the only inquiry is whether the defendant "agreed." [Model Penal Code §5.03(1)]

b. **Wharton's Rule—no conspiracy to commit concerted action crimes:** [§632] Many courts refuse to find a criminal conspiracy in some situations involving an agreement to commit a crime that necessarily involves multiple participants. This rule was first articulated by the early treatise author Francis Wharton and is called "Wharton's Rule."

(1) **Basic prohibition:** [§633] Wharton's Rule holds that where persons agree to commit an offense that by its definition ***necessarily requires a preliminary agreement*** between the parties, there can be no conviction for conspiracy. [Robinson v. State, 184 A.2d 814 (Md. 1962)]

(a) **Examples:** The classic cases coming within Wharton's Rule are prosecutions for adultery, incest, bigamy, and dueling. Since an agreement or concerted action is an essential element of each of these offenses, the two participants cannot be prosecuted for conspiracy to commit the offense.

(b) **Rationale:** Since the object crime always involves concerted preliminary action, an agreement to commit such crimes involves no socially dangerous behavior beyond that involved in the crime itself; thus, the rationale for finding conspiracy liability—the special danger of concerted action—is not presented.

(2) **Exceptions:** [§634] Wharton's Rule is mitigated by several traditional exceptions to its general prohibition against conviction for conspiracy.

(a) **Agreement involving more than essential participants:** [§635] If the number of conspirators exceeds the number of essential participants in the contemplated crime, a number of courts do not apply Wharton's Rule. All the parties to the agreement may be convicted of conspiracy, since in such situations they have formed a group larger than necessary for the commission of the crime and thus the situation presents dangerous concerted action beyond what is necessarily involved in the crime itself. [Baker v. State, 393 F.2d 604 (9th Cir. 1968)]

1) **Example:** D conspires with A and B for the commission of adultery by A and B. Adultery necessarily involves an agreement only by the two persons to the sexual activity. Since here the agreement involves an additional person, it is beyond the scope of Wharton's Rule and D, A, and B may be convicted of conspiracy.

(b) **Objective of agreement not achieved:** [§636] Some courts will apply Wharton's Rule only where the parties have accomplished their objective; *i.e.,* the rule only bars conviction for ***both*** conspiracy and the completed crime. Thus, prosecution for conspiracy to commit adultery is permissible if the co-conspirators did not actually commit adultery or—some courts would say—if the prosecution chooses to ignore the completed adultery and prosecutes only for conspiracy. Others courts, however, criticize this limitation, and many decisions have not recognized it. [Shannon v. Commonwealth, 14 Pa. 226 (1850)]

(3) **Wharton's Rule as presumption of legislative intent:** [§637] The United States Supreme Court has held that Wharton's Rule is merely a presumption of legislative intent. Thus, if the rule would bar conviction in a given case, but there is also evidence of a legislative intent to impose liability, the legislative intent controls and criminal sanctions may be imposed. [Iannelli v. United States, 420 U.S. 770 (1975)—illegal gambling]

c. **Defenses**

(1) **Impossibility of success:** [§638] Most courts take the view that proof that the parties to a conspiracy could not have accomplished their objective (*i.e.,* impossibility of any kind) is ***no defense***. A few decisions disagree, however, and some, analogizing to the law of attempt, suggest that "legal," but not "factual," impossibility is a defense (*see infra,* §§676-679 for distinction between "legal" and "factual" impossibility). [*Compare* Marty v. State, 656 So. 2d 416 (Ala. 1994)—impossibility no defense, *with* Ventimiglia v. United States, 242 F.2d 620 (4th Cir. 1957)—legal impossibility a defense]

(2) **Withdrawal:** [§639] Whether a defendant charged with conspiracy should have a defense of withdrawal or renunciation has given rise to some dispute in criminal law.

(a) **General rule—withdrawal no defense:** [§640] The traditional and still general rule is that a defendant's withdrawal from a criminal conspiracy is ***no defense*** to the crime of conspiracy, no matter when the withdrawal took place or the nature of the defendant's motive. [United States v. Read, 658 F.2d 1225 (7th Cir. 1981)]

(b) **Model Penal Code and modern position:** [§641] The Model Penal Code and modern statutes based on it would extend a defense to a conspirator who proved that she "thwarted the success of the conspiracy under circumstances ***manifesting a complete and voluntary renunciation***" of the criminal purpose. [Model Penal Code §5.03(6)]

(c) **Compare—defense to crimes of co-conspirators:** [§642] While withdrawal is ordinarily no defense to the conspiracy itself, it is sometimes a defense to charges against the defendant for crimes committed by other members of the conspiracy. (*See infra,* §650.)

6. **Liability for Crimes of Co-Conspirators:** [§643] The significance of conspiracy law is especially great because it not only creates a crime but also makes some persons guilty of crimes committed by other persons in situations that would not create liability as an accomplice.

a. **General rule of co-conspirator liability:** [§644] Each member of a conspiracy is liable for those crimes committed by all other members that were: (i) a ***reasonably foreseeable result*** of the conspiracy; and (ii) ***committed in furtherance*** of the conspiracy. This rule is often called the *Pinkerton* Rule, after the leading Supreme Court case adopting it as a matter of federal conspiracy law. [Pinkerton v. United States, 328 U.S. 640 (1946); State v. Bridges, 628 A.2d 270 (N.J. 1993)]

(1) **Example:** D, an attorney, suggested to an underworld figure, X, that V's house would be a good target for a burglary. A year later, X and his companions robbed V and his family at gunpoint, assaulted V's wife, and when police arrived took V's family hostage. Also, in an escape effort X injured several police officers. Since D conspired with X to commit burglary, D could be convicted of the robbery and assault on V's wife, as these crimes were committed in furtherance of the conspiracy and were foreseeable. However, the kidnapping of V's family and assault on police officers by X were not necessary or natural results of the conspiracy and thus were not foreseeable; D could therefore not be convicted of them. [State v. Stein, 360 A.2d 347 (N.J. 1976)]

(2) **Compare—accomplice liability:** [§645] The principle of co-conspirator liability often overlaps with the law of accomplice liability (*see supra,* §§227 *et seq.*). But there are differences. Co-conspirator liability does not require the intent necessary for accomplice liability; nor need it be shown that the person on whom liability is to be placed provided the sort of assistance or encouragement that would otherwise be required to convict as an accomplice. Thus, persons may be liable for the crimes of others under the co-conspirator doctrine even though they would not be liable under the law of accomplice liability.

(3) **Criticism:** [§646] Opposition to the co-conspirator rule has grown in recent years. Critics argue that it extends liability beyond acceptable boundaries. Not only does it impose liability for mere negligence (since the other crimes need only be "foreseeable"), but the defendant can be convicted for crimes without proof that she had any role at all in their commission. [LaFave and Scott, 587-590; People v. McGee, 49 N.Y.2d 48 (1979)—rejecting Pinkerton Rule]

(4) **Limitations on co-conspirator liability**

(a) **Just basis for liability:** [§647] One court has limited co-conspirator liability by requiring that the crime not be too far removed or too remote from the objectives of the conspiracy to constitute a just basis for imposing criminal liability on co-conspirators for the crime. [State v. Bridges, *supra*]

(b) **Due process prohibition against co-conspirator liability where connection "slight":** [§648] Due process may bar imposing liability where the relationship between the defendant and the offense committed by the co-conspirator is "slight," taking into account among other things the degree of involvement in object offense to which the defendant agreed. [United States v. Castaneda, 9 F.3d 761 (9th Cir. 1993)]

b. **Liability for crimes committed prior to joining?** [§649] Language in some opinions suggests that one who joins an already existing conspiracy could be held liable for the crimes committed by other members prior to his joining. [*See, e.g.,* United States v. Knight, 416 F.2d 1181 (9th Cir. 1969)—"One may join a conspiracy already formed and in existence, and be bound by all that has gone on before in the conspiracy, even if unknown to him."] But apparently there have been no actual convictions for such prejoining crimes, and in view of the criticism of the rule creating liability for crimes of other conspirators committed after joining the group (*see* above), it seems very unlikely that any court would permit a conspirator to be convicted of crimes committed ***before*** he entered the scheme.

c. **Withdrawal preventing liability:** [§650] If a defendant ***effectively withdraws*** from a criminal conspiracy, he will not be held liable for crimes ***thereafter*** committed by his former co-conspirators. There are, however, certain prerequisites to a legally effective withdrawal. [Loser v. Superior Court, 78 Cal. App. 2d 30 (1947)]

(1) **Communication to all others:** [§651] The authorities are in general agreement that a withdrawal becomes effective only if and when it is ***communicated to all other members*** of the conspiracy. [Loser v. Superior Court, *supra*] The Supreme Court has noted however that, in some situations, notifying all other members of the group would be an unmanageable task. The Court suggested that affirmative acts inconsistent with the object of the conspiracy and communicated in a manner reasonably calculated to reach co-conspirators would be sufficient. [United States v. United States Gypsum Co., 438 U.S. 422 (1978)]

(2) **Timeliness:** [§652] Some courts require that a withdrawal be "timely." This generally means that it must take place ***in time for the remaining co-conspirators to follow the defendant's example*** and desist from the activity. [People v. Brown, 186 N.E.2d 321 (Ill. 1962)]

(3) **Prevention of target crime:** [§653] At least one court has required that a defendant seeking to withdraw from a conspiracy also ***affirmatively and successfully prevent*** the former co-conspirators from completing the venture. [*See* Eldredge v. United States, 62 F.2d 449 (10th Cir. 1932)] Most decisions, however, have imposed no such limitation.

7. **Duration of the Conspiracy:** [§654] A conspirator is liable for the crimes of his co-conspirators that are committed during (in furtherance of) the conspiracy. Therefore, it is important to determine when the conspiracy ends. Moreover, the determination of when a conspiracy ends frequently affects various procedural matters, such as the statute of limitations and the admissibility of the acts and declarations of one co-conspirator against the others.

a. **General rule—completion of conspiratorial purpose:** [§655] Ordinarily, the conspiracy ends once ***all of the objectives*** of the agreement have been accomplished successfully. However, keep in mind that the agreement might include objectives other than perpetration of the target crime—***e.g.,*** division of the proceeds—in which case the conspiracy terminates only on fulfillment (or abandonment) of these collateral purposes. [*See, e.g.,* People v. Lewis, 222 Cal. App. 2d 136 (1963)]

b. **Efforts to conceal offense:** [§656] In defining the point at which a conspiracy terminates, a major issue may arise as to whether acts to conceal commission of the substantive offense are within the scope of the conspiratorial agreement. A conspiracy containing such an agreement might well last long beyond completion of the offense involved. However, since most offenders attempt to conceal the fact that they have committed a crime, courts have generally held that evidence of overt acts of concealment is ***not sufficient*** to make the act of concealment part of the conspiracy. Indeed, according to the Supreme Court, there must be ***direct evidence*** that the parties ***specifically agreed***, prior to commission of the crime, that they would act together to cover it up or otherwise conceal it. [Grunewald v. United States, 353 U.S. 391 (1957)]

8. **Tactical Advantages for Prosecution:** [§657] Conspiracy law may provide the prosecution with a number of tactical advantages. Whether these advantages are justified is subject to dispute.

   a. **Flexibility:** The looseness and pliability of conspiracy doctrine gives the prosecutor in a conspiracy case substantial flexibility concerning what sort of conduct by the defendant needs to be proved. From defendants' perspective, this makes effective preparation for trial more difficult.

   b. **Increased punishment:** By charging a defendant with both a completed substantive crime and a conspiracy to commit that crime, and perhaps also with crimes committed by co-conspirators, the prosecution can greatly increase the penalty to which a defendant may be subjected upon conviction.

   c. **Choice of venue:** Since venue in a conspiracy prosecution lies in any locale where an overt act was committed, the prosecution can often choose among a broad range of places to try the case and thus can select a place of prosecution in which a conviction is more likely.

   d. **Hearsay exception:** Since statements by conspirators are admissible against their co-conspirators (*see* Evidence Summary), a showing of a conspiracy often increases the evidence that can be used against a defendant.

   e. **Complex joint trials:** Alleged co-conspirators are often tried together and the evidence used in such prosecutions is often extensive and complex. From the prosecution's perspective, this may enable the prosecution to make a more effective case against the defendants as a whole. From the defendants' perspective, of course, this creates the risk that juries may find "guilt by association" rather than objectively evaluating the sufficiency of the evidence against each defendant. [*See* Krulewitch v. United States, 336 U.S. 400 (1949)—Jackson, J., concurring]

C. ATTEMPT

1. **In General:** [§658] At common law, it is a crime to attempt the commission of ***any felony or misdemeanor***. [Rex v. Scofield, Caldecott 397 (1784)] Most modern statutes continue this approach. [Model Penal Code §5.01] Attempt, like most crimes, requires proof of certain conduct—a ***sufficient step*** towards the attempted crime—and the requisite ***intent***.

   a. **Policy considerations in formulating the law of attempt:** [§659] The basic principle that the criminal law does not impose liability for bad thoughts alone (*see supra,* §79) applies no less to attempt than it does to all other crimes. Attempt comes dangerously close to punishing for mere intent, and therefore the requirements for attempt should be defined so as to provide reasonable assurance that those convicted are persons who would commit the target crime if left alone. Such a result can be achieved by a stringent intent requirement and an approach to the act requirement that focuses on whether the defendant's conduct confirms both moral culpability and dangerousness in the sense of an actual willingness to commit the crime.

2. **Elements of Attempt:** [§660] Attempt consists of a ***specific intent*** to commit a crime and an ***act in furtherance*** of that intent that goes far enough towards completion of the crime.

   a. **Mens rea:** [§661] The mens rea of attempt has two components: (i) the intent to commit the acts or cause the result constituting the target crime; and (ii) the intent necessary for the target crime. [People v. Matthews, 258 N.E.2d 378 (Ill. 1970)]

      (1) **Example:** D decided to borrow V's car and return it, even though he knew V had not given him consent to do so. D approached the car but was apprehended as he touched the door handle. D is not guilty of attempted larceny. Attempted larceny requires both the intent to commit the acts constituting larceny (*i.e.*, trespassory taking and asporation of the personal property of another) and the intent necessary for larceny (*i.e.*, intent to permanently deprive the owner of the property). D had the first component of this mental state, since he did intend to take and move V's car. But since he intended to return the car, he did not have the second component—the intent to permanently deprive V of the property.

      (2) **Example:** Evidence showed that D knew he was HIV positive and nevertheless raped V without using a condom. D was prosecuted for attempted murder. Since murder requires that D have caused the death of the victim, the first component of the mens rea required for attempted murder requires proof that D intended to cause that result—V's death. Proof that D was aware of a risk that he would do so or even that he knew he would do so is ***not*** enough. (The jury could, however, infer the necessary intent to cause death from the circumstances.) [Smallwood v. State, 661 A.2d 747 (Md. 1995)]

      (3) **No attempt to commit crimes requiring nonintentional result:** [§662] If a crime requires a result and a mental state less than "intent" regarding that result, most courts hold that there is no crime of attempted commission of that offense. This is because the mens rea requirement of attempt would automatically increase the requirement for the object crime above what was intended. [State v. Dunbar, 817 P.2d 1360 (Wash. 1991)]

         (a) **Example:** D drove recklessly and nearly struck a police officer. It is an offense to recklessly cause injury to a police officer. D could not be convicted for attempted reckless injury to a police officer because the object crime required proof of a result (injury to a peace officer) and a mental state less than intent (recklessness). [State v. Hemmer, 531 N.W.2d 559 (Neb. 1995)]

      (4) **Strict liability crimes:** [§663] Although strict liability offenses do not require proof of any mental state (*see supra*, §113), it is sometimes held

that proof of intent is necessary to conviction for an attempt to commit a strict liability crime. The defendant must therefore be shown to have acted with an intent to bring about the proscribed result. [Gardner v. Akeroyd, [1952] 2 Q.B. 743]

b. **Actus reus:** [§664] The actus reus of attempt is an act that progresses sufficiently towards the commission of the offense or at least sufficiently beyond the mere intent to commit it. Traditionally, courts have applied a number of approaches to determine whether a defendant has done enough in furtherance of his intent to have committed attempt. One approach, the Model Penal Code approach, is gaining increasing acceptance among the courts.

(1) **Act of "perpetration" rather than "preparation":** [§665] Some courts have said that the defendant's acts must have gone ***beyond mere "preparation"*** into the zone of "perpetration." However, since there is much confusion as to when preparation ends and perpetration begins, this formulation is not particularly useful. [State v. Bereman, 276 P.2d 364 (Kan. 1954)]

(2) **Last proximate act:** [§666] An early case intimated that the defendant must have committed the "last proximate act" before the completion of the crime. [Regina v. Eagleton, 6 Cox Crim. Cas. 559 (1855)] This strict approach has been ***universally rejected***; all jurisdictions agree that the defendant need not have come so close to completion of the crime. [Regina v. Roberts, 7 Cox Crim. Cas. 39 (1855)—failure to apply test by same court that earlier suggested it]

(3) **Control over all indispensable elements:** [§667] Some courts require that the defendant have gone far enough to have obtained control over all factors that are indispensable to the commission of the crime. Thus, ***nothing must be left undone*** that would prevent the defendant from committing the crime. [*See, e.g.,* State v. Fielder, 109 S.W. 580 (Mo. 1908)—no attempt to vote illegally until D obtains ballot]

(4) **Physical proximity test:** [§668] Some courts have suggested that the defendant's conduct must be physically proximate to the intended crime. This would focus on ***what remains to be done*** as opposed to what was already done. In applying this test, courts may take into account such factors as the seriousness of the crime, the time and place at which it is to occur, and the uncertainty of the result. [Commonwealth v. Kennedy, 48 N.E. 770 (Mass. 1897)]

(5) **"Probable desistance" test:** [§669] A few courts have found an attempt only where the act is such that in the ordinary course of events it would lead to completion of the crime in the absence of intervening outside factors. Thus, the emphasis is on the ***likelihood that the defendant would cease efforts to commit the crime***, given the conduct he has already committed. [Boyles v. State, 175 N.W.2d 277 (Wis. 1970)]

(6) **"Equivocality" or "res ipsa loquitur" test:** [§670] One variation of the attempt criteria provides that an act amounts to attempt only if—when considered alone—it firmly shows the actor's intent to commit the

crime. Hence, the defendant's behavior is considered without reference to other evidence that may demonstrate criminal intent (such as a confession). The ***act constituting attempt must "speak for itself"*** in establishing intent. [Salmond, Jurisprudence 404 (7th ed. 1925)]

(7) **Model Penal Code—"substantial step strongly corroborative" of intent:** [§671] The Model Penal Code would require (i) an act constituting a ***"substantial step"*** in the course of conduct intended to result in the crime, and (ii) that the conduct be ***"strongly corroborative"*** of the defendant's criminal purpose, although it need not establish purpose by itself. [Model Penal Code §5.01(1)(c)] The Model Penal Code's approach is gaining increasing acceptance in courts and legislatures. [United States v. Jackson, 560 F.2d 112 (2d Cir. 1977)]

(a) **List of potentially sufficient acts:** [§672] The Model Penal Code also enumerates a number of acts that are not to be held insufficient as a matter of law. [Model Penal Code §5.01(2)] If the prosecution proves such conduct, it is entitled to go to the jury on the question of whether the defendant progressed far enough toward commission of the crime. These acts include:

1) ***Lying in wait, searching for, or following*** the contemplated victim of the crime;

2) ***Enticing or seeking to entice the contemplated victim of the crime to go to the place*** where the crime is to be committed;

3) ***Reconnoitering the place*** where the crime is to be committed;

4) ***Unlawfully entering a structure, vehicle, or enclosure*** in which the crime is to be committed;

5) ***Possessing materials to be employed in the commission of the crime***, if those materials are ***specially designed*** for the unlawful use or serve no lawful purpose of the defendant;

6) ***Possessing, collecting, or fabricating materials to be used in the commission of the crime at or near the place*** at which the crime is to be committed, where this serves no lawful purpose of the defendant; and

7) ***Soliciting an innocent agent*** to engage in conduct constituting the crime and a willingness to commit the crime.

(b) **Failure to identify specific victim or target:** [§673] Some courts hold that a defendant's failure to identify the specific victim or target of the intended crime means that the defendant has not gone far enough for attempt. [People v. Smith, 593 N.E.2d 533 (Ill. 1992)]

1) **Example:** Smith took a taxi to a neighborhood and instructed the driver to drive around to look for a Mexican jewelry store Smith intended to rob. He failed to find it. Smith is not guilty

of attempted robbery, even under the Model Penal Code approach. Since he had not identified the store to be robbed, his actions cannot be regarded as reconnoitering the place where the crime is to be committed. [People v. Smith, *supra*]

3. **Defenses**

a. **Impossibility:** [§674] Conduct that would otherwise be sufficient for attempt may not constitute the crime if it would have been "impossible" for the defendant to succeed. Thus, a "defense" of impossibility may be applicable to attempt. In these situations, the defendant believes he can successfully complete the crime he intends to commit but, for reasons unknown to the defendant, such success is in fact impossible.

(1) **Policy considerations:** [§675] Ideally, a defense of impossibility would apply in those situations where despite having done enough with the required mens rea the defendant lacks either the blameworthiness or the dangerousness to justify criminal liability. Whether a defense can be formulated that provides for acquittal of such attempt defendants—and only those defendants—is at best doubtful.

(2) **Traditional rule—only "legal" impossibility is defense:** [§676] The traditional rule is that "legal" but not "factual" impossibility is a defense to attempt. [People v. Dlugash, 41 N.Y.2d 725 (1977)] The major difficulty in applying this rule is distinguishing legal from factual impossibility.

(a) **"True" legal impossibility:** [§677] Sometimes a defendant sets out to do things that he believed would, if completed, constitute a crime but which were not in fact made criminal by the law. The person's only ***misunderstanding*** concerns ***the "law"***: He mistakenly believes that it is a crime to do what he sets out to do. Such a person has not demonstrated a willingness to do things actually prohibited by the law, and thus has not evidenced actual dangerousness. This situation involves clear ***legal impossibility***, and the defendant has a ***defense*** to a charge of attempt.

1) **Example:** D sets out on November 3 intending to shoot a deer that day. D believes that killing a deer in November is a crime. In fact, it is a crime to hunt deer in December but not in November. D is obviously not guilty of killing a deer out of season. Nor is D guilty of an attempt to commit this crime, since what D set out to do (kill a deer in November) is not a crime. D believes this would be a crime, but this mistake as to what the law provides does not create criminal liability.

(b) **Factual impossibility:** [§678] Sometimes a defendant has set out to do something (or to cause a particular result) that would, if accomplished, constitute a crime, but because of factors of which he is unaware, there is ***no chance he will succeed*** in doing these things or causing the result. His actions nevertheless demonstrate his dangerousness and culpability. This is, then, ***factual impossibility*** and is universally ***rejected*** as a defense to a charge of attempt. [People v. Fiegelman, 33 Cal. App. 2d 100 (1939)]

1) **Example:** D reaches into X's pocket intending to steal money that D believes is in the pocket. Unbeknownst to D, X has taken the money out of her pocket. It is thus impossible for D to take the money. Nevertheless, D is guilty of attempted larceny.

(c) **"Mixed" legal and factual impossibility—mistake as to surrounding circumstances:** [§679] In one category of situations, the defendant has set out to do things (or cause results) believing that this would be a crime. In fact, however, because he misunderstands the surrounding circumstances, his conduct, if completed, would ***not actually constitute a crime***, but if the circumstances were as he believes them to be, his intended conduct ***would*** constitute a crime. Whether such a person had adequately demonstrated sufficient blameworthiness and dangerousness to justify convicting him of a crime is a difficult question. Courts have consequently divided on whether defendants in such "mixed" factual and legal impossibility situations are guilty of attempt.

1) **Traditional rule—defense:** [§680] The traditional rule, however, is that the crime of attempt has not been committed, *i.e.,* that a defense of impossibility is available. [People v. Jaffe, 185 N.Y. 497 (1906)]

a) **Example:** D receives property from X that D believes X stole. D thus thinks that he is committing the offense of receiving stolen property. However, the property is actually being used by X with permission of the owner in an effort to apprehend D in possession of stolen property. Since the property is not actually stolen property, D does not, by taking possession of it, commit the crime of receiving stolen property. Whether D is guilty of attempted receipt of stolen property is less clear. D was not mistaken with regard to a pure matter of "law," but rather with regard to the circumstances—*i.e.,* whether the property was still unrecovered by authorities. Under the traditional approach, D has a defense of impossibility and is therefore not guilty of attempted receipt of stolen property. [People v. Jaffe, *supra*]

2) **Modern view—no defense:** [§681] Most courts today, often applying statutes based to some extent on the Model Penal Code (*see* below), hold that a defendant in this situation has no defense to attempt.

a) **Example:** D was shown to have shot a gun into V's dead body. The prosecution claimed D thought V was still alive and intended to kill V; D maintained he knew V was dead. If the prosecution proves that D thought V was still alive,

D can be convicted of attempted murder. It was impossible for D to commit murder by shooting at the thing he shot. But if the circumstances had been as he believed them to be—if the object had been a live person—his conduct in shooting would have been murder. Thus, D would have no defense to attempt under the prosecution's version. (*Note:* If D's version of the facts is believed, he cannot be convicted of attempt because he lacked the mens rea required—the intent to kill.) [People v. Dlugash, *supra*]

(d) **"Inherent" or "obvious" impossibility:** [§682] In a few very unusual situations, it has been held that an attempt is not criminal if it is blatantly obvious that the defendant's chosen methods could not result in the completion of the crime. [Attorney General v. Sillem, 159 Eng. Rep. 178 (1863)]

1) **Example:** D sticks pins in a doll representing X, believing that D's voodoo powers will enable her to cause X's death in this manner. Because of her obvious inability to accomplish her intended result, D is not guilty of criminal attempt. [Attorney General v. Sillem, *supra*]

(e) **Model Penal Code position—only "true legal impossibility" a defense:** [§683] The Model Penal Code and some modern statutes and decisions purport to reject any impossibility defense as defined above. This is accomplished by defining the crime of attempt as consisting of behavior that would constitute a crime (or a substantial step towards commission of a crime) ***if the circumstances were as the defendant believed them to be***. [Model Penal Code §5.01(1)] What under traditional legal analysis would be "true legal impossibility" (*see* above) would probably still require acquittal, however, because in those situations even if all the factual circumstances were as the defendant believed them to be, his actions would not constitute or be a substantial step towards a crime; this would be the case only if the criminal law were as the defendant believed it to be.

b. **"Withdrawal" or abandonment:** [§684] If defendant has, with the requisite intent, proceeded far enough along in a criminal plan to constitute attempt, may he escape liability by abandoning his scheme?

(1) **Policy considerations:** [§685] Those opposing a defense of voluntary abandonment reason that the defendant has demonstrated his dangerousness and culpability by having completed an attempt. They also emphasize the ease with which a defense of abandonment could be falsified, and believe that the small chance of acquittal would not motivate many persons to abandon their efforts to commit crimes. [United States v. Shelton, 30 F.3d 702 (6th Cir. 1994)] On the other hand, those favoring such a defense argue that a truly voluntary abandonment would seldom be found. In those few cases where the defense would be successful, the evidence would show that the defendant is not presently culpable or dangerous. Moreover, the law should provide an incentive for abandonment,

thereby encouraging the actor to desist from his criminal plan. [Model Penal Code §5.01, comment (Tent. Draft No. 10, 1960)]

(2) **Traditional rule—even "voluntary" abandonment no defense:** [§686] The traditional rule is that abandonment is ***never a defense***, regardless of how voluntary it might be. However, the cases in point are usually ones in which there is little credible evidence that the abandonment was truly voluntary within the above-suggested meaning of that term. [United States v. Shelton, 30 F.3d 702 (6th Cir. 1994); People v. Staples, 6 Cal. App. 3d 61 (1970)]

(3) **Model Penal Code position—possible defense:** [§687] The Model Penal Code and modern statutes based on it permit a defendant to avoid liability by proving voluntary abandonment, subject to two conditions:

(i) The abandonment must have been ***entirely voluntary***, which means it must not have been motivated in any way by circumstances not present or apparent earlier which increase the risk of detention or apprehension or which merely increase the difficulty of committing the crime.

(ii) The abandonment must have been ***complete***, which means it must not have been simply a decision to postpone the crime until a better time or until a different victim or opportunity is found.

[Model Penal Code §5.01(4)]

(4) **Compare—abandonment as showing lack of intent:** [§688] If abandonment is not a defense, evidence of abandonment may nevertheless be introduced to show that the defendant had only a "half-formed" or provisional intent and therefore ***lacked the mens rea*** required for liability. [Williams, Criminal Law: The General Part 620-621 (2nd ed. 1961)]

4. **Punishment**

a. **Penalties for attempt:** [§689] While statutes vary widely in the penalties attached to a criminal attempt, many attempts are commonly punishable by a ***lesser penalty*** than the completed crime (*e.g.*, one-half the maximum for the completed crime). The Model Penal Code, however, would authorize the ***same penalty*** as that for the completed crime. [Model Penal Code §5.05(1)]

b. **Relationship of attempt to completed crime:** [§690] Although an attempt does not "merge" into the completed crime, it is clearly a lesser included offense of the completed crime. Therefore, the defendant ***cannot be convicted of both*** attempt and the completed crime (*see supra,* §75).

(1) **Note:** While there is some early authority to the contrary, the better view is that a defendant can be convicted of attempt even if the proof at trial shows that he successfully completed the crime. [People v. Pickett, 175 N.W.2d 347 (Mich. 1970)]

c. **Relationship to other crimes**

(1) **Attempt to commit "attempt-like" crimes:** [§691] It has been suggested that an attempt to commit a crime that is itself an offense consisting of preparatory action (*e.g.*, burglary or assault) should not be made a crime; *i.e.*, there can be no "attempted attempt." Some courts, however, have upheld convictions of this sort. [*See, e.g.*, McQuirter v. State, 63 So. 2d 388 (Ala. 1953)—upholding conviction of attempted assault with intent to rape]

(2) **Solicitation as attempt:** [§692] Although there is authority to the contrary, the better view is that a mere solicitation is not also an attempt. However, if the solicitation is accompanied by additional acts beyond the minimum required for solicitation that also meet the attempt standard, the defendant may of course be punished for attempt. [State v. Green, 861 P.2d 954 (N.M. 1993)]

VIII. HOMICIDE CRIMES

chapter approach

Because of the complex grading schemes relating to homicide offenses, examination questions concerning homicide are quite common. If you find such a question on your exam, decide first whether it should be answered under the common law rules or whether modern-type homicide statutes are applicable. In either case, unless you are asked to apply statutes that provide other distinctions, your analysis of the questions should proceed along the following lines:

1. Did the defendant act with a state of mind that is sufficient to establish malice aforethought:

   — Did the defendant act with ***intent to kill***?

   — Did the defendant act with ***intent to cause serious bodily injury***?

   — Did the defendant act with ***awareness of high risk*** that death or serious bodily injury would be caused?

   — Was death caused in the commission of a felony sufficient to invoke the ***felony murder*** rule?

   If the defendant had any of these states of mind at the time of the defendant's conduct that caused the victim's death, the killing might well be ***murder***.

2. Is there an applicable statute that separates degrees of murder? If so:

   — Are there facts suggesting that the killing was ***premeditated***? Under many such statutes, this will make the killing ***first degree murder***.

   — Was the killing caused during the commission of ***specifically listed felonies***? Often this will be ***first degree murder***.

   Under such schemes, all killings that meet the general definition of murder that are not raised to first degree murder by these two methods will be ***second degree murder***. ***But*** *note:* In the absence of a statute, do not worry about degrees of murder. Common law murder is not divided into degrees.

3. If the facts suggest that the killing was murder, do those facts also include all four elements of ***adequate provocation***?

   — A ***sufficient provocation***;

   — A showing that the provocation did ***in fact stimulate*** the defendant's killing of the victim;

   — A ***lack of a cooling period*** between the provocation and the killing; and

   — The failure of the defendant to have ***actually cooled*** off after the provocation.

If so, the killing will most likely be reduced from murder to ***voluntary manslaughter***.

4. After covering the possibility that the killing might be murder or voluntary manslaughter, consider as an alternative whether the killing might be ***involuntary manslaughter*** under either of the following approaches:

— Did the defendant act without malice aforethought but with ***criminal negligence***?

— Was the death of the victim caused during the commission of an ***unlawful act*** that does not bring into play the felony murder rule?

Also watch for a statute in the question creating the crime of ***criminally negligent homicide.*** If such a statute is applicable, a negligent killing will constitute this crime rather than involuntary manslaughter.

If there is any chance that any of these offenses apply, consider whether there are problems of ***causation***. Consider separately three different possibilities:

— Is there any chance that the victim failed to die within a ***year and a day*** so as to invoke this special rule?

— Was there ***factual causation***; *i.e.*, did the defendant's acts cause the victim to die as and when the victim did die? (*See supra,* §178.)

— Was there ***proximate causation***? Most importantly, was any factor interjected into the chain of causation between the defendant's conduct and the death of the victim that might be regarded as a ***superseding factor***? (*See supra,* §184.)

A. DEFINITION AND CLASSIFICATION

1. **Definition:** [§693] A homicide is the killing of one human being by another human being.

2. **Common Law Classifications:** [§694] At common law, homicides are classified as justifiable, excusable, or criminal. ***Justifiable*** homicides are those commanded or authorized by law; they are not punishable. ***Excusable*** homicides are those in which the killer is to some extent at fault but where circumstances do not justify infliction of full punishment for criminal homicide; the killing remains criminal but the penalty is reduced. Any killing that is not justifiable or excusable is ***criminal*** homicide—either murder or manslaughter. [Clark & Marshall, 469-477]

3. **Classification Under Modern Law:** [§695] Modern statutes tend to abandon the common law scheme above. Excusable homicides are no longer punished, and so the justifiable-excusable distinction is of no significance. Modern statutes often add to homicide law the additional offense of ***negligent homicide***. With regard to murder, a common pattern is to divide murder into two degrees (first degree and second degree). More recently, a number of states have distinguished murder from the separate offense of "capital murder," for which the death penalty may be imposed.

B. MURDER

1. **Murder Defined:** [§696] At common law and under many present statutes, murder is the unlawful killing of another human being with ***malice aforethought***.

2. **"Malice Aforethought":** [§697] "Malice aforethought" is sometimes defined as "the intention to kill, actual or implied, under circumstances which do not constitute excuse or justification or mitigate the offense to manslaughter." The intent to kill is "actual" where the defendant consciously desired to cause death, and "implied" where the defendant intended to cause great bodily harm or where the natural tendency of her behavior was to cause death or great bodily harm. No ill will or hatred of the victim need be shown. [People v. Morrin, 187 N.W.2d 434 (Mich. 1971)]

   a. **Functional definition:** [§698] Malice aforethought is best regarded as a term of art encompassing several different mental states. Absent evidence of adequate provocation (which will reduce the killing to voluntary manslaughter, *see infra,* §§746 *et seq.*), malice aforethought exists if, at the time of the killing, the defendant entertained ***any one*** of the following states of mind [Royal Commission on Capital Punishment, 1949-1953, Report (1953)]:

      (1) **Intent to kill:** [§699] If the defendant ***intended to cause the victim's death***, the killing is with malice aforethought and thus murder.

         (a) **Example:** D shoots V with the intent to cause V's death. Unless there are mitigating circumstances that will reduce the killing to voluntary manslaughter, V's resulting death is clearly murder.

         (b) **"Deadly weapon" doctrine:** [§700] One who intentionally uses a deadly weapon (*i.e.,* a weapon calculated to or likely to produce death or great bodily injury) on another human being, and thereby kills him, is ***"presumed" to have intended the killing***. Under the better view, this is not a mandatory presumption, but rather is a permissive inference, which means that the trier of fact may, but need not, infer from such use of a deadly weapon that the perpetrator did in fact have the intent to kill. [Bantum v. State, 85 A.2d 741 (Del. 1952)]

      (2) **Intent to inflict great bodily injury:** [§701] If the defendant ***intended to inflict serious bodily injury*** upon the victim, even though he did not consciously desire to cause the victim's death, and did in fact cause the victim's death, the killing is with malice aforethought and thus murder. [People v. Geiger, 159 N.W.2d 383 (Mich. 1968)]

         (a) **Example:** H dealt W several blows, caused her to strike her head on the ground and, on discovering that she was unconscious, simply placed her in his car, where she died from the injuries. Although H lacked the intent to kill, he clearly intended to cause W serious bodily injury, and since with this mens rea he caused her death, he is guilty of murder. [People v. Geiger, *supra*]

      (3) **Intent to commit a felony:** [§702] If the defendant was ***in the process of committing a felony*** when she did the act that caused death—and

therefore had the intent to commit a felony—she acted with malice aforethought. This is the basis of the felony murder rule (*see infra,* §§723 *et seq.*)

(4) **Intent to resist lawful arrest:** [§703] Older authorities suggest that a killing caused in the resistance of a lawful arrest is murder even if it does not fall within one of the other categories. [Donehy v. Commonwealth, 186 S.W. 161 (Ky. 1916)] But the modern and better view is that such a killing is murder only if it satisfies one of the other tests of malice aforethought (*i.e.,* intent to kill, felony murder, etc.). In other words, a killing with intent to resist a lawful arrest is ***not a separate type*** of murder. [State v. Weisengoff, 101 S.E. 450 (W. Va. 1919)]

(5) **Awareness of a high risk of death—"depraved mind" or "abandoned and malignant heart" murder:** [§704] Under certain exceptional circumstances, a defendant may be guilty of murder if she acts in the face of an ***unusually high risk that her conduct will cause death or serious bodily injury***. Traditionally, it is said that the risk must have been so great that ignoring it demonstrates an "abandoned and malignant heart" or a "depraved mind." [Commonwealth v. Malone, 47 A.2d 445 (Pa. 1946); N.Y. Penal Law §125.25—statutory "depraved indifference" murder, requiring recklessly causing a grave risk of death to another under circumstances "evincing a depraved indifference to human life" and thereby in fact causing the death of another]

(a) **Example:** D killed V while playing a game of "Russian Poker," which involved loading a revolver with one bullet and, after spinning the chamber, placing the gun to V's head and pulling the trigger. D was guilty of murder. Regardless of whether D intended to kill V or seriously injure him, D acted with the awareness that her conduct created an extremely high risk of V's death. [Commonwealth v. Malone, *supra*]

(b) **Example:** D shot into the caboose of a passing train, unintentionally killing one of the occupants. D is guilty of murder because such conduct indicates an awareness of a sufficiently high risk to human life. [Banks v. State, 211 S.W. 217 (Tex. 1919)]

(c) **Awareness of risk:** [§705] There is dispute as to whether the defendant must have been actually aware of the grave risk involved or whether it is enough that her conduct created that risk. While most of the cases are ambiguous on the matter, the better view would require a subjective realization of the risk—on the theory that anything less is too far removed from intent-to-kill murder to justify treating the two situations alike. [LaFave and Scott, 620-621]

(d) **Compare—reckless and negligent killings:** [§706] More than mere negligence or even recklessness—in modern terms—is required in these cases. The risk of death necessary for either recklessness or negligence is not enough for this type of murder; at most, reckless or negligent killings can be manslaughter (*see infra,* §779). In addition, negligence does not require that the defendant have been actually aware of the risk of death; murders in this category may require actual awareness of the risk (*see* above).

(e) **Creation of risk to many:** [§707] Some jurisdictions limit this sort of murder to those situations in which the defendant has, by her conduct, created a high risk of death to several or many persons. Under this approach, it is not sufficient that the defendant created a high risk of death to only the victim. [*Ex parte* McCormack, 431 So. 2d 1340 (Ala. 1983)]

b. **Previous California requirement—awareness of obligation to obey laws:** [§708] The California Supreme Court held that malice aforethought also requires an awareness of one's obligation to act within the general body of laws regulating society. [People v. Conley, 64 Cal. 2d 310 (1966)]

(1) **Comment:** This decision was an effort to redefine murder so as to make evidence of diminished capacity (*see supra,* §371) a more meaningful method of mitigating the seriousness of the crime committed by an impaired person. Thus, if because of intoxication, mental illness, or mental retardation, the defendant was unable to comprehend the duty, she could not be convicted of murder, although a manslaughter conviction would be permissible.

(2) **Note—legislative abolition of California requirement:** [§709] In 1981, the California statute defining malice was amended specifically to provide that an awareness of the obligation to act within the general body of laws regulating society is ***not*** required. [Cal. Penal Code §188]

c. **Proof of malice aforethought:** [§710] The various states of mind comprising malice aforethought may, of course, be proven by circumstantial evidence. Additionally, it is sometimes said that proof that the defendant killed the victim creates a presumption that she acted with malice aforethought. Under the better view, however, this merely means that the trier of fact may (but need not) infer from the fact of the killing that the defendant had one of the states of mind necessary for murder. If this "presumption" is interpreted as placing the burden of proving lack of malice on the defendant, it is inconsistent with the presumption of innocence and unconstitutional. [State v. Cuevas, 488 P.2d 322 (Hawaii 1971)]

3. **Degrees of Murder:** [§711] At common law, there are no degrees of murder. Statutes, however, often divide murder into first and second degree.

a. **First degree murder:** [§712] The offense of first degree murder has no common law equivalent; it is entirely a creature of statute. While generalization is somewhat difficult, statutes typically classify the following homicides as first degree murder:

(1) **Premeditated killings:** [§713] Premeditated killings are those in which the intent to kill is formed ***with some reflection, deliberation, reasoning or weighing,*** rather than simply on a sudden impulse. Thus premeditation is, in a sense, the process by which intent to kill is formed or the defendant finally decides to act on the intent to kill. While there is general agreement on the abstract definition of premeditation, courts disagree on

the evidence necessary to show it. [State v. Snowden, 313 P.2d 706 (Idaho 1957)]

(a) **Proof of opportunity:** [§714] Some courts defer dramatically to juries' conclusions that defendants did premeditate and tend to uphold a verdict of guilty of premeditated murder if the evidence shows the defendant had sufficient time ***to provide an opportunity to premeditate*** and the jury found she in fact did. [State v. Watson, 449 S.E.2d 694 (N.C. 1994); Commonwealth v. Carroll, 194 A.2d 911 (Pa. 1963)]

1) **No appreciable time needed:** [§715] Courts often do not require a showing that the defendant had a long period of time during which the evidence suggests she might have premeditated. Rather, these courts reason that the formulation of the intent to kill by premeditation and the defendant's final decision to act upon this intent can occur as instantaneously as successive thoughts. [State v. Snowden, *supra*]

a) **Example:** Evidence showed that D shot V four times and one witness testified he heard one shot, a brief pause, and then three more shots. Some courts hold that this is sufficient for a jury to find that D premeditated, since under the "felled victim" rule, a showing of multiple wounds inflicted on the victim shows an adequate opportunity to premeditate between the infliction of the wounds. [State v. Watson, *supra*]

(b) **Proof of actual due consideration:** [§716] A few courts insist on somewhat direct proof that the defendant ***did in fact give the question whether to kill reasonably calm consideration***. This evidence can consist of planning activity prior to the crime or some reasonable substitute, such as proof of a preexisting motive together with evidence that the killing was committed in such a way as to suggest a preconceived plan (*e.g.,* measuring a lethal dose of poison). [People v. Anderson, 70 Cal. 2d 15 (1968)]

1) **Example:** Evidence showed that D raped and strangled V in a pasture and that the process of strangulation must have taken three to five minutes. There was no evidence that D had planned the attack in advance. Although the evidence shows that D could have premeditated, no evidence here shows that in fact D did. Therefore, D cannot be convicted of premeditated murder. [State v. Bingham, 719 P.2d 109 (Wash. 1986)]

(c) **Previous California requirement—"mature and meaningful reflection":** [§717] The California Supreme Court held that premeditation required that the defendant have the ability maturely and meaningfully to reflect upon the gravity of the killing. [People v. Wolff, 61 Cal. 2d 795 (1964)] Under the "diminished capacity" rule (*see supra,* §§371 *et seq.*), evidence of youth, mental illness, or retardation might show the absence of premeditation and thus preclude conviction for first degree murder. In 1981, however, the

California homicide statutes were amended to provide that there is ***no need*** to prove a defendant maturely and meaningfully reflected on the gravity of the killing to convict that defendant of first degree murder. [Cal. Penal Code §189]

(2) **Killing during enumerated felonies:** [§718] Killings committed during the perpetration (or attempted perpetration) of certain ***statutorily enumerated felonies*** are often made first degree murder. The specified felonies typically include arson, rape, robbery, burglary, kidnapping, mayhem, and sexual molestation of a child. [Cal. Penal Code §189]

(a) **Note:** Not all felony murders will be murder in the first degree. If the killing arises out of a felony that is not enumerated in the applicable statute, and does not otherwise qualify for first degree murder, it is second degree murder (*see* below).

(3) **Killing by poison, bomb, lying in wait:** [§719] Killings committed by use of poison or a bomb, or after lying in wait for the victim are sometimes specifically made first degree murder. [Cal. Penal Code §189] Alternatively, however, these categories may be regarded as highly probative of premeditation.

(4) **Killing by torture:** [§720] Statutes sometimes make killings by torture first degree murder. This has been held to require proof of intent to inflict pain and suffering for purposes of revenge, humiliation, or some similar motive, and a causal relationship between the torture and the death of a victim. [State v. Brock, 416 P.2d 601 (Ariz. 1966)]

b. **Second degree murder:** [§721] Under statutes that divide murder into degrees, all killings committed ***with malice aforethought*** that are ***not specifically made first degree murder*** are second degree murder. [People v. Phillips, 64 Cal. 2d 574 (1966)]

(1) **Example:** D is charged with causing V's death in the course of committing the crime of obtaining property by false pretenses (felony murder). Under the governing statute, first degree murder consists of killings committed during the perpetration of certain enumerated felonies. "False pretenses" is not on the list. Therefore, if D is to be convicted of murder, it must be second degree murder. [People v. Phillips, *supra*]

4. **Capital Murder:** [§722] Some modern statutes distinguish the offense of capital murder from murder. The offense of capital murder usually requires proof of at least one of several ***enumerated aggravated factors*** or "***special circumstances***." Under this approach, a defendant may be sentenced to death ***only if*** convicted of the separate offense of capital murder.

a. **Example:** Under the Virginia statute, murder is "capital murder" if it was willful, deliberate, and premeditated, ***and*** the prosecution shows that it was "for hire," that more than one person was killed as part of the same transaction, that the victim was a law enforcement officer, that the killing was related to the commission of rape, abduction, or robbery, or that it came within one of the other similar statutory provisions. [Va. Code §18.2-31]

C. FELONY MURDER

1. **Felony Murder Rule:** [§723] A killing—even if it was accidental—will be murder if it was caused ***with the intent to commit a felony***. This is the "felony murder rule." The felony on which a particular prosecution is based is often called the "***predicate felony***."

   a. **Rationale:** Two justifications have been advanced in support of the rule: The rule is believed to ***deter felonies*** by adding to the threat of conviction and punishment for the felony the additional threat of conviction and punishment for murder if death is caused. Also, the rule is believed to ***discourage the use of violence during the commission of felonies*** by imposing the threat of additional punishment if the felon causes death. Some have questioned whether, in fact, the rule actually functions in either way.

   b. **All co-felons liable for felony murder:** [§724] In situations involving several participants in the predicate felony and one of those felons accidentally caused a death, the other felons as well as the one actually causing the death may be guilty of felony murder. This follows from application to these cases of the co-conspirator rule making all conspirators guilty of foreseeable crimes of their co-conspirators committed in furtherance of the conspiracy. [People v. Friedman, 205 N.Y. 161 (1912); *and see supra,* §644]

   c. **Applies when co-felon is killed:** [§725] Felony murder liability exists even if the person killed is one of the participants in the predicate felony. Courts are likely to be uncomfortable with liability in these cases, however, and thus may well be more willing to find some exception to the rule. [State v. Hoang, 755 P.2d 7 (Kan. 1988)—where two participants in arson were accidentally killed in fire, remaining arsonists were guilty of felony murder]

2. **Limitations on Felony Murder:** [§726] Several limitations on felony murder have developed. These may reflect misgiving regarding the wisdom of the rule itself, at least if it is applied without qualification or limitation.

   a. **Death of another must be "foreseeable":** [§727] Some, but not all, courts require that the death of another have been a foreseeable result of the felony as a condition of applying the felony murder rule. [*Compare* State v. Noren, 371 N.W.2d 381 (Wis. 1985)—foreseeability required *with* People v. Stamp, 2 Cal. App. 3d 203 (1969)—foreseeability not required] In applying this requirement, courts have been quite willing to find the required foreseeable risk of death on the facts of particular cases.

      (1) **Example:** D set a building on fire. Firefighters arrived to fight the fire. V, a firefighter using a breathing apparatus, ignored the alarm that signaled his air was about out and remained in the burning building. V's air ran out and he died of carbon dioxide poisoning. Even though V was considerably negligent, D is guilty of felony murder. A reasonable person would foresee dangerous firefighting as a result of setting fire to a building, and even some negligence on the part of the firefighters is a foreseeable result of arson. Thus, felony murder liability exists. [State v. Leech, 790 P.2d 160 (Wash. 1990)]

b. **Felony must be "dangerous":** [§728] A number of states limit the rule to underlying felonies of a specific nature. Most often, this approach requires that the predicate felony be a ***"dangerous"*** one. [People v. Washington, 62 Cal. 2d 777 (1965)] There are two different approaches for determining whether a felony is dangerous:

(1) **Felony must be "inherently" dangerous:** [§729] A few jurisdictions adopting the dangerous felony approach demand that the felony be ***"inherently" dangerous***, *i.e.,* always dangerous to human life when evaluated in the abstract rather than on the facts of any particular case. [People v. Phillips, 64 Cal. 2d 574 (1966)]

(a) **Example:** Angered over being ripped off in a drug deal, D went to the apartment of the man who ripped D off and fired several shots at the apartment. A young girl in the apartment was killed. D's actions constituted the felony of willful discharge of a firearm at an inhabited dwelling. D could be convicted of felony murder, because the predicate felony was an inherently dangerous one. Although the felony does not require that persons be in the dwelling when the firearm was discharged at it, people are generally in or around such places and thus the offense inherently involves a significant risk of death. [People v. Hansen, 9 Cal. 4th 300 (1994)]

(2) **Felony need only be dangerous as committed:** [§730] Most courts examine the facts of particular cases and the circumstances under which the felony was committed and apply the felony murder rule ***only if the felony as committed*** on the facts of the case involved a special or significant risk to human life. [State v. Stewart, 663 A.2d 912 (R.I. 1995)]

(a) **Example:** D was a convicted felon but nevertheless had a pistol. D went to a friend's house and while D was attempting to unload the pistol it accidentally discharged. V, who lived in a basement apartment at the house, was killed when the bullet went through the floor and into his apartment. D's possession of the pistol was the felony offense of possession of a firearm by a convicted felon. Nevertheless, D could not be convicted of felony murder. Whether a felony suffices as a predicate felony turns on whether it is dangerous as committed. Here, D's commission of the felon of possession of a firearm by a convicted felon was not committed in a dangerous way. [Ford v. State, 423 S.E.2d 255 (Ga. 1992)]

c. **Felony must be "independent"—the "merger" rule:** [§731] Most courts hold that the felony murder rule can be applied only where the ***predicate felony is somewhat independent of the killing***. If the predicate felony is the assault or battery by which the victim's death is caused, the felony "merges" into the killing and thus does not retain sufficient independence to be a predicate felony. [People v. Ireland, 70 Cal. 2d 522 (1969)]

(1) **Rationale:** Since most killings are accomplished by actions constituting assault or battery, permitting these crimes to be used as predicate felonies for felony murder would expand felony murder to cover far more situations than intended by the legislature. [People v. Hansen, *supra*]

(2) **Problem—determining whether felonies are "independent":** [§732] Courts have had considerable difficulty determining whether felonies beyond assaults and batteries are sufficiently independent of the killing that they do not merge into the killing. Some courts say that a felony is independent and does not merge only if the felony involves an intention collateral to and independent of the physical attack on the victim. Others apply a more flexible test and ask whether permitting the felony to be used as a predicate felony would so expand felony murder as to frustrate the legislature's intent to provide for a meaningfully limited felony murder rule. [People v. Hansen, *supra*]

(a) **Example:** In *People v. Hansen, supra,* §729, D was charged with felony murder based on the felony of willful discharge of a firearm at an inhabited dwelling. If a predicate felony requires an intention collateral to and independent of the physical attack on the victim, this felony probably merges into the killing and D cannot be convicted of felony murder. The court, however, reasoned that very few homicides are caused by willful discharge of a firearm at an inhabited dwelling, permitting this felony to be a predicate felony for felony murder would not frustrate legislative intent, and therefore D could be convicted of felony murder.

d. **One of the felons must "directly" cause death:** [§733] Special problems arise when the victim's death was not caused directly by the defendant or one of the co-felons (*e.g.,* they themselves did not pull the trigger of the gun that caused death) but rather by someone else, such as a resisting victim or a pursuing police officer.

(1) **Agency analysis—no felony murder liability:** [§734] Many (probably most) courts reason that felony murder applies only when the death is caused by the defendant or someone acting as the defendant's "agent." Since neither the victim of the felony nor intervening police officers are in any sense agents of the felons, a death directly caused by them cannot give rise to felony murder. [State v. Canola, 374 A.2d 20 (N.J. 1977)]

(2) **Alternative view—felony murder liability exists:** [§735] Some courts have found felony murder liability, reasoning that these situations present all that is necessary—a showing that "but for" the commission of the felony, the victim would not have died. [Commonwealth v. Almeida, 68 A.2d 595 (Pa. 1949), *overruled by* Commonwealth *ex rel.* Smith v. Myers, 261 A.2d 550 (Pa. 1970); People v. Hernandez, 82 N.Y.2d 309 (1993)—reasoning that legislative change in felony murder statute rejected earlier case law finding no liability]

(a) **Compare—co-felon is killed:** [§736] A leading line of cases finding felony murder liability in these situations suggested that felony murder liability would ***not*** be found where the deceased was one of the felons. [Commonwealth v. Redline, 137 A.2d 472 (Pa. 1958)] Other courts, however, reject this distinction. [*See* State v. Oimen, 516 N.W.2d 399 (Wis. 1994)—felony murder statute rejected "majority rule" and imposes liability where resisting robbery victim killed one of robbers]

(3) **Policy analysis—would liability serve purposes of rule?** [§737] Some courts have refused to find felony murder liability in these situations on the ground that the deterrent purposes of the felony murder rule (*supra,* §723) would not be served by applying it where the killing is not actually caused by one of the felons. Since such homicides are not within the direct control of the felons, imposing felony murder liability would discourage neither the commission of felonies nor killings during felonies. [People v. Washington, *supra,* §728—unreasonable to premise a rule of law on so fortuitous a circumstance as the marksmanship of victims and police officers; Commonwealth *ex rel.* Smith v. Myers, *supra*] Other courts, however, have reasoned that imposing felony murder liability even for these killings will add to the incentive the law provides to discourage persons from committing dangerous felonies. [People v. Pugh, 634 N.E.2d 34 (Ill. 1994)]

(4) **Compare—murder liability on other grounds:** [§738] If the felony murder rule does not apply to these situations, the killings may still be murder if the defendant, in addition to committing the felony, has engaged in activity involving such a high risk to human life that malice aforethought can be established under the "awareness of a high risk" rule (*see supra,* §704). [Taylor v. Superior Court, 3 Cal. 3d 578 (1970)]

(a) **Example:** A and B set out to rob C. A waved a gun at C, threatening C. C grabbed the weapon in response and shot and killed A's cofelon, B. Although felony murder did not apply since C rather than one of the felons was the triggerperson, a murder conviction could be obtained if A's actions in threatening C rose to the level of "awareness of high risk" conduct—*i.e.,* if murder could be established without reference to the felony murder rule. [Taylor v. Superior Court, *supra*]

e. **Death must be caused in perpetration of felony:** [§739] All courts agree that the killing must be caused ***in the perpetration*** (or attempted perpetration) of the predicate felony. This does not, however, require that the death occur before the felony is technically completed, only that actions taken before the felony is completed be shown to have caused the death. Even if a felony murder statute requires that the death be caused "in furtherance" of the felony, this means only that the act causing death was part of the felony. [State v. Leech, 790 P.2d 160 (Wash. 1990)]

(1) **Duration of felony:** [§740] Some courts hold that application of the felony murder rule stops immediately after completion or abandonment of the felony, while others apply the rule to killings much further removed from the felony. [*See, e.g.,* State v. Metalski, 185 A. 351 (N.J. 1936)—killing two hours after a robbery many miles away] A middle and probably preferable position is that a killing is felony murder if it is caused during the commission of the felony ***or in immediate flight*** from the crime. Under this approach, "immediate flight" ends when the perpetrators have reached a position of "temporary safety." Subsequently caused deaths are not felony murder. [People v. Lopez, 16 Cal. App. 3d 346 (1971)]

(a) **Example:** D set fire to a building and left. Later, during the fire, a firefighter was killed by the smoke. Although the arson was technically complete considerably before the death occurred, D is still guilty of felony murder. D did the act that caused the death (setting the fire) during and in furtherance of the arson, and this is sufficient. [State v. Leech, *supra*]

3. **Future of Felony Murder:** [§741] The felony murder rule has been a well-established part of American criminal law. Some courts have expressed dissatisfaction with the rule, however, reasoning that it imposes essentially strict liability for a serious crime in violation of basic principles of criminal liability. Nevertheless, many legislatures have not only retained but expanded felony murder liability, sometimes in response to judicial limitations on it.

a. **English abolition:** [§742] England abolished the felony murder rule in 1957. [Eng. Homicide Act, 1957, 5 & 6 Eliz. 2, c. 11, §1]

b. **Model Penal Code position:** [§743] The Model Penal Code does not make felony murder a separate category of murder. It does, however, raise a presumption of "extreme indifference to the value of human life" (sufficient for murder) if the defendant killed while committing or fleeing from a major felony (*e.g.,* robbery, forcible rape, arson, etc.). [Model Penal Code §210.2(1)(b)]

c. **Constitutional considerations:** [§744] A few courts have expressed concern that felony murder liability, or at least broad versions of it, may impose serious criminal liability without sufficient assurance of blameworthiness. Such strict liability, they have reasoned, may run afoul of due process. [State v. Ortega, 817 P.2d 1196 (N.M. 1991)]

d. **Judicial abandonment in the United States:** [§745] Several courts have wholly or in part abandoned the felony murder rule. As a result, the fact that a killing occurred in the course of a felony is simply one of the considerations that can be taken into account in determining whether the defendant acted with actual malice aforethought. [State v. Ortega, *supra*—effectively abandoning felony murder by construing felony murder statute as requiring a mens rea otherwise necessary for murder; People v. Aaron, 299 N.W.2d 304 (Mich. 1980)—abandoning felony murder completely; Commonwealth v. Matchett, 436 N.E.2d 400 (Mass. 1982)—felony murder rule abandoned with regard to statutory felonies less serious than common law felonies and which have no tendency to cause death (*e.g.,* extortion)]

D. VOLUNTARY MANSLAUGHTER

1. **Voluntary Manslaughter Defined:** [§746] A killing that would ***otherwise be murder*** but that was committed in response to certain ***provocation*** has traditionally been regarded as being without malice aforethought and therefore voluntary manslaughter. The defendant must, of course, have acted with one of the states of mind necessary for malice aforethought (*see supra,* §§697-707), but the provocation ***reduces*** the killing from murder to manslaughter.

2. **Roles of the Court and Jury:** [§747] Courts have traditionally mistrusted juries in this area and consequently have been quite willing to find defendants' claims of

adequate provocation insufficient "as a matter of law," on the ground that no reasonable jury could find from the facts that the killing should be reduced to voluntary manslaughter. This is especially the case regarding whether particular kinds of proffered provocation are sufficient under the objective standard. Why juries should be particularly mistrusted on this issue is not clear. The modern trend is clearly away from this view and for courts to more liberally permit juries to decide whether the defendants' showings are adequate. Nevertheless, attention must be carefully paid to two issues: (i) is a case for manslaughter sufficient to "go to the jury" and (ii) if so, is it sufficient to persuade the jury? [Maher v. People, 10 Mich. 212 (1862)—judge is to decide what in law is a reasonable or adequate provocation, but whether facts show this is a question for the jury]

3. **Elements of Provocation Reducing Murder to Manslaughter:** [§748] At common law, a killing is reduced from murder to manslaughter only if the facts show all of the following four elements. Even under modern statutes, all or most of these requirements are often retained.

(i) There must have been ***provocation*** of the kind that would cause a ***reasonable person to lose control*** and act rashly and without reflection;

(ii) The defendant must have ***in fact been provoked***, and the provocation must have caused the defendant to kill the victim;

(iii) The ***interval*** between the provocation and the killing must ***not have been long enough*** for the passions of a reasonable person to cool; and

(iv) The defendant must ***not have actually cooled*** off during the interval between the provocation and the killing.

[LaFave and Scott, 653-663]

a. **Reasonable provocation:** [§749] Whether provocation is reasonable under the circumstances is traditionally judged by an objective standard; *i.e.*, the situation must be one in which a reasonable person would have been provoked. Generally, the provocation must be such as might render ordinary persons of average disposition liable to act rashly, without deliberation, and from passion rather than judgment. [Maher v. People, *supra*]

(1) **Characteristics of the "reasonable person":** [§750] Courts have struggled with the extent to which the reasonable person should be regarded as having the peculiar characteristics that may have made defendant unusually susceptible to provocation. Fairness seems to persuasively argue that some of the defendant's characteristics should be taken into account. At some point, however, giving the reasonable person the defendant's characteristics destroys the objective nature of the standard.

(a) **Purely objective standard:** [§751] Some courts take the position that the reasonable person should not be regarded as having ***any*** of the defendant's peculiar characteristics, because this would deprive the standard of its objective nature. [Bedder v. Director of Public Prosecutions, [1954] 2 All E.R. 801—in deciding whether prostitute's jeering an impotent defendant constituted adequate provocation for his killing her, jeering should not be evaluated according to its impact on a reasonable but impotent person]

(b) **Compromise standard:** [§752] Other courts adopt a compromise position that permits consideration of ***some*** of the defendant's personal characteristics. But under this approach, the reasonable person is not to be regarded as having any unusual reduced capacity for self-control that the defendant may have had, because this would excessively deprive the standard of its objective nature. [State v. Ott, 686 P.2d 1001 (Or. 1984)]

(c) **Model Penal Code position:** [§753] The Model Penal Code provides that the reasonableness of the disturbance that reduces a killing to manslaughter (*see infra,* §775) is to be determined from the viewpoint of a person in the defendant's position under the circumstances as the defendant believed them to be. This allows the court to take into account some of the defendant's special characteristics, but the statutory formulation fails to make clear where the line is to be drawn. [Model Penal Code §210.3(1)(b)]

1) **Example:** Where the evidence showed that D was intoxicated, the trial judge should not instruct the jury that the adequacy of provocation should be determined by using the standard of a reasonable ***sober*** person. But given the modern view that some characteristics of the defendant should be given to the reasonable person, the trial judge should also not require the jury to give no effect to the defendant's intoxication. [State v. Thunberg, 492 N.W.2d 534 (Minn. 1992)]

(2) **Particular situations:** [§754] Because of the traditional tendency of courts to treat some situations as insufficient "as a matter of law" to reduce a killing to voluntary manslaughter, the law has tended to categorize situations presented in these cases. The resulting rules are probably of less importance in modern analysis than they were traditionally, but courts still often invoke them.

(a) **Words alone:** [§755] The traditional view is that mere words, no matter how insulting, are ***not adequate provocation***. [Lang v. State, 250 A.2d 276 (Md. 1969)]

1) **Compare—minority view:** [§756] A few jurisdictions have rejected any such rigid rule, particularly if the words are ***informational*** (*i.e.,* conveying information of a fact that would constitute reasonable provocation if observed) rather than simply insulting or abusive. [State v. Flory, 276 P. 458 (Wyo. 1929)—confession of rape; *and see infra,* §761]

(b) **Battery:** [§757] A minor blow, even if technically a battery, does not constitute adequate provocation, because it would not provoke a reasonable person to a killing passion. But a ***violent and painful*** blow can be sufficient provocation, whether administered with the hand or a weapon. [People v. Harris, 134 N.E.2d 315 (Ill. 1956)—victim severely beat defendant with nightstick]

1) **Compare—defendant provoked blow:** [§758] Even where the defendant has killed in response to a vigorous blow, the homicide will ***not be reduced*** to voluntary manslaughter if the defendant was ***at fault*** in stimulating the blow (as where the defendant was the initial aggressor in the altercation). [State v. Ferguson, 2 Hill 619 (S.C. 1835)]

(c) **Assault:** [§759] The cases are split as to whether an unsuccessful attempt to commit a battery can constitute adequate provocation. The better view, however, is that it may, especially in aggravated cases. [Stevenson v. United States, 162 U.S. 313 (1896)—attacker fired gun at defendant]

(d) **Illegal arrest:** [§760] Courts have also differed as to whether the victim's unlawful arrest of the defendant can constitute adequate provocation. Probably the best view is that it can, particularly where the defendant was aware of the unlawful nature of the arrest. [Bad Elk v. United States, 177 U.S. 529 (1900)]

(e) **Adultery:** [§761] Discovery of one's spouse in the act of committing adultery is ***clearly sufficient*** for a jury to find as provocation. [State v. Thornton, 730 S.W.2d 309 (Tenn. 1987)] Moreover, the modern trend is to extend this rule beyond situations where one spouse actually catches the other in the act. Thus, some courts find sufficient provocation where the defendant is told of the spouse's adultery [Haley v. State, 85 So. 129 (Miss. 1920)] or even simply sees a person known to be having an affair with the spouse [People v. Bridgehouse, 47 Cal. 2d 406 (1956)].

(f) **Mutual quarrel or combat:** [§762] If two persons voluntarily engage in a fight, in the course of which one is killed, the homicide is only manslaughter. Conceptually, the suddenness of the affray, rather than any specific action by the victim, is the provocation. However, while it is not controlling which person struck the first blow, the killing may not be reduced to manslaughter if at the beginning of the fight the defendant was under an unfair advantage. [Whitehead v. State, 262 A.2d 316 (Md. 1970)]

(3) **Mistake concerning provocation:** [§763] On principle, a killing should be reduced to manslaughter as long as the defendant ***reasonably believed*** that a situation constituting adequate provocation existed. In other words, if the defendant was mistaken as to the existence of the provocation but his mistaken belief was a reasonable one, the killing should still be mitigated. [State v. Yanz, 50 A. 37 (Conn. 1901)] The case law is not clear that this is in fact the case, however.

(4) **Provocation by someone other than victim:** [§764] The voluntary manslaughter rule is often stated as requiring that the provocation have been by the person killed, but this may not be entirely true. Situations in which the source of the provocation came from someone other than the person killed by the defendant should be divided into two categories:

(a) **Defendant intends to kill provoking party:** [§765] If the defendant intended to kill the provoking party but killed someone else, either by accident or because he was mistaken as to who had provoked him, the killing is still only voluntary manslaughter. [State v. Griego, 294 P.2d 282 (N.M. 1956)]

(b) **Defendant intends to kill nonprovoking party:** [§766] If the defendant intended to kill someone he knew was not the person who provoked him, the killing is ***not*** reduced to manslaughter. Thus, even if there is adequate provocation, a homicide is murder where the defendant is so enraged that he simply strikes out at some innocent third party. [White v. State, 72 S.W. 173 (Tex. 1902)]

(5) **Injury to persons other than defendant:** [§767] Generally, the defendant must be the target or victim of the provoking conduct. If the subject of the provocation is a ***close relative*** of the defendant, however, at least some courts would hold that the provocation may still be adequate. The case law suggests that this rule would not be applied if the subject of the provocation were a distant relative or a mere friend, but modern courts, reluctant to hold offered provocation inadequate as a matter of law, might well permit such cases to go to the jury. [LaFave and Scott, 658]

b. **Actual provocation:** [§768] No matter how reasonable the provocation, a killing will not be reduced to manslaughter unless the defendant was ***actually provoked***. This is a purely ***subjective*** requirement. In other words, it must be shown that the provocation was such as would cause a reasonable person to lose control ***and*** that ***the defendant in fact*** became so enraged that his conduct was directed by passion rather than reason. [State v. Robinson, 185 S.W.2d 636 (Mo. 1945)]

c. **Absence of reasonable cooling period:** [§769] Voluntary manslaughter law places special emphasis on the time between the provocation and the killing.

(1) **Majority rule—objective standard applied:** [§770] The general rule is that a homicide is not manslaughter if between the provocation and the killing there elapsed sufficient time to enable the ***passions of a reasonable person*** to cool. This is an ***objective*** test, and it is therefore irrelevant that despite the passage of such time the defendant did not in fact cool off. [Sheppard v. State, 10 So. 2d 822 (Ala. 1942)]

(2) **Minority view—subjective standard applied:** [§771] A minority of courts require only that the defendant's own passions not have subsided. Under this approach, it is immaterial that the passions of a reasonable person would have cooled during the lapse of time, as long as the defendant himself was still enraged at the time of the killing. [State v. Hazlett, 113 N.W. 374 (N.D. 1907)]

(3) **Events preceding a final culmination:** [§772] Some courts allow consideration of earlier events as to which considerable time has elapsed if they are part of a development that culminates in an event that provokes the defendant into killing without delay. In such cases, whether the

provocation is sufficient is to be determined by considering both the culminating event and the earlier preceding events in combination. [Commonwealth v. Voytko, 503 A.2d 20 (Pa. 1986)]

(4) **"Reinflaming" occurrences:** [§773] Although an adequate cooling period may have passed, intervening events can remind the defendant of the provoking event and "reinflame" his passions. Courts have varied on whether the cooling period should begin anew with the reinflaming occurrence, although the better view is that it should. [LaFave and Scott, 662]

d. **No actual cooling off:** [§774] Regardless of the period of time between the provocation and the killing, it must be shown that the defendant's passion did ***not in fact*** subside. Thus, if the defendant is unusually controlled and regains composure in a short period of time before killing, the homicide is murder even though the passions of a reasonable person would not have cooled in that time. [*In re* Fraley, 109 P. 295 (Okla. 1910)]

4. **Model Penal Code Position—"Extreme Disturbance":** [§775] Under the Model Penal Code, a killing that would otherwise be murder is reduced to manslaughter if it was committed "under the influence of ***extreme mental or emotional disturbance*** for which there is ***reasonable explanation or excuse***." This embodies much of the concept of adequate provocation. But it also encourages submission of cases to the jury where the matter is doubtful rather than having trial judges find the evidence offered in mitigation inadequate as a matter of law. [Model Penal Code §210.3(1)(b)]

a. **Example:** D returned to his apartment at midnight, to find someone's car parked in D's assigned slot. The police refused to tow the car away. About 2 a.m., V returned to the car and a confrontation between D and V occurred. D stabbed V to death. Some evidence indicated that D was extremely upset, but other testimony was that he was quite calm. Under a modern statute based on the Model Penal Code, the judge was required to submit to the jury whether the killing was under the influence of extreme disturbance. The issue was close enough, however, that a jury verdict rejecting D's contention and convicting D of murder was supported by the evidence. [State v. Raguseo, 622 A.2d 519 (Conn. 1993)]

(1) **Consideration from accused's perspective:** One judge has argued that under statutes of this sort, the jury should determine whether the explanation or excuse for the disturbance would be reasonable from the perception of the defendant, given his own subjective characteristics. Thus, in the example immediately above, the jury should take into account evidence that D was quite paranoid and unusually sensitive regarding his automobile in determining whether V's improper parking was a reasonable excuse for D's emotional disturbance. [State v. Raguseo, *supra*—Berdon, J., dissenting] *But note:* The majority in that case rejected this approach as inconsistent with the objective aspect of the statutory standard.

b. **Compare—anger, embarrassment not enough:** [§776] Even under the liberal Model Penal Code approach, some courts require that the defendant have suffered an identifiable disturbance resulting in loss of self-control. A mere showing that the defendant was made angry or embarrassed by the victim's "provoking" conduct will ***not*** be sufficient. [People v. Walker, 64 N.Y.2d 741 (1984)]

5. **"Imperfect" Defense Situations as Voluntary Manslaughter:** [§777] Some courts have created an additional category of voluntary manslaughter consisting of the so-called imperfect defense cases—*i.e.*, cases in which the defendant has produced evidence tending to establish a defense, but which falls short of doing so, usually because his conduct was not reasonable. [Sanchez v. People, 470 P.2d 857 (Colo. 1970)]

   a. **Example:** D killed V, acting under what D believed to be the need to defend himself, but the evidence showed that D used more force than was reasonably necessary to defend himself. D was held guilty only of manslaughter rather than murder. Since the force used was unreasonable, the case was one of "imperfect" self-defense, thereby mitigating the killing from murder to manslaughter. [Sanchez v. People, *supra*]

E. INVOLUNTARY MANSLAUGHTER

1. **Involuntary Manslaughter Defined:** [§778] An ***unintended*** killing is involuntary manslaughter if it is the result of ***criminal negligence*** or if it is caused during the commission of an ***unlawful act*** that is not a felony or that for some other reason is insufficient to trigger the felony murder rule.

2. **Killing by Criminal Negligence:** [§779] An unintentional killing caused by the commission of any act—even a lawful one—in a criminally negligent manner is involuntary manslaughter. [Commonwealth v. Welansky, 55 N.E.2d 902 (Mass. 1944)]

   a. **More than "civil" negligence required:** [§780] Although it is often unclear what precisely is required for criminal negligence, the courts agree that there must be more than is necessary to establish civil liability for damages. Thus the situation must have been one in which there was both a ***high and unreasonable risk*** of death of another. [Commonwealth v. Aurick, 19 A.2d 920 (Pa. 1941); Commonwealth v. Welansky, *supra*—facts must show "wanton or reckless" conduct, which must go beyond even gross negligence]

      (1) **Example:** D, knowing that his vision was impaired, went hunting with V. The two separated. Both were in camouflage attire. D saw a flash of movement and fired at it, without first ascertaining what it was. The movement was V, who was hit by D's shot and killed. These facts showed the extreme negligence required for criminal liability and D is guilty of involuntary manslaughter. [Cable v. Commonwealth, 415 S.E.2d 218 (Va. 1992)]

   b. **Awareness of risk may be required:** [§781] It may be necessary that the defendant have been actually ***aware of the risk*** for criminal negligence to be present. But this is often left unclear by the case law. If actual awareness is required, the mental state becomes what modern terminology would regard as recklessness rather than negligence. (*See supra,* §152.)

3. **Killing by Commission of an Unlawful Act—"Misdemeanor Manslaughter":** [§782] An unintentional killing caused during the commission of an unlawful "predicate" act is involuntary manslaughter.

   a. **Nature of unlawful act:** [§783] A misdemeanor will, of course, suffice for manslaughter. But the doctrine is broader than this. A felony that, for any reason, will not support felony murder (*see supra,* §§728-732) will be enough for involuntary manslaughter. Moreover, some acts, although not criminal under the law, have been held "unlawful" for manslaughter purposes, although it is unlikely that modern courts would follow this approach. [Commonwealth v. Mink, 123 Mass. 422 (1877)]

      (1) **Example:** D attempted to kill herself with a revolver. Her fiancé intervened, trying to disarm her, but the revolver accidentally discharged and he was killed. Although attempted suicide was not a crime, it was an "unlawful act" and D was therefore convicted of manslaughter. [Commonwealth v. Mink, *supra*]

   b. **Limitations upon doctrine:** [§784] Misdemeanor manslaughter, like felony murder, has sometimes been judicially disfavored because it imposes strict liability for a relatively serious offense. Since involuntary manslaughter is a much less serious crime than murder, however, these courts have generally not regarded misdemeanor manslaughter as suspect as felony murder. [People v. Datema, 533 N.W.2d 272 (Mich. 1995)—although court had abandoned felony murder, misdemeanor manslaughter based on assault as predicate offense is not subject to same objections] Nevertheless, in part because of this judicial disfavor, a number of limitations on misdemeanor manslaughter have developed.

      (1) **Predicate offense must be "malum in se" rather than "malum prohibitum":** [§785] Some jurisdictions hold that the predicate act must be not only unlawful but also ***malum in se*** (*i.e.*, wrong in itself) rather than simply malum prohibitum (*i.e.,* prohibited for convenience). [Estell v. State, 17 A. 118 (N.J. 1889)—driving through tollgate without paying toll not malum in se and thus resulting death of gatekeeper not manslaughter]

         (a) **Example:** Traffic offenses are only malum prohibitum and hence are often held an insufficient predicate for misdemeanor manslaughter. [State v. Collins, 616 N.E.2d 224 (Ohio 1993)—legislature did not intend failure to stop at stop sign to be sufficient for misdemeanor manslaughter]

      (2) **Negligence in addition to unlawful act required:** [§786] Some courts impose the additional requirement that the defendant have acted with criminal negligence, especially where the predicate offense is only malum prohibitum. [People v. Pavlic, 199 N.W. 373 (Mich. 1924)]

      (3) **Unlawful aspect of activity must cause death:** [§787] A few courts require a showing that the ***unlawful aspect*** of the defendant's activity caused the victim's death; *i.e.*, it may not be enough that the course of conduct constituting the unlawful act caused death. [People v. Penny, 44 Cal. 2d 861 (1965)]

(a) **Example:** An unlicensed cosmetologist who caused a patient's death by a poisoned face-lifting treatment was held not guilty of manslaughter. While the lack of a license was a misdemeanor, this was not the aspect of the cosmetologist's activity that caused the death. [People v. Penny, *supra*]

F. MODERN STATUTORY DISTINCTIONS

1. **Model Penal Code Scheme:** [§788] Modern statutes, or at least those that are part of a comprehensive revision of a state's entire criminal code, tend to redefine the homicide offenses by grading them according to the different states of mind as defined by the Model Penal Code (*see supra,* §§147 *et seq.*).

   a. **Murder:** [§789] Under this approach, murder is defined as a killing committed (i) purposely, (ii) knowingly, or (iii) recklessly under circumstances manifesting extreme indifference to the value of human life. [Model Penal Code §210.2(1)]

   b. **Manslaughter:** [§790] The Model Penal Code abandons the distinction between the two traditional types of manslaughter (voluntary and involuntary), and instead creates a single manslaughter offense. Under this scheme, manslaughter is (i) a killing committed recklessly, or (ii) a killing that would otherwise be murder but is committed under the influence of extreme mental or emotional disturbance for which there is reasonable explanation or excuse. [Model Penal Code §210.3(1)]

   c. **Negligent homicide:** [§791] In addition, the Model Penal Code creates the new homicide offense of "negligent homicide" consisting of killings committed negligently. [Model Penal Code §210.4(1)]

2. **Homicide Caused During Operation of a Motor Vehicle:** [§792] Modern criminal codes often contain a separate offense for death caused in the negligent operation of a motor vehicle or by operating a motor vehicle in an unlawful manner. In some states, this offense is a "new" type of manslaughter, but the penalties that may be imposed are often less severe than those assigned to the more traditional kinds of manslaughter. [Cal. Penal Code §§192(3), 193]

G. GENERAL PROBLEMS RELATING TO HOMICIDE LIABILITY

Several collateral problems are common to all the homicide crimes:

1. **Victim Must Be a Living Human Being—Killing of Fetus:** [§793] A killing cannot be a criminal homicide unless the victim is a ***living human being***. [Keeler v. Superior Court, 2 Cal. 3d 619 (1970)] What then is the result if the defendant causes the death of a fetus; is the victim in such cases a "living human being"?

   a. **General rule—fetus not living human being:** [§794] The traditional common law rule is that a fetus is not a living human being until it has been ***"born alive,"*** *i.e.*, fully brought forth from the mother and having an independent circulation. [People v. Ehlert, 654 N.E.2d 705 (Ill. 1995)] At least one case has extended this to include a fetus ***in the process of being born*** if in the natural course of events the birth would have been completed. [People v. Chavez, 77 Cal. App. 2d 621 (1947)] Most courts have been reluctant to make any further inroads on the common law rule. [Keeler v. Superior Court, *supra*—refusing to extend the rule to killing of unborn but viable fetus not in the process of birth]

b. **Minority view—fetus protected by homicide laws:** [§795] One court has reasoned that the traditional rule was based on the difficulty of proving that a defendant in fact caused the "death" of a fetus that would otherwise have been born alive, and that modern medical knowledge has rendered this rationale invalid. Thus that court held that homicide law permits prosecution on the basis that the defendant caused the death of a fetus that would otherwise have been born alive. [Hughes v. State, 868 P.2d 730 (Okla. 1994)]

c. **Statutory changes extending homicide protection to fetus:** [§796] Some states have amended their homicide statutes to include a fetus within the definition of a human being. [Cal. Penal Code §187—defining murder as the unlawful killing of a human being ***or fetus*** with malice aforethought] Statutes of this sort have been upheld against contentions that women's constitutional right to abort a fetus bars criminalization of this conduct. [People v. Davis, 7 Cal. 4th 797 (1994)—women's constitutional right of privacy does not apply if fetus is aborted without woman's consent]

2. **When Does Death Occur—Definition of Death:** [§797] Any of the homicide crimes may also raise issues regarding the definition of death, especially if a defendant argues that the victim's death for legal purposes was actually caused by action taken by treating doctors. For example, suppose a physician removes a victim's organs for purposes of an organ transplant before the victim's legally defined death. If the physician is regarded as having legally caused the death, a defendant who had earlier shot the victim may be relieved of liability for criminal homicide and the physician may be guilty of a crime. It is, therefore, important to determine at what point life ends for purposes of homicide law.

a. **General rule—death is cessation of heartbeat and respiration:** [§798] The traditional rule is that death occurs when the victim's heartbeat and respiratory functions stop. [Thomas v. Anderson, 96 Cal. App. 2d 371 (1950)]

b. **Alternative standard—"brain death":** [§799] A more appropriate criterion would define death as the cessation of the functioning of the brain. Under this standard, death occurs when an electroencephalograph (EEG) reads flat for a given period of time, even if the victim's heart and breathing remain active. [LaFave and Scott, 611] The "brain death" standard for defining the death of a homicide victim has been accepted by some courts. [State v. Fierro, 603 P.2d 74 (Ariz. 1979); People v. Eulo, 63 N.Y.2d 341 (1984)]

3. **Death Must Occur Within a Year and a Day:** [§800] Traditionally, the victim's death must occur within a ***year and a day*** from the time the fatal blow was given or the cause of death (*e.g.*, poison) was administered. The limitation is independent of the ordinary causation requirements; even if the victim would not have died as and when he did "but for" the defendant's acts, there can be no homicide prosecution if the death transpired after the year-and-a-day time period. [Louisville Evansville & St. Louis Railroad v. Clarke, 152 U.S. 230 (1894)]

a. **Rationale:** The rationale for this seemingly arbitrary rule is that otherwise, proof of causation might be so difficult that there is too great a danger of unjustified prosecutions and convictions. [State v. Gabehart, 836 P.2d 102 (N.M. 1992)]

b. **Rule abandoned:** [§801] Reasoning that new advances in crime detection and medicine have rendered the difficulties of proving cause of death virtually nonexistent, some courts have eliminated the specific time limit requirement. [*See* State v. Gabehart, *supra*; People v. Carrillo, 646 N.E.2d 582 (Ill. 1995)] Some states, although not completely abandoning the rule, have extended the time limit by statute. [*See* Cal. Penal Code §194—three years and a day]

4. **Aiding or Causing Suicide:** [§802] Special problems are caused when the victim has requested to be killed or has actually participated in taking her own life.

a. **Common law position—offense is murder:** [§803] Suicide is murder at common law and therefore one who assists another, whether actively or passively, in taking her own life is a party to that offense. [Burnett v. People, 68 N.E. 505 (Ill. 1903)]

b. **Modern position—separate offense:** [§804] Under many modern statutory schemes, suicide itself is not an offense; thus, the aider cannot be guilty of such a crime as a party. However, some statutes create the separate crime of aiding suicide. [Cal. Penal Code §401]

(1) **Compare—actively killing another:** [§805] Some courts limit aiding suicide statutes to persons who passively provide another with the means for the other person to take her own life. Under this approach, one who actively takes the life of another, even at the other person's specific request, is guilty of murder rather than merely of aiding suicide. [People v. Mattock, 51 Cal. 2d 682 (1959)]

IX. OTHER CRIMES AGAINST THE PERSON

chapter approach

In evaluating possible liability for crimes against the person (other than homicide), consider first the nature of the attack upon the victim:

1. Was the attack sexual in nature? (Consider ***rape*** and related offenses.)

2. Did the attack involve restriction of the victim's liberty? (Consider ***false imprisonment*** and ***kidnapping***.)

3. Was the attack of some other type of physical attack? (Consider ***assault***, ***battery***, and ***mayhem***.)

Especially look for these crimes in situations that at first suggest a homicide but where the victim did not die or where there appears to be insufficient causation between the defendant's conduct and the death of the victim. In these cases, although the defendant cannot be convicted of murder or some other form of homicide, it may be possible to find the defendant liable for one of the assaultive crimes discussed in this chapter.

A. ASSAULT AND BATTERY

1. **In General:** [§806] Although the terms "assault and battery" are often used conjunctively, under traditional analysis they represent different and distinct crimes. While there are some similarities between these crimes and the torts of "assault" and "battery," there are also significant differences.

2. **Battery:** [§807] Battery is the unlawful application of force to the person of another. [State v. Hefner, 155 S.E. 879 (N.C. 1930)]

   a. **Actus reus:** [§808] The actus reus of battery is simply the application of force to the person of another.

      (1) **No injury required:** [§809] Traditionally, no injury to the victim need occur; indeed, the touching need not have left any mark at all on the victim. [People v. James, 9 Cal. App. 2d 162 (1935)]

      (2) **Indirect application of force:** [§810] Moreover, the force can be applied directly ***or indirectly***, as where the defendant sets in motion the force that causes the touching. [State v. Monroe, 28 S.E. 547 (N.C. 1897)—D administers poison to V, causing V internal injury; D has committed battery]

         (a) **Example:** D exposed his private organ and compelled a 6-year-old girl to hold it. D is guilty of battery; it is immaterial that the girl did the actual touching. [Beausoliel v. United States, 107 F.2d 292 (D.C. Cir. 1939)]

(3) **Battery under modern statutes:** [§811] As criminalized under modern statutory provisions, battery is somewhat different than it is under traditional law.

(a) **Injury or offensive touching required:** [§812] Modern statutes often abandon the position that any touching constitutes the offense. Instead, such statutes frequently require either that ***bodily injury*** be caused or that the touching is intended or likely to be regarded as ***offensive***.

(b) **Battery made form of assault:** [§813] Modern statutes frequently abandon the "battery" terminology and make the offense one means of committing the crime of assault. [*See* Tex. Penal Code §22.01; Model Penal Code §211.1(1)(a)—injury required]

b. **Mens rea:** [§814] It is sometimes said that the application of force must have been intentional. This is not true, and such statements probably reflect confusion between the crime of battery and the intentional tort of battery.

(1) **Negligence sufficient:** [§815] Generally, battery requires only that the defendant act with criminal negligence, as where he ***should have been aware*** that his conduct would cause the application of force to the person of another. Some cases so holding employ a fiction, saying that intent is necessary but that criminal negligence supplies the intent. [Fish v. Michigan, 62 F.2d 659 (6th Cir. 1933)]

(2) **Unlawful act sufficient:** [§816] Some—but not all—courts traditionally also find a battery simply on the basis that the defendant was engaged in the commission of an unlawful act at the time of the application of force to another. However, some of these courts may require that the unlawful act be malum in se rather than malum prohibitum. [Commonwealth v. Adams, 114 Mass. 323 (1873)] Under modern statutes, an unlawful act is unlikely to be sufficient.

c. **Effect of consent:** [§817] There is no battery if the victim has ***effectively consented*** to the application of force. (*See supra*, §§482-485, for discussion of the circumstances in which consent is legally effective.)

d. **Punishment:** [§818] At common law, battery is a misdemeanor, and "simple" battery is generally a misdemeanor under modern statutes. Most modern statutes also make certain "aggravated" batteries felonies. Aggravated batteries include those committed with intent to kill, rob, or rape; those resulting in serious bodily harm to the victim; and those committed with a dangerous or deadly weapon.

3. **Assault:** [§819] Two different kinds of activity may constitute a criminal assault: (i) an ***attempt to commit a battery***, and (ii) ***intentionally placing another in fear*** of a battery. Not all states punish both types.

a. **Attempted battery as assault:** [§820] Common law criminal assault was apparently limited to attempts to commit a battery. Virtually all jurisdictions now recognize this form of assault. [Perkins and Boyce, 159-161]

(1) **Mens rea:** [§821] Although there is some confusion concerning the mens rea required for an attempted battery type of assault, it is clear that an intent to frighten the victim will ***not*** suffice for this type of assault. [Chapman v. State, 78 Ala. 463 (1885)]

(a) **Intent to commit a battery:** [§822] The general rule is that the defendant must have intended to commit a battery, which means she must have intended the application of force to the victim. Thus, there can be no conviction for assault where the evidence shows that the defendant was only reckless, that is, only aware of a substantial risk that her conduct would result in a battery.

(b) **Intent to commit dangerous act:** [§823] At least one court has held that assault simply requires an intent to willfully commit an act, the direct, natural, and probable consequences of which (if successfully completed) would be injury to another. Under this approach, the defendant need not have intended the injury. [People v. Rocha, 3 Cal. 3d 893 (1971)]

(2) **Actus reus:** [§824] By application of the rules applicable to attempts (*see supra,* §§664 *et seq.*), the defendant must have come reasonably close to successfully completing the battery. [People v. Lilley, 5 N.W. 982 (Mich. 1880)]

(3) **Present ability to succeed:** [§825] Under statutes in some states (although not under the common law definition), assault requires proof that the defendant had the ***present ability to succeed*** in an attempt to commit a battery. Accordingly, in these jurisdictions that make the ability to succeed an element of the crime, "factual impossibility" (*supra*, §678) will prevent liability. [People v. Sylva, 143 Cal. 62 (1904)—attempt to shoot V with unloaded gun that D believed to be loaded was not an assault]

(4) **Conditional assault:** [§826] It is no bar to a conviction of assault that the defendant expressly or impliedly represented that she would not commit a battery if the victim complied with certain demands.

(a) **Example:** D points a gun at V, saying, "Put up your hands." D is guilty of assault. D's words and actions imply that she will shoot V, although ***only if*** V does not comply with the demand to raise his hands. The fact that the assault is conditional, because the victim could avoid the threatened harm by giving in to the demand, is immaterial. [People v. Thompson, 93 Cal. App. 2d 780 (1949)]

b. **Intentional placing in fear as assault:** [§827] A probable majority of states extend the crime of assault to include the intentional putting of another in fear of immediate bodily harm. Hence, in these jurisdictions, an assault can be committed ***either*** by an attempted battery ***or*** by intentionally putting another in fear. [Perkins and Boyce, 162]

(1) **Intent to cause apprehension of harm:** [§828] Under this form of assault the defendant must have ***intended to put the victim in fear***, although a showing that the defendant intended to actually harm the victim will also suffice. [Mihas v. United States, 618 A.2d 197 (D.C. 1992)]

(2) **Victim must be apprehensive:** [§829] In addition, proof that the victim was ***aware*** of the assault is essential, as is a showing that the victim ***in fact*** experienced ***apprehension of immediate harm***. [State v. Barry, 124 P. 775 (Mont. 1912)]

(3) **Conduct sufficient to create reasonable apprehension:** [§830] The defendant's conduct must have been of the sort ***likely to induce a fear*** of immediate harm ***in a reasonable person***. [Mihas v. United States, *supra*] Thus, ***mere words*** are usually ***not*** enough for this kind of assault, although words accompanied by some action may be sufficient. [State v. Hazen, 165 P.2d 234 (Kan. 1946)]

(a) **Example:** D, a homeless person, was cleaning his fingernails with a knife when V passed and glanced at D. D said, "What are you looking at, punk? Get out of here!" and—still holding the knife—took several steps towards V. V testified that he was afraid D might cut him with the knife. This evidence permitted a jury to find that D committed intent-to-frighten assault, since given D's actions a reasonable person in V's position would have felt concern for his safety. [Mihas v. United States, *supra*]

(b) **Compare:** D verbally threatens to strike V but makes no physical move to do so. This is not criminal assault, although it could be if D also raises her fist as if to act on her threats. [State v. Hazen, *supra*]

c. **Model Penal Code position:** [§831] The Model Penal Code defines an assault as including:

(i) An attempt to cause bodily injury to another; ***or***

(ii) An attempt by physical menace to put another in fear of imminent serious bodily harm.

[Model Penal Code §211.1(1)(c)]

(1) **Note:** This latter type of assault differs from the traditional "putting in fear" form of assault in two ways: (i) no actual fear need exist in the victim, since an attempt to put in fear is enough; and (ii) the attempt must be to put the victim in fear of ***serious*** bodily harm.

d. **Punishment:** [§832] Assault is a misdemeanor at common law, and "simple" assault remains so today. However, modern statutes often make certain "aggravated" assaults felonies. The aggravated assaults generally include assaults with intent to kill, rob, or rape; assaults on a police officer; and assaults with a deadly weapon.

B. MAYHEM

1. **In General:** [§833] At early common law, mayhem consisted of maliciously depriving another of the use of such of his members as might render him less able to fight. The crime was later extended by English statute to cover injuries that disfigured but did not disable the victim. [Perkins and Boyce, 239]

a. **Modern statutes:** [§834] Modern statutes often retain the crime of mayhem, generally defining it to require either that the defendant ***disable or disfigure***. [Perkins and Boyce, 241; Cal. Penal Code §203—defining crime of mayhem as disabling, disfiguring, or rendering useless a member of another's body, depriving another of such a member of the body, or cutting or disabling the tongue, putting out an eye, or slitting the nose, ear, or lip]

2. **Actus Reus:** [§835] The defendant must have caused the victim bodily injury that permanently disfigures or disables him.

a. **Disablement defined:** [§836] "Disablement" requires the ***loss of use*** of a major part of the body (*e.g.,* arm, hand, finger, leg, foot, eye, front tooth, or testicle), although that part need not actually be removed. [Bowers v. State, 7 S.W. 247 (Tex. 1888)]

(1) **Example:** D commits mayhem by biting off a portion of V's thumb only if the injury substantially deprived V of the use of the thumb. [Bowers v. State, *supra*]

b. **Disfigurement defined:** [§837] "Disfigurement" requires an ***alteration*** of the victim's face or body that changes his normal appearance, such as severing or slitting the nose, lip, ear, or tongue. [State v. Raulie, 59 P.2d 359 (N.M. 1936)]

c. **Limitation—permanent damage required:** [§838] For either disablement or disfigurement, the injury must be ***permanent***. [State v. Raulie, *supra*—cutting of V's lip not mayhem where lip was stitched and healed, leaving no mark]

3. **Mens Rea:** [§839] It is often said that the defendant must have acted "maliciously," and statutes sometimes require an "intent to disable or disfigure." Nevertheless, an ***intent to injure*** the victim will generally suffice. Moreover, some courts have even held it enough that the defendant intended to commit a minor battery on the victim, even though she had no intent to inflict serious injury at all. [State v. Hatley, 384 P.2d 252 (N.M. 1963)]

4. **Punishment:** [§840] Mayhem is a felony at common law, punishable by mutilation (*i.e.,* loss of the same member as suffered by the victim). Although the penalty is not as drastic today, the crime ordinarily remains a felony under modern statutes.

C. RAPE AND RELATED OFFENSES

1. **In General:** [§841] At common law, rape is unlawful sexual intercourse with a female person without her consent. For analytical purposes, it is useful to distinguish between cases in which the intercourse is accomplished by means of force, threats, or fraud ("forcible" rape) and those in which consent is given but is ineffective because of the victim's age ("statutory" rape). Modern statutes often redefine the offense and rename it as sexual assault, and classify it as a crime against the person rather than a sexual offense.

2. **Forcible (or Common Law) Rape:** [§842] Common law rape consists of unlawful carnal knowledge of a woman against her will. [State in the Interest of

M.T.S., 609 A.2d 1266 (N.J. 1992)] Several aspects of this definition have given rise to difficulty.

a. **Carnal knowledge—sexual intercourse:** [§843] The requirement of carnal knowledge means that the defendant must have completed an act of sexual intercourse. However, only the slightest penetration of the female sexual organ is required; emission is not necessary. [De Armond v. State, 285 P.2d 236 (Okla. 1955)]

b. **"Unlawful"—husband cannot rape wife:** [§844] Traditionally, the intercourse must be "unlawful." Thus, at common law, a husband cannot be convicted of raping his wife, even if he compels her to submit to intercourse.

(1) **Rationale:** The term "unlawful" was originally used to mean "not authorized by law," and intercourse between a husband and wife was authorized. A wife was regarded as "consenting" to intercourse with her husband during the marital relationship.

(2) **Compare—termination of marriage:** [§845] A male who engages in intercourse with his ***former*** wife (*i.e.,* after a divorce) without her consent can be convicted of rape. [State v. Parsons, 285 S.W. 412 (Mo. 1926)]

(3) **Compare—liability as party:** [§846] While a husband cannot commit common law rape by having sexual intercourse with his wife, he can be convicted as a ***party*** to a rape of his wife by some other male (*see supra,* §265).

(4) **Modern statutes:** [§847] A number of jurisdictions now define rape (or its equivalent, *see infra,* §873) so that it can be committed, at least under certain circumstances, by a husband upon the wife. [Cal. Penal Code §262]

(a) **Example:** California law creates the offense of "rape of a spouse," consisting of sexual intercourse by the defendant with his spouse against the spouse's will and accomplished by force or threats. Prosecution requires either that the victim have reported the offense within one year or that the victim's allegations be corroborated. [Cal. Penal Code §§262, 264]

c. **Against the will of the woman—without consent:** [§848] The requirement that the intercourse be against the will of the woman has proven the most difficult to apply. Several situations must be distinguished. All effectively involve situations in which the act is accomplished without the effective consent of the woman.

(1) **Intercourse accomplished by force:** [§849] Intercourse accomplished by force is, of course, without consent. However, there is no rape if the victim resisted during the early portion of the encounter but consented before the actual act of intercourse. [Wade v. State, 138 S.E. 921 (Ga. 1927)]

(2) **Intercourse accomplished by threats:** [§850] Consent or submission obtained by placing the victim in fear of great and immediate bodily harm is legally ***ineffective***, and the intercourse is rape. [State v. Schuster, 282 S.W.2d 553 (Mo. 1955)]

(3) **Incapacity to give effective consent:** [§851] If the victim was incapable of giving a legally effective consent—because of intoxication, mental deficiency, or insanity—intercourse with her is against the woman's will and is rape; it is immaterial that she may have expressed words indicating consent. [Commonwealth v. Burke, 105 Mass. 376 (1870)]

(4) **Consent obtained by fraud:** [§852] Under certain limited circumstances, consent obtained by fraud renders the consent ineffective, and the intercourse is against the will of the woman and hence rape.

(a) **Fraud as to whether act is intercourse:** [§853] If the defendant deceives the victim into believing that the act involved is ***something other than intercourse***, her consent to that act will not bar a rape conviction. This is regarded as "fraud in the factum"—*i.e.*, fraud as to the ***nature of the act***. [State v. Ely, 194 P. 988 (Wash. 1921)]

1) **Example:** D told V that in the course of medical treatment it would be necessary for him to insert a medical instrument into her sexual parts. V consented to this. D in fact had sexual intercourse with her. D was guilty of rape, as there was no effective consent to the sexual act. [State v. Ely, *supra*]

2) **Compare—fraud as to medical value of intercourse:** [§854] On the other hand, if the defendant does not deceive the victim as to the nature of the act but simply misrepresents its medical (or other) value, the intercourse is ***not*** rape. Here there is only "fraud in the inducement"; the victim has clearly consented to the act of sexual intercourse and is only deceived ***as to the inducement*** for submitting thereto. [Boro v. Superior Court, 163 Cal. App. 3d 1224 (1985); Moran v. People, 25 Mich. 356 (1872)]

(b) **Fraud as to whether defendant is husband:** [§855] There is a split of authority where the defendant has intercourse with the victim after fraudulently inducing her into believing that a marital relationship exists between them—*e.g.*, by pretending to be her husband or by deceiving her into believing that a sham ceremony has caused them to be married. Some courts find that intercourse under these circumstances is not rape on the theory that the victim has not been deceived as to the nature of the act (*i.e.,* whether it is sexual intercourse). [State v. Brooks, 76 N.C. 1 (1877)] But other courts have found the fraud sufficiently related to the nature of the act to support a rape conviction. [People v. Crosswell, 13 Mich. 427 (1865)]

(c) **Fraud as to identity:** [§856] If the defendant deceived the victim regarding his identity in a manner not involving a marriage relationship, the fraud will not render the intercourse rape. [People v. Hough, 159 Misc. 2d 997 (1994)]

1) **Example:** D came late at night to the apartment of his twin brother's girlfriend, V. Leaving the lights low, he led V to believe that he was his twin brother and V willingly engaged in intercourse with D. This was not rape, as D's deception did not render V's consent ineffective. [People v. Hough, *supra*]

d. **Mens rea:** [§857] The mens rea required for rape is not clearly defined. The major question is whether the defendant must be aware that the act is being performed against the will of the woman. Essentially this poses the question whether the accused must be aware of the lack of consent or whether negligence will suffice, *i.e.*, whether it is sufficient that a reasonable person in the defendant's position would have been aware of a lack of consent. Often this is of significance because it determines the effect of the defendant's claim that he believed the victim consented. If the proof shows that the victim did not consent, such a claim presents a contention of mistake of fact (*see supra*, §§395-407). Uncertainty regarding the necessary mens rea makes resolution of a mistake of fact question difficult, of course, because a mistake of fact will ordinarily preclude conviction only if it at least negates the mens rea required by the crime. Whether in addition the mistake must be reasonable is a troublesome question, discussed *supra*, §§399-400.

(1) **Mistaken belief that victim consented must be reasonable:** [§858] Several courts have held that a defendant's mistaken belief that the victim consented to the sexual activity will prevent conviction only if ***both*** (i) the defendant ***honestly and in good faith*** had such a belief; and (ii) the facts were such that mistake was ***objectively reasonable***. [United States v. Short, 4 C.M.A. 437 (1954); People v. Mayberry, 15 Cal. 3d 143 (1975); Tyson v. State, 619 N.E.2d 276 (Ind. 1993)]

(a) **Requirement of equivocal conduct by victim:** [§859] Several leading mistake cases hold that no issue of mistake of fact is raised for jury consideration unless the facts tend to show equivocal conduct by the victim that could have led the defendant to reasonably believe the victim consented. [People v. Mayberry, *supra*; Tyson v. State, *supra*]

1) **Example:** D was tried for raping V. D testified that V consented; V testified that she resisted D's efforts but D—the current heavyweight boxing champion—overcame her resistance. The jury did not have to be instructed on mistake as to consent, because D presented no evidence of equivocal conduct on V's part that could have led him to reasonably believe she consented. [Tyson v. State, *supra*]

(2) **Compare—unreasonable mistake can be sufficient:** [§860] In a leading decision, the House of Lords held that under English rape law then in effect a rape defendant's even unreasonable mistaken belief that the victim was consenting would prevent conviction, since it showed the lack of the mens rea required by the crime. [Regina v. Morgan, [1976] A.C. 182] *Note:* If rape requires that the defendant have been aware that

the act was performed against the will of the woman, *Morgan* is consistent with the position of the Model Penal Code that acquittal is required by any mistake of fact that negates the state of mind required, even if that mistake was unreasonable (*see supra,* §401). American courts, however, have been reluctant to adopt that view in this situation.

e. **Special problems**

(1) **Corroboration of victim's testimony:** [§861] Some states require that the rape victim's testimony be corroborated, on the rationale that a charge of rape is easy to make and difficult to disprove. [81 Yale L.J. 1365 (1972)]

(2) **Requirement of resistance "to the utmost":** [§862] Some courts traditionally applied a rigorous requirement that the victim have resisted the defendant's efforts with all her powers. But such resistance need not be established where the evidence shows it would have been futile or was prevented by threats of the defendant. [People v. Taylor, 268 N.E.2d 865 (Ill. 1971)] *Note:* The requirement of resistance is often abolished, sometimes by statute. [*See, e.g.*, 18 Pa. Stat. Ann. §3107—the victim "need not resist"]

(3) **Effect of victim's promiscuity:** [§863] Rape imposes no formal requirement that the victim have been chaste, but evidence of the victim's prior sexual activity has traditionally been admissible on the question of whether she consented. The modern trend, however, is to ***limit the use of such evidence***, at least to those situations in which it is shown to have some direct and meaningful relationship to the consent issue. [*See, e.g.*, Mich. Stat. Ann. §750.520j—evidence of victim's prior sexual behavior not admissible unless and to the extent that trial judge finds the evidence material to a fact at issue and that its inflammatory or prejudicial nature does not outweigh its probative value]

f. **Special age defense:** [§864] The common law rule is that a boy under the age of 14 is incapable of committing rape. This is a ***conclusive presumption***; it cannot be refuted by evidence showing the boy's ability to have sexual intercourse. [King v. Groombridge, 173 Eng. Rep. 256 (1836); State v. Rogers, 168 S.E.2d 345 (N.C. 1969)]

(1) **Compare—rebuttable presumption:** [§865] Statutes in some jurisdictions have modified the rule to a rebuttable presumption. Accordingly, a boy under age 14 can be convicted of rape where the evidence proves his ability to have intercourse beyond a reasonable doubt. [*See, e.g.*, Va. Code §18.2-61(c)—rebuttable presumption that juvenile over age of 10 but less than 14 does not have physical capacity to commit rape]

(2) **Compare—no special age rule:** [§866] Many jurisdictions have explicitly abolished the traditional presumptions and thus no special age rule applies to defendants charged with rape. [N.C. Stat. §14-27.9—no presumption that person under age 14 is physically incapable of committing rape; Fla. Stat. §794.02]

3. **"Statutory" Rape:** [§867] In most jurisdictions, intercourse with a female under the age of consent is rape, regardless of whether or not she consented.

   a. **Age of consent:** [§868] The age of consent varies by statute among the states. [*See, e.g.,* Cal. Penal Code §261.5—age 18]

   b. **Awareness of victim's age not necessary:** [§869] Under most statutory schemes, this form of rape is a ***strict liability crime*** (*see supra,* §131) in that the defendant need not be aware of the victim's age. Consequently, even a reasonable mistaken belief that the victim was over the age of consent will not prevent a conviction. [State v. Superior Court, 454 P.2d 982 (Ariz. 1969)]

      (1) **Compare—"defense" of reasonable mistake:** [§870] A small number of jurisdictions have provided for the acquittal of one accused of statutory rape upon an affirmative defensive showing that he reasonably believed that the victim was over the age of consent. [People v. Hernandez, 61 Cal. 2d 529 (1964)]

   c. **Defense—minor age discrepancy between defendant and victim:** [§871] Some states permit a defendant to avoid conviction or reduce the seriousness of the offense by showing that there was only a small difference between his age and that of the victim. The purpose is to limit this crime to situations in which it is most likely that the defendant exercised undue influence or persuasion over the victim. [*See, e.g.,* Cal. Penal Code §261.5—distinguishing for penalty purposes between perpetrators not more than three years older or younger than victims and others; Tex. Penal Code §22.011(e)—affirmative defense to sexual assault on "child" that D was not more than three years older than victim, and victim was age 14 or older]

4. **Equal Protection Issues Regarding Sex Offenses:** [§872] Insofar as rape and related offenses apply only to—or fall most heavily on—male persons, it can be argued that equal protection has been denied such male offenders. However, statutes creating such sex crimes will be upheld if the distinction realistically reflects a difference in the actual situation of the sexes. [Michael M. v. Superior Court, 450 U.S. 464 (1981)]

   a. **Example:** Statutory rape statutes typically impose a penalty on the male participant in consensual intercourse. But the statutes are aimed at the important problem of teenage sexual activity and resulting pregnancies. Since the male participants in the sexual activity incur far fewer risks relating to such pregnancies, it is not unreasonable for states to address the problem by imposing penalties only on the male participants. [Michael M. v. Superior Court, *supra*]

5. **Modern Trend—"Sex Neutral" Offense of Sexual Assault:** [§873] A number of jurisdictions have replaced rape with a new offense—sexual assault or criminal sexual conduct—that is designed to be sexually neutral. The Michigan statute is a widely-followed model. [Mich. Stat. Ann. §§750.520a *et seq.*]

   a. **Victim can be of either sex:** [§874] Under these new statutes, the offense need not involve a female victim but rather covers nonconsensual sexual behavior on victims of either sex.

b. **Offense expanded to cover more than vaginal penetration:** [§875] Under these new statutes, the offense is expanded to cover conduct other than the vaginal penetration of the victim necessary for the traditional crime of rape. Thus the new statutes cover nonconsensual cunnilingus, fellatio, anal intercourse, any other intrusion of a part of the perpetrator's body or of any object into the genital or anal openings of the victim's body, and the intentional touching of the intimate parts of the victim's body for purposes of sexual arousal or gratification. [Mich. Stat. Ann. §750.520a(l)—defining sexual penetration]

6. **Deemphasis on Consent Under Modern Statutes—Intercourse "By Forcible Compulsion":** [§876] Critics of traditional rape law regarded rape's requirement that the intercourse be "against the will" of the victim—and thus without her consent—as inherently and undesirably focusing rape prosecution on the victim rather than on the conduct of the defendant. Responding to this concern, some jurisdictions have eliminated this traditional element and rather have redefined the offense in terms of the ***defendant's*** conduct. [18 Pa. Stat. Ann. §3121—rape consists of engaging in sexual intercourse with another "by forcible compulsion"; N.J. Stat. Ann. 2C:14-2c(1)—sexual assault defined as sexual penetration of another where the actor "uses physical force"] Under these statutes, courts are faced with a difficult task in defining what kind and degree of force an accused must have used to be guilty of the offense. Often courts are unable to define the required force without resort to the concept of consent, which the legislature seems to have eliminated as a part of the offense.

   a. **Example:** Under the Pennsylvania statute (above), proof that the defendant used only the force or effort necessary to complete the act of intercourse was not sufficient to show "forcible compulsion," although the victim said, "No," during the activity. Rape as defined in the statute requires force establishing lack of consent and inducement of the victim to submit without additional resistance. Thus, despite the efforts of the statute's reformers, the court reintroduced lack of consent as part of the definition of "forcible compulsion" which the defendant must be shown to have used. [Commonwealth v. Berkowitz, 641 A.2d 1161 (Pa. 1994)]

   b. **Example:** Under the New Jersey sexual assault statute (above), sexual assault requires no more force or effort by the accused than that required to accomplish sexual penetration ***but*** it also impliedly requires the absence of what a reasonable person would believe to be affirmative and freely-given permission by the victim. [State in the Interest of M.T.S., *supra,* §842]

D. FALSE IMPRISONMENT

1. **Definition:** [§877] Both at common law and under modern statutes, false imprisonment is the intentional unlawful confinement or restraint of another person. [Model Penal Code §212.3—restraining another so as to substantially interfere with his liberty]

2. **Actus Reus—Confinement:** [§878] The defendant must have compelled the victim to remain where he did not want to remain or go where he did not want to go. [People v. Agnew, 16 Cal. 2d 655 (1940)]

a. **Means used:** [§879] The confinement may, of course, be accomplished by actual physical restraint. However, the application of force is ***not*** essential; the confinement may also be accomplished by ***threats***. But in such cases, the victim must have been aware of the threats and have submitted to them. [Pike v. Hanson, 9 N.H. 491 (1838)]

b. **Compare—preventing person from proceeding:** [§880] It is not confinement simply to prevent a person from going in one direction, as long as the person may proceed in another direction and is aware of this opportunity. [Perkins and Boyce, 224]

3. **Mens Rea:** [§881] The weight of authority apparently requires that the defendant have ***intended to confine*** the victim. [Clark & Marshall, 746] However, the Model Penal Code departs from this position, requiring only that the restraints be ***"knowingly"*** accomplished. Thus, it would be sufficient if the defendant was aware that her conduct was practically certain to restrain another unlawfully. [Model Penal Code §212.3]

4. **Unlawful:** [§882] The confinement must have been "unlawful," meaning that there must have been ***no legal authority*** for the detention. Thus, for example, one who acts in situations creating a right to make an arrest (*see supra,* §§554 *et seq.*) is not guilty of false imprisonment.

5. **Punishment:** [§883] False imprisonment is a common law misdemeanor and generally remains such under modern statutes.

a. **Model Penal Code position:** [§884] The Model Penal Code makes false imprisonment a misdemeanor. However, if the restraint was effectuated under circumstances exposing the victim to a risk of serious bodily injury or involved holding the victim in a condition of involuntary servitude, the offense would be "felonious restraint," a felony. [Model Penal Code §§212.3—false imprisonment, 212.2—felonious restraint]

E. KIDNAPPING

1. **Common Law:** [§885] Common law kidnapping consists of the forcible abduction or stealing away of a person from his own country and sending him into another country. [4 Blackstone, Commentaries 219]

2. **Modern Statutes:** [§886] In virtually all jurisdictions, kidnapping has been substantially expanded beyond the common law definition. Thus, movement of the victim into another country is no longer required. Instead, modern kidnapping is generally regarded as a form of ***aggravated false imprisonment***, requiring the same unlawful restraint as does false imprisonment but also some aggravating characteristic.

a. **Confinement and movement (or asportation):** [§887] Kidnapping is frequently defined as including forcible movement of a person into another place. [*See, e.g.,* Cal. Penal Code §207] Under such statutes, the major issue concerns the amount and nature of movement required.

(1) **Any movement sufficient:** [§888] A number of courts have concluded that ***any movement*** is sufficient, reasoning that it is the fact and not the

distance of forcible removal that controls. [State v. Padilla, 474 P.2d 821 (Ariz. 1970); People v. Chessman, 38 Cal. 2d 166 (1951), *overruled in* People v. Daniels, 71 Cal. 2d 1119 (1969)]

(2) **Substantial movement necessary:** [§889] Other courts and statutes tend to require that the movement be ***substantial***, on the theory that otherwise, the defendant's behavior has not become sufficiently reprehensible to justify the heavy penalty attaching to kidnapping. [Model Penal Code §212.1—requiring movement of victim a substantial distance from vicinity where he was found]

(3) **Compare—relationship to other crimes:** [§890] The question of what movement or confinement is necessary for kidnapping is also raised by contentions that kidnapping must be defined so as to meaningfully distinguish it from what are often closely-related crimes, such as rape and robbery (*see infra*, §902).

b. **Confinement in secret place:** [§891] Kidnapping is often defined as including restraint of the victim in a secret place, *i.e.*, a place where he is unlikely to be found. [Tex. Penal Code §20.03]

c. **Confinement accomplished by deadly force:** [§892] In addition, some states punish a confinement of the victim that is accomplished by the use or threat of deadly force as kidnapping. [Tex. Penal Code §20.03]

d. **Confinement for extortion or ransom:** [§893] Abducting another for purposes of holding him for ransom or extortion is sometimes a kind of kidnapping. [Cal. Penal Code §209]

e. **Confinement for sexual abuse:** [§894] Sometimes kidnapping includes confinement of the victim for purposes of sexually abusing him. [Tex. Penal Code §20.04(a)(4)]

3. **Confinement—How Accomplished:** [§895] Kidnapping statutes differ as to how the detention or confinement must be accomplished:

a. **Force or threats:** [§896] Generally, a confinement or movement accomplished by force or threats of force is sufficient. [Tex. Penal Code §20.01(1)(A)]

b. **Deception:** [§897] Under some statutes, it is enough that the confinement or movement was accomplished by deception. [*But see* People v. Stephenson, 10 Cal. 3d 652 (1974)—deception not enough under statute defining crime as "forcibly" carrying away another]

c. **Minors and incompetents:** [§898] Some statutes provide that the mere ***persuading*** of a minor or incompetent to remain in one place or to move will suffice, despite the acquiescence of the victim, ***if*** the victim's parents have not acquiesced. [Tex. Penal Code §20.01(1)(B)]

d. **Subsequent restraint of initially willing victim:** [§899] If movement of the victim is required for kidnapping and the victim willingly accompanies the defendant, the crime is still committed if the defendant later uses force or threats and compels the victim to accompany the defendant further. But there must be some movement of the victim ***after*** the defendant has found it necessary to use force or threats. [People v. Camden, 16 Cal. 3d 808 (1976)]

4. **Mens Rea:** [§900] Case law does not clearly define the mens rea required for kidnapping. If compelled to address the issue, however, the courts are likely to require an actual intent to confine or move the victim.

   a. **Compare—specific intents required by statute:** [§901] Those statutes that define kidnapping as abduction for some specified purposes clearly require proof of a specific intent. [Tex. Penal Code §20.04(a)(1)—abduction with the intent to hold victim for ransom or reward]

5. **Relationship of Kidnapping to Other Crimes:** [§902] Kidnapping is sometimes defined simply as the forcible confinement or movement of the victim. However, in many instances such confinement or movement is merely ***incidental*** to the commission of another crime, such as robbery or rape. When this happens, is the defendant guilty of kidnapping as well as the robbery or rape?

   a. **Broader view—independent convictions allowed:** [§903] A literal application of the statutes would support liability for both crimes or either crime. Accordingly, some courts continue to permit conviction for kidnapping in these situations, regardless of whether the kidnapping was incidental to another offense. [State v. Jacobs, 380 P.2d 998 (Ariz. 1963)]

   b. **Modern trend—unusually high risk to victim required:** [§904] Many and perhaps most courts hold that in such situations, kidnapping is ***not*** committed unless the compelled detention or movement ***substantially increased the risk*** to the victim, beyond the risk always or generally created by the other crime. If no such movement or detention was involved, the defendant may be guilty of the underlying robbery or rape but not of kidnapping. [People v. Adams, 205 N.W.2d 415 (Mich. 1973); State v. Anthony, 817 S.W.2d 299 (Tenn. 1991)]

      (1) **Example:** D walks into a restaurant where X and Y are working, pulls a gun, and compels X and Y to go to another room in the back of the restaurant where D demands they open the safe. Upon being told the safe is in the front of the store, D directs X to remain in the back room and directs Y to the front of the store where D compels Y to open up the safe. X is clearly guilty of armed robbery. Kidnapping in this jurisdiction consists of confining or carrying away another. D also "technically" meets all requirements of kidnapping, since D confined X and carried away both X and Y. Under the modern trend, however, D is not guilty of kidnapping because the detention and movement of the victims were incidental to the commission of armed robbery and did not increase the risk of harm to the victim beyond what is involved in armed robbery. [State v. Anthony, *supra*]

6. **Punishment:** [§905] Kidnapping is generally a felony and was traditionally a capital crime. However, it is likely that courts today would find the death penalty disproportionately severe for the offense.

a. **"Simple" versus "aggravated" kidnapping:** [§906] Many states recognize a distinct crime of aggravated kidnapping and provide for a more severe penalty than would otherwise follow under the general kidnapping statute. [Cal. Penal Code §209—kidnapping for ransom, reward, extortion or robbery]

b. **Mitigating circumstances:** [§907] Some statutes authorize a ***reduced*** penalty if the defendant has released the victim in a safe condition. [Model Penal Code §212.1]

X. CRIMES AGAINST THE HABITATION

chapter approach

The traditional crimes of ***burglary*** and ***arson*** protect a citizen's security in the habitation. The common law crimes are rather limited in scope (*e.g.,* burglary could take place only in the nighttime), but modern statutes have expanded these crimes.

In answering questions involving possible habitation offenses, consider the following general issues. If your question has provided you with a statute, be sure to consider these issues in light of any statutory modification of the common law.

1. Was the structure or place one protected by the statutory or common law definition of the crimes? (Traditionally, it must be the ***dwelling of another***.)

2. Was there sufficient intrusion upon protected interests? (Traditionally, there must be an ***entry by breaking*** for burglary or a ***burning*** for arson.)

3. Was the intrusion made with the requisite intent? (Traditionally, this requires intent to ***commit a felony*** for burglary or ***malice*** for arson.)

A. BURGLARY

1. **Common Law:** [§908] At common law, burglary is the breaking and entering of the dwelling house of another in the nighttime with the intent to commit a felony. [4 Blackstone, Commentaries 224]

   a. **Entry:** [§909] There must be an ***actual*** or ***constructive entry*** into the structure.

      (1) **Entry of person:** [§910] The slightest intrusion into the structure by the defendant or some ***part of the defendant's body*** is sufficient. This is true whether the intrusion of a part of the defendant's body was for the purpose of actually committing the intended offense or only to gain entry. [Regina v. O'Brien, 4 Cox Crim. Cas. 400 (1850)]

      (2) **Entry of an instrument:** [§911] An "entry" is also accomplished by the defendant's insertion of a tool or other instrument into the structure, ***provided*** the purpose of the intrusion is ***to commit the intended felony***.

         (a) **Example:** D drills a hole into the floor of a grainery, intending to steal the grain by having it run through the hole into sacks below. As D completes the hole, the tip of the auger goes into the grainery. This is an entry of the grainery for purposes of burglary, since D inserted an instrument into the structure for the purpose of committing the intended felony. [Mattox v. State, 101 N.E. 1009 (Ind. 1913)]

         (b) **Compare—instrument used to gain entry:** [§912] If, on the other hand, the tool or instrument is inserted simply to enable the defendant himself to gain entry, this is ***not sufficient***. [Mattox v. State, *supra*] A few jurisdictions, however, make any entry by an instrument for any purpose sufficient. [People v. Moore, 131 Cal. App. 4th 489 (1994)]

(3) **"Constructive" entry by innocent agent:** [§913] A "constructive" entry occurs (and will suffice for burglary) where the defendant causes a person incapable of committing a criminal offense or who is under his control (*e.g.,* a child or insane person) to enter the structure to achieve his felonious purpose.

(4) **Note—entry of part of dwelling:** [§914] Although burglary is most often committed by entering the dwelling structure as a whole, the entry can also be made of a part of dwelling, as long as all the requirements for the offense are established.

b. **Breaking:** [§915] The entry must have been accomplished by a "breaking." This requires the use of ***actual or constructive force*** to create an ***opening*** of the structure ***by trespass***. [Perkins and Boyce, 246-247] (Note, however, that the creating of an opening of ***any closed part*** of the structure will suffice; *see infra*, §928.)

(1) **Use of force to create opening:** [§916] It is sufficient for a breaking that the defendant used force—albeit only a small amount of force—to create an opening where none previously existed. Thus, it is a "breaking" to push open a closed but unlatched door.

(2) **Compare—use of force to enlarge existing opening:** [§917] Traditionally, the application of force to ***enlarge*** an already existing opening—as by further pushing open a door that is already open—would ***not*** suffice. *But note:* A number of courts now hold to the contrary. [State v. Sorenson, 138 N.W. 411 (Iowa 1912); LaFave and Scott, 793]

(3) **"Constructive" force:** [§918] Several situations involve "constructive" force and therefore constitute a "breaking":

(a) Obtaining entry ***by fraud***;

(b) Obtaining entry ***by threatening the use of force***;

(c) Entering ***through a chimney***; and

(d) Obtaining entry by ***having a servant or some other co-conspirator within the structure open the door***. [Clarke v. Commonwealth, 66 Va. 908 (1874)]

(4) **Compare—breaking to leave:** [§919] There is dispute as to whether burglary is committed if the defendant does not use force to enter the structure but effectuates a breaking in order to leave. Most courts, however, hold that this is ***not*** burglary. [Rolland v. Commonwealth, 82 Pa. 306 (1876)]

(5) **Requirement of trespass—effect of consent to enter:** [§920] The breaking for purposes of burglary must be ***trespassory*** (*i.e.*, without the occupant's authority). Therefore, one who has permission to enter is not guilty of burglary. [Smith v. State, 362 P.2d 1071 (Alaska 1961)]

(a) **Example:** D opens the door of a store and enters during regular business hours with the intent to rob the storekeeper. There is no breaking and hence no burglary; as a member of the public, D has entered with consent. [State v. Stephens, 91 So. 349 (La. 1922)]

(b) **Limitation—scope of consent:** [§921] The scope of any purported consent to enter must be examined: The defendant must have had authority to be on the premises ***at the time*** in question and in the ***particular part*** of the premises he entered. [State v. Corcoran, 143 P. 453 (Wash. 1914)]

1) **Example:** If A provides D with a key to A's house and gives D the ***unrestricted*** right to enter, D is not guilty of burglary even if he uses the key to gain entry for purposes of stealing A's jewels. However, D would be guilty of burglary if A had authorized D to enter only during the daytime and D actually entered at night. [State v. Corcoran, *supra*]

(6) **Causal relationship between breaking and entry:** [§922] The breaking must be the means by which the entry is accomplished. [Regina v. Davis, 6 Cox Crim. Cas. 369 (1854)]

(a) **Example:** D opened a window to X's house, intending to crawl through, but D then noticed an open door and entered through the door. D is not guilty of burglary, because the breaking (*i.e.,* the opening of the window) was not the means by which the entry was ultimately accomplished. [Regina v. Davis, *supra*]

c. **Dwelling house:** [§923] The structure entered must be a dwelling, which means a place ***regularly used to sleep***. [*Ex parte* Vincent, 26 Ala. 145 (1855)]

(1) **Use for other purposes:** [§924] As long as the building is used to sleep in on a regular basis, the fact that it is also used for business or other purposes will not prevent it from being a dwelling. [State v. Hudson, 430 P.2d 386 (N.M. 1967)]

(2) **Yet unoccupied structures:** [§925] A structure intended for use as a residence, but which is not yet occupied as such, is ***not*** a dwelling—even if a guard sleeps there to protect it. [Fuller's Case, 1 Leech's Cr. Cas. 186 (1782)]

(3) **Temporary absence of resident:** [§926] On the other hand, a structure used as a dwelling remains such despite the ***temporary absence*** of those living in it (*e.g.,* summer cottage burglarized in winter). However, it ceases to be a dwelling if the residents ***permanently leave***. [Henderson v. State, 86 So. 439 (Fla. 1920)]

(4) **Other buildings within "curtilage":** [§927] Buildings not used as living quarters but which are within the fenced-in area known as the "curtilage" are regarded as dwellings. Thus, barns, stables, garages, and similar structures can be the subject of a burglary.

(a) **But note:** Merely breaking and entering the fenced-in area is not burglary; there must be a breaking into a ***structure*** within the curtilage.

(5) **Entry of closed parts of a dwelling:** [§928] Burglary does not require an entry into the structure itself by breaking. A breaking and entry of any closed part of the structure (such as a room, closet, or wall safe) is sufficient. However, the area entered must be ***part of the structure***. Consequently, entry into a trunk within the dwelling is not enough. [Allen v. State, 231 P. 96 (Okla. 1924)]

(a) **Example:** D enters X's house without any intent to commit a crime therein. Once inside, however, D remembers that X keeps money in the refrigerator and decides to steal it. D opens the refrigerator to commit the larceny and inserts his hand. D probably has not committed burglary, because the refrigerator he entered with intent to commit larceny was not a part of the dwelling structure. If the refrigerator were constructed as a part of the structure (*i.e.*, a built-in), D would be guilty of burglary. [Allen v. State, *supra*]

d. **Of another:** [§929] The structure must be the dwelling of another person. [Clarke v. Commonwealth, 66 Va. 908 (1874)]

(1) **Right of habitation determinative:** [§930] The ***right of habitation*** rather than ownership or title controls whose dwelling a structure is. Thus, a landlord can commit burglary in a house or apartment that she owns but has leased to another to use as a residence, because the house or apartment is the dwelling of the tenant and not of the landlord. [White v. State, 49 Ala. 344 (1873)]

(2) **Premises occupied by defendant and another:** [§931] If the defendant jointly occupies the premises with others, the defendant cannot commit burglary by entering the jointly-occupied premises because the premises are his own dwelling. [People v. Gauze, 15 Cal. 3d 709 (1975)] An argument can be made, however, that this position ignores the legitimate interests of others who occupy the premises.

(a) **Example:** D and X share a dwelling. If D enters the structure by force to steal X's money, there is no burglary. Nor would Y, a third person, be guilty of burglary if he entered by force for the same purpose, if he was authorized by D to enter. [McCreary v. State, 212 P. 336 (Ariz. 1923); People v. Gauze, *supra*]

(b) **Compare:** A court order has been issued giving X exclusive possession of the joint dwelling of D and X. D enters by breaking with the requisite intent. D commits burglary, because the premises are the dwelling of X even if title to those premises is in D's name. [*Ex parte* Davis, 542 S.W.2d 192 (Tex. 1976)]

(3) **But note—part of premises may constitute dwelling of another:** [§932] Premises that are jointly occupied may be separated so that some parts are the dwelling of one occupant and other parts are the dwelling of the other. In such cases, one occupant can commit burglary by entering those parts of the structure that constitute the dwelling of the other. [State v. Rio, 230 P.2d 308 (Wash. 1951)]

(a) **Example:** X hired D to work on his farm and permitted D to live in X's house. D did not, however, have access to X's bedroom. D entered X's bedroom intending to commit felony assault on X. D committed burglary by entering a part of the house that was the dwelling of another and not his own dwelling. [State v. Rio, *supra*]

e. **In the nighttime:** [§933] The breaking and entry must occur in the nighttime. [4 Blackstone, Commentaries 224]

(1) **"Nighttime" defined:** [§934] "Nighttime" is the period when the countenance of a person cannot be discerned by natural sunlight. [Blackstone, *supra*]

(2) **Breaking and entering on different nights:** [§935] Although there must be a causal relationship between the breaking and entering (*supra*, §922), they do not have to occur on the same night. Thus, the breaking can be made on one night and the entry (made possible by the breaking) the next. [1 Hale, Pleas of the Crown 551 (1778)]

f. **With the intent to commit a felony:** [§936] At the ***time of the entry***, the defendant must ***intend to commit a felony*** within the structure. There is no burglary if the felonious intent is formed ***after*** the entry is completed. [People v. Hill, 67 Cal. 2d 105 (1967)]

(1) **Intent to commit misdemeanor not sufficient:** [§937] The intent must be to commit a crime that is presently a felony under the governing law. An intent to commit a misdemeanor will not support a burglary conviction. [Commonwealth v. Newell, 7 Mass. 245 (1810)]

(2) **Actual commission of felony not required:** [§938] All that is required is the felonious ***intent***. Thus the defendant need not complete his plan to commit a felony. In this sense, then, burglary is a "preparatory crime" similar to attempt.

(3) **Abandonment of intent irrelevant:** [§939] Abandonment of the plan once entry is obtained will not prevent conviction for burglary. The crime is ***complete at the moment entry is made with the requisite intent***.

(4) **"Within" the structure:** [§940] The traditional definition of burglary requires an intent to commit a felony "in" the structure entered. However, even where the felony was not to be committed in the structure itself, courts have sometimes held it sufficient that the defendant intended the entry to be an important part of his felonious scheme. [*See* People v. Wright, 206 Cal. App. 2d 184 (1945)—intent to commit felony in vicinity of place entered sufficient for burglary if entry was made to facilitate commission of the crime; entry into one structure with intent to commit

felony in another structure sufficient if two structures were so closely connected that entry into one and commission of the crime in the other would constitute a practically continuous transaction]

(a) **Example:** D entered a dwelling of another with the intent to take a child to the roof and there commit the felony of child molesting. D was guilty of burglary, although he did not literally intend to commit a felony "in" the dwelling. His plan required him to pass through the dwelling to reach the situs of the intended crime; therefore, the place of entry and situs of felonious intent were sufficiently connected to support a burglary conviction. [People v. Shields, 70 Cal. App. 2d 628 (1962)]

2. **Modern Statutes:** [§941] Modern statutes have significantly modified common law burglary. [Model Penal Code §221.1; Cal. Penal Code §459] The following changes are typical:

a. **Breaking not required:** [§942] Often the requirement that the entry be accomplished by a breaking is eliminated. As a result, ***any entry***—however accomplished—is sufficient. [Model Penal Code §221.1(1); Cal. Penal Code §459]

(1) **Compare—entry must be unlawful or without consent:** [§943] Modern statutes dispensing with the need for a breaking often explicitly or implicitly require that the entry be "unlawful" or at least without consent. [LaFave and Scott, 794]

(2) **Premises open to the public:** [§944] Under modern statutes, the requirement that entry be without consent often means that burglary is not committed by entry of premises, such as a store, that are at the time open to the public. [Model Penal Code §221.1(1)] Some courts, however, reason that one who enters such premises concealing his criminal purpose engages in deception that nullifies the consent. Thus entry of a store open to the public can constitute burglary. [People v. Barry, 94 Cal. 481 (1892)]

b. **Structure need not be dwelling:** [§945] Many structures ***other than dwellings*** can often be the subject of a burglary. Some statutes also extend the crime to entry of motor vehicles and sometimes to other things.

(1) **Examples:** Under the Model Penal Code, entry of any building would be burglary if the other requirements are met. [Model Penal Code §221.1(1)] The California Penal Code covers entry of a house, room, apartment, tenement, shop, warehouse, store, mill, barn, stable, outhouse or other building, tent, vessel, floating home, railroad car, cargo container, trailer coach, house car, inhabited camper, vehicle (if doors are locked), aircraft, or mine. [Cal. Penal Code §459]

(2) **But note—different punishment:** [§946] Burglary of a dwelling or its equivalent is often made punishable by a more severe penalty than other burglaries. [Cal. Penal Code §461—burglary of inhabited dwelling or portion of building is burglary of first degree]

c. **Time of entry irrelevant:** [§947] Modern statutes typically dispense with the requirement that the breaking and entry be in the nighttime. [Model Penal Code §221.1(1); Cal. Penal Code §459]

(1) **But note—different punishment:** [§948] Burglary in the nighttime is sometimes punished more severely than other burglary. [Conn. Penal Code §53a-102]

(2) **Redefinition of nighttime:** [§949] Modern codes distinguishing between burglary in the daytime and burglary in the nighttime often define nighttime in relationship to sunrise and sunset. [Conn. Penal Code §53a-100(a)(3)—night is period between 30 minutes after sunset and 30 minutes before sunrise]

d. **Intent to commit misdemeanor sufficient:** [§950] The intent element of burglary is frequently broadened to include certain offenses that are not felonies. Thus, statutory schemes often require an intent to commit a felony ***or any theft*** (whether felony theft or not). [Cal. Penal Code §459—"with intent to commit grand or petit larceny or any felony"] The Model Penal Code would go further and require only an intent to commit ***any crime***. [Model Penal Code §221.1]

e. **Punishment:** [§951] Burglary is a common law felony and remains such in most (if not all) jurisdictions. However, statutes commonly divide burglary into ***degrees***, and authorize more severe penalties for one degree than the other. [Cal. Penal Code §460]

(1) **"Aggravated" or "first degree" burglary:** [§952] Those burglaries included within the more severely punishable degree often include:

(a) Burglary of an ***inhabited dwelling*** [Cal. Penal Code §460];

(b) Burglary while ***armed with a deadly weapon*** [Model Penal Code §221.1(2)(b)]; or

(c) Burglaries involving ***assault*** upon a person [Model Penal Code §221.1(2)].

(2) **Conviction for both burglary and intended crime:** [§953] Under generally applicable rules, if the defendant successfully completes the crime that he intended to commit at the time of entry, he can be convicted and punished for ***both*** the burglary and the target crime (*see supra,* §§61 *et seq.*). The Model Penal Code, however, would bar conviction for both crimes unless the target offense was an extremely serious one. [Model Penal Code §221.1(3)]

B. ARSON

1. **Common Law:** [§954] At common law, arson is the malicious burning of the dwelling house of another. [Perkins and Boyce, 273-274]

a. **Dwelling house:** [§955] The structure burned must be a dwelling house. The definition of "dwelling house" in the context of burglary applies to the crime of arson as well. (*See supra,* §§923-928.)

b. **Of another:** [§956] As in burglary, the dwelling house must be that of another. Again, it is the ***right to possession*** rather than ownership that controls. Thus, a landlord's burning of her own structure is arson if the tenant was entitled to use it as a residence. [Harris' Case, 168 Eng. Rep. 56 (1753)]

(1) **Compare—misdemeanor of "houseburning":** [§957] One who intentionally burns her own dwelling commits the common law misdemeanor of "houseburning" if the house is located in a city or town or sufficiently close to other houses to create a risk of their burning. [Rex v. Holmes, 2 East P.C. 1022 (1634)]

c. **Burning:** [§958] There must be an actual "burning" of some part of the structure.

(1) **Definition of burning:** [§959] "Burning" requires some consuming ***by fire*** of the material from which the structure is made. ***But note:*** It is not necessary that the structure be destroyed or even seriously damaged.

(2) **Dwelling must be burned:** [§960] The burning must involve some ***part of the dwelling structure***. Arson is not committed by burning something—such as personal property—inside of a dwelling.

(3) **Scorching versus charring:** [§961] Some combustible part of the structure must have been at least ***charred***. Thus there need not be an open flame or "blaze." However, mere discoloration by heat (a "scorching") or blackening by smoke is ***not*** sufficient. [State v. Hall, 93 N.C. 571 (1885)]

(a) **Example:** D sets fire to a chest of drawers in B's house, but the only damage to the structure itself is a blackening of the ceiling from smoke. D is not guilty of arson. There has been no "burning" of a part of the structure. The burning of the chest, which is not a part of the dwelling, is not arson, and the ceiling, which is a part of dwelling, was not burned.

(4) **Damage by explosion not sufficient:** [§962] Common law arson is not committed if the only damage to the dwelling is that done by an explosion. If the explosion causes a fire which in turn "burns" a part of the structure, however, the crime is committed. [State v. Landers, 47 S.W. 100 (Tex. 1898)]

d. **Mens rea—malice:** [§963] The mens rea required for arson is "malice." However, this does not require ill will towards the occupant or the structure itself. Rather, malice exists if the defendant (i) ***intended to burn*** the structure; (ii) ***knew*** that it would burn; or (iii) intentionally and without justification or excuse created an ***obvious fire hazard*** to the structure. [Perkins and Boyce, 274-277]

(1) **Negligence not sufficient:** [§964] A burning caused by mere negligence is not common law arson. [Morris v. State, 27 So. 336 (Ala. 1900)]

(2) **Commission of crime not sufficient:** [§965] No arson is committed where a building is accidentally burned during the commission of a crime; *i.e.,* there is no "felony arson" rule analogous to the felony murder rule. [Regina v. Faulkner, 13 Cox Crim. Cas. 550 (1877)]

(3) **High risk created by burning own dwelling:** [§966] If a person sets fire to her own dwelling and this creates a high risk that other residences will catch fire, she is guilty of arson if one of them does. This person has acted with the third type of malice above (*see supra,* §963). [Isaac's Case, 2 East P.C. 1031 (1799)]

2. **Modern Statutes:** [§967] Modern statutes tend to expand the common law crime of arson. [Model Penal Code §220.1; Cal. Penal Code §451] Common modifications are as follows:

a. **Structures other than dwellings:** [§968] The burning of many structures other than dwellings is often punished as arson, and some statutes expand the offense to cover property other than structures. [Model Penal Code §220.1(1)(a)—"building or occupied structure"; Cal. Penal Code §450—any structure, forest land, or property]

b. **Ownership and occupancy:** [§969] Modern arson statutes sometimes prohibit burning of structures without regard to ownership or occupancy. Thus the offense can be committed by burning a structure that the ***defendant*** owns and occupies. [Cal. Penal Code §451—burning of structure or property made arson without regard to ownership or identity of inhabitants]

(1) **Limitation—state of mind required:** [§970] The effect of this expansion of the crime of arson is limited by the requirement of a state of mind. Burning one's own structure or dwelling is unlikely to be arson under these modern statutes if the defendant was unaware of any risk to others created by her actions. [Brown v. State, 403 A.2d 788 (Md. 1979)]

c. **"Burning" not required:** [§971] The problems associated with the common law concept of "burning" are eliminated under some statutory schemes that simply require that the defendant start a fire ***with the intent of damaging or destroying the structure*** concerned. [Model. Penal Code §220.1(1)—starting a fire with the purpose of destroying a building or occupied structure of another]

d. **Explosion sufficient:** [§972] Arson statutes are often expanded to cover damage done—or the risk created—by explosion as well as by fire. [Model Penal Code §220.1(1)—starting a fire or causing an explosion with necessary intent; Tex. Penal Code §28.02]

e. **Personal property of another:** [§973] Some states have even broadened the crime to include the burning of another's ***personal property***, although this is generally punishable by a less severe penalty than arson involving a structure. [Cal. Penal Code §450]

f. **Arson with intent to defraud insurer:** [§974] The burning of property ***with intent to defraud an insurer*** (*i.e.*, an intentional burning for the purpose of collecting insurance by misrepresenting that the damage was caused by someone else) is frequently made a separate (but related) crime. Some statutes go even further, prohibiting the ***starting*** of a fire with the intent to damage property and collect the insurance on it. [Cal. Penal Code §451(d)—burning of property not inhabited or personal property owned by defendant is arson if done with intent to defraud; Tex. Penal Code §28.02(a)(2)(B)—starting fire with intent to damage building knowing it is insured]

3. **Punishment:** [§975] Arson is a common law felony and remains a felony by statute in virtually all jurisdictions.

XI. CRIMES AGAINST PROPERTY—ACQUISITION OFFENSES

chapter approach

An examination question involving a possible wrongful appropriation of property by a defendant will be governed either by a modern theft statute or by the traditional property offenses. If the question does not include an applicable theft statute or otherwise refer you to the modern crime of theft, you should consider the following questions to determine whether the appropriation constitutes one of the traditional property offenses:

1. Begin by asking whether the defendant has committed ***larceny*** (*i.e.*, the trespassory taking and asportation of the personal property of another with the intent to permanently deprive the owner of possession).

2. At the time of the wrongful acquisition of the property, was it arguable that the defendant was already in possession of the property? (Consider ***embezzlement***.)

3. Is it arguable that the property was obtained with permission of the victim but that this permission was obtained by misrepresentations? (Consider ***false pretenses*** as well as ***larceny by trick***.)

4. Is it arguable that the defendant obtained the property by means of force or threats? (Consider ***robbery*** and perhaps ***extortion***.)

Note that if the question includes reference to a statutorily defined offense of ***theft***, it is likely that many of these traditionally different offenses will be lumped together in the definition of that offense.

A. INTRODUCTION

1. **Distinctions Between Offenses:** [§976] The basic crimes against property are those involving a ***wrongful acquisition*** of property. At common law, the "acquisition offenses" have detailed technical requirements which reflect a begrudging expansion of the crimes by the early courts to cover more and more situations. The important distinctions between the offenses can be summarized as follows:

   a. **Larceny:** The wrongful ***taking*** of property ***from the possession of another*** person who has a superior right to its possession, with the ***intent to permanently deprive***.

   b. **Embezzlement:** A ***misappropriation*** of property by a person who ***already has it*** in his possession, with intent to defraud.

   c. **False pretenses:** Distinguishable from larceny in that the perpetrator obtains ***title and possession*** from another by means of ***deception***. (But note that the taking for purposes of larceny can also be rendered wrongful if accomplished by deception.)

gilbert LAW SUMMARIES

SUMMARY OF CRIMES AGAINST PROPERTY

Property Offense	Act	Intent	Title
Larceny	wrongful ***taking*** of property ***from the possession of another***	intent to ***permanently deprive*** owner of possession	title remains with the owner
Embezzlement	***misappropriation*** of property by a person ***already in possession*** of the property	intent ***to defraud*** the owner of ownership	title remains with the owner
False Pretenses	wrongful taking of ***title*** to property ***by misrepresentation*** to the owner	***knowledge of falsity*** of the misrepresentation ***and*** intent ***to defraud*** owner	the owner transfers title to the perpetrator
Robbery	wrongful taking of property ***from victim's person or presence by violence or intimidation***	intent to ***permanently deprive*** owner of possession	title remains with the owner
Extortion	obtaining or attempting to obtain property ***by threats*** not sufficient to constitute robbery	intent ***to obtain property*** through wrongful threats	title may remain with owner or be transferred (most states do not even require possession to pass)
Receipt of Stolen Property	***acceptance*** of property after it has wrongfully been taken from another	intent ***to deprive*** owner of property ***known to be stolen***	title remains with the owner

d. **Robbery:** Larceny ***from the victim's person or presence*** where the taking is accomplished ***by force or threats***.

e. **Extortion:** Obtaining or attempting to obtain property from the victim by ***threats not sufficient to constitute robbery***.

f. **Receipt of stolen property:** The ***acceptance*** of property after the larceny by which it was acquired has been completed.

2. **Modern Statutes—Theft:** [§977] In modern criminal codes, a single offense is often created that includes what previously was larceny, embezzlement, false pretenses, receipt of stolen property, and sometimes other offenses (such as extortion). This offense is generally labeled ***theft***. [Model Penal Code §223.1]

B. LARCENY

1. **Elements:** [§978] Larceny is primarily an infringement of another's ***possessory*** interest in property. The elements of the offense are:

a. A ***trespassory***

b. ***Taking*** (or "caption") and

c. ***Asportation*** (carrying away) of

d. The ***personal property***

e. ***Of another***

f. With the ***intent to permanently deprive*** the owner of possession of the property.

2. **Subject Matter of Larceny—Personal Property:** [§979] Only ***tangible personal property*** (*i.e.,* goods and chattels) can be the subject of larceny.

a. **Realty and fixtures:** [§980] As a general rule, neither realty nor fixtures (*i.e.,* items permanently affixed to the land) are within the scope of larceny. [State v. Jackson, 11 S.E.2d 149 (N.C. 1940)—tombstone]

(1) **Compare—severed fixtures:** [§981] However, once fixtures, crops, or minerals are ***severed*** from the realty, they become personal property and can be the subject of larceny—***provided*** they come into the possession of the landowner and are then taken from his possession. Severed items come into the possession of the landowner if the defendant relinquishes possession of them after they are severed and while they are still on the land. [State v. Jackson, *supra*]

(a) **Example:** D dug up five pounds of potatoes from L's garden and placed them in a pile. D then dug up another five pounds but placed them in a sack as he removed them from the ground and carried the sack away as soon as it was full. Later, D returned and took the first five pounds of potatoes. D is guilty of larceny only of the ***first five pounds***. Although these potatoes were initially part of the realty, D severed them and left them on the property long enough that they came into the possession of the owner prior to D's taking and asportation of them. But since his severance and asportation of the second five pounds were part of the ***same act***, those potatoes were never in the possession of the owner, and their removal, therefore, could not be larceny. [Bell v. State, 63 Tenn. 426 (1874)]

b. **Animals:** [§982] Whether animals can be the subject of larceny requires that several distinctions be drawn.

(1) **Domestic versus "base" animals:** [§983] Livestock and animals of domestic value (horse, pig, chicken, and the like) can be the subject of larceny. On the other hand, "base animals" (*i.e.,* household pets) cannot be.

(2) **Wild animals:** [§984] Wild animals are not considered to be the property of anyone and thus cannot be the subject of larceny. If, however, a wild animal is killed or captured, it is treated in the same fashion as a severed fixture—the animal becomes personal property. If it remains on the property long enough to come into the possession of the landowner, taking it can be larceny; if it is killed (or captured) and removed in the same continuous transaction, however, there is no larceny, as the landowner never came into possession. [Regina v. Townly, 12 Cox Crim. Cas. 59 (1871)]

c. **Intangible property:** [§985] Intangible personal property cannot be the subject of larceny. Documents, records, and choses in action are regarded as being merged into the thing they represent, and therefore are not "property" themselves. [People v. Caridis, 29 Cal. App. 166 (1915)]

d. **Services:** [§986] Services are clearly not property. Thus, the wrongful acquisition of the benefits of one's services (*e.g.*, a train ride, a night's lodging, or theater admission) is not larceny. [Chappell v. United States, 270 F.2d 274 (9th Cir. 1959)]

e. **Electricity:** [§987] Under the common law definition, it is questionable whether electricity is sufficiently tangible to be "taken," and therefore it might not be the subject of larceny. Nevertheless, courts tend to hold that larceny is committed when electrical power is "taken," as when it is diverted by improperly hooking up to a transmission line. [People v. Menagas, 11 N.E.2d 403 (Ill. 1937)]

f. **Stolen property and contraband:** [§988] Since larceny is a crime against possession (rather than title), stolen property and contraband can be the subject of larceny. [People *ex rel.* Koons v. Elling, 190 Misc. 998 (1948)]

g. **Compare—modern statutes:** [§989] Statutes often broaden the scope of property that can be the subject of larceny or theft.

(1) **Real property:** [§990] It may be theft to unlawfully transfer real property (or an interest therein) with the requisite intent, and it is now commonly theft to take fixtures, crops, or similar items. [Model Penal

Code §223.2(2)—theft of "immovable property"; Cal. Penal Code §469—specifically incorporating into theft offenses the removal of fixtures and things attached to realty]

(2) **Intangible property:** [§991] Likewise, intangible property (such as documents or records) is frequently brought within the purview of modern theft or larceny statutes. [Tex. Penal Code §§31.01(5)(B)—property includes intangible personal property and anything severed from land, 31.01(5)(C)—property includes a document presenting or embodying anything of value]

(a) **Contents of documents:** [§992] It is arguably theft under some statutes to take the contents of documents, as by copying them. [State v. Telek, 216 A.2d 242 (N.J. 1966)]

(3) **Services:** [§993] Additionally, it may also be theft to wrongfully acquire the advantages of another's services. [Model Penal Code §223.7; Tex. Penal Code §31.04—separate offense of theft of services]

(4) **Gas:** [§994] Whether natural gas can be the subject of common law larceny is uncertain. But it has been held to constitute "property" under a modern larceny statute. [People v. Neiss, 73 App. Div. 2d 938 (1980)]

h. **Computer-related issues:** [§995] Misappropriation of the new types of "property" created by computers gives rise to special problems.

(1) **Not covered by larceny or theft:** [§996] A computer program may not be the subject of larceny or theft. [Hancock v. State, 402 S.W.2d 906 (Tex. 1966)] Unauthorized use of a computer may not be larceny under a statute that defines the crime as taking any "thing of value." [Lund v. Commonwealth, 232 S.E.2d 745 (Va. 1977)]

(2) **Modern trend—property crimes cover computer-related "property":** [§997] In some jurisdictions the protection of larceny or theft has been expanded to such property. [*See* Mass. Gen. Laws Ann. ch. 266, §30(2)—property that can be the subject of larceny includes "electronically processed or stored data, either tangible or intangible" and "data while in transit"]

3. **Asportation:** [§998] Larceny requires that the property be ***"carried away."*** This is the requirement of asportation.

a. **Slightest movement sufficient if part of "carrying away":** [§999] All that is required for asportation is the ***slightest movement***. But this movement must be ***part of the process of carrying away*** the property; movement as part of preparation to begin carrying away will not suffice.

(1) **Example:** D intended to steal a barrel of turpentine. D turned the barrel over from its head to its side, but before he could roll it off, he was apprehended. No "carrying away" movement of the barrel had occurred; D had merely changed the barrel's position. D is therefore not guilty of larceny. [State v. Jones, 65 N.C. 395 (1871)] But if he had rolled it a few inches, he would have asported it.

b. **Modern statutes:** [§1000] Modern statutes that make larceny one type of theft (*see infra,* §§1149 *et seq.*) often dispense with the requirement of asportation entirely. [*See* Model Penal Code §223.2(1)—requiring only a "taking" or "exercise of control" over property; Tex. Penal Code §31.03(a)]

4. **Taking:** [§1001] The defendant must have completed a taking, or "caption," of the property. This means that the defendant must have acquired ***dominion and control*** (*i.e.*, possession) over the property. [Thompson v. State, 10 So. 520 (Ala. 1892)]

   a. **Compare—asportation:** [§1002] Usually, the movement that suffices for asportation will also show sufficient dominion and control to also establish the taking necessary. This is not always the case, however.

   b. **Means of caption:** [§1003] The caption can be effected by the defendant directly or by an innocent agent. A defendant may therefore commit larceny by causing possession to be taken by another. [Smith v. State, 74 S.E. 1093 (Ga. 1912)]

      (1) **Example:** D wrongfully sells V's bicycle to X, and X rides it away thinking he has bought it from the true owner. D is guilty of larceny. Having caused X to take possession of the bicycle, D is no less guilty than he would have been had he ridden it away himself with the intent to sell it later. [Smith v. State, *supra*]

   c. **Modern statutes:** [§1004] Modern statutes often define larceny-type crimes in terms of a "taking," an "appropriation," or an "exercise of control" over the property. Accordingly, it is likely that the traditional common law analysis regarding a "caption" will still be applied. [Model Penal Code §223.2(1); Tex. Penal Code §§31.01(4), 31.03(a)—theft consists of appropriation, defined as exercising control over property]

5. **Requirement of a "Trespass":** [§1005] Larceny requires that the taking be ***trespassory***, *i.e.*, wrongful. [State v. Lewis, 433 P.2d 617 (Or. 1967)]

   a. **Taking without consent:** [§1006] The taking is trespassory if it is without the consent of the victim. Thus, if the person from whom possession of the property is acquired acquiesces in the taking, there is ordinarily no larceny. [Perkins and Boyce, 303-304]

   b. **Taking with consent induced by deception—"larceny by trick":** [§1007] A taking with the victim's permission can be sufficient for larceny if the permission is obtained by deception. The courts reason that, in light of the fraud or deception, the victim retains constructive possession of the property and the defendant therefore misappropriates it from that possession. Larceny committed in this fashion is traditionally called "larceny by trick." [Hufstetler v. State, 63 So. 2d 730 (Ala. 1953)]

      (1) **Fraud required—past or present fact:** [§1008] It is often stated that larceny by trick (as well as false pretenses) requires a misrepresentation concerning a ***past or present fact***. Under this view, a false promise (which is a misrepresentation of a "future fact") will not suffice. *But*

note: There is some authority, however, for the proposition that a false promise can give rise to larceny by trick, if the prosecution shows that in making the promise the defendant misrepresented his present intent to carry out the promise—a matter of "present fact." [People v. Miller, 169 N.Y. 339 (1902)]

(a) **Example:** In a leading English case, D asked V for V's horse, saying that he wanted to borrow it for the day and promising to return it that evening. Actually, D intended to keep the horse permanently. V consented to D's taking the horse. The fact that D obtained the horse by means of a promise he did not keep would ***not*** be enough to establish the fraud required to make his taking of the horse larceny. In this case, the court found larceny was proved but on a very narrow ground: It held that D obtained the horse by misrepresenting his intentions for use of the horse, a present fact. [Rex v. Pear, 168 Eng. Rep. 208 (1779)] Some courts, inclined to define the crime more broadly, would find larceny on a different and broader ground—that D obtained the horse by means of a promise that he misrepresented he intended to keep, and this would be a sufficient misrepresentation of present fact for larceny.

1) **But note:** If at the time D promised to return the horse, he actually meant to do so, the mere failure of D to keep his promise would not make his actions larceny.

(2) **Consent to taking for purposes of a trap:** [§1009] In some situations, the owner of the property anticipates the defendant's actions and is aware of the defendant's taking of the property. Even so it is generally held that this awareness and passive acquiescence in the defendant's action does not constitute consent; the defendant's conduct is still larceny. [Smith v. United States, 291 F.2d 220 (9th Cir. 1961)] However, some cases hold that there is no larceny if the owner or an employee acting on his order goes so far as to actually hand the property over to the defendant. [Topolewski v. State, 109 N.W. 1037 (Wis. 1906)]

(3) **Limitation—defendant must obtain possession only:** [§1010] Larceny by trick is committed only if the defendant uses deception to obtain ***possession***. If title is also obtained, the crime may be false pretenses (*see infra,* §1071]), but it is not larceny. [People v. Ashley, 42 Cal. 2d 246 (1954)]

c. **"Shoplifting":** [§1011] Determining whether the taking, asportation, and trespass required for larceny occur in a shoplifting context presents special problems. Some handling of the items by customers is with the owner's consent. But a shoplifter can complete larceny without actually leaving the store with the merchandise. This can be done if the shoplifter conceals the item and perhaps moves towards an exit, so as to move the property (thus ***asporting*** it) and exercise control over it that is inconsistent with the owner's rights (thus ***taking*** it) and clearly beyond what the owner has authorized customers to do (thus acting in a ***trespassory*** manner). The intent to steal (*see infra,* §§1023 *et seq.*) must of course exist as well. [People v. Olivo, 52 N.Y.2d 309 (1981)]

d. **Modern statutes:** [§1012] Modern statutes typically define theft as requiring that the defendant exercise ***unlawful*** control over the property and define "unlawful" as including without effective consent. Deception renders consent ineffective. [Tex. Penal Code §§31.01(3), 31.03]

(1) **False promises sufficient:** [§1013] If a defendant obtained property by making a promise that ***at the time*** he did ***not*** intend to keep, his exercise of control over the property will generally be considered unlawful and will constitute theft.

(2) **Compare—unkept promise:** [§1014] If a defendant obtained property by making a promise that at the time he intended to keep, his exercise of control over the property does not become theft simply because he ***later*** failed to keep the promise. Moreover, a failure to keep a promise by itself will not permit the inference that the defendant intended at the time the promise was made not to keep it. [Model Penal Code §223.3(1)]

(3) **"Possession/title" distinction irrelevant:** [§1015] Under modern statutes, the false pretenses-larceny by trick distinction is ***abolished***, and whether the defendant obtained possession or title is therefore irrelevant.

6. **"Of Another":** [§1016] The property involved must be that of another. However, since larceny is basically a crime against possession this means only that the defendant must have taken the property from the possession of another person who had a ***right to possession superior to that of the defendant***. [Perkins and Boyce, 296-298]

a. **Larceny by owner's taking from another:** [§1017] Thus, a person can commit larceny by taking her ***own*** property from the possession of someone else who has a superior right to possession. [State v. Cohen, 263 N.W. 922 (Minn. 1935)]

(1) **Example:** D takes her coat to X for alterations. X does the work and thereby acquires a possessory lien on the coat to secure his right of payment. D then takes the coat with the intent to deprive X of his interest. D is guilty of larceny; the property was that "of another" (X as a lienholder) although title to it is in D. [State v. Cohen, *supra*]

b. **"Possession" versus "custody":** [§1018] There is ***no larceny*** where the defendant had ***possession*** at the time of the misappropriation (although the defendant may be guilty of embezzlement; *see infra*, §1055). On the other hand, there may well be a larceny if the defendant simply had custody. Thus, the distinction between custody and possession is crucial.

(1) **Possession requires significant authority:** [§1019] Ordinarily, the issue is a factual one and turns on the amount of control vested in the defendant. If the defendant was given significant authority over the property, she has possession; but if she was given only limited authority over it, she has only custody. [Morgan v. Commonwealth, 47 S.W.2d 543 (Ky. 1932)]

(a) **Example:** D was in charge of the local telegraph office and was the only person with the combination to the office safe. According to routine practice, money was placed in the safe until it was forwarded to the company's main office. D broke into the safe and took the money inside. D was held ***not guilty*** of larceny. *Rationale:* D had sufficient authority over the money at the time of the misappropriation to give D possession, and so D did not take it from the possession of another. [Morgan v. Commonwealth, *supra*]

(2) **Employee misappropriation cases:** [§1020] The possession/custody issue becomes particularly important where property has been entrusted to and then misappropriated by an employee. Here, the special rules applicable depend on whether the property was delivered to the employee by a third party or by the employer. (*See* detailed discussion, *infra*, §§1048 *et seq.*)

c. **Joint owners:** [§1021] If two or more persons jointly own property, most courts hold that a misappropriation by one is not larceny. *Rationale:* Both owners have the right to possession, and thus the property is not that of another. [State v. Elsbury, 175 P.2d 430 (Nev. 1946)]

d. **Larceny from spouse:** [§1022] At common law, one spouse cannot commit larceny of the other spouse's property because of the identity of the husband and wife—spouses are considered as "one." Some courts, however, have upheld convictions where the guilty spouse had separated from the other or was in the process of doing so at the time of the theft. [61 Colum. L. Rev. 73 (1961)]

7. **Mens Rea—"Intent To Permanently Deprive":** [§1023] Larceny requires an intent to ***permanently*** deprive the victim of his interest in the property. It is not necessary that the victim be permanently deprived; rather, what controls is what the defendant intends at the time of taking.

a. **Intent to keep:** [§1024] Intent to permanently deprive exists, of course, if the defendant intends to personally and permanently keep the property.

(1) **Compare—intent to borrow and return:** [§1025] If the defendant takes the property with the intention of returning it, the taking does not amount to larceny. [People v. Brown, 105 Cal. 66 (1894)]

b. **Intent to create substantial risk of permanent loss:** [§1026] If the defendant takes the property with the intent of doing something with the property that would create a ***substantial risk*** of its ***permanent loss*** to the owner, this is sufficient for larceny. [State v. Langis, 444 P.2d 959 (Or. 1968)]

(1) **Example:** D takes V's car, intending to drive it some distance away and abandon it there. D may be convicted of larceny, but only if the jury determines that the circumstances of the intended abandonment would involve a substantial risk that the car would never be returned to V. [State v. Langis, *supra*]

(2) **Indifference as to owner's interest:** [§1027] A few courts have held that ***indifference*** as to whether the owner ever gets the property back is sufficient for larceny. [State v. Gordon, 321 A.2d 352 (Me. 1974)] Under

this approach, the prosecution apparently need not establish that the intended disposition of the property involved a high or even substantial risk of loss to the owner.

c. **Intent to sell to owner or to pledge:** [§1028] It is also sufficient for larceny that the defendant intended to return the property to the owner but only upon payment or that the defendant intended to pledge the property as security or to pawn it. This is on the theory that the owner may refuse or be unable to pay the price or to redeem it, and thus the defendant's intended disposition of the property involves a ***sufficient risk of permanent loss***. [Regina v. Holloway, 169 Eng. Rep. 285 (1848)]

d. **Intent to pay for property:** [§1029] If property is for sale and the defendant takes it with the intent and present ability to pay, no larceny has taken place. However, taking property with only a vague intent to pay for it sometime in the future ***is*** generally held to be larceny. Courts vary on in-between situations. A sound approach is to find larceny despite an intent to pay unless the defendant reasonably believes the owner would be willing to sell the property for the amount the defendant intends to tender to the owner. [Mason v. State, 32 Ark. 238 (1877)]

e. **Intent to return equivalent property:** [§1030] The cases are not clear as to whether it is larceny to take property with the intent to return the ***equivalent but not the identical item***. Under the better view, there is no larceny if the property is such that it is unlikely to make any difference to the owner whether she has the original or an equivalent substitute. [State v. Savage, 186 A. 738 (Del. 1916)—not larceny to take gasoline intending to return an identical amount]

f. **Intent to collect debt or taking under claim of right:** [§1031] It is not larceny to take specific money reasonably believed due one as a debt [People v. Gallegos, 274 P.2d 608 (Colo. 1954)] or to take property as security for payment of a debt honestly believed to exist [*In re* Bayles, 47 Cal. App. 517 (1920)]. Such takings under "claim of right" show the defendant's belief that she had a legal right to the property taken (*i.e.,* she thought it was "hers") and therefore that she did not intend, by taking it, ***to deprive anyone else of his interest*** in the property.

(1) **Compare—taking to satisfy a general claim:** [§1032] The cases are split where the defendant takes property with no claim that she has a right to that property but only pursuant to a claim that the defendant is owed an amount equal to the value of the property taken (*e.g.*, jewelry taken in satisfaction of $500 debt). Probably the best approach is to find that larceny was committed ***unless*** the defendant took the property honestly believing that she had a legal right to engage in this sort of "self-help" and thus believed she had an interest in the property that entitled her to take it. Only in such cases does the defendant lack the intent to deprive another of property she knows belongs to the other person.

g. **Modern statutes:** [§1033] Modern theft statutes tend to retain the essence of the common law requirement of intent to permanently deprive. [People v. Jaso, 4 Cal. App. 3d 767 (1970)—Cal. Penal Code §484 requires specific intent to deprive owner of his property]

(1) **Model Penal Code—intent to deprive:** [§1034] "Theft" under the Model Penal Code requires that the defendant act with the purpose of depriving another person of the property involved. "Deprive" is defined as including any of the following:

(i) ***Withholding property of another permanently or for so extended a period*** as to appropriate a major portion of its economic value;

(ii) ***Withholding property with intent to restore it only upon payment*** of a reward or other compensation; or

(iii) ***Disposing of property in such a way as to make it unlikely that the owner will recover it.***

[Model Penal Code §§223.2, 223.0(1)]

(2) **Model Penal Code—claim of right and similar matters:** [§1035] The Model Penal Code accommodates a defendant's claim that she believed she had a right to take the property by recognizing three affirmative defenses applicable to theft. These must be raised by the defendant, but once raised the burden of proof is on the prosecution. It is an affirmative defense to theft that:

(i) The defendant was ***unaware that the property was that of another***;

(ii) The defendant acted under an ***honest claim of right*** to the property or a claim that she had a right to acquire or dispose of it as she did; or

(iii) The defendant took property exposed for sale ***intending to promptly purchase and pay*** for it or reasonably believing that the owners, if present, would have consented to her taking of it.

[Model Penal Code §223.1(3)]

(3) **Special problem—vehicles and "joyriding":** [§1036] Although generally it is not a crime to take property of another without the intent to deprive, many jurisdictions make special provision for such takings of vehicles. It is an offense—frequently called joyriding—to take or operate the vehicle of another without the consent of the owner. ***No intent to deprive*** is required. [Model Penal Code §223.9—"unauthorized use of automobile and other vehicle"; Cal. Penal Code §499b—taking vehicle for the purpose of temporarily using or operating it]

8. **Taking and Intent Must Coincide:** [§1037] As a general rule, the mens rea and actus reus must concur in a point of time (*see supra,* §170). Thus, for larceny the intent to permanently deprive must exist ***at the very moment of the taking***. [Ennis v. State, 167 P. 229 (Okla. 1917)]

a. **Example:** D had V's corn in his possession and, pursuant to V's direction, D sold the corn and received the money. D thereafter decided to steal the money. D did not commit larceny, because his intent to steal did not exist at the time he took possession of the money. [Ennis v. State, *supra*]

b. **Exception—"continuing trespass" situations:** [§1038] Under certain circumstances, the wrongful intent need not exist at the time the property is first taken. If the defendant's act of taking the property is ***wrongful*** (although not necessarily criminal) and later, while in possession of the property, defendant forms the requisite intent, the initial trespass is said ***to "continue"*** until the formulation of the intent, at which point the necessary concurrence is established and the actions constitute larceny. [State v. Coombs, 55 Me. 477 (1868)]

(1) **Example:** D obtained a horse and sleigh, lying as to his intended destination and length of absence but intending to return them. Later, D decided to steal the property and sold it. By reason of D's concealed intent, the initial taking was trespassory. Hence, D became guilty of larceny when he subsequently converted the property to his own use. [State v. Coombs, *supra*]

(2) **Compare—possession rightfully obtained:** [§1039] The "continuing trespass" doctrine will ***not*** apply if the defendant's initial possession was ***rightfully*** obtained. Thus, if D in the above example had not misrepresented his intended use, his misappropriation would not be larceny.

9. **Special Problem Areas:** [§1040] Special problems are raised by several situations that should be considered individually.

a. **Property acquired by finding:** [§1041] Whether a person commits larceny of property he found depends on whether the property was ***abandoned or only lost or mislaid***.

(1) **Abandoned property:** [§1042] Abandoned property (*i.e.,* property that has been ***intentionally cast away*** by its owner with the intent of relinquishing all rights therein) has no owner and therefore is not the "property of another." Accordingly, it ***cannot be the subject of larceny***. [United States v. Smiley, 27 F. Cas. 1132 (1864)]

(2) **Lost or mislaid goods:** [§1043] Lost or mislaid goods, on the other hand, ***can*** be the subject of larceny, subject to the application of special rules.

(a) **Definitions:** [§1044] Property is ***"lost"*** when the owner has ***accidentally given up possession*** not knowing where it is. If the owner has ***intentionally placed*** the property somewhere but later ***forgot where***, the property is ***"mislaid."*** Conversely, property is not lost or mislaid simply because the owner does not know exactly where it is at the moment. [People v. Stay, 19 Cal. App. 3d 166 (1971)]

(b) **Special requirements for larceny of lost or mislaid goods:** [§1045] Property that is lost or mislaid is regarded as being still in the ***constructive possession of the owner,*** so that one who finds it and takes possession does so from the possession of the owner. [Foulke v. New York Consolidated Railroad, 228 N.Y. 269 (1920)] Nonetheless, the taking is larceny only if the following two requirements are met:

1) **Clue to ownership:** [§1046] A "clue to ownership" is required. This means that the defendant must either ***know who the owner is*** or have reason to believe that the owner ***can be located*** at the time he finds the property. It is not sufficient that extraordinary diligence by the defendant would have led to discovery of the owner; it is necessary that ***reasonable efforts*** by the defendant would have disclosed the owner's identity. [Brooks v. State, 35 Ohio St. 46 (1878)]

2) **Intent must exist at time of finding:** [§1047] In addition, the defendant must have the intent to steal ***at the time he finds the property*** and takes it into his possession. If he takes it innocently and thereafter forms the intent to steal, he is not guilty of larceny. [Regina v. Thurborn, 169 Eng. Rep. 293 (1848)]

b. **Misappropriations by employee:** [§1048] Employee misappropriations of property belonging to the employer present special problems. The issues differ depending on whether the property at issue was delivered to the employee ***by a third party*** or ***by the employer***.

(1) **Delivery by third party:** [§1049] If property is delivered ***by a third party*** to a servant or employee on behalf of the employer, the servant or employee receives ***possession***. Therefore, if the servant or employee subsequently misappropriates the property, larceny is not committed because the property has not been taken from the possession of another. [125 A.L.R. 367 (1940)]

(a) **Example:** Owner delivered two jewels to Employer's store and handed them to the clerk, D. D placed one in his pocket and the other in the safe, which was where Employer had told him to deposit all delivered jewels. Before leaving for the day, D went to the safe, took the second jewel, and put it in his pocket. D did all of this intending to steal the jewels. D is guilty of larceny of the second jewel only. The first jewel was never in Employer's possession—since it was not placed in the safe as was the second—so D did not take it from the possession of another.

(b) **Duration of possession:** [§1050] The servant or employee keeps possession until he delivers the property to his employer or places it in a receptacle provided by the employer for the employer's purpose. If he ***thereafter*** misappropriates the property, he commits larceny. [Bazeley's Case, 2 East P.C. 571 (Cr. Cas. Res. 1799); Nolan v. State, 131 A.2d 851 (Md. 1957)]

(c) **Compare—liability for embezzlement:** [§1051] An employee who misappropriates such property before it goes into the possession of the employer may commit embezzlement. Thus, in the example above, D may be guilty of embezzlement of the first jewel. (*See* below.)

(2) **Delivery by employer:** [§1052] When property is entrusted to a servant or employee ***by the master or employer***, a different set of rules apply. The result turns on the amount of trust placed in the servant or employee.

(a) **Ordinary servant or employee:** [§1053] Ordinarily, a servant or employee merely has ***custody*** of the employer's property. Thus, any misappropriation by the servant or employee is from the possession of the employer and therefore larceny. [Warren v. State, 62 N.E.2d 624 (Ind. 1945)]

(b) **"Trusted" employee:** [§1054] However, if the employer has delegated significant authority to the employee, the employee obtains ***possession*** of the property. He therefore does not commit larceny by subsequently misappropriating the property. [Morgan v. Commonwealth, 47 S.W.2d 543 (Ky. 1932); *and see supra,* §1020]

C. EMBEZZLEMENT

1. **Statutory Crime:** [§1055] Embezzlement is a statutory crime, and thus, its definition varies among jurisdictions. Generally, however, it involves the ***fraudulent conversion of the property of another by one who is already in lawful possession*** of it. Unlike larceny, which is a crime against possession, embezzlement is a crime against ***ownership***.

2. **Historical Background:** [§1056] The first of the statutes making embezzlement a crime was enacted in England in 1799 and was clearly designed to close the "loopholes" created by courts' definition of larceny as requiring a taking ***from the possession of another***. [Perkins and Boyce, 351-354]

3. **Elements of the Crime:** [§1057] Embezzlement requires proof that the defendant (i) converted; (ii) property; (iii) of another; (iv) in his lawful possession; (v) with intent to defraud.

   a. **Conversion:** [§1058] "Conversion," as used in embezzlement, requires a ***serious act of interference*** with the owner's rights. Mere movement of the property is not sufficient. Generally, conversion requires some use of the property that is materially inconsistent with the terms of the arrangement under which the defendant has possession of the property. [People v. Schnepp, 200 N.E. 338 (Ill. 1936)]

      (1) **Example:** D, a deputy sheriff, was in possession of a departmental patrol car. In the early morning, D drove it to a lawn mower repair shop, placed someone else's mower in it, and sped away from and eluded another police officer. D is guilty of embezzlement, since the use of the patrol car was clearly inconsistent with the owner's rights and the trust reposed in D. [People v. Redondo, 19 Cal. App. 4th 1428 (1993)]

   b. **Property:** [§1059] The property that can be the subject of embezzlement is often ***defined more broadly*** than it is in larceny. It may, for example, include real property. Thus, it would be embezzlement to claim ownership in land held for another. [People v. Roland, 134 Cal. App. 675 (1933)]

   c. **Of another:** [§1060] Clearly, one who converts her own property cannot be guilty of embezzlement. Cases sometimes raise a difficult question as to whether the property at issue was given to the defendant and thus is not the property "of another," or rather was simply entrusted to the defendant and thus remains property of another which can be the subject of embezzlement. [LaFave and Scott, 732-733]

(1) **Example:** V hires D, a contractor, to build a swimming pool. V gives D an advance payment of $2,000, believing that D will use this to buy materials for construction of the pool. In fact, D uses the money to pay for materials used on her last job. Is D guilty of embezzlement? Most likely there was no agreement between V and D that D would receive the money for the limited purpose of conveying it to a seller of materials for V's pool; if there had been such an agreement, the money would have remained V's and D's actions would most likely have been a fraudulent conversion. However, since V simply gave D the money, the money became D's, and although D did not live up to V's expectations she did not "convert" property "of another."

(2) **Compare—co-owners and agents:** [§1061] Generally, a co-owner of property does not commit embezzlement by misappropriating jointly owned property in her possession because it is not property of another. Similarly, an agent authorized to collect money for her principal and to keep a certain portion as a commission is often regarded as a co-owner of the money collected and thus does not commit embezzlement if she misappropriates it. *But note:* Embezzlement statutes sometimes address this specifically and make such agents guilty of embezzlement if they misappropriate the collected money. [People v. Riggins, 132 N.E.2d 519 (Ill. 1956)—independent collection agent committed embezzlement by misappropriating money collected for principal]

d. **Lawful possession:** [§1062] The requirement that the defendant be in ***lawful possession*** of the property at the time of the conversion is the primary distinguishing characteristic of embezzlement. Some statutes specifically set forth those persons who can come within the scope of the crime (*e.g.,* employees, bailees, bankers). Others are worded broadly enough to cover any persons entrusted with property. [Cal. Penal Code §503—"Embezzlement is the fraudulent appropriation of property by a person to whom it has been entrusted"]

e. **Fraudulent intent:** [§1063] At the time of the conversion, the defendant must have a fraudulent intent. Unfortunately, precisely what is sufficient to constitute the required fraudulent intent is not entirely clear. Arguably, all that embezzlement requires is that the defendant have deceived the victim by impliedly misrepresenting that the defendant was not converting the property—*i.e.,* by withholding from the owner that the defendant was converting the property.

(1) **Intent to return:** [§1064] A conversion is not without fraudulent intent because the defendant intended to return the property or to make restitution. One court has gone so far as to say that intent to return or repay cannot even be considered in determining whether the defendant acted with the necessary intent to defraud. [State v. Joy, 549 A.2d 1033 (Vt. 1988)]

(a) **Compare—mitigation of punishment:** [§1065] Evidence that the accused intended to or actually did restore the property may be used to mitigate punishment. [Cal. Penal Code §§512-513—restoration of property before accused is charged is no defense but may mitigate punishment]

(2) **Claim of right:** [§1066] If the defendant honestly believed that she was entitled to the property (*see supra,* §1031), her conversion is not embezzlement. [People v. LaPique, 120 Cal. 25 (1898)]

(3) **Modern view—statutory schemes requiring intent to permanently deprive:** [§1067] Under some modern theft statutes, what was previously the separate crime of embezzlement is made one way of committing theft. This means that the defendant must have acted with the ***intent required for theft***, which is usually intent to permanently deprive the owner of the property.

(a) **Compare—related offense of misapplication of property:** [§1068] The Model Penal Code takes the above approach but also contains a somewhat overlapping offense, misapplication of entrusted property, which requires that the accused misapply property entrusted to her and do so with ***knowledge that this misapplication creates a substantial risk of loss or detriment*** to the owner. [Model Penal Code §224.13]

4. **Demand for Return:** [§1069] A demand for the return of the property is ***not a formal requirement*** of embezzlement. In some situations, however, proof of a conversion is facilitated by evidence that the victim demanded the property and the defendant refused. Indeed, in a few cases it is likely that a conversion could not be shown without evidence of demand and refusal. [People v. Ward, 134 Cal. 301 (1901)]

a. **Compare—demand not substitute for proof of conversion:** [§1070] While "demand and refusal" may be relevant evidence, it is ***not a substitute*** for showing a conversion of the property by the defendant. The prosecution must prove that the defendant did something with the property constituting a conversion. [State v. Williams, 179 N.W.2d 756 (Iowa 1970)]

D. FALSE PRETENSES

1. **Statutory Crime:** [§1071] False pretenses, like embezzlement, is a statutory crime and so its definition varies among jurisdictions. But in general, the offense consists of ***obtaining title*** to property ***by means of a material false representation*** and ***with intent to defraud*** the victim.

2. **Historical Background:** [§1072] Under technicalities of the law of larceny (and specifically larceny by trick), one who obtained ***title*** (rather than mere possession) by means of deception could not be guilty of larceny (*see supra,* §1010). In 1757, Parliament closed this "loophole" by creating the statutory crime of obtaining property by false pretenses. Most American jurisdictions have enacted similar statutes.

3. **Policy Considerations:** [§1073] Courts are often concerned that false pretenses and similar crimes will be applied so as to make what are really only breaches of

contract into criminal offenses. These crimes are consequently often interpreted narrowly to minimize this risk. [People v. Norman, 85 N.Y. 2d 609 (1995)]

4. **Elements of the Crime:** [§1074] False pretenses requires proof that the defendant (i) obtained title; (ii) to property; (iii) by a false representation; (iv) with ***both*** knowledge of the misrepresentation's falsity ***and*** intent to defraud.

   a. **Obtaining title:** [§1075] False pretenses requires that the defendant acquire ***title*** to the property; it is not enough that the victim parts only with possession. Usually, the victim's intention determines what the defendant receives: If the victim intends to transfer title to the defendant, the defendant gets title; if the victim intends to transfer only possession, the defendant gets no more than possession. [Franklin v. State, 214 So. 2d 924 (Ala. 1968)]

      (1) **Absolute title not required:** [§1076] It is not essential that the defendant acquire an absolute title. Thus, for example, D purchased a new car from V, giving D's old car in trade and representing to V that the old car was completely paid for. The new car was purchased on a conditional sales contract, in which V retained title to the car as security for the loan to D. D's representations as to having paid for the old car were untrue, and D was held guilty of false pretenses. The court acknowledged that any title obtained by fraud is arguably voidable but held that nevertheless D had obtained a sufficient property interest to support conviction of the crime. [Franklin v. State, *supra*]

      (2) **Compare—larceny by trick:** [§1077] One who obtains possession and not title by means of a false representation may be guilty of larceny by trick. (*See supra,* §1007.)

   b. **Property:** [§1078] As with embezzlement, the property that can be the subject of false pretenses is often broader in scope than that which can be the subject of larceny. Thus, the crime may be committed by obtaining title to real property, instruments or securities, and—under some statutes—services, credit, and board and lodging. [Stokes v. State, 366 P.2d 425 (Okla. 1961)—telephone service is a "valuable thing" within meaning of false pretenses statute]

   c. **False representation:** [§1079] The defendant must have obtained the property by means of a false representation. There are, however, several traditional limits on the situations that will qualify.

      (1) **Nature of false representation:** [§1080] Courts' concern that false pretenses not be applied so as to criminalize essentially contractual breaches and unpaid debts is reflected in the somewhat limited definition of the misrepresentations that will suffice for this offense.

         (a) **Past or existing fact:** [§1081] Clearly, a misrepresentation of a past or existing fact will suffice. [Ross v. State, 424 S.W.2d 168 (Ark. 1968)]

         (b) **Future facts or false promises:** [§1082] Most courts hold that the crime of false pretenses ***cannot*** be premised on misrepresentations of "future facts" or false promises, even if the defendant did not intend to keep the promise at the time it was made. [Chaplin v. United States, 157 F.2d 697 (D.C. Cir. 1946)]

1) **Rationale:** This position has been defended on the ground that it is not the purpose of the criminal law to provide redress for every victim of a bad bargain. Civil remedies suffice for such situations. [Chaplin v. United States, *supra*]

2) **Modern trend:** [§1083] There is nevertheless an apparent trend among more modern cases and statutes to hold that false promises ***will*** suffice ***if*** the prosecution proves that the defendant intended when the promise was made not to perform it. [People v. Ashley, 42 Cal. 2d 246 (1954)—promise made without intent to perform is sufficient for false pretenses, but D's intent must be proved by more than the failure to perform the promise; N.Y. Penal Law §155.05—larceny "by false promise"]

(c) **Passive nondisclosure:** [§1084] Ordinarily, a defendant does ***not*** commit false pretenses simply by the failure to correct a false impression that she knew was harbored by the victim. [Stumpff v. People, 117 P. 134 (Colo. 1911)] Courts may be persuaded to find that silence is enough, however, if the defendant was responsible (even innocently) ***for creating the false impression***.

(2) **Materiality:** [§1085] The misrepresentation must concern a material fact; *i.e.*, it must have been a "controlling inducement" for the victim's parting with the property. However, it need not be the sole inducing reason; it is enough that the misrepresentation was one of several factors relied on by the victim in deciding to transfer the property to the defendant. [Whitmore v. State, 298 N.W. 194 (Wis. 1941)]

(3) **Causal factor (reliance):** [§1086] In addition, the misrepresentation must ***cause*** the victim to transfer the property to the defendant. Thus, if the victim was not in fact deceived by the misrepresentation, the crime of false pretenses has not been committed. [Commonwealth v. Johnson, 167 A. 344 (Pa. 1933)]

(a) **Example:** D misrepresented certain facts to V, hoping to persuade V to give D money. Although V did not believe D's lies, V wanted to catch D in the commission of a crime and therefore gave D the money. Since V was not deceived by the misrepresentations, D is not guilty of false pretenses. [Commonwealth v. Johnson, *supra*]

(b) **Compare—liability for attempt:** [§1087] However, even though the victim was not deceived, the defendant can be convicted of ***attempted*** false pretenses. [Commonwealth v. Johnson, *supra*]

d. **Mens rea:** [§1088] The mens rea for false pretenses is twofold:

(1) **Knowledge of falsity:** [§1089] The defendant must have "***knowledge***" that the representations were false. If she believes them to be true—even

though her belief is unreasonable—she has not committed false pretenses. On the other hand, if the defendant makes the representations but does not know whether or not they are true ("conscious ignorance"), this is probably sufficient. [People v. Marsh, 58 Cal. 2d 732 (1962)—false representations made "either recklessly or without information on which the defendant could base a belief" that they were true sufficient]

(2) **Intent to defraud:** [§1090] Moreover, it must also be shown that the defendant had the intent to defraud the victim. Precisely what this requires is not entirely clear.

(a) **Situations precluding intent to defraud:** [§1091] Generally, there is no intent to defraud if (i) the defendant believed the property to be her own; (ii) she intended to restore the property; or (iii) she believed that she was entitled to the property because of a debt owed her by the victim. [20 A.L.R.2d 1266 (1951)—intent to obtain payment of debt by misrepresentation will usually, but not always, prevent conviction for false pretenses]

(b) **Less required than for larceny:** [§1092] It has been held that the intent to defraud for purposes of false pretenses demands less than the intent to permanently deprive required by larceny. However, the precise difference between the two "specific intents" has not been developed by the courts. [*See, e.g.*, State v. Mills. 396 P.2d 5 (Ariz. 1964)—intent to repay loan will not prevent conviction for false pretenses based on obtaining loan by misrepresentations, even though intent to repay would preclude conviction for larceny]

5. **Special Evidentiary Requirement:** [§1093] Some jurisdictions impose special evidentiary requirements (*e.g.*, corroboration) in false pretenses cases. These rules are apparently designed to prevent convictions based solely on the victim's testimony. For instance, in California certain false pretenses cases require a handwritten misrepresentation, two witnesses to the misrepresentation, or one witness to the misrepresentation and corroborating circumstances. [Cal. Penal Code §532(b)]

E. ROBBERY

1. **Elements:** [§1094] Robbery is basically aggravated larceny. It requires proof of all of the elements for larceny (*see supra*, §§978 *et seq.*) ***plus*** two other things:

(i) The property must be taken ***from the victim's person or presence***; and

(ii) The taking of the property must be accomplished ***by means of violence or intimidation***.

[Cal. Penal Code §211—robbery is "taking of personal property in the possession of another, from his person or immediate presence, . . . accomplished by means of force or fear"]

2. **Taking from Victim's Person or Presence:** [§1095] Robbery requires a taking from the ***presence*** of the victim. The crime is sometimes described as requiring that the property be taken from the person of another, but this is not correct. [People v. Braverman, 173 N.E. 55 (Ill. 1930)]

a. **"Presence":** [§1096] Property is within the victim's presence for purposes of robbery if it is close to the victim and ***within his control*** in the sense that he could have prevented its taking had it not been for the defendant's use of violence or threats. [People v. Braverman, *supra*]

(1) **Example:** D forced V at gunpoint to enter a room and locked V in it. D then went to another room in the same building and took money from a safe. D is guilty of robbery because the money was in the presence of V, even though in a different room. [People v. Braverman, *supra*]

b. **Compare—Model Penal Code:** [§1097] The Model Penal Code, departing from traditional formulations of the crime, would not require that the taking be from the person or the presence of the victim. Rather, it is only necessary under the Code that violence or threats be used in the course of committing theft. [Model Penal Code §222.1] This approach is followed in many modern criminal codes, although some require that the defendant have made the threats or engaged in the violence with the intent of obtaining the property being stolen. [*See, e.g.*, Tex. Penal Code §29.02]

3. **Taking by Violence or Intimidation:** [§1098] The taking of the property must be accomplished by violence or intimidation.

a. **Violence:** [§1099] The taking is accomplished by violence within the meaning of robbery if ***any force*** is used to obtain the property.

(1) **"Pickpocket" situations:** [§1100] It is ***not*** robbery to stealthily take property from the pocket of the victim because ***no use of force*** is involved; the crime is simply larceny, although the fact that it is "larceny from the person" often means that it is punishable by a more severe penalty than ordinary larceny. Such pickpocket situations escalate into robbery, however, if the defendant pushes or jostles the victim or if the victim becomes aware of what is happening and the defendant struggles with the victim to keep possession of the property. [Bauer v. State, 43 P.2d 203 (Ariz. 1935)]

(2) **"Snatching" situations:** [§1101] The defendant also does not commit robbery by simply snatching property from the victim's grasp so suddenly that the victim offers no resistance, because the taking of the property involves ***no use of force*** within the meaning of robbery. But there is a robbery if the items are attached to the victim's person (as by a chain) so that force is required to effect a removal. [State v. Broderick, 59 Mo. 318 (1875)—watch chain fastened to watch and buttonhole] Robbery may even be committed if the victim becomes aware that the object is being taken and resists by grabbing the item so the defendant must ***wrest*** it from the victim's grasp over resistance. [State v. Sein, 590 A.2d 665 (N.J. 1991)]

(3) **Victim rendered helpless:** [§1102] It is robbery to render the victim helpless by use of force and then take the property. This is true even if the victim is rendered helpless by the administration of a drug or an intoxicating substance, since this amounts to a battery (unlawful application of force; *see supra,* §810). [State v. Snyder, 172 P. 364 (Nev. 1918)]

(4) **Compare—Model Penal Code requirement of serious injury:** [§1103] The Model Penal Code would limit this type of robbery (*i.e.*, a taking by violence) to situations in which the defendant inflicts ***serious bodily injury***. [Model Penal Code §222.1(1)(a)]

b. **Intimidation:** [§1104] Even where actual violence is not employed, a taking of property is nonetheless robbery if accomplished by means of intimidation (*i.e.*, ***threats***).

(1) **Victim must be placed in fear:** [§1105] Robbery by intimidation requires that the victim have ***actually been placed in fear***. Sometimes this requirement is put as requiring that the taking have been accomplished by threats, which means that the threats must have instilled fear in the victim and caused that victim to give up the property. [S.W. v. State, 513 So. 2d 1088 (Fla. 1987)—robbery conviction improper where evidence showed victim was not in fear]

(a) **Compare—threats sufficient:** [§1106] The Model Penal Code and some modern statutes based on it do not require that the victim be placed in fear ***if*** the defendant threatened serious bodily injury. [Model Penal Code §222.1(1)(b)]

(2) **Objectively sufficient threatening conduct necessary:** [§1107] Intimidation requires that the victim's fear be attributable to the defendant's actions; simply showing that the victim was placed in fear is not sufficient by itself. Moreover, the victim's fear must be ***reasonable***, which means that the defendant's actions must have been such that a reasonable person would have felt the necessary fear. The threat need not, however, be explicit and an implied threat is sufficient. [People v. Hollingsworth, 457 N.E.2d 1062 (Ill. 1983)]

(a) **Example:** D approached V, a convenience store cashier. D then placed his hand in the cash drawer, and when V grabbed his wrist and demanded, "What are you doing?" D clenched his fist and glared at V. V released D's wrist and D left with money from the drawer. V testified that she feared that V would hurt her if she did not let him go. D is guilty of robbery. V's fear alone is not enough. Here, however, D's clenching his fist and glaring was an implied threat that would place a reasonable person in fear. V's testimony showed V was placed in fear and this caused V to give up the property. [Wilmeth v. State, 808 S.W.2d 703 (Tex. 1991)]

(b) **Compare—purposely putting in fear sufficient:** [§1108] The Model Penal Code and modern statutes based on it do not require that the defendant's conduct meet any objective standard but instead require that the defendant have ***purposely*** put the victim in fear. This reflects the view that robbery should be found even if the victim was unusually susceptible to threats and the defendant both knew and intentionally exploited this to place the victim in fear although by conduct that would not have had this impact on others. [Model Penal Code §222.1(1)(b)]

(3) **Nature of threat:** [§1109] Traditionally, the injury threatened must be of ***death***, ***bodily injury***, or ***destruction of the victim's dwelling house***. Threats to ***accuse the victim of sodomy*** have also been held sufficient, but threats to accuse the victim of other crimes are not enough. [Montsdoca v. State, 93 So. 157 (Fla. 1922)]

(a) **Compare—Model Penal Code:** [§1110] The Model Penal Code would require that the threat be of ***serious bodily injury***. [Model Penal Code §222.1(1)(b)]

(4) **Target of threat:** [§1111] The threat need not be directed at the owner of the property; one can commit robbery by threatening harm to a ***member of the owner's family or other relative***, or to ***anyone in the owner's presence***. [Lear v. State, 6 P.2d 426 (Ariz. 1931)]

(5) **Immediacy required:** [§1112] The threat must be of ***immediate injury***. A general threat to harm the subject at some time in the future will not suffice. [People v. Rudelt, 6 App. Div. 2d 640 (1958)—statement, "I must have that money; I could kill you but I won't," could be construed as creating necessary fear of immediate injury]

c. **Violence or intimidation used to take property:** [§1113] The force or intimidation must be used to take the property. Thus, it is necessary that the violence or threats occur ***before or during the taking*** of the property. If the taking is complete before the force or intimidation is used, this requirement is not met. [State v. Long, 675 P.2d 832 (Kan. 1984)]

(1) **Taking may be broadly construed:** [§1114] In order to bring situations within robbery, courts may broadly construe the taking, even perhaps interpreting that term differently than in the larceny context.

(a) **Example:** D entered a small building; he then took money from a cash box and put it in his pocket. When D was surprised by the owner, V, he pushed V out of the way and rushed out. D is guilty of robbery, because he had not completed his taking of the property when he used the force against V since he had not yet removed the money from V's immediate presence. It is likely, however, that this court would have said that for purposes of larceny, D had completed the necessary taking when he put the money in his pocket. [State v. Long, *supra*]

(2) **Situations created for other purposes:** [§1115] According to the weight of authority, the violent or intimidating acts need not in all cases be committed for the very purpose of taking the victim's property. Thus, a defendant who uses violence or intimidation for some other purpose commits robbery if he takes advantage of that situation to obtain property from the person or presence of another. [Carey v. United States, 296 F.2d 422 (D.C. Cir. 1961)]

(a) **Example:** During an argument with V, D stabbed V to death, and then—for the first time—decided to steal the money that V had on her person. Even though the intent to steal did not arise until after the violence was used, D was guilty of robbery. [Carey v. United States, *supra*]

d. **Model Penal Code position:** [§1116] The Model Penal Code and many modern statutes dispense with the need for the use of force or intimidation to obtain the property. Under this approach, it is only necessary that the defendant seriously wound another, threaten another with serious bodily injury, or commit or threaten to commit a serious felony "in the course of committing" theft. "In the course of committing theft" is defined as including immediate escape from committing or attempting to commit theft. [Model Penal Code §222.1(1)]

(1) **Example:** D entered the premises, committed theft, and then concealed himself there. A police officer was called to the scene. When the officer arrived, D attacked the officer. Since the attack on the officer was "in the course of committing" the theft, D is guilty of robbery. [State v. Mirault, 457 A.2d 455 (N.J. 1983)]

4. **Possible Defense—Taking Under Claim of Right:** [§1117] Since robbery requires that the defendant be committing larceny, the elements of larceny must also be proved and this includes the intent to permanently deprive. Facts showing that the defendant lacked this intent therefore show the defendant did not commit robbery. Thus, it is generally held that a defendant does not commit robbery if he honestly believes he is entitled to the property taken, even though he takes the property from the person or presence of another by violence or intimidation; his claim of right shows he lacked the intent to deprive another of that other person's property. [People v. Butler, 65 Cal. 2d 569 (1967); *and see supra,* §1031]

a. **Compare—refusal to apply claim of right law:** [§1118] Because self-help involving violence or threats poses risks of escalating dangerous conduct, courts have sometimes strained to avoid applying claim of right law to robbery, even if they would apply it to simple larceny situations. For example, some courts have held that claim of right does not apply to robberies where the behavior involved would be illegal even if it was with the full consent of the victim. [Jupiter v. State, 616 A.2d 412 (Md. 1992)—intoxicated D who took beer from bartender at gunpoint and paid for it cannot rely on claim of right defense to robbery charge because bartender could not legally sell beer to intoxicated person; hence, transaction effected by robbery (*i.e.*, the sale of beer) would have been illegal even if done with victim's consent]

5. **Punishment:** [§1119] Robbery is a common law felony and remains a felony in most if not all modern jurisdictions, ***regardless of the value of the property taken***. [Cal. Penal Code §213; Tex. Penal Code §29.02(b)] However, for purposes of punishment, statutes often distinguish between simple robbery and aggravated robbery, imposing a heavier penalty for the latter. [*See* Tex. Penal Code §29.03—robbery raised to aggravated robbery if perpetrator causes serious bodily injury to another or uses or exhibits a deadly weapon]

F. EXTORTION (OR BLACKMAIL)

1. **Common Law:** [§1120] Common law extortion is the corrupt collection of an unlawful fee by a public officer under color of office. It is a misdemeanor. [Perkins and Boyce, 442-443]

2. **Modern Statutes:** [§1121] Modern statutes have expanded the crime of extortion to include what is generally regarded as ***blackmail***, although they may denominate the crime by various names. [Cal. Penal Code §518—"extortion"; Ky. Penal Code §509.080—"criminal coercion"]

   a. **Statutory schemes:** [§1122] Modern extortion statutes typically fall into two distinct patterns:

      (1) **Property obtained by threats:** [§1123] Some statutory schemes require that the defendant actually ***obtain property*** by means of threats or coercion. [Cal. Penal Code §518—obtaining property with subject's consent where the consent is induced by wrongful use of force or fear or under color of office; Model Penal Code §223.4—obtaining property by certain enumerated threats]

         (a) **Compare—liability for attempt:** [§1124] Under these statutes, a defendant who has only threatened the victim but not yet received the property he wants cannot be convicted of the completed offense, but he may be liable for attempted extortion. [People v. Franquelin, 109 Cal. App. 2d 777 (1952)]

      (2) **Threats alone sufficient:** [§1125] Most statutes, on the other hand, require only the making of certain prohibited ***threats with the intent to thereby obtain property*** or some thing of value. [Ky. Penal Code §509.080—defining criminal coercion as threats made with intent to compel person to engage in conduct or refrain from conduct]

   b. **Type of threats required—in general:** [§1126] Jurisdictions vary as to the type of threats that will suffice for the crime. Typically, however, the threats covered are those that are insufficient for robbery because they do not involve the harm necessary for robbery or because the harm is not threatened immediately. Often, extortion or blackmail is committed by threats to do things that themselves could be done without violating the law; thus, it is a crime to threaten to do certain things as a means of seeking property even though the things threatened could be lawfully done.

      (1) **Typically sufficient threats:** [§1127] Extortion statutes commonly define the following threats as sufficient:

         (a) Threats to unlawfully ***injure the person or property*** of another [Cal. Penal Code §519(1)];

         (b) Threats to ***accuse*** the individual threatened or a relative or family member ***of a crime*** [Cal. Penal Code §519(2)];

         (c) Threats to ***expose or impute*** to the individual threatened or any of these persons ***"any deformity, disgrace, or crime"*** [Cal. Penal Code §519(3)];

         (d) Threats to ***expose any secret*** affecting these persons. [Cal. Penal Code §519(4)].

(2) **Example:** D, a lawyer, represented X in a divorce proceeding. D obtained photographs of X's spouse, Y, in a criminal sexual act. D showed the photos to Y and told Y that unless Y agreed to a property settlement in the divorce proceedings, D would use the photos in court and thus reveal Y's commission of the criminal sexual act. D was guilty of extortion under a statute defining the offense as maliciously threatening to accuse another of an offense with intent to extort money. [State v. Harrington, 260 A.2d 692 (Vt. 1969)]

c. **Limitation—causation required:** [§1128] Under statutes requiring that property actually be acquired by the prohibited threats, it is also necessary to show a ***causal connection*** between the threats and the victim's surrendering the property. In fact, it has been held that the threat must have been the ***"operating or controlling cause"*** of the payment; a showing that the threat was merely a factor in the victim's decision would be insufficient. [People v. Williams, 127 Cal. 212 (1899)]

d. **Claim of right defense:** [§1129] Some, but not all, jurisdictions recognize a defense consisting of a good faith belief by the defendant that he was entitled as a matter of legal right to the money or property he sought to obtain by the threat. The defense may be limited to some types of extortion.

(1) **Example:** Under New York law, a defendant charged with larceny by extortion committed by instilling fear in the victim that he would be charged with a crime may assert an affirmative defense consisting of proof that (i) the defendant reasonably believed the threatened charge to be true; and (ii) the defendant's sole purpose was to induce the victim to make good the wrong that was the subject of the threatened charge. [N.Y. Penal Law §155.15]

(2) **Defense inapplicable where damage uncertain:** [§1130] Jurisdictions recognizing the claim of right defense are unlikely to apply it to situations in which the defendant claims to be entitled to the property because of wrong done by the victim that caused damage or harm of an ***uncertain value***. [State v. Greenspan, 374 S.E.2d 884 (N.C. 1989)]

e. **Punishment:** [§1131] Extortion is generally punished as a felony. [Cal. Penal Code §520]

G. RECEIVING STOLEN PROPERTY

1. **Historical Background:** [§1132] At early common law, one who simply received stolen property incurred no criminal liability—not even as an accessory after the fact—because he did not harbor the thief himself. While later English statutes provided for accomplice liability in such situations (even if the thief himself had not been convicted), it was not until 1827 that a separate statutory crime of receiving stolen property knowing it to be stolen was promulgated.

2. **Elements Under Modern Statutes:** [§1133] Although modern statutes differ to some extent in their definitions of the crime, generally four elements are included:

(i) ***Receiving***

(ii) ***Stolen*** property

(iii) ***Knowing*** it to be stolen, and

(iv) With the ***intent to deprive*** the owner of the property.

a. **Stolen property:** [§1134] It is essential that the property have been "stolen" within the meaning of the statutory language. Two problems arise in applying this requirement:

(1) **Property acquired by crimes other than larceny:** [§1135] Although the statutes are usually interpreted to include property obtained by robbery or burglary, some courts have construed the language narrowly, finding it not to cover property obtained by embezzlement or false pretenses. [State v. George, 173 S.W. 1077 (Mo. 1915)] Some statutes avoid such interpretative problems by specifically including property obtained by any of the acquisition offenses.

(2) **Property recovered:** [§1136] If the owner (or law enforcement authorities acting on the owner's behalf) recovers the property, it is no longer "stolen." Therefore, a person who subsequently receives it has not "received stolen property," even though she may erroneously believe she has done so. [People v. Rojas, 55 Cal. 2d 252 (1961)]

(a) **Compare—liability for attempt:** [§1137] While such a defendant cannot be convicted of the completed offense, she may be guilty of attempted receipt of stolen property. (But recall that some courts find this involves legal impossibility, thereby precluding liability for attempt; *see supra,* §677.)

b. **Receiving:** [§1138] The property must be received by the defendant. But this does not mean that she must take actual personal possession of the property. It is sufficient if she ***indirectly exercises control*** over it, as where she has the thief deposit the property in a designated place. [LeFanti v. United States, 259 F. 460 (3d Cir. 1919); People v. Candiotto, 183 Cal. App. 2d 348 (1960)—D guilty of receipt of stolen goods if someone else with D's knowledge or consent concealed stolen goods on D's premises]

c. **Knowing goods to be stolen:** [§1139] Most statutes require that the defendant ***know*** the goods were stolen at the time she received them. This knowledge need not have come from personal observation of the crime by which the goods were acquired and can be inferred from circumstantial evidence, such as proof that the goods were acquired from a person of questionable character or that the defendant paid a disproportionately low price for them. [People v. Boyden, 116 Cal. App. 2d 278 (1953)]

(1) **Reason to believe goods stolen:** [§1140] In some jurisdictions, it is enough that there existed reasonable grounds to believe the goods were stolen. As long as such grounds were present, the defendant is guilty whether or not she actually knew the goods were stolen. This imposes liability for negligence regarding this element. [Ala. Crim. Code §13A-8-16]

(2) **Abolition of knowledge requirement—constitutionality:** [§1141] A few statutes have imposed liability without regard to whether the recipient knew or should have known that the goods were stolen (*i.e.*, imposed strict liability). However, some such statutes have been struck down as violative of due process (*see supra,* §145). [People v. Estreich, 272 App. Div. 698 (1947), *aff'd,* 297 N.Y. 910 (1948)]

d. **Intent to deprive owner:** [§1142] Some courts hold that the defendant must have a "bad" intent in addition to knowledge of the stolen nature of the goods, even if the statute defining the crime does not explicitly require this. Otherwise, for example, a police officer who takes stolen property from an apprehended thief would be guilty of the crime. These courts often require a showing that the defendant ***intended to deprive the owner*** of the property. [People v. Block, 540 N.E.2d 512 (Ill. 1989)]

(1) **No intent to restore:** [§1143] Occasionally, statutes approach this subject negatively, defining the crime as committed by the knowing receipt of stolen property in the absence of an intent to restore it to the owner. [Model Penal Code §223.6(1)—receipt of stolen property criminal "unless the property is received . . . with intent to restore it to the owner"; Ala. Crim. Code §13A-816—offense committed by receipt of stolen property unless this is done "with intent to restore it to the owner"]

(2) **"Bad" intent not uniformly required:** [§1144] Some statutes are silent as to the requirement of a "bad" intent, and the case law under some of them contains no suggestion that such an intent is essential. [People v. Wielograf, 101 Cal. App. 3d 488 (1980)—receiving stolen property requires only "general criminal intent" to aid thief, render recovery of property by owner more difficult, or to deprive owner of property]

3. **Conviction of Thief for Receiving Stolen Property:** [§1145] Several situations raise an issue as to whether one who participates in the larceny by which the property was acquired can be convicted of receiving it.

a. **Where defendant was the actual thief:** [§1146] Clearly, the person who actually stole the property cannot be convicted of receiving it. The thief, in other words, cannot receive from himself. [People v. Taylor, 4 Cal. App. 2d 214 (1935)]

b. **Other participants in crime:** [§1147] Whether participants in the theft other than the actual thief—the person who took the property—can be convicted of receiving stolen property is less clear. Most courts hold that if the defendant was a party to the crime but was ***not an active participant*** in its commission (*i.e.,* an accessory before the fact), she can be convicted of receiving property from the participant who actually stole it. But the courts are about evenly divided on whether a participant who was ***actually present*** (*i.e.,* a principal in the second degree) can be convicted of receiving the property. [136 A.L.R. 1087 (1942)]

c. **Conviction of both offenses:** [§1148] The better rule is that one who could be convicted of either the crime by which the property was acquired or receiving it (as in §1142, above) ***cannot*** be convicted of ***both*** and given consecutive sentences, although there is some authority to the contrary. [Milanovich v. United States, 365 U.S. 551 (1961)]

H. CONSOLIDATION OF ACQUISITION OFFENSES—THEFT

1. **In General:** [§1149] As indicated earlier (*supra*, §977), modern criminal codes often consolidate some or nearly all of the property acquisition offenses into a single offense called "theft." This crime, purely a creature of modern statutes and unknown to the common law, requires proof that the defendant: (i) exercised control (*see supra*, §§1000, 1004) (ii) over property (*see supra*, §§989-997) of another (iii) unlawfully (*see supra*, §1012) (iv) with intent to permanently deprive that person of the property (*see supra*, §§1033-1034).

2. **Statutory Patterns:** [§1150] Modern codes reflect several approaches towards the consolidation of the property acquisition crimes:

   a. **Single crime of theft:** [§1151] Some codes create a single crime of theft designed to encompass many of the same situations covered by the traditional offenses. However, robbery is seldom included in this consolidation; it is usually preserved as a separate crime. [*See, e.g.,* Tex. Penal Code §§31.03—defining theft; 31.02—expressing legislative intent to create single crime superseding prior separate offenses of theft, theft by false pretext, acquisition of property by threat, embezzlement, extortion, and receiving stolen property]

   b. **Multiple theft crimes:** [§1152] An alternative approach creates multiple theft crimes that correspond to the traditional common law crimes. [*See, e.g.,* Cal. Penal Code §§484—theft defined as including larceny, false pretenses, and embezzlement; 485—theft by appropriating lost property; 496—receiving stolen goods as separate crime; 499—theft of water as separate crime]

   c. **Model Penal Code approach:** [§1153] The Model Penal Code adopts a single crime of theft but contains numerous sections setting forth the different methods by which it may be committed. The Code's intention is to permit a prosecutor simply to charge a defendant with theft and then at trial prove that it was committed in any of the enumerated ways, unless failure to specify the appropriate subsection in advance would deprive the defendant of fair notice. [Model Penal Code §§223.1(1)—providing for single theft offense; 223.2—theft by unlawful taking or disposition; 223.3—theft by deception; 223.4—theft by extortion; 223.6—theft by receipt of stolen property]

3. **Punishment:** [§1154] Theft is often divided into degrees, typically grand theft (a felony) and petty theft (a misdemeanor). Some statutes, however, simply provide different penalties for the crime without formally designating two degrees. Among those thefts commonly designated as felonies are:

   (i) Theft of ***property or services of a value above a given level*** (*e.g.,* $400);

   (ii) Theft of ***items regarded as especially important*** without regard to value (*e.g.,* automobiles, firearms, or farm animals); and

   (iii) Thefts ***from the person*** of another, without regard to the value of the property taken.

   [Cal. Penal Code §487]

XII. OFFENSES AGAINST GOVERNMENT

chapter approach

Treason and related offenses are of limited applicability on criminal law exams. But where they may apply, watch especially for two considerations:

1. The defendant must have had ***allegiance to the government***.

2. There may be ***special proof requirements***, ***e.g.***, proof often requires testimony of two witnesses to the defendant's conduct.

A. TREASON

1. **Ancient Definition:** [§1155] Under ancient English law, it was "high treason" to kill the king, promote revolt in the kingdom or armed forces, or counterfeit the great seal. "Petit treason" consisted of a killing of a husband by his wife, a master or mistress by a servant, or a prelate by a clergyman. Treason was neither a felony nor a misdemeanor but a crime in a separate class by itself.

2. **Modern Formulations of the Crime:** [§1156] Treason is now a statutory crime, and its definition is fixed both by the United States Constitution and state criminal codes.

   a. **Federal crime:** [§1157] Treason is the only crime provided for in the United States Constitution. It is there defined as levying war against the United States, adhering to their enemies, or giving their enemies aid and comfort. [U.S. Const. art. 39, §3, cl. 1]

   b. **State crimes:** [§1158] Where treason is made a crime under state statutes, the definitions often emphasize action directed against state government. [Cal. Penal Code §37—treason consists of levying war against the state, adhering to its enemies, or giving its enemies aid and comfort]

3. **Requirements**

   a. **Allegiance:** [§1159] Since treason is essentially a breach of allegiance, the defendant can be convicted only if he owed allegiance to the prosecuting government. Thus, one who has lost or renounced his American citizenship cannot commit treason against the United States. [Kawakita v. United States, 343 U.S. 717 (1952)]

   b. **Overt act:** [§1160] Disloyal thoughts alone are not enough for treason. Some overt act of aid—such as affirmative encouragement of the enemy—is required. [Cramer v. United States, 325 U.S. 1 (1945)]

   c. **Intent to betray:** [§1161] The defendant must have had the ***intent to betray*** the government, but a showing that ***he was aware*** that his actions would assist an enemy of the government will suffice. [D'Aquino v. United States, 192 F.2d 338 (9th Cir. 1951)]

d. **Special evidentiary requirement:** [§1162] Under federal law and the law of many states, conviction for treason requires either (i) the testimony of ***two witnesses to the overt act*** or (ii) the defendant's ***confession in open court***. [U.S. Const. art. 3, §3, cl. 1; Cal. Const. art. 1, §20]

4. **Misprision of Treason:** [§1163] Misprision of treason is ***concealment*** of the known treason of another. It is punishable under federal law and the law of some states. [18 U.S.C. §2382; Cal. Penal Code §38]

B. TREASON-LIKE CRIMES [§1164]

There are a number of offenses resembling treason that proscribe certain activities thought to constitute a threat to the government. For instance:

1. **Rebellion:** [§1165] It is a federal crime to incite or engage in any rebellion against the United States. [18 U.S.C. §2383]

2. **Advocating Overthrow of Government:** [§1166] It is also a violation of federal criminal law knowingly or willfully to advocate the overthrow or destruction of the government of the United States or any state. [18 U.S.C. §2385]

XIII. OFFENSES AGAINST THE ADMINISTRATION OF JUSTICE

chapter approach

If an examination question involves action by a participant that frustrates efforts to ***capture, prosecute, or convict another suspect,*** be certain to consider possible liability for one or more of the following offenses. Consider specifically the nature of the participant's action:

1. Did the participant conceal the suspect or otherwise attempt to assist the suspect in avoiding conviction? (Consider ***misprision of felony*** or ***hindering apprehension or prosecution***.)
2. Did the participant enter into an agreement that involved his nonparticipation in the prosecution? (Consider ***compounding***.)
3. Did the participant misrepresent facts during in-court testimony? (Consider ***perjury***.)

A. HINDERING APPREHENSION OR PROSECUTION OF FELON

1. **Liability as Accessory After the Fact:** [§1167] Under common law "party" rules, one who assists a known felon in escaping arrest, prosecution, or conviction can incur liability for the felony committed as an accessory after the fact (*see supra,* §§202, 210). This approach, however, has been universally abandoned.

2. **Modern Statutes**

   a. **Accessory after the fact:** [§1168] If the terminology of "accessory after the fact" is retained in modern criminal statutes, it is used to identify a ***specific offense*** punishable by its ***own penalty*** rather than a basis for making a person guilty of a crime previously committed by another. [*See, e.g.,* Cal. Penal Code §§32, 33—one who "harbors, conceals, or aids" another who has committed a felony with knowledge that the person had committed a felony and with intent that the person escape from arrest, trial, conviction, or punishment is an accessory to the felony, which is punishable by one year imprisonment, a fine of not more than $5,000, or both]

   b. **Hindering apprehension or prosecution:** [§1169] Modern statutes sometimes create a ***new crime*** for former liability as an accessory after the fact, punishing much the same behavior (*i.e.,* aiding or warning another with the intent to hinder that person's apprehension, conviction, or punishment). [*See, e.g.,* Tex. Penal Code §38.05]

B. MISPRISION OF FELONY

1. **Common Law:** [§1170] At common law, one who fails to report or prosecute a person known to have committed a felony is guilty of the misdemeanor of misprision of felony. Apparently, however, persons who merely had knowledge of the

commission of a felony and failed to report it were rarely (if ever) actually prosecuted for this offense. [LaFave and Scott, 600]

2. **Modern Statutes:** [§1171] Federal statutes and those in some states retain misprision of felony as a crime. Federal law defines the offense as: (i) having knowledge of the actual commission of a felony cognizable by federal courts; and (ii) concealing and failing as soon as possible to make this known to a judge or other person of authority under the United States. [18 U.S.C. §4]

   a. **Limitation—active assistance required:** [§1172] The federal crime has been interpreted to require some ***affirmative steps to conceal*** the person known to have committed a felony, although this is arguably not a necessary reading of the statutory terminology. Thus, one who simply has knowledge of the commission of a felony and fails to report it is not punishable. [United States v. Warters, 885 F.2d 1266 (5th Cir. 1989)]

C. COMPOUNDING A CRIME

1. **Common Law:** [§1173] It is the common law misdemeanor of compounding a crime to agree for consideration not to prosecute another for a felony. [Perkins and Boyce, 578]

2. **Modern Statutes:** [§1174] Compounding often remains an offense under modern statutes. The crime is often defined as agreeing to forgo prosecution of ***any*** offense—felony or misdemeanor. [Model Penal Code §242.5; Cal. Penal Code §153—defining crime as accepting or agreeing to accept a benefit in consideration of refraining from reporting an offense or information relating to an offense]

3. **Elements:** [§1175] Compounding consists of (i) an agreement (ii) for valuable consideration (iii) to fail to report or cooperate in the prosecution of a crime.

   a. **Agreement:** [§1176] An ***agreement*** is an essential element of the crime. Thus, compounding is not committed if the defendant simply provides aid or fails to assist in the prosecution of another, hoping for a reward from that person. [Fidelity & Deposit Co. v. Grand National Bank, 69 F.2d 177 (8th Cir. 1934)]

   b. **Valuable consideration:** [§1177] It must be shown that pursuant to the agreement the defendant was entitled to valuable consideration (*i.e.*, money or anything of value or advantage) in return for her failure to prosecute. [Commonwealth v. Pease, 16 Mass. 91 (1819)]

4. **"Settlement" of Crimes:** [§1178] It is unclear under many compounding crimes to what extent the victim of a crime will be exposed to liability for compounding if she accepts restitution from the offender and in return agrees not to press charges. Some states permit certain compromises. [Cal. Penal Code §153—offense of compounding does not apply to certain statutorily-permitted compromises of misdemeanors] The Model Penal Code would provide for an affirmative defense to the crime of compounding consisting of a showing that the amount received under an agreement not to prosecute does not exceed an amount which the defendant believed to be due her as restitution or indemnification for the harm done by the crime. [Model Penal Code §242.5]

D. PERJURY

1. **Common Law:** [§1179] At common law, the misdemeanor of perjury is the willful giving of a false statement under oath in a judicial proceeding. [4 Blackstone Commentaries 137]

2. **Modern Statutes:** [§1180] Perjury is still a crime under modern law. However, modern statutes have sometimes modified the common law definition:

   a. **Any false testimony where oath may be administered:** [§1181] Generally, perjury is no longer limited to the context of a judicial proceeding. It is therefore perjury to give false testimony under oath ***in any proceeding*** wherein the law authorizes the administration of an oath. Thus, perjury can be committed before a legislative or administrative committee or board, if that body has authority by law to administer an oath to witnesses who appear before it. [Cal. Penal Code §118]

   b. **Limitation—"material" matter:** [§1182] There is no perjury unless the false statement is shown to have been "material," meaning that the statement could probably have ***influenced the outcome*** of the proceeding in which it was given. Thus, a false statement under oath concerning a matter that has no bearing on the proceeding is not perjury. [People v. Pierce, 66 Cal. 2d 53 (1967)]

3. **Special Evidentiary Requirements:** [§1183] At common law, perjury must be proved by the testimony of at least two witnesses. Some jurisdictions have now relaxed this requirement, but many still imposed a higher than ordinary requirement of proof. [Cal. Penal Code §1103a—conviction for perjury cannot rest on testimony by a single person, although falsity of the testimony can be proved by "indirect" evidence]

4. **Effect of Retraction:** [§1184] Courts have divided on the significance of a witness's retraction of perjured testimony. Some hold there can be no conviction if the witness retracts her testimony in the same proceeding and before its falsity has been established. [People v. Ezaugi, 2 N.Y.2d 439 (1957)] Others, however, find no defense in such a showing. [United States v. Norris, 300 U.S. 564 (1937)]

5. **Subornation of Perjury:** [§1185] The different offense of subornation of perjury is closely related to perjury.

   a. **Definition:** [§1186] One who intentionally causes another to commit perjury is guilty of the common law misdemeanor of subornation of perjury. This often remains an offense under modern statutes. [*See, e.g.*, Cal. Penal Code §127]

   b. **Requirements:** [§1187] Two requirements are often imposed for conviction: (i) the defendant must have ***known*** that the testimony to be given by the witness would be false, and (ii) the defendant must have ***actually caused*** the witness to actually give the false testimony. [Niehoff v. Sahagian, 103 A.2d 211 (Me. 1954)]

REVIEW QUESTIONS

FILL IN ANSWER

CLASSIFICATION OF CRIMES

1. Diane is charged with a statutory crime that is punishable by up to two years in the state prison. Upon conviction, however, the judge sentences Diane to only a period of probation. Has Diane been convicted of a felony? ________

BURDEN OF PROOF

2. D is prosecuted for intentionally causing damage to the property of Jones. The jury will be instructed that the prosecution must prove beyond a reasonable doubt that D intended to cause the damage. May the judge also instruct the jury that the law presumes a person intends the ordinary consequences of his voluntary acts? ________

BASIC LEGAL LIMITS UPON CRIMINAL LAW

3. Police officers executing a search warrant for Dirtbag's apartment find pornographic literature in a dresser drawer. May Dirtbag be convicted of possession of pornographic items? ________

4. Donald is charged with violating a statute that prohibits "any conduct infringing upon the public welfare." Is the statute constitutionally valid? ________

5. In the following situations, can D be sentenced to death without violating the Eighth Amendment's prohibition against cruel and unusual punishment?

   a. D is convicted of raping V at a time when D was 23 years old and V was 21. ________

   b. D is convicted of murdering V at a time when D was 15 years of age. ________

   c. D is convicted of murdering V at a time when D was 17 years old. ________

6. Cinder Pete throws a match under V's porch, intending to burn V's house and to kill V, who is sleeping inside. The house burns down and V is killed. May Cinder be convicted of both arson and murder if he is tried for both crimes at the same time? ________

7. A and B agree to kill V. Pursuant to the plan, A obtains a gun and the two of them break into V's house at night. B then shoots V to death.

   a. At common law, can A and B be convicted of conspiracy, burglary, and murder? ________

   b. Would the result be different under modern law? ________

8. Defenda was arrested while cruising the streets. Criminal charges are brought against her pursuant to an ordinance that prohibits "being a common prostitute." May she be convicted? ________

9. Suppose the same arrest as in question 8., but the charge is for "loitering for purposes of prostitution." Now may Defenda be convicted? ________

ELEMENTS OF CRIMES

10. Denise slips while walking on the sidewalk. She instinctively reaches out to grasp some support. Instead, her finger pokes out the eye of Vernon, who was also walking on the sidewalk. Has Denise committed an "act" upon which a criminal battery charge can be based? ________

11. Drowsier is a sleepwalker. One night, while sleepwalking, she pushes over and destroys a valuable vase belonging to a neighbor. Has Drowsier committed an "act" upon which a prosecution for malicious mischief can be based? ________

12. Def is walking down a street when he hears a person scream. He turns around and sees a woman being dragged into a dark alley by a man with a knife in his hand. Def decides to do nothing and walks away.

    a. Has Def "acted" so as to be guilty of a crime against the woman? ________

    b. Assume Def recognized the woman as a neighbor whom he despised. He was glad to witness her peril and intentionally decided not to intervene. If the woman is killed, can Def be convicted of any form of criminal homicide? ________

    c. Assume instead that Def recognized the woman as his wife but still chose not to intervene. Has Def "acted" so as to be guilty of a crime against his wife? ________

13. Dinah Dasanova is having a clandestine love affair with Vinny Virile, who is married to another woman. While in Dinah's apartment, Vinny becomes violently ill and begs Dinah to call a doctor for him. However, Dinah refuses, fearing that Vinny's wife will find out about the affair. If Vinny dies because of lack of medical attention, is Dinah guilty of some form of criminal homicide? ________

14. Dan Drownder is employed as a lifeguard on a public beach. During a period when he is supposed to be working, he leaves his guard station to visit a friend. While Dan is gone, a bather drowns. If the bather was a stranger to Dan, can Dan be convicted of some form of criminal homicide? ________

15. D is speeding down a highway at night when his car strikes and injures V. Because of the darkness, D is unaware of the accident and does not stop. Has D "acted" so as to be guilty of violating a hit-and-run statute? ________

16. Dad's child is ill and doctors report that surgery is essential. Dad does not have money to pay for further medical care and therefore does nothing. If the child dies because the surgery is not performed, is Dad guilty of some homicide offense? ________

17. D is charged with selling alcoholic beverages in a "dry" county. At trial, he testifies that he did not know the beverages in question were alcoholic. Must the jury be instructed that D should be acquitted unless the proof shows he was aware that the beverages were alcoholic? ________

18. During the course of an argument, Def shoved Vic, causing Vic serious injury when he fell and struck his head on the ground. Def is charged with aggravated battery under a statute defining the crime as "purposefully or knowingly causing serious bodily injury to another." Should Def be convicted? ________

19. D threw a rock intending to break the window of V's house. However, D's aim was off and the rock struck and broke a window of X's house. Can D be convicted of malicious mischief based upon the accidental damage to X's home? ________

20. Don Dillon intends to kill Vance Villain and buys a rifle for this purpose. While Dillon is engaged in target practice in his own backyard, Villain unexpectedly walks by and is killed by a bullet that ricochets from the target. Is Dillon guilty of murder? ________

21. Intending to kill Missy, Danny takes a shot at her while she is standing in a street. Although Danny is a champion shooter, he surprisingly misses his target. However, seconds later a truck hits Missy and kills her.

    a. Is Danny guilty of murder? ________

    b. Assume instead that the truck strikes Missy first. While she is lying near death in the middle of the street, Danny lives up to his champion reputation and shoots Missy, killing her instantly. It is clear that Missy would have died shortly from the truck wound alone. Is Danny guilty of murder? ________

22. While V is standing on the side of a busy highway, D approaches her from behind and stabs her. V pulls away, falling onto the highway. Shortly thereafter, a passing car strikes V and V dies from the combined effects of the knife wound and the injuries inflicted by the car. Is D guilty of any form of criminal homicide? ________

23. Dudley Disconcerted, an aging, soon-to-retire pitcher for the Lost Angels Bums, decides to kill T.T. Terrific, predicted by sportswriters to be the only one standing in the way of Dudley's last chance to receive the Cy Young Award. Pursuant to his plan, Dudley substitutes a knife for the baseball when T.T. comes to bat. The knife strikes T.T. in the chest and he collapses, whereupon he is immediately rushed to the hospital. Is Dudley guilty of any form of criminal homicide in the following situations?

    a. At the hospital, Nurse mistakenly gives T.T. a lethal gas instead of oxygen and T.T. dies. ________

    b. Surgery was successfully performed on T.T., and he is slowly recovering. However, because of his prolonged absence from the team he is eliminated from Cy Young contention. T.T. becomes despondent over this development and kills himself at the hospital. ________

    c. T.T's wound turned out to be only a superficial laceration; he is treated immediately and released. As he walks out of the hospital, however, he is struck by an arriving ambulance and dies instantly. ________

SCOPE OF CRIMINAL LIABILITY

24. A, who harbored a grudge against V, encouraged B and C to rob V's store. Upon their arrival at the store, B stood guard outside while C went in and robbed it. Following the robbery, V called the police who responded in immediate pursuit of the perpetrators. Fearful of their probable apprehension, B and C approached D for help; D permitted B and C to live in his basement until police concern with them subsided.

    a. Identify the principal(s) in the first degree to the robbery of V. ________

    b. Identify the principal(s) in the second degree. ________

    c. Identify the accessory(ies) before the fact. ________

    d. Identify the accessory(ies) after the fact. ________

25. Assume the same facts as in question 24., above. At common law, could A be convicted if B and C had been tried and acquitted? ________

26. Dorian leases an apartment to Natalie, knowing that Natalie intends to use the apartment as her headquarters for a bookmaking operation. Is Dorian an accomplice to Natalie's offense of bookmaking? ________

27. Clerk Dent is approached by Harry Habit and asked to help Habit take drugs from the store in which Dent works. Pursuant to the scheme, Dent leaves the door unlocked for Habit who enters later that night and takes the drugs. Both are soon apprehended and Dent is charged as an accessory before the fact to Habit's larceny. Dent, however, can establish that Habit was entrapped into committing the crime. Is Dent guilty? ________

    a. Suppose instead that before Habit left to enter the store, Dent telephoned him and reported that he, Dent, was withdrawing from the scheme. Dent, however, had already unlocked the door and Habit proceeded with the larceny. Ignoring any entrapment question, is Dent guilty as an accessory before the fact? ________

28. Virginia, age 16, invites her boyfriend Adam to have intercourse with both her and her younger sister, Sissy, who is 15. Assuming Adam responds affirmatively to the invitation—

    a. Is Virginia an accomplice to Adam's "statutory rape" of her? ________

    b. Is Virginia an accomplice to Adam's "statutory rape" of Sissy? ________

29. Sam, a tavern owner, employs Woody as bartender. Woody sells liquor to minors in violation of a state statute.

    a. Can Sam be convicted of selling liquor to minors? ________

    b. Can Sam be convicted even if he was unaware that Woody was selling liquor to minors? ________

c. Would Sam be guilty if Woody had deliberately violated Sam's previous instructions not to sell to minors? ________

30. Acme Tavern is owned by Acme Corporation. The corporation employs a bartender who sells liquor to minors in violation of a local ordinance making this a misdemeanor and, on one occasion, commits a felony assault on a patron whom he dislikes.

a. Can Acme be convicted of a misdemeanor? ________

b. Can Acme be convicted of felony assault? ________

DEFENSES

31. D suffers from a severe mental illness, most recently manifested by his erroneous belief that V has maliciously slandered him to all his friends. Upset over this, D purchases a gun and kills V. A defense psychiatrist testifies at the murder trial that D knew killing was wrong but was compelled by his illness to take V's life.

a. Would D be entitled to acquittal by reason of insanity under the *M'Naghten* rule? ________

b. Would D be entitled to acquittal under the irresistible impulse test? ________

c. Would D be entitled to acquittal under the *Durham* rule? ________

32. D is severely retarded. He shoots V, killing him. Later he asks when V will come to visit him and cannot understand why V does not show up. In a prosecution for murder, would D be entitled to acquittal under the *M'Naghten* rule? ________

33. Ben Drinken goes into a bar for a couple of drinks. He has more than a few and comes out hours later quite intoxicated. On his way home, he gets into an altercation with Victor, who had inadvertently bumped into Ben while crossing the street. Ben strikes Victor; Victor falls down. Ben takes Victor's wallet and leaves.

a. Can Ben be convicted of larceny of the wallet? ________

b. Can Ben be convicted of assault and battery on Victor? ________

c. Suppose instead that Ben orders a nonintoxicating drink, but as a practical joke, the bartender spikes it with a substantial amount of an intoxicating substance. Does Ben now have a defense to an assault and battery charge? ________

34. Dudley drives away in Vanessa's car, honestly but unreasonably believing that it is his own car. Is Dudley guilty of larceny? ________

35. D has intercourse with V, honestly believing that V has consented. In fact, V was objecting and resisting with sufficient seriousness that a reasonable person would have perceived that she was not consenting to the intercourse. Is D guilty of rape? ________

36. Following the death of his father, Moby, Dick takes all of Moby's money and spends it on frivolous items for himself. Charges are later brought against Dick for larceny. At trial Dick testifies that when he took the money he thought the

laws of intestate succession made him Moby's sole heir; in fact, the law was otherwise. Assuming his testimony is believed, should Dick be convicted of larceny? ________

a. Would the result be different if Dick testified that he knew the money was not his but that he talked with a lawyer and, on the basis of that conversation, concluded that there was no criminal penalty involved in taking the money from family members? ________

37. Partin is charged with willful failure to pay federal income tax due on the wages he received from his employer, Acme Refrigerator Company. Would he be entitled to acquittal in either of the following situations?

a. Partin convinces the jury that he actually believed that under the federal income tax law "wages" are not included within the "income" subject to tax, and the prosecution responds with convincing testimony that no reasonable person could entertain such an erroneous view of federal tax law. ________

b. Partin convinces the jury that he actually believed that because of technical irregularities in adoption of the Sixteenth Amendment authorizing a federal income tax, the amendment is not effective and thus the federal income tax system is unconstitutional and hence unenforceable. ________

38. Dogood sees a forest fire burning towards a town. Believing that the only way to stop the fire is to set a backfire that would destroy Nel's home, Dogood sets the backfire. Does Dogood have a defense to an arson charge? ________

39. Badman forces Hapless at gunpoint to drive him away from the scene of a robbery. Badman then compels Hapless to drive into a roadblock, whereupon a police officer is struck and killed.

a. Should Hapless be convicted as an accessory after the fact to Badman's robbery? ________

b. Does Hapless have a defense to the charge of intentionally murdering a police officer? ________

40. Narcotics agents operating undercover approach D and, representing that one of them is suffering from withdrawal, ask D to get them some heroin. D first refuses but after several pleas, she complies, procuring the heroin and selling it to the agents. D is promptly arrested.

a. In a prosecution for illegal sale of narcotics, can D successfully claim entrapment? ________

b. Would the result in a. be different if it were proven that D regularly sold narcotics? ________

c. Can D claim entrapment after testifying at her trial that she had not provided the agents with the heroin? ________

41. V decides to mutilate himself to protest the government's increase in taxes and asks D to assist him. D complies by amputating V's arms. D is charged with battery.

a. Does evidence of V's request establish a defense? ______

b. If V testifies that he forgives D, does D have a defense? ______

42. Stu Suspicious accuses Slick Vic of making advances to Stu's spouse. Vic raises his arm as if to strike Stu who, fearing the blow, strikes first. Vic sustains minor injuries.

a. Does Stu have a defense to a battery charge? ______

b. Would Stu have a defense to a battery charge if it were proven that Vic only raised his hand to scratch his head? ______

c. Assume that instead of striking Vic, Stu shot and killed him. Would Stu have a defense to a murder charge? ______

43. A plainclothes police officer is attempting validly to arrest Winnie on a public drunkenness charge. Darren comes by and, reasonably believing that Winnie is the victim of an unlawful assault, intervenes and injures the officer. If charged with battery, does Darren have a defense? ______

44. Diego's automobile was stolen. Three days later, he sees it parked on the street with Vance sitting inside. Diego tries to take possession, but Vance resists. In overcoming the resistance, Diego strikes and injures Vance.

a. If charges are brought against Diego for battery, does he have a defense? ______

b. Suppose Diego announced he was arresting Vance for larceny and then used force to overcome Vance's resistance. When charged with battery, would Diego then have a defense? ______

PRELIMINARY OR INCHOATE CRIMES

45. Dumbo approaches Mickey and says, "I'll give you $500 if you'll beat up Goofy." Mickey is an undercover police officer and arrests Dumbo. Has Dumbo committed a criminal offense? ______

46. A knows where a large amount of counterfeit money can be purchased and decides to ask B to help him pass the bills if he obtains them. Upon disclosure of the scheme to B, B responds, "What a break for you. You'll make a fortune." On the basis of these facts alone, are A and B guilty of criminal conspiracy? ______

47. Hillary, Bill, and Chelsea agree to rob a bank. Pursuant to the plan, Bill, who is to provide a getaway vehicle, steals a car and parks it in Chelsea's garage. The next day, Hillary tells Chelsea that she has changed her mind and will not join in the crime. Chelsea informs Bill of Hillary's change of heart at their meeting just before the robbery. Chelsea and Bill nevertheless carry out the robbery themselves.

a. Are Hillary, Bill, and Chelsea all guilty of criminal conspiracy? ______

b. Are Hillary, Bill, and Chelsea all guilty of the larceny of the car? ______

c. Are Hillary, Bill, and Chelsea all guilty of robbery? ______

48. A is charged with conspiring with B and C to kill V. B and C are acquitted. Can A be convicted? ________

49. Madame X, a married woman, is having an affair with her secretary, Sam Slade. The two agree to spend the night together at the Bijou Hotel. Can they be convicted of criminal conspiracy? ________

50. Desperate has amassed a huge gambling debt at the local casino and has no resources to pay it back. He decides to kill his father and use the inheritance to satisfy the debt. Pursuant to this plan, he buys a gun. Is Desperate guilty of attempted murder? ________

    a. Suppose that after buying the gun Desperate goes to his father's house and conceals himself in the bushes waiting to take his father by surprise. Is Desperate guilty of attempted murder? ________

51. D plans to buy stolen property from X, who he knows will be at a given location at midnight. D arrives at the location as scheduled, but X has since been arrested and will not show up. Is D guilty of attempted receipt of stolen property? ________

    a. Suppose a plainclothes police officer arrives at the location and offers to sell D a purportedly stolen radio. The radio in fact belongs to the police officer. If D buys the radio thinking it is stolen, is he guilty of receipt of stolen property or attempted receipt of stolen property? ________

HOMICIDE CRIMES

52. Can Deadly be convicted of murder in the following situations?

    a. Deadly intentionally stabs Vicky in the leg. The wound proves fatal and Vicky dies. ________

    b. Deadly throws a bottle in Vicky's direction, intending to frighten her. The bottle shatters against the wall; a piece of glass strikes Vicky, and she bleeds to death. ________

    c. Deadly, showing off to friends, pilots his new speedboat through a crowd of swimmers. Going at full speed, he intends only to scatter the swimmers, but one of them is hit by the boat and dies. ________

53. Dan Gerous is charged with first degree murder for the premeditated killing of Vic Tim. The prosecution establishes that Dan killed Vic with a pistol. If Dan shows that he formed the intent to kill Vic only seconds before the homicide actually took place, may he be convicted of first degree murder? ________

54. Starkmad and Disgusting rob a bank. During the robbery, Disgusting becomes attracted to Teller and forces his attentions upon her, despite Starkmad's urging to avoid this. Finally, Starkmad strikes Disgusting with the butt of his gun to discourage the attack on Teller; the gun discharges accidentally and kills Disgusting. Is Starkmad guilty of felony murder? ________

55. Sipowitz and Simone are in the process of burglarizing Fancy's gas station at night when Kelly, a police officer, comes upon the scene. Sipowitz and Simone

run into nearby woods with Kelly in pursuit. Simone accidentally drops a gun he is carrying; the gun discharges and Kelly is killed.

a. Is Simone guilty of felony murder? ________

b. Assuming Simone is guilty of felony murder, is Sipowitz also guilty? ________

56. Domino is in the process of holding up a liquor store with a toy pistol which appears to be real. The police arrive and order Domino to throw down his weapon; Domino runs instead. The police open fire, but they miss Domino and kill Vega, an innocent bystander. Would all courts find Domino guilty of felony murder? ________

57. Would the killings in the following situations more likely be voluntary manslaughter than murder?

a. V calls D several names that reflect on D's ethical standards and her mother's sexual practices. D becomes irate and kills V. ________

b. D and V are arguing over a place in a theater line. They agree to settle the matter by fighting it out. During the fight, V is killed. ________

c. While D, V, and X are sitting around a table, X tells D that V has committed adultery with D's spouse. D immediately kills V. ________

d. V throws a rock at D and runs away. The next day, D sees V and kills him. ________

e. V throws a rock at D and runs away. D, frustrated at her inability to obtain revenge against V, sees X, an innocent bystander, and kills X. ________

58. Should the following killings be charged as involuntary manslaughter?

a. D intentionally drops a large rock from a highway overpass. Distracted by the approaching rock, V loses control of her car on the highway and is killed in the ensuing crash. ________

b. D is cleaning his gun when the telephone rings. He leaves the gun on the table while he goes to the adjoining room to answer the phone. Meanwhile, V, D's four-year-old son, wanders into the room and takes the gun to play with it; it discharges, killing V instantly. ________

c. D is carefully carrying a concealed weapon which accidentally discharges, killing V. ________

d. D is attempting to commit suicide. V intervenes to prevent this, and in the struggle the gun that D was using discharges, killing V. ________

OTHER CRIMES AGAINST THE PERSON

59. Can D be convicted of battery in the following situations?

a. D puts poison in V's drink, and V drinks it. ________

b. D intentionally spits on V's shoe. ________

c. D, driving her car in a highly negligent manner, strikes Pedestrian. D did not intend to injure anyone. ________

60. Don points a gun at Vivian and pulls the trigger. Unknown to Don, the gun is defective and will not fire. Is Don guilty of assault? ________

61. Danielle attacks Violet as a result of which Violet's face is severely disfigured. Danielle is charged with mayhem, but at the time of the trial, two years later, Violet's face has returned to normal. Can Danielle be convicted? ________

62. Dance and Vance are at a party. Both have consumed great amounts of liquor. Vance passes out, and Dance engages in an act of intercourse with her while she is unconscious. Is Dance guilty of rape? ________

63. Dennis tells Vanna that unless she submits to intercourse with him, he will report her to the police as a prostitute. Vanna submits. Is Dennis guilty of rape? ________

64. Dunbar tells Veronica that if she will engage in intercourse with him, he will pay her $150. He does not intend to pay her, and after the act is complete he refuses to do so. Is Dunbar guilty of rape? ________

65. Deitrich and Val have been living together for two years but Val refuses to have intercourse with Deitrich until they are married. Deitrich arranges a sham marriage ceremony and convinces Val that they are married. Val then consents to intercourse. Is Deitrich guilty of rape? ________

66. In D's prosecution for rape of V, D testifies that V consented to the intercourse. V testifies for the prosecution that she did not consent but rather physically resisted as much as she could. D asks that the jury be instructed that D should be acquitted if the jury determines that D reasonably believed V consented, whether or not she actually did. Does the prosecution have a viable argument that this instruction should not be given? ________

67. While Slim is walking down a hall in a public building, Bull moves in front of him and refuses to permit him to proceed. Is Bull guilty of false imprisonment? ________

68. Doug Delude, as part of an extortion scheme, tells Dupe that his wife is in the hospital calling for him. Dupe willingly accompanies Delude to his car and drives away with him. Is Delude guilty of kidnapping? ________

69. D breaks into V's house and finds her in the kitchen. He compels her to go into the adjoining room and rapes her there. Is D guilty of kidnapping as well as rape? ________

CRIMES AGAINST THE HABITATION

70. Delilah, intending to kill Samson, throws a bomb through a closed window in Samson's house at night. Has Delilah committed burglary? ________

71. Digby, intending to steal Villareal's family jewels, pushes open a partially opened window in Villareal's house and crawls in. Has Digby committed burglary? ________

72. D persuades V's cook to let him into V's house late one night to steal V's valuable Picasso. The cook does so. Is D guilty of burglary? ________

73. Darlene owns a house that she rents to Vi. One night while Vi is away, Darlene decides to steal Vi's money and enters the house with her passkey. Has Darlene committed burglary? ________

74. To escape a rampaging storm one night, Desperate breaks and enters Handy's home. Once inside, Desperate sees Handy's wallet lying on the floor and decides to steal it. Has Desperate committed burglary? ________

75. D breaks and enters V's house during the nighttime. Will the following facts preclude D's conviction for common law burglary?

    a. V and all other occupants were on vacation, and so no one was present in the house. ________

    b. Once inside, D abandoned her intent to steal. ________

    c. D was voluntarily intoxicated at the time of entry. ________

    d. D's intent on entering was to find a place to sleep for the night. ________

76. Delinquent throws a firebomb into Violet's house. It lands on a sofa, burns the fabric, and then goes out. Is Delinquent guilty of arson? ________

77. Klutz, while burglarizing a house, accidentally leaves a cigarette burning. The cigarette sets fire to the house, and before help arrives the house burns down. Is Klutz guilty of arson? ________

78. Tenant sets fire to his apartment in protest of Landlord's failure to repair the premises. The fire accidentally spreads to other units in the building, causing them severe damage. Is Tenant guilty of arson? ________

CRIMES AGAINST PROPERTY

79. Can the following items be the subject of common law larceny?

    a. A purebred Siamese cat of champion stock. ________

    b. An Angus bull. ________

    c. Stock certificates in a corporation. ________

    d. Corn growing in a field. ________

    e. A stolen car. ________

    f. A wallet lost by its owner. ________

80. Lucy leaves her TV with Vic for repairs. Vic repairs it but refuses to return it to Lucy until she pays for the work. When Vic is not looking, Lucy takes the TV and runs, intending never to pay the repair bill. Is Lucy guilty of larceny? ________

81. Scully and Mulder own a taxi business together. Scully takes Cab 804 (which belongs to the business) and refuses to return it. Is Scully guilty of larceny? ________

82. Husband takes Wife's jewelry and gives it to Beggar as a gift. Is Husband guilty of common law larceny? ________

83. Looking for some fuel to feed his furnace, Cheapskate takes some old posts lying in Neighbor's backyard. He intends to pay Neighbor for them should Neighbor complain about the taking. Is Cheapskate guilty of larceny? ________

84. Smart picks up a briefcase in a public restroom at an airport believing it to be his own. When he opens it later that day, however, he finds it belongs to Chaos, whose name is on the papers inside. The briefcase also contains over $100,000 in cash. After giving the matter a few days thought, Smart decides to keep the briefcase and its contents. Is Smart guilty of larceny? ________

85. Aldo goes to Betty's office to give Betty $500. Betty's receptionist, Cassandra, accepts the money and, as Aldo leaves, places it in her purse and walks out, intending to keep it. Is Cassandra guilty of larceny? ________

86. Busy gives her errand clerk, Delivery, $500 to deposit for her in the bank. On the way to the bank, Delivery decides he has better uses for the money and absconds with it. Is Delivery guilty of larceny? ________

87. A loans B $5,000 and agrees to hold B's diamond ring as security. A immediately sells the ring for $7,500. Is A guilty of embezzlement? ________

88. Botticelli promises to deliver a rare painting to DaVinci for $5,000. DaVinci gives Botticelli the $5,000, who then absconds. Is Botticelli guilty of false pretenses? ________

    a. Suppose instead that Botticelli does deliver the painting, but that it has damage to the back of it which substantially reduces its value. Botticelli knew of the defect all along but did not call the matter to DaVinci's attention. Is Botticelli guilty of false pretenses? ________

89. D enters V's jewelry store and misrepresents that X has sent him to pick up certain emeralds for X's inspection and possible purchase. V gives the jewels to D and D agrees to return with the jewels or the cash for their purchase later that day. Immediately thereafter, D converts the emeralds to his own use as he had intended to do all along. Is D guilty of false pretenses? ________

90. Slight O'Hand, a professional pickpocket, lifts Bozo's wallet at a circus. Bozo was busy watching the elephants perform at the time and did not feel a thing. Is O'Hand guilty of robbery? ________

91. After an illegal gambling game, Loser, one of the participants, pulls a gun and demands his losses back. The money is quickly handed over, and Loser runs off. Is Loser guilty of robbery? ________

92. D attempts to rape V, but V escapes, leaving her purse behind. D finds the purse and keeps it. Is D guilty of robbery? ________

93. Brutus enters Tiny's home, ties him up, and forces him to tell where his money is hidden. Brutus then goes into another room to get the money from the hiding place. Is Brutus guilty of robbery? ________

94. D threatens to harm V's child when the child returns from school, unless V gives D all the money in V's home. Fearful for her child's life, V complies.

   a. Assuming the child is away at boarding school and will not be home for a week, is D guilty of robbery? ________

   b. Is D guilty of extortion? ________

95. Mel and Vera are having an adulterous affair. Mel threatens to tell Vera's spouse about the affair unless Vera pays Mel $10,000. Assuming Vera has not yet paid Mel the money, is Mel guilty of extortion? ________

96. Marla purchased a dog from Harold for $1,500, with the understanding that the dog was well trained. The first time Marla took the dog outside, it ran away despite her commands to "come." Marla told Harold that unless he gave her $1,500, she would contact the district attorney and press criminal charges for criminal fraud. As a result, Marla is charged with extortion. Does she have a defense? ________

97. Delbert encourages Xena to steal certain items from Viceroy. Delbert is not present when Xena commits the crime. Xena sells the items to Delbert. Delbert is convicted of the larceny as an accessory before the fact. Can Delbert also be convicted of receiving stolen property? ________

OFFENSES AGAINST GOVERNMENT AND THE ADMINISTRATION OF JUSTICE

98. Claudine, a Canadian citizen, is visiting the United States. She obtains certain U.S. military secrets and passes them to Country X, which is at war with the United States. Is Claudine guilty of treason? ________

99. Loyal knows that her dear friend Zip has committed robbery but neither reports this information to authorities nor tells them where Zip can be found. As a result, Zip avoids capture and conviction. Is Loyal guilty of misprision of felony under federal law? ________

   a. Assume instead that Loyal knows Zip is hiding in the apartment next door. Police come by and ask Loyal if she has seen Zip, and Loyal tells them that she believes he is hiding in another neighborhood. The police leave to check this out, and Zip escapes. Is Loyal now guilty of misprision of felony? ________

100. D observed X kill Z. When police question D about the incident, D falsely tells them that Z attacked X and that X killed in self-defense. D hopes that X will reward him for this help. Is D guilty of compounding a crime? ________

ANSWERS TO REVIEW QUESTIONS

1. **YES**	Whether or not a crime is a felony depends upon the punishment that ***may be*** imposed upon conviction—not the punishment actually imposed. Accordingly, under any of the tests used to distinguish felonies from misdemeanors, this crime would be a felony. [§9]
2. **NO**	The jury might understand the instruction as requiring that D prove he did not intend to cause the damage. Thus, the instruction would violate D's due process right to have all elements of the crime proved beyond a reasonable doubt. [§20]
3. **NO**	The right of privacy embodied in the First Amendment prohibits punishing a person for possession of obscene materials in the privacy of his home. [§42]
4. **NO**	The statute is clearly "void for vagueness" under the Due Process Clauses of the Fifth and Fourteenth Amendments because it is lacking in certainty as to the conduct made criminal. [§§44 *et seq.*]
5.a. **NO**	The death penalty is constitutionally excessive for the crime of rape of an adult woman. [§55]
b. **NO**	The death penalty is constitutionally excessive if the defendant was under age 16 at the time of the crime. [§58]
c. **YES**	The Eighth Amendment does not limit the availability of the death penalty on age grounds if the defendant was 16 years or older at the time of crime. [§58]
6. **PROBABLY YES**	The federal constitutional prohibition against double jeopardy is not violated by conviction for several overlapping offenses if this occurs in a single trial. [§66] However, legislative intent may have been to have the arson "merge" into the murder and thus to bar conviction for both. [§75] If the intent is to bar conviction for both, the constitutional provision would be violated by multiple conviction. [§67] The *Blockburger* test suggests that the legislative intent was to permit conviction for both because each crime requires proof of something that the other does not (arson requires the burning of a dwelling while murder does not, and murder requires the death of the victim while arson does not). [§76] *But note:* There may be more stringent state statutory or constitutional law prohibiting multiple convictions for what is essentially the same conduct. [§72]
7.a. **NO**	At common law, conspiracy (a misdemeanor) merges into the object crimes (which are felonies). But there is no merger of crimes of the same degree, and thus A and B can be convicted of burglary and murder. [§63]
b. **YES**	Merger is not recognized under modern law. [§64]
8. **NO**	A crime punishing a given status offends the Eighth Amendment prohibition against cruel and unusual punishment. [§80]
9. **YES**	There is no prohibition against making specific acts criminal, even if those acts are closely related to a status which cannot itself be made a crime. [§81]

10. **NO** This was not volitional action and so does not meet the legal requirements for an "act." [§§83, 85]

11. **NO** Where criminal liability is predicated on an affirmative act, there must be a showing of some ***conscious*** and ***volitional*** movement. [§85]

12.a. **NO** From the facts given, Def had no legal duty to assist the woman (a moral obligation alone is not enough). Therefore, his failure to help her does not constitute an "act." [§§89 *et seq.*]

b. **NO** He still has not "acted" within the meaning of the criminal law. The fact that Def and the woman were neighbors does not create a legal duty to act, and his bad or "criminal" intent alone cannot render him liable. [§§78-79, 89 *et seq.*]

c. **YES** The marriage relationship obligated Def to do whatever he was capable of doing to avert the peril (whether by intervening personally or seeking others to help). Having failed to perform a legal duty where it was possible to do so, Def has "acted" for purposes of criminal liability. [§§91, 105]

13. **POSSIBLY** The modern trend is to expand on the common law legal duties. Thus, a court might find that the relationship between Dinah and Vinny obliged her to act to save Vinny's life. If such a duty is found, Dinah's omission will support a criminal homicide conviction. [§§91, 102]

14. **YES** Dan breached a contractual duty (to maintain his post and aid swimmers in distress), and that omission was an "act" that caused death. [§94]

15. **NO** Although the statute may have imposed a duty to act, there is no "act" for criminal law purpose unless D was ***aware*** of the facts creating that duty. Here, D was not. [§101]

16. **POSSIBLY** An omission is an "act" only if the defendant could have ***performed*** the duty violated. Thus, if Dad could not have obtained medical assistance, his failure to do so will not support a homicide conviction. However, Dad's own financial straits are not conclusive; he can be held criminally liable if other sources of help (such as welfare agencies) were available. [§§105-106]

17. **NO** This crime is a "regulatory offense" and thus will most probably be interpreted as imposing strict liability. Accordingly, no intent is necessary as to the critical element of the nature of the beverages sold. [§§131 *et seq.*; *and see* United States v. Balint, §139]

18. **PROBABLY NOT** The apparent inference to be drawn from the facts is that Def did not consciously desire, nor contemplate to a practical certainty, the ***serious*** injury to Vic that actually occurred; had he intended to cause such severe harm he no doubt would have dealt Vic a blow (or the like) rather than simply giving Vic a shove. Therefore, in regard to the nature of the result, Def did not act with "purpose" or "knowledge" as these terms are defined in modern codes. [§§149-150]

19. **YES** Although D did not intend the harm actually caused (damage to X's home), there was considerable similarity between the contemplated harm and the resulting harm (broken window). Therefore, the doctrine of "transferred intent"

applies and D will be treated as if he intended to break X's window. [§§167-168]

20. **NO** While Dillon had the intent required [§§697 *et seq.*] and performed an act causing death, there was not the requisite ***concurrence*** between the intent and the act; *i.e.,* since the act was not attributable to Dillon's culpable state of mind, he cannot be convicted of murder. [§§170-171] (*Compare:* If engaging in target practice in the backyard is found to be criminally negligent, Dillon could be found guilty of involuntary manslaughter; but here, there would be the necessary concurrence between act and intent.) [§779]

21.a. **NO** There was no factual causation between the death and Danny's action. (Missy would have been hit by the truck whether or not Danny fired at her.) [§§175-178]

b. **YES** The facts now show "but for" causation. It is immaterial that Danny merely hastened the inevitable—"but for" his act Missy would not have died when and as she did. [§§170, 190]

22. **YES** Although death was caused in an uncontemplated manner, there is nothing here to break the chain of causation; it was clearly foreseeable that a struggling victim along the side of a highway might accidentally fall into traffic. [§§184 *et seq.*]

23.a. **PROBABLY** In the absence of evidence that the medical mistreatment was grossly negligent, it will not break the chain of proximate causation (*i.e.,* Nurse's mistake is not a superseding factor). [§§191-193]

b. **PROBABLY** T.T.'s depression was directly related to the injury inflicted by Dudley. Hence, a court will most likely find that T.T.'s conduct in taking his own life was a foreseeable intervening factor that does not break the chain of proximate causation. [§194]

c. **NO** Here T.T.'s death was caused by an ***unforeseeable*** accident that broke the chain of proximate causation. [§§184-197]

24.a. **C** The actual perpetrator of the crime is the principal in the first degree. [§205]

b. **B** B facilitated C's perpetration of the robbery and by acting as a lookout was constructively (if not actually) present at its commission. [§§206-207]

c. **A** A encouraged C to commit the robbery but was not present at its commission. [§208]

d. **D** D assisted B and C in their efforts to avoid apprehension by police, knowing that they had committed a felony. [§210]

25. **NO** At common law, conviction of the principal was essential to conviction of an accessory. [§214] (However, the rule is otherwise in most jurisdictions today. [§225])

26. **SPLIT** Some jurisdictions require that an accessory act with the purpose of aiding the principal; and under these facts, it does not appear that Dorian had such intent. (Knowledge of Natalie's illegal activity alone would not be enough.) [§241]

But other jurisdictions require only that the accessory be aware that his actions will assist the commission of a crime, in which case, Dorian would be guilty. [§243]

27. **UNCLEAR** Whether an accessory can assert defenses available to the actual perpetrator is subject to a split of authority (although at least one circuit court has held that an accessory could not rely on the perpetrator's entrapment defense). [§247] If the defense does not extend to Dent, he can be convicted for abetting Habit's commission of the crime. [§208]

a. **YES** Dent was an ***abettor*** (not simply an inciter), since he physically assisted commission of the crime. An abettor cannot withdraw by a renunciation alone, but must deprive his earlier action of its effectiveness. This Dent did not do (door remained unlocked), and his attempted withdrawal is therefore ineffective. [§§255-258]

28.a. **NO** She is within the class of persons protected by the statutory rape statute and therefore is not liable despite her participation. [§261]

b. **YES** Virginia was not the "victim" of this crime. Moreover, the fact that she could not commit rape upon Sissy directly does not preclude her conviction as an accessory to Adam's rape of Sissy. [§265]

29.a. **PROBABLY** Statutes of this sort are often read as imposing vicarious liability on an employer for the acts of employees, but the matter is ultimately one of legislative intent. [§§280-282]

b. **PROBABLY** But note that this is an issue of ***strict*** rather than ***vicarious*** liability. This statute is likely to be interpreted as imposing both strict and vicarious liability, but the questions are separate. [§§279, 134-144]

c. **SPLIT** Some courts hold employers liable despite such instructions, while others find that such instructions relieve employers of vicarious liability. Even in these latter jurisdictions, however, it may be necessary for Sam to show that the instructions were vigorously given and unambiguous. [§§284-285]

30.a. **YES** This is a minor offense (misdemeanor) committed by an employee in the course of his employment. [§301]

b. **SPLIT** Some courts would invoke the standard governing minor crimes, in which case Acme would be liable. But in other jurisdictions, a corporation is liable for a serious crime only if the offense was authorized or tolerated by a management official. Since the felony was perpetrated because of the bartender's personal grudge, it is unlikely that Acme would be found liable under the latter approach. [§§302-305]

31.a. **NO** Any compulsion that D experienced is irrelevant under *M'Naghten*. Here, D had not lost the capacity to know his act was legally wrong, since his symptoms did not cause him to believe he was legally justified in killing. Moreover, the fact that he purchased a gun to accomplish the killing demonstrates that he did know the nature and quality of his act. [§§237-342]

b. **PERHAPS** A jury might find that because of his illness, D could not control the urge to act as he did. He would then be entitled to acquittal. [§§345-346]

c. **YES** The evidence establishes that "but for" his mental illness, D would not have killed V. [§350]

32. **YES** Retardation can give rise to insanity, and here D clearly did not understand the nature and quality of the act of killing (otherwise, he would not have been awaiting V's visit). [§§330, 338]

33.a. **DEPENDS** Larceny requires proof of the specific intent to steal. If because of his voluntary intoxication Ben lacked that intent, he cannot be convicted of larceny. [§§385-386]

b. **YES** Assault and battery are not specific intent crimes. Therefore, Ben's voluntary intoxication is no defense. [§§385-386]

c. **DEPENDS** Under these facts, Ben's intoxication would be involuntary, since he was unaware of the intoxicating nature of the drink. However, involuntary intoxication is only a complete defense if it renders the defendant insane within the meaning of the jurisdiction's insanity test. [§§381-382]

34. **NO** He has a mistake of fact defense. Because Dudley thought he was driving his own car, he clearly lacked the intent to deprive Vanessa of ***her*** car. Moreover, it is irrelevant that the mistake was unreasonable, since it disproves a ***specific*** intent required for larceny. [§§395, 1023 *et seq.*]

35. **YES** Rape is not a specific intent crime. Therefore, an unreasonable mistake of fact cannot be used to prove lack of intent. [§§395, 858]

36. **NO** He has a "mistake of law" defense. His mistake concerning intestate succession law shows he lacked the intent to steal required by larceny and therefore prevents liability. [§410]

a. **YES** A belief that one's acts will not be criminal is generally not a defense. This situation does not come within any of the exceptions; none of the exceptions covers a belief based on advice of counsel. [§§409, 427]

37.a. **YES** "Willfulness" as used in this crime requires that the accused be shown to have failed to pay tax that he knew was due. Partin's testimony establishes that he did not know the tax was due and thus the prosecution's evidence fails. Since his testimony actually establishes his lack of the required mens rea, it is irrelevant that his belief was objectively unreasonable. [§§410-411]

b. **NO** "Willfulness" as required by this crime does not require knowledge that the statutes imposing the tax are constitutionally valid. Hence his testimony does not show that he lacked the mens rea required by the crime and he can be convicted. [§413]

38. **YES** This is a classic necessity defense situation; *i.e.,* Dogood reasonably believed that burning Nel's home was the only way to prevent the occurrence of a greater harm (destruction of the town). [§429]

39.a. **NO** — Hapless can successfully assert the defense of duress since he was compelled to act under threat of immediate serious bodily harm. [§§439-445]

b. **NO** — Duress is not a defense to the intentional killing of another, and no other defenses are apparent from the facts. (Duress may be offered to negate premeditation, however, and thus it may preclude conviction for first degree murder.) [§§446-449]

40.a. **PROBABLY** — The facts set forth a persuasive case for entrapment. Applying the traditional standard, the agents' repeated requests and their appeals to D's sympathy indicate D was not predisposed to commit the crime. And, under the modern standard, it is likely that the agents' perseverance would have induced a reasonable person to commit the crime. [§§462-465, 468-471]

b. **YES** — Now it appears that D was predisposed to commit the crime and that the agents merely provided her with the opportunity to do so. Hence, there would be no entrapment under the traditional approach. [§465] However, D would probably still have a defense if the jurisdiction adopts the minority ("objective") standard, under which her own predisposition would be immaterial. [§468]

c. **PROBABLY NOT** — In many and perhaps most jurisdictions, the accused cannot both claim entrapment and deny commission of the crime. [§459]

41.a. **NO** — Consent is not a defense to crimes involving serious bodily injury. [§480]

b. **NO** — The victim's forgiveness is never a defense. [§486]

42.a. **YES** — Stu reasonably believed he was about to suffer imminent harm and so was entitled to act in self-defense. [§§490-496]

b. **YES** — The defense of self-defense is available as long as it ***reasonably appeared*** to the defendant that force was necessary to prevent imminent harm. [§494]

c. **NO** — Deadly force can be used in self-defense only if the defendant reasonably believed he was threatened with death or serious bodily injury; Vic's raising his arm did not pose such a threat. [§498]

43. **SPLIT** — Courts disagree on whether force can be used in defense of others where the person defended would not have had the right to act in self-defense. [§§527-529]

44.a. **NO** — Not even nondeadly force can be used to retake property wrongfully in the possession of another. The actor must resort to legal process. [§540]

b. **PROBABLY** — A private citizen can use nondeadly force to make a felony arrest if the felony was in fact committed and the citizen reasonably believes the arrested person committed it. [§565]

45. **YES** — This is a completed solicitation; the person incited need not respond affirmatively. [§§578-580]

46. **NO** — An ***agreement*** to combine is essential to the crime of conspiracy. Here, however, B did not agree to anything; B simply expressed approval of A's participation. [§§591, 602]

47.a. **YES** All entered into the agreement, and Hillary's later withdrawal is no defense. [§§602, 640]

b. **YES** The theft was foreseeable and committed in furtherance of the conspiratorial objective. [§644] Moreover, there is no question of withdrawal as a defense to Hillary's liability since she did not renounce the scheme until after the larceny was committed. [§650]

c. **NO (most courts)** Hillary is not liable for the robbery, because she effectively withdrew from the conspiracy before the robbery took place. (While at least one court has required the withdrawing member to prevent her co-conspirators from completing the object crime, most courts hold that a timely communication is enough.) [§§650-653]

48. **NO** Since there must be an agreement between at least two persons, acquittal of all other members of the alleged conspiracy means that the remaining member cannot be guilty. [§§626-627]

49. **NO** Under "Wharton's Rule," there can be no conviction for conspiracy to commit an offense which by its definition requires a preliminary agreement between the parties (here, adultery). [§§632-633]

50. **NO** Although there are various tests for determining whether or not a person has gone far enough to constitute attempt, it is unlikely that merely purchasing the gun is enough under any of these tests. [§§664-672]

a. **PROBABLY** Under most tests, Desperate has now gone far enough toward commission of the crime. He may not, however, have met the "last proximate act" test or the "control over all indispensable elements" test. [§§664-672]

51. **YES** This is a case of "factual impossibility"; *i.e.,* D has done everything he could do to consummate the crime and failed only because of X's intervening arrest. Factual impossibility will not prevent liability. [§676]

a. **PROBABLY NOT** He is not guilty of receipt of stolen property, because the property was not in fact "stolen." [§§1134-1136] Moreover, since it is "legally impossible" to commit the crime by receiving this item, some courts, applying the traditional rule, would find no liability for attempt. (Other courts, however, reject this rule and would permit D's conviction.) [§§677-683, 1137]

52.a. **YES** Deadly acted with intent to inflict serious bodily injury and this is enough. [§701]

b. **NO** Deadly's intent to frighten Vicky and the fortuitous events that followed do not demonstrate malice aforethought. [§§697-704]

c. **YES** Deadly's conduct evidences an awareness of a high risk of death or serious bodily injury to the swimmers and this is sufficient. [§§704-705, 707]

53. **DEPENDS** Courts disagree on whether premeditation requires proof of an opportunity for extended reflection. Some jurisdictions require proof of an appreciable period of time during which deliberation could have occurred; others do not. [§§713-715]

54. **DEPENDS** Some courts require the death to have been a foreseeable consequence of the felony. In these jurisdictions it is unlikely that the felony murder rule would be applied since Disgusting was on an independent venture of his own; *i.e.,* the incident that prompted the killing was not a foreseeable result of commission of the robbery. [§727]

55.a. **PROBABLY** Although the felony itself had terminated, many courts apply the felony murder rule to deaths caused after technical completion of the felony—particularly if the death is caused before the felons reach a place of temporary safety. [§740]

b. **YES** Each felon is liable for those killings by his co-felons that are the natural and probable result of the felony. [§724]

56. **NO** The modern trend limits application of the felony murder rule to situations in which one of the ***felons*** directly causes death. (Here death was caused by the act of a police officer.) However, the modern view is not universally accepted; some courts might convict Domino for felony murder on the theory that "but for" his attempted perpetration of the robbery, Vega would not have been killed. [§§733-735]

57.a. **PROBABLY NOT** Traditionally, mere words are not adequate provocation. [§755]

b. **YES** A killing during mutual combat is voluntary manslaughter. [§762]

c. **DEPENDS** Some courts find adequate provocation only where one spouse actually observes the other spouse committing adultery; others also find it where the defendant-spouse is told of the adultery. [§761]

d. **NO** While a battery is adequate provocation if it is a serious one [§757], here the time that elapsed between the provocation and the killing was most probably sufficient for the passions of a reasonable person to cool. [§770]

e. **NO** A killing is not reduced to voluntary manslaughter where the provocation causes the defendant intentionally to strike out at innocent third persons. [§766] (Note that the result would be different if D intended to kill V but accidentally killed X. [§765])

58.a. **NO** This involves such a high risk to human life that it would properly be charged as murder. [§§778, 704]

b. **YES** Inadvertently leaving the gun within the reach of a four-year-old child most likely involves criminal negligence. [§§779-781]

c. **DEPENDS** While the killing was caused during the commission of a prohibited act, some jurisdictions also require that the act be malum in se. Here the unlawful act was only malum prohibitum and so is not necessarily sufficient to make the killing manslaughter. [§785]

d. **PROBABLY** This is an unintentional killing caused during the commission of an unlawful act. [§§782-783] However, a few courts might find no liability, and if suicide is still murder in the jurisdiction (as it is at common law) there may be liability for felony murder. [§803]

59.a. **YES** Indirect application of force is still a battery. [§810]

b. **YES** No injury is necessary. [§809]

c. **YES** Battery need not be intentional; criminal negligence will suffice. [§§814-815]

60. **DEPENDS** Some jurisdictions in which assault is defined as an attempted battery also require a showing that the defendant had the present ability to succeed. Here, however, the gun was defective and therefore Don could not be convicted. [§825] Other jurisdictions extend the crime of assault to include intentionally putting another in fear of immediate bodily harm; arguably, Don has done just that here. [§827]

61. **NO** Violet's normal appearance was only temporarily impaired; mayhem requires a ***permanent*** disfigurement. [§838]

62. **YES** If the victim is unable to give consent, intercourse with her is rape. [§851]

63. **NO** Consent obtained by use of threats is vitiated only where the threats are of bodily harm. [§850]

64. **NO** This is not one of the types of fraud that will invalidate consent. [§§852-856]

65. **SPLIT** Courts disagree as to whether fraud concerning the existence of a marital relationship invalidates consent. [§855]

66. **YES** Some courts hold that such an instruction is appropriate ***only if*** there is some evidence of equivocal conduct on the victim's part that might have supported a belief by the defendant that the victim consented. [§§858-859]

67. **NO** Simply preventing the victim from proceeding is not a "confinement" for purposes of false imprisonment. [§880]

68. **DEPENDS** Statutes differ on whether causing the movement of the victim by deception is sufficient. [§§895, 897]

69. **DEPENDS** D might be guilty under statutes defining kidnapping as detention and movement of the victim, although there may be a question as to whether the forced movement was substantial enough. [§§887-889] But here the detention and movement of the victim were incidental to the commission of another serious crime, rape. In this situation, many courts would require that the risk to the victim have been increased beyond what is involved in rape. [§§902-904]

70. **YES** Entry by an instrument with which Delilah intended to commit the underlying crime is enough. [§911]

71. **DEPENDS** The issue here is whether there was a "breaking." Some courts require that force be used to ***create*** an opening. But others hold it sufficient that force is used to enlarge an existing opening. [§916]

72. **YES** Obtaining entry with the aid of a co-conspirator already in the dwelling is "constructive force" and will suffice for a breaking. [§§915, 918]

73. **YES** Since Vi had the right to use the house to live in, it was Vi's dwelling. [§§929-930]

74. **NO** The felonious intent must exist at the time of entry. [§936]

75.a. **NO** Temporary absence of the residents does not mean the structure is not a dwelling. [§926]

b. **NO** The crime is complete on entry. The intent need not be carried out. [§938]

c. **DEPENDS** Only if the intoxication proves the lack of intent to commit a felony in the structure will the conviction be barred. [§§385, 936-937]

d. **YES** D did not intend to commit a felony at the time of entry. [§936]

76. **NO** For arson, some part of the structure itself must be "burned." [§960]

77. **NO** Neither negligence nor the commission of another crime (here, burglary) will supply the malice required for arson. [§§963-965]

78. **YES** Creating a high risk of damage to other dwellings by setting one's own dwelling on fire establishes the malice necessary for arson. [§§963, 966]

79.a. **NO** Household pets cannot be the subject of larceny. [§983]

b. **YES** Domestic animals of value can be the subject of larceny. [§983]

c. **NO** Intangible personal property cannot be the subject of larceny. [§985]

d. **NO** Crops are part of the realty and thus not the subject of larceny. [§980]

e. **YES** Even stolen property or contraband can be the subject of larceny. [§988]

f. **YES** Lost property can be the subject of larceny (although a defendant can be convicted only if there was a "clue to ownership" and the defendant intended to steal the item when he found it). [§§1045-1047]

80. **YES** Since Vic had a right to possession superior to that of Lucy, Lucy's taking is larceny. [§§1016-1017]

81. **NO** Most courts hold that one joint owner cannot commit larceny from the other joint owner. [§1021]

82. **NO** At common law, spouses are regarded as "one." Hence, one spouse cannot commit larceny by taking the property of the other. [§1022]

83. **PROBABLY** Cheapskate's vague and conditional intent to pay for the property (which was apparently not for sale) is probably insufficient to prevent his actions from being larceny. [§1029]

84. **NO** The misappropriation of lost property is not larceny unless the intent to steal exists at the time of the finding. [§1047]

85. **NO** Since Cassandra received possession of the money when it was delivered to her, her placing of it in her purse did not involve a taking from the possession of another. Betty never got possession of it, so the money was not taken from the possession of Betty. [§§1049-1050]

86. **PROBABLY** As an errand clerk, it is doubtful that Delivery was a "trusted employee." Thus, Delivery most probably received only custody from Busy, and when Delivery misappropriated the money he did so from the possession of another (Busy). [§§1052-1053]

87. **YES** A had lawful possession of the ring pursuant to the security agreement and converted it with fraudulent intent. [§§1057-1063]

88. **NO (most courts)** Botticelli has not made a misrepresentation of past or present ***fact***. The crime of false pretenses traditionally cannot be premised on a false promise. [§§1079-1082]

a. **NO** Ordinarily, passive nondisclosure of facts is not enough for false pretenses. [§1084]

89. **NO** D did not obtain ***title*** to the jewelry by means of the false representation; he only obtained possession and so cannot be guilty of false pretenses. [§1075] He is, however, guilty of larceny by trick. [§§1077, 1007-1010]

90. **NO** The property was not taken by means of violence or intimidation. [§§1098-1100]

91. **DEPENDS** The issue is whether Loser had the requisite intent to permanently deprive another of his property. If Loser believed he was legally entitled to reclaim his money because the game was illegal, he was taking it under a claim of right and has not committed robbery. However, the facts are unclear as to what Loser's belief was. [§§1031, 1117]

92. **NO** The property was not taken from V's person or presence. [§§1095-1096]

93. **YES** Although the property was not taken from Tiny's person, it was taken from his "presence"—*i.e.,* from a place close enough to him that he could have prevented the taking had Brutus not tied him up. [§§1095-1096]

94.a. **NO** The threats for purposes of robbery must be to do ***immediate*** harm. [§1112]

b. **PROBABLY** The threats are of the sort likely to suffice for extortion; immediacy is not essential. [§1126]

95. **SPLIT** Although the threats are of the sort likely to constitute extortion [§1126], some statutes require that the defendant actually obtain the property; others punish the mere making of the threats with the intent to obtain property. [§§1122-1125]

96. **PERHAPS** Many jurisdictions recognize a defense of "claim of right" to extortion. If this jurisdiction does, Marla has a defense based on her belief that she was entitled to the money she demanded from Harold. The fact that her claim was of a specific amount tends to support the defense, if the jurisdiction recognizes it. [§§1129-1130]

97. **PROBABLY NOT** One who was a party to, but not an active participant in, the larceny can probably be convicted of receipt of the stolen property. [§1147] But under the better view, such a person cannot be convicted of both the larceny and receipt of the property. [§1148]

98. **NO** Treason cannot be committed by a person who does not owe allegiance to the government. Therefore, Claudine, as a Canadian citizen, cannot be convicted. [§1159]

99. **NO** The federal statute has been interpreted to require the rendering of some affirmative assistance to the felon. Thus, Loyal's nondisclosure alone will not support a federal conviction. [§1172]

a. **YES** Loyal has taken affirmative steps to conceal Zip, knowing he committed a felony. [§1172]

100. **NO** Compounding a crime requires an agreement between the defendant and the person assisted. Here, no such agreement exists. [§1176]

SAMPLE EXAM QUESTION I

Marvin Rutledge approaches Vera Parks and suggests that the two join in a scheme to defraud one Jim Kelp of a large amount of money. The scheme involves the sale to Kelp of a complicated-appearing machine that the two will represent to Kelp as having the ability to change glass into a substance indistinguishable from diamonds. Parks wishes to learn more about the matter. The two approach Mike Mechanic, a handyman, to tell him of the plan and ask him if he can construct a device that will suit their needs. Mechanic is about to leave the country but says he will delay his departure to prepare such a device if Rutledge and Parks will pay him half of his $500 fee in advance and the balance upon delivery of the device. Rutledge pays Mechanic $250. Rutledge and Parks then proceed to a restaurant where Rutledge has reason to believe Kelp can be found. While Parks waits in the bar, Rutledge makes contact with Kelp. After about an hour, Rutledge returns to Parks, informing her that Kelp is suspicious and may want to check out Rutledge with the local bunco squad. "I can't let him do that," Rutledge says, to which Parks responds, "Now that I can see what you're getting into, I want no part of it." Parks then leaves the bar. Rutledge joins Kelp. They leave the restaurant and, as they pass an alley, Rutledge pulls a knife and stabs Kelp. Kelp dies immediately.

Discuss the possible criminal liability of Mechanic and Parks.

SAMPLE EXAM QUESTION II

Ken Hite parks his Ford pickup near the tightly-guarded warehouse of Acme Chemicals, intending to gain entry and steal a quantity of "Bango," a new and highly efficient explosive. He has wirecutters, a flashlight, and a .45 pistol. He uses the wirecutters to gain entry to the building and immediately spots the cabinet with the explosives. He fills his knapsack with Bango and leaves the building. As he is reentering his pickup, a guard sees him and orders him to halt. Instead, Hite slams the car door shut and speeds away. About five miles from the warehouse, a police officer who has been alerted by radio to the break-in and given a description of Hite's auto observes Hite pass. The officer begins pursuit. As Hite's car careens around a corner, it leaves the road and strikes a tree. The knapsack with the Bango is thrown clear of the car but lands in a campfire built by two boy scouts and their scoutmaster. In the resulting explosion, the scoutmaster suffers a severe stomach wound. He is rushed to a nearby hospital where surgery is begun. After successfully administering to the wound, the surgeon notices that the scoutmaster has a small hernia and decides to repair it, since he has opened the body cavity anyway. While he is doing so, the scoutmaster suddenly dies. Later, conflicting evidence on the immediate cause of death is produced. One physician testifies that the anesthesiologist must have simply not been watching because had he been observing the patient he could have prevented the death. Another testifies that the death was sudden, unforeseeable, and unpreventable. The state statute defines murder as "the killing of another human being with malice aforethought, either express or implied."

What issues are presented by a charge of murder against Hite, based on the death of the scoutmaster? Discuss.

SAMPLE EXAM QUESTION III

Fen Dant is the foreperson of a loading dock crew. During a noonday break, Dant enters a partially loaded boxcar where Vic Tem, one of the crew members, is eating his bag lunch.

Dant and Tem begin talking, and Dant complains bitterly about the company's failure to pay him the overtime he believes he has coming. Dant sees an apparently expensive wrench lying on a box. He picks it up and comments that the company owes him 10 times what the wrench is worth. Tem then asserts that whatever an employee's "beef" against the company, there is no excuse for stealing company property. The discussion becomes more heated and the two come to blows. Dant strikes Tem and Tem falls to the floor, unconscious. Dant then picks up the wrench and jumps out of the boxcar. He is immediately confronted by company security personnel who take him into custody and retrieve the wrench. The wrench in fact belongs to the company.

What is Dant's possible criminal liability? Discuss.

SAMPLE EXAM QUESTION IV

Martin Roke is charged with burglary, rape, and murder. The rape and murder victim was Bess Franks; the burglary charge is based on Roke's entry into Franks's residence with intent to rape her. At the trial, the prosecution introduces evidence establishing that on the date in question, Roke broke into Franks's apartment, compelled her to have intercourse with him against her wishes, and then shot her six times, causing her death. The defense produces a psychiatrist who testifies that Roke has a long history of mental illness and is a paranoid schizophrenic. He has been undergoing treatment for this disorder for years and has been taking powerful medication for the illness. The psychiatrist further testifies that in his opinion Roke's condition caused him to believe that Franks was a witch with supernatural powers and that she was using these powers against him. It was because of these beliefs that Roke entered Franks's residence and attacked her. In response to a question from defense counsel, the psychiatrist testifies that if Roke consumed intoxicating beverages while taking his medication, the intoxicants would have a far more serious effect upon him than they would have on a person not taking such drugs. Another defense witness testifies that he observed Roke and a companion, "Smokey," drinking in a bar the night of the crime. Both appeared to be intoxicated. According to the witness, Roke told Smokey of his belief in Franks's supernatural powers and Smokey encouraged this belief. The witness further adds that Smokey helped Roke leave the bar and by following them he, the witness, was able to observe Smokey confirming Roke's conclusion regarding Franks and telling Roke that he, Roke, had to do something about the situation. The witness then says that he saw the two stop before an apartment building, later identified as that of Franks, and that Smokey appeared to be cajoling and almost pushing Roke into the building. After this testimony, the defense rests.

Discuss the various theories, if any, upon which Roke might rely in attempting to avoid conviction for any of the offenses charged.

SAMPLE EXAM QUESTION V

Peter Linin has been charged with a violation of the following criminal statute:

> §567.89. Criminal Nonsupport.
> An individual commits an offense, punishable by a fine of no more than $500 and by a jail term of no more than 30 days, if he fails to provide for the lawfully required support of his children.

The prosecution's evidence will show that Linin was approached by Elizabeth Holden and told by her that her soon-to-be-born child had been fathered by him. Holden further demanded that Linin make arrangements for reasonable support of the child.

It is undisputed and the prosecution will show that Holden's child was born and that for a year Linin provided no support for the child. The prosecution will also introduce evidence tending to show that Linin is the father of the child and was financially able to provide support.

The defense will produce evidence tending to show that Linin is not in fact the father of the child. In addition, defense evidence will tend to show that after Holden initially approached Linin, Linin called Lawyer's Referral Service (run by the State Bar) and was referred to I. M. Shyster, a local attorney. Shyster, after listening to Linin's story (including a denial of paternity based upon what Linin understood to be Holden's reputation for sexual promiscuity), informed Linin that in light of the dispute as to paternity he was not liable for the support of the child. Moreover, he advised Linin that he had nothing to lose by refusing to provide support, because the worst that could happen would be that Holden would bring a civil action on behalf of the child and, if Linin lost, he would simply have to pay the support. Shyster was unaware of the statute under which Linin is now being prosecuted.

Identify and briefly discuss the issues presented by Linin's prosecution.

SAMPLE EXAM QUESTION VI

Lois Kane is the owner of Lois's Pawn Shop in state X. Because her various business ventures require much of her time, she hired a manager, Clark Lent, to assume general operating responsibility for the shop. Under the law of state X, it is a misdemeanor to sell a handgun to any person with an unexpunged felony conviction. On June 14, while Kane is in another state tending to her earthworm farm there, Lent is in charge of the shop. Mary Parks enters the store and tells Lent she would like to purchase a small revolver, but she has been unsuccessful in other stores because everybody knows about her five-year-old conviction for armed robbery. Lent indicates that he cannot sell her a gun either and informs her of the statutory prohibition. Parks then tells Lent that she and her three-year-old son are forced by financial considerations to live in an undesirable area of the city, that on two occasions persons have attempted to break into their apartment, and that her son's safety depends upon her being able to secure a weapon for use in self-defense. Lent, with tears running down his cheeks, removes a small revolver from the display case and hands it to Parks, saying, "Well, look this over and see if it will do." At this point, another person who has entered the store during this discussion identifies himself as a police officer and tells Lent he is under arrest. Evidence is available to establish that Parks was acting as a paid agent of the police in an effort to identify pawn shops illegally selling guns and that she in fact had no felony convictions. Kane is ultimately charged with attempted violation of the statute prohibiting sale of handguns to convicted felons.

Discuss the issues presented by this charge.

SAMPLE EXAM QUESTION VII

Jim Looper was walking down a street at 9:30 p.m., when he was approached by a uniformed police officer, Kim Readings. Readings informed Looper that he was under arrest for the robbery of a nearby convenience store. When Looper protested that he knew nothing about it, Readings struck him repeatedly with her nightstick. Looper noticed that he was near the apartment of a friend, Martin Doubt, and ran towards the apartment. The door was open and Looper, with Readings in pursuit, rushed in. Seeing Doubt sitting at a table eating, Looper shouted, "Help me get rid of this killer cop!" But Doubt, seeing Readings at the door, responded, "You handle your own problems." Readings then took custody of Looper. Later, it was determined that Readings had no basis for believing Looper to be the perpetrator of the robbery and the arrest was therefore clearly invalid. Looper, however, is charged with burglary. He is prepared to testify that he cannot recall any of the events of that evening that occurred after the first blow struck by Readings with her nightstick.

Among the criminal statutes in the jurisdiction are the following:

> §23. Burglary. It is a felony offense to enter the habitation of another with the intent to commit a felony or any theft.
>
> §36. Solicitation. It is an offense to solicit another to commit any offense. Solicitation is a felony if the offense solicited is a felony.
>
> §76. Battery.
> a. The offense of battery consists of causing the application of force upon the person of another.
> b. Battery is a felony under the following circumstances: . . . (5) It is committed upon the person of one known to be a police officer.

Identify and discuss the issues raised by the burglary charge against Looper.

SAMPLE EXAM QUESTION VIII

Marvin Tubb is charged with the rape of Myna Winters. The facts show that Winters is 26 years of age and is retarded; tests show that her I.Q. is approximately 45. Police interviews with Winters resulted in eliciting the following version of the relevant events: Tubb and Winters had been neighbors and friends for several months. On August 14, Tubb suggested to Winters that the two of them enter into a common law marriage after eloping. Winters agreed, with reservations. That night, the two left their homes about 8:00 p.m. and went to a nearby park where they exchanged rings. Tubb assured Winters that they were then married. They then went to Tubb's apartment where he began making sexual advances to Winters. She tells the officers that they ultimately had intercourse and that "I didn't want to, and I told him so. But he made me do it." When asked if she fought him, she responds, "I was afraid. He just said we had to do it because we were married." Tubb, on the other hand, tells the officers that he never specifically represented to Winters that the exchange of rings was a legal marriage. He also denies compelling her to engage in intercourse. "I had to urge her on," he says, "but you always have to guide her. She's not too smart, you know." The jurisdiction has no common law marriage doctrine and the state courts have specifically rejected arguments that the doctrine should be accepted.

Identify and discuss the issues presented by the pending charge against Tubb.

ANSWER TO SAMPLE EXAM QUESTION I

Mechanic's Liability

Conspiracy: The issue is whether Mechanic may be guilty of criminal conspiracy. Conspiracy requires an agreement between two or more persons to accomplish an unlawful purpose. Having committed himself to participate in what he knew was a joint undertaking, the major issue is whether he had the requisite ***intent***; however, the law is not entirely clear on this matter. If knowledge that his participation would aid in the accomplishment of the object crime is sufficient, Mechanic is most probably guilty; he knew what the device would be used for. But if intent to further that objective is required, he is probably not guilty. He was to be fully paid upon delivery of the device and therefore had no financial interest in the crime's success. In fact, he would not even be in the country. Consequently, the most likely inference is that Mechanic was indifferent as to the scheme's success. The prosecution can argue that knowledge should be sufficient, since those who participate in criminal schemes with knowledge that their assistance will facilitate the commission of a crime are both blameworthy and dangerous. The defense can argue that purpose should be necessary because otherwise there is not sufficient assurance that defendants are in fact both blameworthy and socially dangerous enough to justify criminal liability. It can also be argued that since the object crime is not a very serious one (*i.e.,* a nonviolent fraud crime), intent or purpose should be required; *i.e.,* the need to hold such minor participants liable is not great in light of the nature of the crime. Both arguments are persuasive, and the issue ultimately turns on which view the court adopts.

Murder: It is unlikely that Mechanic will be found liable for the murder of Kelp. The issue is whether Mechanic is guilty of murder even though he is not the one who stabbed Kelp. Since he did not perpetrate the homicide himself, Mechanic can only be convicted under the rule of co-conspirator liability. However, even assuming Mechanic was a member of the conspiracy, it must be shown that the killing was a foreseeable result of the conspiracy and committed in furtherance of it. Here, Marvin's killing of Kelp was arguably not pursuant to the conspiracy's objectives but was part of an independent effort on his part to avoid being reported to officials. Moreover, it is very doubtful that, given the nondangerous nature of the scheme and the lack of any indication that violence was to be used or even threatened, the act of killing was foreseeable, at least from Mechanic's perspective. If these arguments are not sufficiently persuasive, it can also be contended that the co-conspirator liability rule should be abandoned on policy grounds. Although the rule might discourage criminal schemes of the sort involved here, it is arguably inconsistent with general notions of personal responsibility and therefore imposes unjustified vicarious liability. Should the court agree with this theory, Mechanic should not be convicted even if the killing is found to have been foreseeable and perpetrated pursuant to the conspiracy's objectives.

Parks's Liability

Conspiracy: Parks probably will be found guilty of conspiracy. The initial question is whether she actually joined Marvin's scheme. She at no point expressly indicated a willingness to actively participate, and at no point did she accept a specific role. In fact, such a role was never identified. However, the requisite agreement can be implied from the actions of the parties, and Parks's actions do suggest a more than tentative willingness to be part of the criminal design.

Assuming Parks did enter into an agreement with Marvin (and perhaps Mechanic), the intent issue is more easily overcome than in Mechanic's case (above). The most likely interference is that she acted with the intent of participating in and benefiting from the scheme and thus joined with the purpose of furthering the object crime.

It is unlikely that Parks's abandonment of the scheme at the bar will have any effect on her liability for the conspiracy itself, because most courts find that abandonment after the agreement has been reached is no defense. Arguably, the policy of encouraging conspirators to abandon their schemes justifies acceptance of the minority rule making withdrawal a defense to conspiracy. However, even if the court follows the minority view, Parks will have difficulty bringing herself within it. It is likely that the court would require a showing of "voluntary" withdrawal. But here, the voluntariness of Parks's withdrawal is questionable; *i.e.,* arguably it was occasioned by the fear of apprehension (Kelp was "suspicious") rather than an honest and sincere desire to avoid involvement in a venture that she did not understand fully until Marvin revealed his willingness to use violence.

Murder: Although the same issues are raised as in the discussion of Mechanic's liability, the prosecution might have a stronger case against Parks for murder. Parks's liability turns on the co-conspirator theory. Since Parks was further involved in the scheme than Mechanic and knew more details, it is arguable that the killing was foreseeable from her perspective. Moreover, a convincing argument can be made that as the criminal scheme developed in the bar, its objectives expanded to include thwarting Kelp's efforts to contact authorities.

If Parks is potentially liable for the killing on a co-conspirator theory, the remaining question is whether she effected an abandonment before the killing so as to prevent liability. Although Parks clearly communicated her abandonment to Marvin, she did not communicate it to Mechanic. If he was a member of the conspiracy, it can be argued that her efforts to abandon the scheme would not have been successful until he was notified. On the other hand, perhaps the more just rule would be to require that notice be given only to those members of the conspiracy who are presently active in the part of the scheme at issue; to demand more would arguably pose an impossible burden and destroy the incentive to withdraw from a complex criminal design.

ANSWER TO SAMPLE EXAM QUESTION II

Two theories might be used to support the murder charge against Hite—felony murder and murder based on his awareness of a high risk of death.

Felony Murder: The issue is whether a felony murder conviction might be sought on the ground that death was caused in the commission of statutory burglary (trespassory breaking and entering of the warehouse with intent to steal Bango) and theft, or larceny (trespassory taking and carrying away of Bango with intent to steal). Many jurisdictions require that death be a ***foreseeable result*** of the felony, but arguably, death—especially the sort of death involved here—was not foreseeable to Hite. This was a simple burglary and theft rather than a life-threatening robbery. On the other hand, Hite not only had a pistol with him (and so may have contemplated a killing) but knew the dangerous nature of the substance he was stealing; thus it can be argued that the accidental explosion and resulting death were foreseeable. It can also be argued by the prosecution that foreseeability should not be essential, because the deterrent purpose of felony murder requires that the law impose a dramatic and inescapable penalty upon all of those who cause death in the commission of a felony.

In addition, a number of states limit the felony murder rule to "dangerous" felonies. Indeed, some courts require that the felony be "inherently" dangerous, but arguably the burglary and theft involved here are not inherently dangerous to human life. Given the questionable nature of the felony murder rule, the defense can argue that the inherently dangerous felony requirement approximately limits the rule to those situations where it is most necessary. But it can also be argued by the prosecution that the crimes here were sufficiently dangerous ***as they were committed*** and that this should suffice for felony murder, on the theory that the purpose of the felony murder rule is to encourage felons to avoid dangerous situations; such purpose would be best accomplished by applying the rule to any situation where the felony was committed in a dangerous way (*i.e.,* where the felons did what the rule seeks to deter).

A final problem under the felony murder theory is that the death took place after both the burglary and the larceny had been completed. Does the felony murder rule still apply? Under the better view, probably so, since this was most likely "immediate flight" and thus, part of the felony.

Awareness of a High Risk of Death: If the felony murder theory fails, Hite might still be found liable for murder on the theory that he acted with awareness of sufficient risk of death to bring into play the "abandoned and malignant heart" doctrine. The major question here is whether the risk Hite took (and of which he seems to have been aware) was serious enough to bring him within the doctrine. In arguing that it was, the prosecution can emphasize not only the illicit obtaining of a dangerous material but also Hite's attempting to evade escape in a manner that greatly increased the risk. The defense, on the other hand, can point to the absence of specific evidence that Hite knew what sort of handling of the explosive would cause it to detonate and argue that while he was aware of a risk, it should not be regarded as a risk high enough to be legally equivalent to an intent to cause death.

Causation: Assuming either of the above theories is successful, there is still a problem of "proximate causation." Here, the scoutmaster's death was directly caused by a means outside the scope of the risks involved under both murder theories. The question then is whether the manner in which death actually occurred "broke the chain of causation." Under one version of the facts, death was seemingly caused by such gross negligence on the part of the anesthesiologist (not even watching the patient) that the immediate cause of death was not foreseeable and thus broke the chain. On the other hand, the scoutmaster's hernia was a preexisting condition and even if it played a role in directly causing death, the court should not find the chain of causation broken. Moreover, a strong argument can be advanced that there was no unforeseeable intervening factor entering into the causal chain at all; *i.e.,* the primary factor in causing death was the surgery made necessary by Hite's action, and extending that surgery to correct minor additional problems and errors by the medical staff is arguably foreseeable.

ANSWER TO SAMPLE EXAM QUESTION III

Larceny: Dant is probably guilty of larceny. Guilt turns on the resolution of three subissues. First, did he "take" or "capture" the wrench? Although moving the wrench was clearly an asportation, the capture element requires Dant's exercise of dominion and control over the property. Here, however, Dant never removed the property from the premises; in fact, he was only out of the boxcar for a matter of seconds before he was apprehended. Nonetheless, a capture is not necessarily measured in units of time. Dant did disable the person who apparently had prior control of the wrench and did have it within his own control after knocking Tem unconscious. Thus, a persuasive argument can be made that there was a sufficient capture.

Assuming there was a capture, did Dant take the wrench from the "possession" of another? Dant was the foreperson of the crew and, as such, exercised some control over the area in which the activity took place. It is also reasonable to assume that he had certain control over company property in that area, including the wrench he is charged with stealing. If his control over the wrench amounted to possession, he could not have taken it from the possession of another and therefore could not be guilty of larceny. But here, it is likely (although more facts would be helpful) that as a "mere" employee without special rights, his authority over company property such as the wrench was such that at most he had only "custody" of it. As a result, he most likely did take it from the possession of the company.

The final subissue is whether Dant had the requisite intent, given the evidence that he may have taken the wrench because of his belief that the company was indebted to him. Larceny requires the intent to permanently deprive another of ***its*** property. However, if Dant honestly (although perhaps unreasonably) believed that the wrench was rightfully his because of the company's failure to pay him overtime, he did not have the intent to deprive the company of ***its*** wrench. The facts are unclear as to what Dant actually was thinking. Arguably, he was not acting out a belief that the wrench was his but, rather, simply thought he was morally justified in engaging in conduct he knew constituted larceny. Under this theory, it can be concluded that he had the requisite intent.

Attempted Larceny: If Dant did not "take" the wrench he cannot be convicted of larceny, but he may be guilty of attempted larceny. The issue is whether he had clearly progressed far enough towards commission of the crime to satisfy any of the tests for attempt. However, as with the completed crime, the major issue concerns Dant's intent—if he lacked the intent necessary for larceny, he lacked it for attempted larceny as well.

Embezzlement: If Dant did not take the wrench from the "possession of another," he may be guilty of embezzlement, on the theory that he had possession of the wrench pursuant to a trust agreement and converted it. Again, however, the problem is one of intent—if he believed the wrench was his, he probably lacked the requisite intent to defraud.

Robbery: The issue is whether Dant can be convicted for the more serious offense of robbery, assuming he is guilty of larceny. This presents two additional issues. First, did Dant take the wrench from the presence of his victim as is required for robbery? The wrench was not on Tem's person. Moreover, it was arguably not within Tem's presence, absent evidence that he had used it and temporarily set it down or otherwise had some special relationship to the wrench. On the other hand, the wrench was clearly within Tem's reach and had it not been for the fight he probably could have retained control. This strongly suggests that it was in his presence.

Second, was the taking accomplished by force? Dant will contend that he and Tem simply had an argument over the ethical propriety of stealing from the company in general and that Tem's participation in the fight was not resistance to Dant's removal of the wrench. In fact, the evidence arguably reveals no effort to remove the wrench, or even a solidified intent to do so, until after the use of force on Tem was completed. Thus, at most, the facts show a battery upon Tem (*see* below) followed by larceny of the wrench. The prosecution, on the other hand, can make an equally strong argument that Dant formed the intent to take the wrench and communicated this to Tem before the brawl. Tem then physically attempted to thwart Dant's efforts and only by his use of force did Dant accomplish the taking. Under this interpretation of the facts, the taking was clearly accomplished by force and constituted robbery.

Battery: Dant will be found guilty of battery. Battery is: the unlawful application of force to the person of another, resulting in bodily injury or an offensive touching. Both elements are present in the facts; *i.e.,* Dant struck Tem in the course of a fight, and Tem suffered an injury resulting in loss of consciousness. Specific intent is not required for battery, although the intent to strike Tem is apparent in this case.

ANSWER TO SAMPLE EXAM QUESTION IV

Insanity: Roke will be entitled to an acquittal if he was legally insane at the time of the crimes. If the defense psychiatrist is believed, Roke was clearly mentally ill. But whether this should result in acquittal depends upon which "insanity test" the jurisdiction follows. If this is a *M'Naghten* jurisdiction, the prosecution can argue that the evidence falls short of establishing insanity. Even if the beliefs induced by Roke's mental illness had been accurate (*i.e.,* if Franks had been a witch and had been using her powers against Roke), Roke would not have been legally entitled to enter Franks's apartment, rape her, and kill her. Even so, the defense might prevail on the theory that because of his mental illness and the beliefs it caused, Roke did not understand the nature and quality of raping and killing Franks or the acts (such as the burglary) that were incident thereto. This latter theory will satisfy the *M'Naghten* test.

If the jurisdiction applies one of the control tests (*i.e.,* the irresistible impulse test or the Model Penal Code test), the issue is still a difficult one. The defense can argue that one who believes that another has such supernatural powers and intends to use them against him has lost the capacity to avoid responding violently towards the victim; it is unreasonable to expect that normal influences will prevent such action. But the prosecution can argue that this does not explain why Roke raped Franks and therefore a jury could find that the crimes were not simply the result of such delusions. Moreover, the prosecution could also argue that even if Roke believed Franks was a witch with supernatural powers, this did not deprive Roke of the ability to seek less violent solutions to the situation.

Diminished Capacity: Should the insanity defense fail, Roke might rely upon the psychiatric testimony as showing lack of capacity to form the intent required for at least some of the crimes charged. However, not all courts recognize the diminished capacity doctrine; therefore, it may be incumbent upon defense counsel to convince the court of the propriety of considering evidence of mental illness as bearing upon intent. Arguably, the requirement of intent logically calls for consideration of all relevant evidence; moreover, considering mental illness as bearing upon intent provides a desirable vehicle for mitigating punishment and, at the same time, not excusing a defendant. If the court agrees, it will be urged that at most Roke should be convicted of less serious offenses, such as trespass rather than burglary and manslaughter rather than murder. The prosecution, however, can counter with several arguments: Evidence of mental illness should be restricted to the insanity defense and therefore the doctrine of diminished responsibility should be rejected. And even if accepted, it should be limited to specific intent crimes; therefore, it should not prevent conviction for rape. Regarding burglary and murder, the defense evidence arguably does not tend to demonstrate an inability to form the requisite intents. If it does not tend to do so, no issue of diminished capacity is raised, and whether the doctrine is accepted is irrelevant.

Intoxication: Roke will have a complete defense if he was ***involuntarily*** intoxicated at the time of the crimes and because of that intoxication met either the *M'Naghten* test or any of the control tests (described above). Roke's intoxication might be found involuntary if he was unaware of the reaction that would result from his mixing the medication and liquor. However, the prosecution can argue that since Roke voluntarily consumed the beverages knowing of their intoxicating nature, his intoxication should be regarded as ***voluntar***y only. And even if regarded as involuntary, it does not necessarily establish a defense; *i.e.,* arguably, there is no basis in the facts for concluding that because of his intoxication Roke lacked the ability to understand the wrongfulness of his actions, to understand their nature and quality, or to avoid committing them.

If Roke's intoxication is characterized as voluntary, the defense might argue that it demonstrates the lack of intent required for the crimes charged. In response, the prosecution might stress that voluntary intoxication is irrelevant to guilt of rape, since it should be available only to disprove specific intents and rape is not a specific intent crime. Moreover, in regard to burglary and murder, the facts as proved provide no basis for concluding that because of his intoxication, Roke lacked the intent to commit rape (and therefore was not guilty of burglary) or lacked the intent to kill (and therefore was not guilty of murder). In the absence of more specific evidence showing the effect of his voluntary intoxication upon his ability to formulate intent, no apparent bar to conviction exists.

Duress; Absence of "Voluntary" Act: Finally, it can be urged that Smokey's actions in reinforcing Roke's beliefs and in encouraging Roke to act on those beliefs give rise to a defense based either on duress or the lack of a "voluntary" act. (Entrapment is, of course, unavailable since there is no evidence that Smokey was a government agent or was acting under the direction and control of such an agent.) Duress is raised only by evidence tending to show that the defendant was acting in response to threats of serious bodily harm to himself or another. No such evidence exists here, however; Smokey may have encouraged Roke, but he did not threaten him. Thus, there is little possibility of the duress defense succeeding. Arguably, Smokey's conduct when considered in light of the other factors (including Roke's mental illness and intoxication) rendered Roke's behavior involuntary and thus not an "act" upon which liability can be based. But this argument is weak at best; from the facts given, it does not appear that Smokey's actions were compelling enough to so override Roke's ability to exercise volitional control as to render his subsequent behavior involuntary within the meaning of the "act" requirement.

ANSWER TO SAMPLE EXAM QUESTION V

Application of Statute to Linin: Prosecution of Linin will not succeed if the statute does not apply to him. The issue is whether Linin is, in fact, the father of the child. If it is established that he is not, he must be acquitted because one element of the crime is that the unsupported person be the child of the defendant. If, however, it is determined that the evidence does in fact show paternity, several more complex issues will be presented.

Mistake of Fact: Will Linin's belief that he was not the parent of the child prevent liability? This is a "mistake of fact" issue, and the question becomes whether the state of mind required by the crime is such that the mistake establishes the lack of that intent. Since the statute does not expressly address the question of state of mind, the issue becomes a matter of interpretation and legislative intent. There are four possibilities:

(1) The statute requires ***knowledge***, *i.e.,* that the defendant be aware to a practical certainty that the person is his child;

(2) The statute requires ***recklessness***, *i.e.,* that the defendant be aware of a substantial and unjustified risk that the person is his child;

(3) The statute requires ***negligence***, *i.e.,* that there be a substantial and unjustified risk that the person is the defendant's child and that a reasonable person would have been aware of this risk; and

(4) The statute imposes ***"strict liability,"*** *i.e.,* that it does not require any intent or negligence in regard to the fact of paternity.

Arguments that this is a strict liability crime would stress that the crime is not a traditional one, it involves only a minor penalty, and it is part of a broad scheme to regulate support of children; therefore, the legislative intent must have been to dispense with any requirement of intent and Linin's mistake is irrelevant. However, an equally strong argument can be made that conviction for nonsupport involves a moral condemnation and the legislature could not have intended to impose such condemnation upon a person who was unaware that he had a child to support; therefore, strict liability could not have been intended. Moreover, to impose such liability absent a showing of some intent might violate due process.

If the statute is held not to impose strict liability, the prosecution might argue that it requires no more than negligence or recklessness, on the ground that this would assure blameworthiness but would not impose so great a hurdle to enforcement as to make the statute worthless. In light of Holden's claim about paternity, and the only evidence contradicting that being Linin's perception of Holden's general reputation for promiscuity, the facts show awareness of a risk of paternity (if recklessness is required) or at least a risk of which Linin should have been aware (if negligence will suffice). Linin, on the other hand, would argue for a requirement of knowledge, on the ground that limiting the statute to those who know the person not supported is their child is the only way to sufficiently assure blameworthiness. Usually, such knowledge would not be difficult to show, so the requirement would not impair the statute's general effectiveness. Applying this standard, the facts seemingly show a good faith dispute concerning paternity and therefore establish the absence of the knowledge that should be required for liability.

Assuming the facts show a mistake of fact that is logically inconsistent with Linin having the requisite state of mind, it might still be contended that the mistake should be given no legal effect unless it was a reasonable one. Reliance might be placed on the traditional rule that if a mistake of fact is offered to "disprove" a "general intent," it must be a reasonable error. Any mistake that Linin in fact made in regard to paternity, the prosecution would assert, was unreasonable—especially since it was based only upon what Linin believed to be Holden's reputation. The defense might argue, however, that whatever the traditional rule, even an unreasonable mistake should be given legal significance if it in fact negates the essential state of mind. Any other rule would in effect abrogate the "intent" requirement of the crime and be arbitrary. Moreover, an argument can be made that Linin's error was, in fact, reasonable. A person's general reputation is something that is widely relied upon in many contexts, and Linin was therefore justified in relying upon Holden's reputation in formulating a doubt as to whether he was the father.

Mistake of Law: Will the advice Linin received from Shyster and the state of mind that advice created prevent liability? The issue is whether, where a person has done all he reasonably can do to ascertain the law (*i.e.,* consult an apparently reputable attorney), there is no reason to hold him liable if the advice given is wrong. Linin will contend that courts should recognize this defense of "mistake of law." However, no court has gone this far, the general rule being that ignorance of the law is no excuse. Although reasonable reliance upon an official interpretation of the law or a court decision has been recognized as a defense, similar treatment has not been given to advice from a privately retained attorney. Hence, it is almost certain that the defense will lose on this argument.

But the possibility remains that Shyster's advice will have some effect. The statute requires proof that the support was "lawfully required." Applying state of mind analysis, Linin must be shown to have been ***at least*** reckless in regard to each element of the offense; thus, the prosecution must show that Linin was aware of a substantial and unjustifiable risk that the support he was not paying was required by law. If Linin believed Shyster's advice, a judge or jury could reasonably conclude that Linin was unaware of a risk that the support was in fact legally required. On the other hand, the facts do not necessarily preclude a finding of recklessness. Linin may not have believed Shyster fully and, in light of Holden's claims, might still have been aware of a high enough risk that Shyster was wrong and that the support was legally required. Moreover, in light of the difficulty of proving that defendants charged under the statute were aware of the legal situation, the legislature might have intended to impose strict liability in regard to the element of "lawfully required support" (in which case even a complete and honest mistake by Linin as to his duty to pay the support is totally irrelevant). Or, perhaps negligence should suffice, in which case the prosecution can rely on Holden's claim and Shyster's off-the-cuff and cavalier opinion to establish that a reasonable person would have been aware of a substantial risk that the support at issue was legally required. The question of whether strict liability or liability for negligence was intended can be argued in much the same way as was the question of the intent required in regard to paternity (discussed above).

ANSWER TO SAMPLE EXAM QUESTION VI

Kane: Since Kane did not directly participate in the offense and did not know of its commission, she cannot be liable as a party to the offense committed directly by Lent. She can be liable only if vicarious liability and strict liability are imposed. Further, she may not be vicariously liable because entrapment or impossibility may establish that Lent was himself not guilty of attempted violation of the statute.

Vicarious Liability: Kane can be convicted only if the statute was intended to impose vicarious liability, *i.e.,* only if she is liable for crimes committed by her employees. Here, a strong argument can be made that the apparent legislative intent is to impose such liability. The underlying conduct (sale of handguns) is of the sort likely to be engaged in by employees of stores. The legislative purpose of preventing handguns from getting into the hands of felons would arguably be frustrated if sales by employees are excluded. The crime is only a misdemeanor and there is no indication of an intent to require personal fault on the part of the defendant.

Kane may be able to escape liability if she can show that she instructed Lane to abide by the statute and that his actions were in disregard of this instruction, or that she took all reasonable steps to prevent any sales in violation of the statute. The facts here, however, do not suggest that the arguments have any basis.

Strict Liability: The facts make clear that Kane did not have any awareness that the attempted sale was being made, so if the crime requires proof of mens rea she almost certainly lacked it. While the fact that the statute may be intended to impose vicarious liability may suggest that it was also intended to impose strict liability, the strict liability issue is a separate one that must be addressed independently. This offense appears to be a "public welfare" offense and thus is likely to impose strict liability; it is part of a general scheme regulating the availability of handguns. It is not a traditional crime for which mens rea has been required, and it holds only a misdemeanor penalty. On the other hand, it can be urged that imposing liability without regard to the actor's awareness of the facts—especially the buyer's felony record—would result in convictions of persons who are not culpable and whose conduct is not directly contrary to the legislative scheme. On balance, however, it appears likely that the statute was intended to impose strict liability and therefore Kane's lack of awareness concerning the sale and its circumstances will not prevent liability.

Lent's Guilt: Kane is vicariously liable for Lent's crime only if Lent himself is guilty of attempted violation of the statute. There are two possible barriers to a conclusion that Lent is guilty.

(1) **Entrapment:** Here, a police agent arguably entrapped Lent into the actions relied upon to constitute the offense. Lent initially resisted Parks's urging that he sell the gun in violation of the statute. There is no showing of predisposition to sell in contravention of the bar. Further, she secured his willingness only by making pleas of an essentially personal nature that invoked his sympathy for the plight of her alleged son. It can be urged that the facts here show that Lent's intention to commit the crime was stimulated or created by Parks's entreaties and thus constituted entrapment. (Since there was no evidence of predisposition, it is irrelevant whether the objective or subjective standard is used to resolve the issue.)

(2) **Impossibility:** The facts show that Parks did not in fact have a felony conviction. Therefore, if Lent had actually sold her the gun, the sale would not have violated the statute even though Lent mistakenly believed that it would have. But this means that the case presents a classic example of "legal impossibility": Lent could not have committed the crime by completing the course of conduct which he began. The question is whether this does or should prevent his having committed attempt. Under traditional rules, this does prevent liability, and it can be urged that this is an appropriate position because Lent and others like him have not demonstrated a willingness to engage in conduct that in fact creates a social danger. On the other hand, a number of courts have abandoned the traditional rule and have held that even legal impossibility does not prevent conviction for attempt. It can be argued that Lent and others like him have demonstrated a willingness to break the law and therefore are both dangerous and culpable; the fact that fortuitously their conduct would not have constituted a violation if completed does not negate this. Whether or not Lent's conduct constituted attempt will depend upon the court's willingness to adopt the traditional approach or the more modern one.

ANSWER TO SAMPLE EXAM QUESTION VII

The burglary charge must rest on the proposition that Looper entered Doubt's apartment with the intent of committing the felony offense of soliciting a felony battery, *i.e.,* a battery upon Readings. There are three problems here: whether the conduct constituted burglary; whether the conduct in which Looper intended to engage was a felony, given the potential availability of the right of self-defense; and whether in view of his possible unconsciousness he has committed an "act" upon which liability of any sort can be based.

Burglary: The statute here is a modern burglary statute that dispenses with the traditional requirement of breaking. There is no doubt that the apartment was the habitation of another or that Looper entered it. Apart from the question of whether his intent was "to commit a felony" (discussed in the next section), the only issue presented is whether he had the intent at the time of entry. If he did not form the intent to solicit the battery upon Readings until after he entered the apartment, he is not guilty of burglary. Here, it can be argued that Looper probably did not decide to ask Doubt for help until he found that Doubt was actually in the apartment; his entry into the apartment was with the intent only of avoiding apprehension, not shown here to be a felony. It is important to note that he did not cry out and thus give evidence of his intent to solicit the battery until after he was in the apartment. On the other hand, it can be urged that the natural inference from the circumstances is that he expected to find Doubt there, that he ran into the apartment with the intent of soliciting Doubt's help, and thus that the entry was made with the requisite intent.

Was the Solicitation a Felony? If an application of force by Doubt upon Readings was not subject to some defense, it would be a felony under section 76; therefore, soliciting Doubt to engage in this conduct would be a felony solicitation under section 36. The solicitation was complete when the request was made; the instant rejection of it by Doubt does not prevent it from being the offense of solicitation. If, however, Looper had the right to strike Readings in self-defense, and if Doubt had the right to assist Looper in self-defense, then the conduct would not be an offense and its solicitation would not be an offense under section 36.

(1) **Looper's Right of Self-Defense:** Under the traditional rule, a person has the right to use force to defend against an unlawful arrest and that use of force is not itself a crime. If this rule applies, Looper had the right to use force against Readings; the arrest was unlawful and it appears that he intended to use no more force than reasonably appeared necessary to avoid the arrest. But in view of the trend towards abandonment of this rule, Looper might be found to have no right of self-defense. The prosecution might well urge the court to adopt the modern view that force used to resist arrest, especially an arrest being made by a person known to be a police officer, is not privileged; in support of this, the prosecution would argue the strong policy of discouraging resolution of disputes concerning arrests by fights in the streets, and would urge that persons like Looper be encouraged to save their objections until a legal forum is provided.

But even under the modern position, an arrestee is entitled to resist excessive force used to make an arrest. Looper may argue that even if he had no right to resist the arrest being attempted by Readings, he nevertheless had the right to resist the excessive force that she had demonstrated a willingness to use (by hitting him with the nightstick) despite his nonresistance. In support of this position, Looper could urge that any legal remedy he might have for the detention resulting from the arrest would not undo the effect of the excessive force, so he should be entitled to use self-help in response to that. While the prosecution might urge that Readings's use of force here was not excessive given Looper's "protests," the facts suggest he merely verbally objected to the arrest and therefore Readings's actions in striking him were unreasonable in response.

(2) **Doubt's Right to Assist Looper:** If Looper had the right to defend himself against Readings, Doubt would have the privilege of acting to assist him. Therefore, the conduct by Doubt which Looper solicited would not constitute the crime of assault. Even if Looper had no actual right to defend himself, it can be argued that Doubt would be entitled to act on reasonable appearances and to protect Looper if it reasonably appeared that Looper had the right to use force in self-defense. Arguably, however, Doubt could not reasonably conclude that Looper had the right to defend himself against a uniformed officer attempting to make an arrest.

Commission of "Act": Looper's loss of memory concerning the events suggests that he may, as the result of the blow struck by Readings, have been unconscious at the time of the entry into the apartment. If this was the case, his movements did not constitute a willed "act" upon which liability can be based; therefore, he cannot be convicted. The prosecution might argue, however, that loss of memory is not sufficient proof of unconsciousness at the time of the entry. Moreover, it can urge that if Looper was rendered unconscious by the blow, this blow was caused by Looper's improper resistance to the arrest and thus cannot be given this immunizing significance. Looper, of course, can respond by urging that his protests were not resistance and do not make him responsible for Readings's violent response.

ANSWER TO SAMPLE EXAM QUESTION VIII

Tubb's conduct might be rape under any of three theories: (a) Winters's consent was invalid because of her incapacity; (b) Winters's consent was invalid because of Tubb's deception; and (c) the intercourse was accomplished by force without Winters's consent. Under each theory, there are possible mens rea problems. It is also conceivable that the facts raise a problem of corroboration of Winters's testimony.

Mens Rea: The mens rea required for rape unfortunately is unclear. Specifically, it is uncertain whether the defendant must be aware that the circumstances making the intercourse unlawful actually exist, or at least aware of a substantial risk that they exist. Tubb, of course, would urge that he is culpable only if the proof shows actual awareness of the circumstances. The state could argue that this presents an unrealistic burden on it, and at most that a showing of awareness of a risk be required.

Incapacity Theory: Intercourse amounts to rape regardless of the woman's articulated consent, if she was by reason of mental impairment incapable of giving effective consent. The prosecution would urge here that Winters's I.Q. demonstrates that she was unable to comprehend what is involved in consenting to intercourse and thus, that her consent was not effective. Tubb would argue that Winters still retained at least the capacity to understand the nature of intercourse and thus could give consent. If Winters was in fact incapable of giving consent, Tubb most likely had the required mens rea. His admission to the officers shows that he was actually aware of her impairment, so even under that standard most favorable to him, he had the awareness required under this theory.

Deception Theory: Under limited circumstances, intercourse accomplished pursuant to the woman's consent is rape where the consent was induced by fraud. The issue is whether the fraud that can be shown here, even under the prosecution's evidence, is the kind of fraud that invalidates the woman's consent. The courts are split on whether deceiving a woman into believing that a marital relationship exists will invalidate consent. The prosecution would argue that this involves deception concerning a matter so important to the conduct as to be equivalent to deception concerning whether the conduct constitutes intercourse. Tubb, on the other hand, would argue that only deception as to whether the act was intercourse should invalidate consent, because otherwise there is no reasonable way to limit the sorts of deception that will invalidate consent. If the trier of fact accepts Tubb's version of the facts, of course, it is quite clear that no deception invalidating the consent took place.

There may also be an issue under this theory as to whether Tubb had the requisite mens rea. If Winters understood the events in the park to be a purportedly valid marriage but Tubb did not so intend them, it can be urged on behalf of Tubb that even if Winters was deceived he was unaware of that and therefore lacked the required mens rea. Tubb would urge that rape be interpreted to require actual awareness of the fact that the woman was deceived concerning the existence of a marital relationship. The prosecution, however, would urge that it should be sufficient that Tubb was or should have been aware of a risk that Winters so construed the events and that, in light of his awareness of her mental disability, it can be shown that he was conscious of a high risk that she was misled.

Rape by Force Theory: Winters's statement suggests that she submitted to intercourse because she believed Tubb would use force to compel her to do so if she did not submit. Whether this proves rape by force is problematical. Winters did not resist at all, and certainly not to the "utmost." But the prosecution can argue that resistance should not be required where it is prevented by the victim's perception that resistance will be met by force and harm. Tubb, however, can respond that while threats as well as actual force can give rise to rape, there must be some specific threats shown and that none can be shown here. The prosecution, on the other hand, may rely upon what Winters perceived as the coercive nature of the situation in Tubb's apartment as effectively communicating to her that resistance would be useless and in fact harmful.

An important mens rea issue is also presented under this theory: If Winters was in fact coerced into submission by the nature of the circumstances, did Tubb possess adequate awareness of this? Again, he can argue that his awareness of Winters's feeling coerced should be required and that such awareness cannot be shown here. The prosecution can argue that the circumstances, including Winters's reluctance, either did or should have alerted him to a risk that she perceived herself as coerced and that this is sufficient.

Corroboration: It appears that the only testimony bearing upon the events will be that of Winters. Some courts require corroboration of the woman's testimony. Tubb can argue that such corroboration should be required because a charge of rape is easy to make and hard to challenge, especially in cases such as this where relatively subtle matters are at issue. The prosecution, on the other hand, can argue that the issues in rape cases are no different from those in other prosecutions and there is no justification for a special corroboration requirement in rape cases.

TABLE OF CASES

INDEX

Notes

Notes

Notes

Notes

Notes

Publications Catalog

Publishers of America's Most Popular Legal Study Aids!

All Titles Available At Your Law School Bookstore.

AMERICA'S BEST SELLING OUTLINES

gilbert LAW SUMMARIES

Gilbert Law Summaries are the best selling outlines in the country, and have set the standard for excellence since they were first introduced more than twenty-five years ago. It's Gilbert's unique combination of features that makes it the one study aid you'll turn to for all your study needs!

Accounting and Finance for Lawyers
Professor Thomas L. Evans, University of Texas
Basic Accounting Principles; Definitions of Accounting Terms; Balance Sheet; Income Statement; Statement of Changes in Financial Position; Consolidated Financial Statements; Accumulation of Financial Data; Financial Statement Analysis.
ISBN: 0-15-900382-2 Pages: 232 $19.95

Administrative Law
By Professor Michael R. Asimow, U.C.L.A.
Separation of Powers and Controls Over Agencies; (including Delegation of Power) Constitutional Right to Hearing (including Liberty and Property Interests Protected by Due Process, and Rulemaking- Adjudication Distinction); Adjudication Under Administrative Procedure Act (APA); Formal Adjudication (including Notice, Discovery, Burden of Proof, Finders of Facts and Reasons); Adjudicatory Decision Makers (including Administrative Law Judges (ALJs), Bias, Improper Influences, Ex Parte Communications, Familiarity with Record, Res Judicata); Rulemaking Procedures (including Notice, Public Participation, Publication, Impartiality of Rulemakers, Rulemaking Record); Obtaining Information (including Subpoena Power, Privilege Against Self-incrimination, Freedom of Information Act, Government in Sunshine Act, Attorneys' Fees); Scope of Judicial Review; Reviewability of Agency Decisions (including Mandamus, Injunction, Sovereign Immunity, Federal Tort Claims Act); Standing to Seek Judicial Review and Timing.
ISBN: 0-15-900000-9 Pages: 306 $20.95

Agency and Partnership
By Professor Richard J. Conviser, Chicago Kent
Agency: Rights and Liabilities Between Principal and Agent (including Agent's Fiduciary Duty, Right to Indemnification); Contractual Rights Between Principal (or Agent) and Third Persons (including Creation of Agency Relationship, Authority of Agent, Scope of Authority, Termination of Authority, Ratification, Liability on Agents, Contracts); Tort Liability (including Respondeat Superior, Master-Servant Relationship, Scope of Employment). Partnership: Property Rights of Partner; Formation of Partnership; Relations Between Partners (including Fiduciary Duty); Authority of Partner to Bind Partnership; Dissolution and Winding up of Partnership; Limited Partnerships.
ISBN: 0-15-900327-X Pages: 172 $17.95

Antitrust
By Professor Thomas M. Jorde, U.C. Berkeley, Mark A. Lemley, University of Texas, and Professor Robert H. Mnookin, Harvard University
Common Law Restraints of Trade; Federal Antitrust Laws (including Sherman Act, Clayton Act, Federal Trade Commission Act, Interstate Commerce Requirement, Antitrust Remedies); Monopolization (including Relevant Market, Purposeful Act Requirement, Attempts and Conspiracy to Monopolize); Collaboration Among Competitors (including Horizontal Restraints, Rule of Reason vs. Per Se Violations, Price Fixing, Division of Markets, Group Boycotts); Vertical Restraints (including Tying Arrangements); Mergers and Acquisitions (including Horizontal Mergers, Brown Shoe Analysis, Vertical Mergers, Conglomerate Mergers); Price Discrimination—Robinson-Patman Act; Unfair Methods of Competition; Patent Laws and Their Antitrust Implications; Exemptions From Antitrust Laws (including Motor, Rail, and Interstate Water Carriers, Bank Mergers, Labor Unions, Professional Baseball).
ISBN: 0-15-900328-8 Pages: 236 $18.95

Bankruptcy
By Professor Ned W. Waxman, College of William and Mary
Participants in the Bankruptcy Case; Jurisdiction and Procedure; Commencement and Administration of the Case (including Eligibility, Voluntary Case, Involuntary Case, Meeting of Creditors, Debtor's Duties); Officers of the Estate (including Trustee, Examiner, United States Trustee); Bankruptcy Estate; Creditor's Right of Setoff; Trustee's Avoiding Powers; Claims of Creditors (including Priority Claims and Tax Claims); Debtor's Exemptions; Nondischargeable Debts; Effects of Discharge; Reaffirmation Agreements; Administrative Powers (including Automatic Stay, Use, Sale, or Lease of Property); Chapter 7-Liquidation; Chapter 11-Reorganization; Chapter 13-Individual With Regular Income; Chapter 12-Family Farmer With Regular Annual Income.
ISBN: 0-15-900442-X Pages: 368 $21.95

Business Law
By Professor Robert D. Upp, Los Angeles City College
Torts and Crimes in Business; Law of Contracts (including Contract Formation, Consideration, Statute of Frauds, Contract Remedies, Third Parties); Sales (including Transfer of Title and Risk of Loss, Performance and Remedies, Products Liability, Personal Property Security Interest); Property (including Personal Property, Bailments, Real Property, Landlord and Tenant); Agency; Business Organizations (including Partnerships, Corporations); Commercial Paper; Government Regulation of Business (including Taxation, Antitrust, Environmental Protection, and Bankruptcy).
ISBN: 0-15-900005-X Pages: 289 $17.95

California Bar Performance Test Skills
By Professor Peter J. Honigsberg, University of San Francisco
Hints to Improve Writing; How to Approach the Performance Test; Legal Analysis Documents (including Writing a Memorandum of Law, Writing a Client Letter, Writing Briefs); Fact Gathering and Fact Analysis Documents; Tactical and Ethical Considerations; Sample Interrogatories, Performance Tests, and Memoranda.
ISBN: 0-15-900152-8 Pages: 229 $18.95

Civil Procedure
By Professor Thomas D. Rowe, Jr., Duke University, and Professor Richard L. Marcus, U.C. Hastings
Territorial (Personal) Jurisdiction, including Venue and Forum Non Conveniens; Subject Matter Jurisdiction, covering Diversity Jurisdiction, Federal Question Jurisdiction; Erie Doctrine and Federal Common Law; Pleadings including Counterclaims, Cross-Claims, Supplemental Pleadings; Parties, including Joinder and Class Actions; Discovery, including Devices, Scope, Sanctions, and Discovery Conference; Summary Judgment; Pretrial Conference and Settlements; Trial, including Right to Jury Trial, Motions, Jury Instruction and Arguments, and Post-Verdict Motions; Appeals; Claim Preclusion (Res Judicata) and Issue Preclusion (Collateral Estoppel).
ISBN: 0-15-900447-0 Pages: 460 $22.95

Commercial Paper and Payment Law
By Professor Douglas J. Whaley, Ohio State University
Types of Commercial Paper; Negotiability; Negotiation; Holders in Due Course; Claims and Defenses on Negotiable Instruments (including Real Defenses and Personal Defenses); Liability of the Parties (including Merger Rule, Suits on the Instrument, Warranty Suits, Conversion); Bank Deposits and Collections; Forgery or Alteration of Negotiable Instruments; Electronic Banking.
ISBN: 0-15-900367-9 Pages: 194 $19.95

Community Property
By Professor William A. Reppy, Jr., Duke University
Classifying Property as Community or Separate; Management and Control of Property; Liability for Debts; Division of Property at Divorce; Devolution of Property at Death; Relationships Short of Valid Marriage; Conflict of Laws Problems; Constitutional Law Issues (including Equal Protection Standards, Due Process Issues).
ISBN: 0-15-900422-5 Pages: 188 $18.95

Call To Order: 1-800-787-8717 or Order On-Line at http://www.gilbertlaw.com

gilbert LAW SUMMARIES

America's Best Selling Outlines

Conflict of Laws
By Dean Herma Hill Kay, U.C. Berkeley

Domicile; Jurisdiction (including Notice and Opportunity to be Heard, Minimum Contacts, Types of Jurisdiction); Choice of Law (including Vested Rights Approach, Most Significant Relationship Approach, Governmental Interest Analysis); Choice of Law in Specific Substantive Areas; Traditional Defenses Against Application of Foreign Law; Constitutional Limitations and Overriding Federal Law (including Due Process Clause, Full Faith and Credit Clause, Conflict Between State and Federal Law); Recognition and Enforcement of Foreign Judgments.

ISBN: 0-15-900424-1 Pages: 273 $20.95

Constitutional Law
By Professor Jesse H. Choper, U.C. Berkeley

Powers of Federal Government (including Judicial Power, Powers of Congress, Presidential Power, Foreign Affairs Power); Intergovernmental Immunities, Separation of Powers; Regulation of Foreign Commerce; Regulation of Interstate Commerce; Taxation of Interstate and Foreign Commerce; Due Process, Equal Protection; "State Action" Requirements; Freedoms of Speech, Press, and Association; Freedom of Religion.

ISBN: 0-15-900375-X Pages: 355 $21.95

Contracts
By Professor Melvin A. Eisenberg, U.C. Berkeley

Consideration (including Promissory Estoppel, Moral or Past Consideration); Mutual Assent; Defenses (including Mistake, Fraud, Duress, Unconscionability, Statute of Frauds, Illegality); Third-Party Beneficiaries; Assignment of Rights and Delegation of Duties; Conditions; Substantial Performance; Material vs. Minor Breach; Anticipatory Breach; Impossibility; Discharge; Remedies (including Damages, Specific Performance, Liquidated Damages).

ISBN: 0-15-900014-9 Pages: 326 $21.95

Corporations
By Professor Jesse H. Choper, U.C. Berkeley, and Professor Melvin A. Eisenberg, U.C. Berkeley

Formalities; "De Jure" vs. "De Facto"; Promoters; Corporate Powers; Ultra Vires Transactions; Powers, Duties, and Liabilities of Officers and Directors; Allocation of Power Between Directors and Shareholders; Conflicts of Interest in Corporate Transactions; Close Corporations; Insider Trading; Rule 10b-5 and Section 16(b); Shareholders' Voting Rights; Shareholders' Right to Inspect Records; Shareholders' Suits; Capitalization (including Classes of Shares, Preemptive Rights, Consideration for Shares); Dividends; Redemption of Shares; Fundamental Changes in Corporate Structure; Applicable Conflict of Laws Principles.

ISBN: 0-15-900342-3 Pages: 319 $21.95

Criminal Law
By Professor George E. Dix, University of Texas

Elements of Crimes (including Actus Reus, Mens Rea, Causation); Vicarious Liability; Complicity in Crime; Criminal Liability of Corporations; Defenses (including Insanity, Diminished Capacity, Intoxication, Ignorance, Self-Defense); Inchoate Crimes; Homicide; Other Crimes Against the Person; Crimes Against Habitation (including Burglary, Arson); Crimes Against Property; Offenses Against Government; Offenses Against Administration of Justice.

ISBN: 0-15-900217-6 Pages: 317 $20.95

Criminal Procedure
By Professor Paul Marcus, College of William and Mary, and Professor Charles H. Whitebread, U.S.C.

Exclusionary Rule; Arrests and Other Detentions; Search and Seizure; Privilege Against Self-Incrimination; Confessions; Preliminary Hearing; Bail; Indictment; Speedy Trial; Competency to Stand Trial; Government's Obligation to Disclose Information; Right to Jury Trial; Right to Counsel; Right to Confront Witnesses; Burden of Proof; Insanity; Entrapment; Guilty Pleas; Sentencing; Death Penalty; Ex Post Facto Issues; Appeal; Habeas Corpus; Juvenile Offenders; Prisoners' Rights; Double Jeopardy.

ISBN: 0-15-900449-7 Pages: 271 $20.95

Estate and Gift Tax
By Professor John H. McCord, University of Illinois

Gross Estate; Allowable Deductions Under Estate Tax (including Expenses, Indebtedness, and Taxes, Deductions for Losses, Charitable Deduction, Marital Deduction); Taxable Gifts; Deductions; Valuation; Computation of Tax; Returns and Payment of Tax; Tax on Generation-Skipping Transfers.

ISBN: 0-15-900425-X Pages: 327 $20.95

Evidence
By Professor Jon R. Waltz, Northwestern University, and Roger C. Park, University of Minnesota

Direct Evidence; Circumstantial Evidence; Rulings on Admissibility; Relevancy; Materiality; Character Evidence; Hearsay and the Hearsay Exceptions; Privileges; Competency to Testify; Opinion Evidence and Expert Witnesses; Direct Examination; Cross-Examination; Impeachment; Real, Demonstrative, and Scientific Evidence; Judicial Notice; Burdens of Proof; Parol Evidence Rule.

ISBN: 0-15-900385-7 Pages: 387 $22.95

Federal Courts
By Professor William A. Fletcher, U.C. Berkeley

Article III Courts; "Case or Controversy" Requirement; Justiciability; Advisory Opinions; Political Questions; Ripeness; Mootness; Standing; Congressional Power Over Federal Court Jurisdiction; Supreme Court Jurisdiction; District Court Subject Matter Jurisdiction (including Federal Question Jurisdiction, Diversity Jurisdiction); Pendent and Ancillary Jurisdiction; Removal Jurisdiction; Venue; Forum Non Conveniens; Law Applied in the Federal Courts (including Erie Doctrine); Federal Law in the State Courts; Abstention; Habeas Corpus for State Prisoners; Federal Injunctions Against State Court Proceedings; Eleventh Amendment.

ISBN: 0-15-900232-X Pages: 313 $21.95

Future Interests & Perpetuities
By Professor Jesse Dukeminier, U.C.L.A.

Reversions; Possibilities of Reverter; Rights of Entry; Remainders; Executory Interest; Rules Restricting Remainders and Executory Interest; Rights of Owners of Future Interests; Construction of Instruments; Powers of Appointment; Rule Against Perpetuities (including Reforms of the Rule).

ISBN: 0-15-900218-4 Pages: 185 $19.95

Income Tax I - Individual
By Professor Michael R. Asimow, U.C.L.A.

Gross Income; Exclusions; Income Splitting by Gifts, Personal Service Income, Income Earned by Children, Income of Husbands and Wives, Below-Market Interest on Loans, Taxation of Trusts; Business and Investment Deductions; Personal Deductions; Tax Rates; Credits; Computation of Basis, Gain, or Loss; Realization; Nonrecognition of Gain or Loss; Capital Gains and Losses; Alternative Minimum Tax; Tax Accounting Problems.

ISBN: 0-15-900421-7 Pages: 312 $21.95

Income Tax II - Partnerships, Corporations, Trusts
By Professor Michael R. Asimow, U.C.L.A.

Taxation of Partnerships (including Current Partnership Income, Contributions of Property to Partnership, Sale of Partnership Interest, Distributions, Liquidations); Corporate Taxation (including Corporate Distributions, Sales of Stock and Assets, Reorganizations); S Corporations; Federal Income Taxation of Trusts.

ISBN: 0-15-900384-9 Pages: 238 $19.95

Labor Law
By Professor James C. Oldham, Georgetown University, and Robert J. Gelhaus

Statutory Foundations of Present Labor Law (including National Labor Relations Act, Taft-Hartley, Norris-LaGuardia Act, Landrum-Griffin Act); Organizing Campaigns, Selection of the Bargaining Representative; Collective Bargaining (including Negotiating the Agreement, Lockouts, Administering the Agreement, Arbitration); Strikes, Boycotts, and Picketing; Concerted Activity Protected Under the NLRA; Civil Rights Legislation; Grievance; Federal Regulation of Compulsory Union Membership Arrangements; State Regulation of Compulsory Membership Agreements; "Right to Work" Laws; Discipline of Union Members; Election of Union Officers; Corruption.

ISBN: 0-15-900340-7 Pages: 260 $19.95

Legal Ethics
By Professor Thomas D. Morgan, George Washington University

Regulating Admission to Practice Law; Preventing Unauthorized Practice of Law; Contract Between Client and Lawyer (including Lawyer's Duties Regarding Accepting Employment, Spheres of Authority of Lawyer and Client, Obligation of Client to Lawyer, Terminating the Lawyer-Client Relationship); Attorney-Client Privilege; Professional Duty of Confidentiality; Conflicts of Interest; Obligations to Third Persons and the Legal System (including Counseling Illegal or Fraudulent Conduct, Threats of Criminal Prosecution); Special Obligations in Litigation (including Limitations on Advancing Money to Client, Duty to Reject Certain Actions, Lawyer as Witness); Solicitation and Advertising; Specialization; Disciplinary Process; Malpractice; Special Responsibilities of Judges.

ISBN: 0-15-900026-2 Pages: 258 $20.95

Legal Research, Writing and Analysis
By Professor Peter J. Honigsberg, University of San Francisco

Court Systems; Precedent; Case Reporting System (including Regional and State Reporters, Headnotes and the West Key Number System, Citations and Case Finding); Statutes, Constitutions, and Legislative History; Secondary Sources (including Treatises, Law Reviews, Digests, Restatements); Administrative Agencies (including Regulations, Looseleaf Services); Shepard's Citations; Computers in Legal Research; Reading and Understanding a Case (including Briefing a Case); Using Legal Sourcebooks; Basic Guidelines for Legal Writing; Organizing Your Research; Writing a Memorandum of Law; Writing a Brief; Writing an Opinion or Client Letter.

ISBN: 0-15-900436-5 Pages: 187 $17.95

Multistate Bar Examination
By Professor Richard J. Conviser, Chicago Kent

Structure of the Exam; Governing Law; Effective Use of Time; Scoring of the Exam; Jurisdictions Using the Exam; Subject Matter Outlines; Practice Tests, Answers, and Subject Matter Keys; Glossary of Legal Terms and Definitions; State Bar Examination Directory; Listing of Reference Materials for Multistate Subjects.

ISBN: 0-15-900246-X Pages: 776 $24.95

Personal Property
Gilbert Staff

Acquisitions; Ownership Through Possession (including Wild Animals, Abandoned Chattels); Finders of Lost Property; Bailments; Possessory Liens; Pledges, Trover; Gift; Accession; Confusion (Commingling); Fixtures; Crops (Emblements); Adverse Possession; Prescriptive Rights (Acquiring Ownership of Easements or Profits by Adverse Use).

ISBN: 0-15-900360-1 Pages: 140 $14.95

Professional Responsibility
(see Legal Ethics)

Call To Order: 1-800-787-8717 or Order On-Line at http://www.gilbertlaw.com

gilbert LAW SUMMARIES

Property
By Professor Jesse Dukeminier, U.C.L.A.

Possession (including Wild Animals, Bailments, Adverse Possession); Gifts and Sales of Personal Property; Freehold Possessory Estates; Future Interests (including Reversion, Possibility of Reverter, Right of Entry, Executory Interests, Rule Against Perpetuities); Tenancy in Common; Joint Tenancy; Tenancy by the Entirety; Condominiums; Cooperatives; Marital Property; Landlord and Tenant; Easements and Covenants; Nuisance; Rights in Airspace and Water; Right to Support; Zoning; Eminent Domain; Sale of Land (including Mortgage, Deed, Warranties of Title); Methods of Title Assurance (including Recording System, Title Registration, Title Insurance).

ISBN: 0-15-900426-8 Pages: 515 $22.95

Remedies
By Professor John A. Bauman, U.C.L.A., and Professor Kenneth H. York, Pepperdine University

Damages; Equitable Remedies (including Injunctions and Specific Performance); Restitution; Injuries to Tangible Property Interests; Injuries to Business and Commercial Interests (including Business Torts, Inducing Breach of Contract, Patent Infringement, Unfair Competition, Trade Defamation); Injuries to Personal Dignity and Related Interests (including Defamation, Privacy, Religious Status, Civil and Political Rights); Personal Injury and Death; Fraud; Duress, Undue Influence, and Unconscionable Conduct; Mistake; Breach of Contract; Unenforceable Contracts (including Statute of Frauds, Impossibility, Lack of Contractual Capacity, Illegality).

ISBN: 0-15-900325-3 Pages: 390 $22.95

Sale and Lease of Goods
By Professor Douglas J. Whaley, Ohio State University

UCC Article 2; Sales Contract (including Offer and Acceptance, Parol Evidence Rule, Statute of Frauds, Assignment and Delegation, Revision of Contract Terms); Types of Sales (including Cash Sale Transactions, Auctions, "Sale or Return" and "Sale on Approval" Transactions); Warranties (including Express and Implied Warranties, Privity, Disclaimer, Consumer Protection Statutes); Passage of Title; Performance of the Contract; Anticipatory Breach; Demand for Assurance of Performance; Unforeseen Circumstances; Risk of Loss; Remedies; Documents of Title; Lease of Goods; International Sale of Goods.

ISBN: 0-15-900219-2 Pages: 234 $19.95

Secured Transactions
By Professor Douglas J. Whaley, Ohio State University

Coverage of Article 9; Creation of a Security Interest (including Attachment, Security Agreement, Value, Debtor's Rights in the Collateral); Perfection; Filing; Priorities; Bankruptcy Proceedings and Article 9; Default Proceedings; Bulk Transfers.

ISBN: 0-15-900231-1 Pages: 224 $18.95

Securities Regulation
By Professor David H. Barber, and Professor Niels B. Schaumann, William Mitchell College of Law

Jurisdiction and Interstate Commerce; Securities Act of 1933 (including Registration Requirements and Exemptions); Securities Exchange Act of 1934 (including Rule 10b-5, Tender Offers, Proxy Solicitations Regulation, Insider Transactions); Regulation of the Securities Markets; Multinational Transactions; State Regulation of Securities Transactions.

ISBN: 0-15-9000437-3 Pages: 478 $22.95

Torts
By Professor Marc A. Franklin, Stanford University

Intentional Torts; Negligence; Strict Liability; Products Liability; Nuisance; Survival of Tort Actions; Wrongful Death; Immunity; Release and Contribution; Indemnity; Workers' Compensation; No-Fault Auto Insurance; Defamation; Invasion of Privacy; Misrepresentation; Injurious Falsehood; Interference With Economic Relations; Unjustifiable Litigation.

ISBN: 0-15-900220-6 Pages: 452 $22.95

Trusts
By Professor Edward C. Halbach, Jr., U.C. Berkeley

Elements of a Trust; Trust Creation; Transfer of Beneficiary's Interest (including Spendthrift Trusts); Charitable Trusts (including Cy Pres Doctrine); Trustee's Responsibilities, Power, Duties, and Liabilities; Duties and Liabilities of Beneficiaries; Accounting for Income and Principal; Power of Settlor to Modify or Revoke; Powers of Trustee Beneficiaries or Courts to Modify or Terminate; Termination of Trusts by Operation of Law; Resulting Trusts; Purchase Money Resulting Trusts; Constructive Trusts.

ISBN: 0-15-900465-9 Pages: 274 $20.95

Wills
By Professor Stanley M. Johanson, University of Texas

Intestate Succession; Simultaneous Death; Advancements; Disclaimer; Killer of Decedent; Elective Share Statutes; Pretermitted Child Statutes; Homestead; Formal Requisites of a Will; Revocation of Wills; Incorporation by Reference; Pour-Over Gift in Inter Vivos Trust; Joint Wills; Contracts Relating to Wills; Lapsed Gifts; Ademption; Exoneration of Liens; Will Contests; Probate and Estate Administration.

ISBN: 0-15-900040-8 Pages: 312 $21.95

Gilbert Law Summaries FIRST YEAR PROGRAM

Includes Five Gilbert Outlines:

- **Civil Procedure**
  By Professor Thomas D. Rowe, Jr. Duke University Law School, and Professor Richard L. Marcus U.C. Hastings School Of Law
- **Contracts**
  By Professor Melvin A. Eisenberg U.C. Berkeley School Of Law
- **Criminal Law**
  By Professor George E. Dix University Of Texas School Of Law
- **Property**
  By Professor Jesse Dukeminier U.C.L.A. Law School
- **Torts**
  By Professor Marc A. Franklin Stanford University Law School

Plus—

- **Gilbert's Dictionary Of Legal Terms**
- **The 8 Secrets Of Top Exam Performance In Law School**
  By Professor Charles H. Whitebread USC Law School

All titles are packaged in a convenient carrying case with handle. $130 if purchased separately. $95 if purchased as a set. Save $35.

ISBN: 0-15-900254-0 Set $95

Gilbert's Pocket Size Law Dictionary
Gilbert

A dictionary is useless if you don't have it when you need it. If the only law dictionary you own is a thick, bulky one, you'll probably leave it at home most of the time — and if you need to know a definition while you're at school, you're out of luck!

With Gilbert's Pocket Size Law Dictionary, you'll have any definition you need, when you need it. Just pop Gilbert's dictionary into your pocket or purse, and you'll have over 4,000 legal terms and phrases at your fingertips. Gilbert's dictionary also includes a section on law school shorthand, common abbreviations, Latin and French legal terms, periodical abbreviations, and governmental abbreviations.

With Gilbert's Pocket Size Law Dictionary, you'll never be caught at a loss for words!

Available in your choice of 5 colors

■ Brown	ISBN: 0-15-900252-4	$7.95
■ Blue	ISBN: 0-15-900362-8	$7.95
■ Burgundy	ISBN: 0-15-900366-0	$7.95
■ Green	ISBN: 0-15-900365-2	$7.95

Limited Edition: Simulated Alligator Skin Cover

■ Black	ISBN: 0-15-900364-4	$7.95

The Eight Secrets Of Top Exam Performance In Law School
Charles Whitebread

Wouldn't it be great to know exactly what your professor's looking for on your exam? To find out everything that's expected of you, so that you don't waste your time doing anything other than maximizing your grades?

In his easy-to-read, refreshing style, nationally recognized exam expert Professor Charles Whitebread will teach you the eight secrets that will add precious points to every exam answer you write. You'll learn the three keys to handling any essay exam question, and how to add points to your score by making time work for you, not against you. You'll learn flawless issue spotting, and discover how to organize your answer for maximum possible points. You'll find out how the hidden traps in "IRAC" trip up most students… but not you! You'll learn the techniques for digging up the exam questions your professor will ask, before your exam. You'll put your newly-learned skills to the test with sample exam questions, and you can measure your performance against model answers. And there's even a special section that helps you master the skills necessary to crush any exam, not just a typical essay exam — unusual exams like open book, take home, multiple choice, short answer, and policy questions.

"The Eight Secrets of Top Exam Performance in Law School" gives you all the tools you need to maximize your grades — quickly and easily!

ISBN: 0-15-900323-7 $9.95

Call To Order: 1-800-787-8717 or Order On-Line at http://www.gilbertlaw.com

LAW SCHOOL LEGENDS
SERIES
America's Greatest Law Professors on Audio Cassette
Wouldn't it be great if all of your law professors were law school legends — the kind of professors whose classes everyone fights to get into? The professors whose classes you'd take, no matter what subject they're teaching. The kind of professors who make a subject sing. You may never get an opportunity to take a class with a truly brilliant professor, but with the Law School Legends Series, you can now get all the benefits of the country's greatest law professors...on audio cassette!
Call To Order: 1-800-787-8717 or Order On-Line at http://www.gilbertlaw.com

LAW SCHOOL LEGENDS SERIES

America's Greatest Law Professors on Audio Cassette

We found the truly gifted law professors most law students can only dream about — the professors who draw rave reviews not only for their scholarship, but for their ability to make the law easy to understand. We asked these select few professors to condense their courses into a single lecture. And it's these lectures you'll find in the Law School Legends Series. With Law School Legends, you'll get a brilliant law professor explaining an entire subject to you in one simple, dynamic lecture. The Law School Legends make even the most difficult concepts crystal clear. You'll understand the big picture, and how all the concepts fit together. You'll get hundreds of examples and exam tips, honed over decades in the classroom. But best of all, you'll get insights you can only get from America's greatest law professors!

Administrative Law
Professor Patrick J. Borchers
Albany Law School of Union University

TOPICS COVERED: Classification Of Agencies; Adjudicative And Investigative Action; Rulemaking Power; Delegation Doctrine; Control By Executive; Appointment And Removal; Freedom Of Information Act; Rulemaking Procedure; Adjudicative Procedure; Trial-Type Hearings; Administrative Law Judge; Power To Stay Proceedings; Subpoena Power; Physical Inspection; Self Incrimination; Judicial Review Issues; Declaratory Judgment; Sovereign Immunity; Eleventh Amendment; Statutory Limitations; Standing; Exhaustion Of Administrative Remedies; Scope Of Judicial Review.
4 Audio Cassettes
ISBN: 0-15-900189-7 $45.95

Agency & Partnership
Professor Thomas L. Evans
University of Texas

TOPICS COVERED: Agency: Creation; Rights And Duties Of Principal And Agent; Sub-Agents; Contract Liability — Actual Authority: Express And Implied; Apparent Authority; Ratification; Liabilities Of Parties; Tort Liability — Respondeat Superior; Frolic And Detour; Intentional Torts. Partnership: Nature Of Partnership; Formation; Partnership By Estoppel; In Partnership Property; Relations Between Partners To Third Parties; Authority of Partners; Dissolution And Termination; Limited Partnerships.
4 Audio Cassettes
ISBN: 0-15-900351-2 $45.95

Antitrust
Professor Thomas D. Morgan
George Washington University Law School

TOPICS COVERED: Antitrust Law's First Principle; Consumer Welfare Opposes Market Power; Methods of Analysis; Role of Reason, Per Se, Quick Look; Sherman Act §1: Civil & Criminal Conspiracies In Unreasonable Restraint Of Trade; Sherman Act §2: Illegal Monopolization, Attempts To Monopolize; Robinson Patman Act Price Discrimination, Related Distribution Problems; Clayton Act §7: Mengers, Joint Ventures; Antitrust & Intellectural Property; International Competitive Relationships; Exemptions & Regulated Industries; Enforcement; Price & Non-Price Restraints.
4 Audio Cassettes
ISBN: 0-15-900341-5 $39.95

Bankruptcy
Professor Elizabeth Warren
Harvard Law School

TOPICS COVERED: The Debtor/Creditor Relationship; The Commencement, Conversion, Dismissal, and Reopening Of Bankruptcy Proceedings; Property Included In The Bankruptcy Estate; Secured, Priority And Unsecured Claims; The Automatic Stay; Powers Of Avoidance; The Assumption And Rejection Of Executory Contracts; The Protection Of Exempt Property; The Bankruptcy Discharge; Chapter 13 Proceedings; Chapter 11 Proceedings; Bankruptcy Jurisdiction And Procedure.
4 Audio Cassettes
ISBN: 0-15-900273-7 $45.95

Civil Procedure
By Professor Richard D. Freer
Emory University Law School

TOPICS COVERED: Subject Matter Jurisdiction; Personal Jurisdiction; Long-Arm Statutes; Constitutional Limitations; In Rem And Quasi In Rem Jurisdiction; Service Of Process; Venue; Transfer; Forum Non Conveniens; Removal; Waiver; Governing Law; Pleadings; Joinder Of Claims; Permissive And Compulsory Joinder Of Parties; Counter-Claims And Cross-Claims; Ancillary Jurisdiction; Impleader; Class Actions; Discovery; Pretrial Adjudication; Summary Judgment; Trial; Post Trial Motions; Appeals; Res Judicata; Collateral Estoppel.
5 Audio Cassettes
ISBN: 0-15-900322-9 $59.95

Commercial Paper
By Professor Michael I. Spak
Chicago Kent College Of Law

TOPICS COVERED: Types Of Negotiable Instruments; Elements Of Negotiability; Statute Of Limitations; Payment-In-Full Checks; Negotiations Of The Instrument; Becoming A Holder-In-Due Course; Rights Of A Holder In Due Course; Real And Personal Defenses; Jus Teril; Effect Of Instrument On Underlying Obligations; Contracts Of Maker And Indorser; Suretyship; Liability Of Drawer And Drawee; Check Certification; Warranty Liability; Conversion Of Liability; Banks And Their Customers; Properly Payable Rule; Wrongful Dishonor; Stopping Payment; Death Of Customer; Bank Statement; Check Collection; Expedited Funds Availability; Forgery Of Drawer's Name; Alterations; Imposter Rule; Wire Transfers; Electronic Fund Transfers Act.
3 Audio Cassettes
ISBN: 0-15-900275-3 $39.95

Conflict Of Laws
Professor Patrick J. Borchers
Albany Law School

TOPICS COVERED: Domicile; Jurisdiction—In Personam, In Rem, Quasi In Rem; Court Competence; Forum Non Conveniens; Choice Of Law; Foreign Causes Of Action; Territorial Approach To Choice/Tort And Contract; "Escape Devices"; Most Significant Relationship; Governmental Interest Analysis; Recognition Of Judgments; Foreign Country Judgments; Domestic Judgments/Full Faith And Credit; Review Of Judgments; Modifiable Judgments; Defenses To Recognition And Enforcement; Federal/State (Erie) Problems; Constitutional Limits On Choice Of Law.
4 Audio Cassettes
ISBN: 0-15-900352-0 $39.95

Constitutional Law
By Professor John C. Jeffries, Jr.
University of Virginia School of Law

TOPICS COVERED: Introduction; Exam Tactics; Legislative Power; Supremacy; Commerce; State Regulation; Privileges And Immunities; Federal Court Jurisdiction; Separation Of Powers; Civil Liberties; Due Process; Equal Protection; Privacy; Race; Alienage; Gender; Speech And Association; Prior Restraints; Religion—Free Exercise; Establishment Clause.
5 Audio Cassettes
ISBN: 0-15-900373-3 $45.95

Contracts
By Professor Michael I. Spak
Chicago Kent College Of Law

TOPICS COVERED: Offer; Revocation; Acceptance; Consideration; Defenses To Formation; Third Party Beneficiaries; Assignment; Delegation; Conditions; Excuses; Anticipatory Repudiation; Discharge Of Duty; Modifications; Rescission; Accord & Satisfaction; Novation; Breach; Damages; Remedies; UCC Remedies; Parol Evidence Rule.
4 Audio Cassettes
ISBN: 0-15-900318-0 $45.95

Copyright Law
Professor Roger E. Schechter
George Washington University Law School

TOPICS COVERED: Constitution; Patents And Property Ownership Distinguished; Subject Matter Copyright; Duration And Renewal; Ownership And Transfer; Formalities; Introduction; Notice, Registration And Deposit; Infringement; Overview; Reproduction And Derivative Works; Public Distribution; Public Performance And Display; Exemptions; Fair Use; Photocopying; Remedies; Preemption Of State Law.
3 Audio Cassettes
ISBN: 0-15-900295-8 $39.95

Corporations
By Professor Therese H. Maynard
Loyola University Law School

TOPICS COVERED: Ultra Vires Act; Corporate Formation; Piercing The Corporate Veil; Corporate Financial Structure; Stocks; Bonds; Subscription Agreements; Watered Stock; Stock Transactions; Insider Trading; 16(b) & 10b-5 Violations; Promoters; Fiduciary Duties; Shareholder Rights; Meetings; Cumulative Voting; Voting Trusts; Close Corporations; Dividends; Preemptive Rights; Shareholder Derivative Suits; Directors; Duty Of Loyalty; Corporate Opportunity Doctrine; Officers; Amendments; Mergers; Dissolution.
4 Audio Cassettes
ISBN: 0-15-900320-2 $45.95

Criminal Law
By Professor Charles H. Whitebread
USC School of Law

TOPICS COVERED: Exam Tactics; Volitional Acts; Mental States; Specific Intent; Malice; General Intent; Strict Liability; Accomplice Liability; Inchoate Crimes; Impossibility; Defenses; Insanity; Voluntary And Involuntary Intoxication; Infancy; Self-Defense; Defense Of A Dwelling; Duress; Necessity; Mistake Of Fact Or Law; Entrapment; Battery; Assault; Homicide; Common Law Murder; Voluntary And Involuntary Manslaughter; First Degree Murder; Felony Murder; Rape; Larceny; Embezzlement; False Pretenses; Robbery; Extortion; Burglary; Arson.
4 Audio Cassettes
ISBN: 0-15-900279-6 $39.95

Call To Order: 1-800-787-8717 or Order On-Line at http://www.gilbertlaw.com

Criminal Procedure

By Professor Charles H. Whitebread
USC School of Law

TOPICS COVERED: Incorporation Of The Bill Of Rights; Exclusionary Rule; Fruit Of The Poisonous Tree; Arrest; Search & Seizure; Exceptions To Warrant Requirement; Wire Tapping & Eavesdropping; Confessions (Miranda); Pretrial Identification; Bail; Preliminary Hearings; Grand Juries; Speedy Trial; Fair Trial; Jury Trials; Right To Counsel; Guilty Pleas; Sentencing; Death Penalty; Habeas Corpus; Double Jeopardy; Privilege Against Compelled Testimony.

3 Audio Cassettes
ISBN: 0-15-900281-8 $39.95

Evidence

By Professor Faust F. Rossi
Cornell Law School

TOPICS COVERED: Relevance; Insurance; Remedial Measures; Settlement Offers; Causation; State Of Mind; Rebuttal; Habit; Character Evidence; "MIMIC" Rule; Documentary Evidence; Authentication; Best Evidence Rule; Parol Evidence; Competency; Dead Man Statutes; Examination Of Witnesses; Present Recollection Revived; Past Recollection Recorded; Opinion Testimony; Lay And Expert Witness; Learned Treatises; Impeachment; Collateral Matters; Bias, Interest Or Motive; Rehabilitation; Privileges; Hearsay And Exceptions.

5 Audio Cassettes
ISBN: 0-15-900282-6 $45.95

Family Law

Professor Roger E. Schechter
George Washington University Law School

TOPICS COVERED: Marital Relationship; Formalities And Solemnization; Common Law Marriage; Impediments; Conflict Of Laws; Non-Marital Relationship; Void And Voidable Marriages; Annulment; Divorce; Separation; Full Faith And Credit; Temporary Orders; Property Division; Community Property Principles; Equitable Distribution And Reimbursement; Marital And Separate Property; Alimony; Child Support; Enforcement Of Orders; Antenuptial And Postnuptial Agreements; Separation And Settlement Agreements; Custody; Visitation Rights; Termination Of Parental Rights; Adoption; Illegitimacy; Paternity Actions.

3 Audio Cassettes
ISBN: 0-15-900283-4 $39.95

Federal Courts

Professor John C. Jeffries
University of Virginia School of Law

TOPICS COVERED: History Of The Federal Court System; "Court Or Controversy" And Justiciability; Congressional Power Over Federal Court Jurisdiction; Supreme Court Jurisdiction; District Court Subject Matter Jurisdiction—Federal Question Jurisdiction, Diversity Jurisdiction And Admiralty Jurisdiction; Pendent And Ancillary Jurisdiction; Removal Jurisdiction; Venue; Forum Non Conveniens; Law Applied In The Federal Courts; Federal Law In The State Courts; Collateral Relations Between Federal And State Courts; The Eleventh Amendment And State Sovereign Immunity.

3 Audio Cassettes
ISBN: 0-15-900372-5 $39.95

Federal Income Tax

By Professor Cheryl D. Block
George Washington University Law School

TOPICS COVERED: Administrative Reviews; Tax Formula; Gross Income; Exclusions For Gifts; Inheritances; Personal Injuries; Tax Basis Rules; Divorce Tax Rules; Assignment Of Income; Business Deductions; Investment Deductions; Passive Loss And Interest Limitation Rules; Capital Gains & Losses; Section 1031, 1034, and 121 Deferred/Non Taxable Transactions.

4 Audio Cassettes
ISBN: 0-15-900284-2 $45.95

Future Interests

By Dean Catherine L. Carpenter
Southwestern University Law School

TOPICS COVERED: Rule Against Perpetuities; Class Gifts; Estates In Land; Rule In Shelley's Case; Future Interests In Transferor and Transferee; Life Estates; Defeasible Fees; Doctrine Of Worthier Title; Doctrine Of Merger; Fee Simple Estates; Restraints On Alienation; Power Of Appointment; Rules Of Construction.

2 Audio Cassettes
ISBN: 0-15-900285-0 $24.95

Law School Exam Writing

By Professor Charles H. Whitebread
USC School of Law

TOPICS COVERED: With "Law School Exam Writing," you'll learn the secrets of law school test taking. Professor Whitebread leads you step-by-step through his innovative system, so that you know exactly how to tackle your essay exams without making point draining mistakes. You'll learn how to read questions so you don't miss important issues; how to organize your answer; how to use limited exam time to your maximum advantage; and even how to study for exams.

1 Audio Cassette
ISBN: 0-15-900287-7 $19.95

Professional Responsibility

By Professor Erwin Chemerinsky
USC School of Law

TOPICS COVERED: Regulation of Attorneys; Bar Admission; Unauthorized Practice; Competency; Discipline; Judgment; Lawyer-Client Relationship; Representation; Withdrawal; Conflicts; Disqualification; Clients; Client Interests; Successive And Effective Representation; Integrity; Candor; Confidences; Secrets; Past And Future Crimes; Perjury; Communications; Witnesses; Jurors; The Court; The Press; Trial Tactics; Prosecutors; Market; Solicitation; Advertising; Law Firms; Fees; Client Property; Conduct; Political Activity.

3 Audio Cassettes
ISBN: 0-15-900371-7 $39.95

Real Property

By Professor Paula A. Franzese
Seton Hall Law School

TOPICS COVERED: Estates—Fee Simple, Fee Tail, Life Estate; Co-Tenancy—Joint Tenancy, Tenancy In Common, Tenancy By The Entirety; Landlord-Tenant Relationship; Liability For Condition Of Premises; Assignment & Sublease; Easements; Restrictive Covenants; Adverse Possession; Recording Acts; Conveyancing; Personal Property.

4 Audio Cassettes
ISBN: 0-15-900289-3 $45.95

Remedies

By Professor William A. Fletcher
University of California at Berkeley, Boalt Hall School of Law

TOPICS COVERED: Damages; Restitution; Equitable Remedies; Tracing; Rescission and Reformation; Injury and Destruction of Personal Property; Conversion; Injury to Real Property; Trespass; Ouster; Nuisance; Defamation; Trade Libel; Inducing Breach of Contract; Contracts to Purchase Personal Property; Contracts to Purchase Real Property (including Equitable Conversion); Construction Contracts; and Personal Service Contracts.

4 Audio Cassettes
ISBN: 0-15-900353-9 $45.95

Sales & Lease of Goods

By Professor Michael I. Spak
Chicago Kent College of Law

TOPICS COVERED: Goods; Contract Formation; Firm Offers; Statute Of Frauds; Modification; Parol Evidence; Code Methodology; Tender; Payment; Identification; Risk Of Loss; Warranties; Merchantability; Fitness; Disclaimers; Consumer Protection; Remedies; Anticipatory Repudiation; Third Party Rights.

3 Audio Cassettes
ISBN: 0-15-900291-5 $39.95

Secured Transactions

By Professor Michael I. Spak
Chicago Kent College of Law

TOPICS COVERED: Collateral; Inventory; Intangibles; Proceeds; Security Agreements; Attachment; After-Acquired Property; Perfection; Filing; Priorities; Purchase Money Security Interests; Fixtures; Rights Upon Default; Self-Help; Sale; Constitutional Issues.

3 Audio Cassettes
ISBN: 0-15-900292-3 $39.95

Securities Regulation

By Professor Therese H. Maynard
Loyola Marymount School of Law

TOPICS COVERED: Securities Markets; IPOs; Brokers-Dealers; Securities Acts (1933, 1934); Self-Regulatory Organizations; Insider Trading; the SEC; Securities—*Howey* Test; Publicly Held Corporation; Underwriting; Who is Subject to Section 5 of 1933 Securities Act; Offers; Prospectuses; Registration Statements; Liability for Material Misstatements; Exemptions from Section 5 Registration; Foreign Issuers and Offshore Offerings; Regulations A and D; Rules 504, 505, 506, 701; Liability Provisions of 1933 Act; Due Diligence Defense; Damages; Liability Under Sections 12 (a)(1) and (2).

5 Audio Cassettes
ISBN: 0-15-900359-8 $45.95

Torts

By Professor Richard J. Conviser
Chicago Kent College of Law

TOPICS COVERED: Essay Exam Techniques; Intentional Torts—Assault, Battery, False Imprisonment, Intentional Infliction Of Emotional Distress, Trespass To Land, Trespass To Chattels, Conversion; Defenses. Defamation—Libel, Slander; Defenses; First Amendment Concerns; Invasion Of Right Of Privacy; Misrepresentation; Negligence—Duty, Breach, Actual And Proximate Causation, Damages; Defenses; Strict Liability, Products Liability; Nuisance; General Tort Considerations.

4 Audio Cassettes
ISBN: 0-15-900293-1 $45.95

Wills & Trusts

By Professor Stanley M. Johanson
University of Texas School of Law

TOPICS COVERED: Attested Wills; Holographic Wills; Negligence; Revocation; Changes On Face Of Will; Lapsed Gifts; Negative Bequest Rule; Nonprobate Assets; Intestate Succession; Advancements; Elective Share; Will Contests; Capacity; Undue Influence; Creditors' Rights; Creation Of Trust; Revocable Trusts; Pourover Gifts; Charitable Trusts; Resulting Trusts; Constructive Trusts; Spendthrift Trusts; Self-Dealing; Prudent Investments; Trust Accounting; Termination; Powers Of Appointment.

4 Audio Cassettes
ISBN: 0-15-900294-X $45.95

Law School Legends Series
FIRST YEAR PROGRAM

Includes Five Law School Legends Titles:

- **Civil Procedure**
  By Professor Richard D. Freer
  Emory University Law School
- **Contracts**
  By Professor Michael I. Spak
  Chicago Kent College Of Law
- **Criminal Law**
  By Professor Charles H. Whitebread
  USC School of Law
- **Real Property**
  By Professor Paula A. Franzese
  Seton Hall Law School
- **Torts**
  By Professor Richard J. Conviser
  Chicago Kent College of Law

Plus—

- **Law School Exam Writing**
  By Professor Charles H. Whitebread
  USC Law School

All titles are packaged in a convenient carry case. $250 if purchased separately. $195 if purchased as a set. Save $55.

ISBN: 0-15-900306-7 Set $195

If you accidentally damage a tape within five years from the date of purchase we'll replace it for FREE— No questions asked!

GILBERT LAW AUDIO TAPES · FIVE YEAR · TAPE REPLACEMENT GUARANTEE

Call To Order: 1-800-787-8717 or Order On-Line at http://www.gilbertlaw.com

NO QUESTIONS

ASKED.

We stand behind our products... even if someone stands on them!

With the Law School Legends Series you get America's Greatest Law Professors on audio cassette — plus one of the best audio tape guarantees in the business! If you accidentally damage a Law School Legends tape within 5 years from the date of purchase, we'll replace it for free — **no questions asked!**

The Law School Legends Series
America's Greatest Law Professors on Audio Cassette

Available in Many Popular Titles. All Titles Fully Indexed for Quick Reference.

Administrative Law
Agency & Partnership
Antitrust Law
Bankruptcy
Civil Procedure
Commercial Paper
Conflict of Laws
Constitutional Law
Contracts
Copyright Law
Corporations
Criminal Law
Criminal Procedure
Evidence
Family Law
Federal Courts
Federal Income Tax
First Year Program
Future Interests
Law School Exam Writing
Prof. Responsibility
Real Property
Remedies
Sale & Lease of Goods
Secured Transactions
Securities Regulation
Torts
Wills & Trusts

Call To Order: 1-800-787-8717 or Order On-Line at http://www.gilbertlaw.com

SAVE

Hundreds Of HOURS On Your READING Assignments!

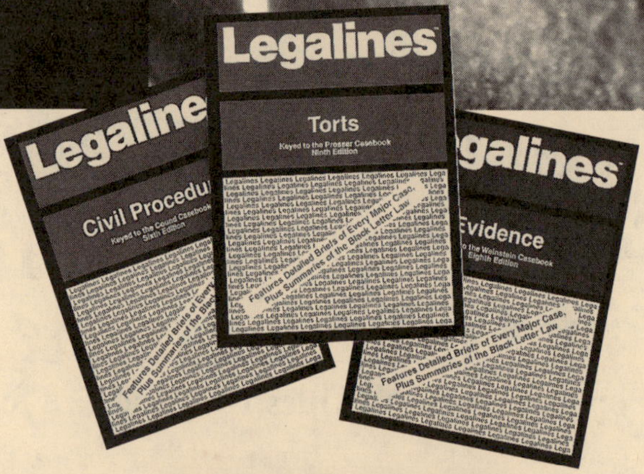

Legalines

Detailed Briefs of Every Major Case Plus Summaries Of The Black Letter Law!

Call To Order: 1-800-787-8717 or Order On-Line at http://www.gilbertlaw.com

Legalines

Legalines gives you authoritative, detailed briefs of every major case in your casebook. You get a clear explanation of the facts, the issues, the court's holding and reasoning, and any significant concurrences or dissents. Even more importantly, you get an authoritative explanation of the significance of each case, and how it relates to other cases in your casebook. And with Legalines' detailed table of contents and table of cases, you can quickly find any case or concept you're looking for. But your professor expects you to know more than just the cases. That's why Legalines gives you more than just case briefs. You get summaries of the black letter law, as well. That's crucial, because some of the most important information in your casebooks isn't in the cases at all … it's the black letter principles you're expected to glean from those cases. Legalines is the only series that gives you both case briefs and black letter review. With Legalines, you get everything you need to know—whether it's in a case or not!

Administrative Law

Keyed to the Breyer Casebook
ISBN: 0-15-900169-2 176 pages $19.95
Keyed to the Gellhorn Casebook
ISBN: 0-15-900170-6 186 pages $21.95
Keyed to the Schwartz Casebook
ISBN: 0-15-900171-4 145 pages $18.95

Antitrust

Keyed to the Areeda Casebook
ISBN: 0-15-900405-5 165 pages $19.95
Keyed to the Handler Casebook
ISBN: 0-15-900390-3 158 pages $18.95

Civil Procedure

Keyed to the Cound Casebook
ISBN: 0-15-900314-8 241 pages $21.95
Keyed to the Field Casebook
ISBN: 0-15-900415-2 310 pages $23.95
Keyed to the Hazard Casebook
ISBN: 0-15-900324-5 206 pages $21.95
Keyed to the Rosenberg Casebook
ISBN: 0-15-900052-1 284 pages $21.95
Keyed to the Yeazell Casebook
ISBN: 0-15-900241-9 206 pages $20.95

Commercial Law

Keyed to the Farnsworth Casebook
ISBN: 0-15-900176-5 126 pages $18.95

Conflict of Laws

Keyed to the Cramton Casebook
ISBN: 0-15-900331-8 113 pages $16.95
Keyed to the Reese (Rosenberg) Casebook
ISBN: 0-15-900057-2 247 pages $21.95

Constitutional Law

Keyed to the Brest Casebook
ISBN: 0-15-900338-5 172 pages $19.95
Keyed to the Cohen Casebook
ISBN: 0-15-900378-4 301 pages $22.95
Keyed to the Gunther Casebook
ISBN: 0-15-900467-5 367 pages $23.95
Keyed to the Lockhart Casebook
ISBN: 0-15-900242-7 322 pages $22.95

Constitutional Law (cont'd)

Keyed to the Rotunda Casebook
ISBN: 0-15-900363-6 258 pages $21.95
Keyed to the Stone Casebook
ISBN: 0-15-900236-2 281 pages $22.95

Contracts

Keyed to the Calamari Casebook
ISBN: 0-15-900065-3 234 pages $21.95
Keyed to the Dawson Casebook
ISBN: 0-15-900268-0 188 pages $21.95
Keyed to the Farnsworth Casebook
ISBN: 0-15-900332-6 219 pages $19.95
Keyed to the Fuller Casebook
ISBN: 0-15-900237-0 184 pages $19.95
Keyed to the Kessler Casebook
ISBN: 0-15-900070-X 312 pages $22.95
Keyed to the Murphy Casebook
ISBN: 0-15-900387-3 207 pages $21.95

Corporations

Keyed to the Cary Casebook
ISBN: 0-15-900172-2 383 pages $23.95
Keyed to the Choper Casebook
ISBN: 0-15-900173-0 219 pages $21.95
Keyed to the Hamilton Casebook
ISBN: 0-15-900313-X 214 pages $21.95
Keyed to the Vagts Casebook
ISBN: 0-15-900078-5 185 pages $18.95

Criminal Law

Keyed to the Boyce Casebook
ISBN: 0-15-900080-7 290 pages $21.95
Keyed to the Dix Casebook
ISBN: 0-15-900081-5 103 pages $15.95
Keyed to the Johnson Casebook
ISBN: 0-15-900175-7 149 pages $18.95
Keyed to the Kadish Casebook
ISBN: 0-15-900333-4 167 pages $18.95
Keyed to the La Fave Casebook
ISBN: 0-15-900084-X 202 pages $20.95

Criminal Procedure

Keyed to the Kamisar Casebook
ISBN: 0-15-900336-9 256 pages $21.95

Decedents' Estates & Trusts

Keyed to the Ritchie Casebook
ISBN: 0-15-900339-3 204 pages $21.95

Domestic Relations

Keyed to the Clark Casebook
ISBN: 0-15-900168-4 119 pages $16.95
Keyed to the Wadlington Casebook
ISBN: 0-15-900377-6 169 pages $18.95

Estate & Gift Taxation

Keyed to the Surrey Casebook
ISBN: 0-15-900093-9 100 pages $15.95

Evidence

Keyed to the Sutton Casebook
ISBN: 0-15-900096-3 271 pages $19.95
Keyed to the Waltz Casebook
ISBN: 0-15-900334-2 179 pages $19.95
Keyed to the Weinstein Casebook
ISBN: 0-15-900097-1 223 pages $20.95

Family Law

Keyed to the Areen Casebook
ISBN: 0-15-900263-X 262 pages $21.95

Federal Courts

Keyed to the McCormick Casebook
ISBN: 0-15-900101-3 195 pages $18.95

Income Tax

Keyed to the Freeland Casebook
ISBN: 0-15-900361-X 134 pages $18.95
Keyed to the Klein Casebook
ISBN: 0-15-900383-0 150 pages $18.95

Labor Law

Keyed to the Cox Casebook
ISBN: 0-15-900238-9 221 pages $18.95
Keyed to the Merrifield Casebook
ISBN: 0-15-900177-3 195 pages $20.95

Real Property

Keyed to the Browder Casebook
ISBN: 0-15-900110-2 277 pages $21.95
Keyed to the Casner Casebook
ISBN: 0-15-900111-0 261 pages $21.95
Keyed to the Cribbet Casebook
ISBN: 0-15-900239-7 328 pages $22.95
Keyed to the Dukeminier Casebook
ISBN: 0-15-900432-2 168 pages $18.95
Keyed to the Nelson Casebook
ISBN: 0-15-900228-1 288 pages $19.95
Keyed to the Rabin Casebook
ISBN: 0-15-900262-1 180 pages $18.95

Remedies

Keyed to the Re Casebook
ISBN: 0-15-900116-1 245 pages $22.95
Keyed to the York Casebook
ISBN: 0-15-900118-8 265 pages $21.95

Sales & Secured Transactions

Keyed to the Speidel Casebook
ISBN: 0-15-900166-8 202 pages $21.95

Securities Regulation

Keyed to the Jennings Casebook
ISBN: 0-15-900253-2 324 pages $22.95

Torts

Keyed to the Epstein Casebook
ISBN: 0-15-900335-0 193 pages $20.95
Keyed to the Franklin Casebook
ISBN: 0-15-900240-0 146 pages $18.95
Keyed to the Henderson Casebook
ISBN: 0-15-900174-9 162 pages $18.95
Keyed to the Keeton Casebook
ISBN: 0-15-900406-3 252 pages $21.95
Keyed to the Prosser Casebook
ISBN: 0-15-900301-6 334 pages $22.95

Wills, Trusts & Estates

Keyed to the Dukeminier Casebook
ISBN: 0-15-900337-7 145 pages $19.95

Call To Order: 1-800-787-8717 or Order On-Line at http://www.gilbertlaw.com

Dictionary *of* Legal Terms

Every Legal Term You'll Ever Need To Know... Just A Keystroke Away!

You're working away on your computer. Suddenly, you come across a legal term you don't understand. Are you going to have to waste precious time searching for your dictionary? Not anymore! The definition you're looking for will be on screen in the blink of an eye — with Gilbert's new On-Screen Dictionary of Legal Terms.

With Gilbert's on-screen dictionary, you simply highlight the word you need defined, or type it in. Then your on-screen dictionary takes over, giving you the definition you're looking for, right away. You get more than 3,500 legal terms and phrases — and that means every word you'll need throughout law school, and beyond!

But what if you come across an abbreviation you don't understand? Or one of those Latin words that show up so often in legal opinions, terms like pro tanto and res gestae? That's no problem with Gilbert's on-screen dictionary! You can instantly access the meaning of any Latin legal term (and French terms too!). You get all kinds of abbreviations, including periodical and governmental ones. You even get a complete listing of law school shorthand. No matter what kind of reference help you need, you'll find it in Gilbert's!

Features over 3,500 legal terms and phrases, law school shorthand, common abbreviations, Latin and French legal terms, periodical abbreviations, and governmental abbreviations.

Includes Free Pocket Size Law Dictionary!

ISBN: 0-15-900250-8
Macintosh $27.95

ISBN: 0-15-900249-4
Windows $27.95

Call To Order: 1-800-787-8717 or Order On-Line at http://www.gilbertlaw.com

100% Comprehensive, 100% Authoritative, 100% of What You Need

CASEBRIEFS

FOR WINDOWS

Detailed Briefs Of Every Major Case— At Your Fingertips!

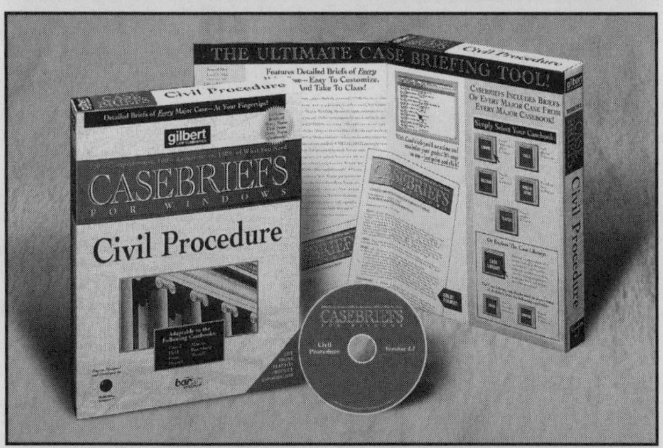

Casebriefs Interactive Software For Windows

As a law student you can't afford to waste a minute. That's why you need Casebriefs Software. With Casebriefs you simply click on the name of the case you're looking for, and you instantly have an expert brief of it at your fingertips! The facts. The issue. The holding. The rationale. Expert commentary. You'll get everything you need, whether you're preparing for class or studying for your final exam!

When you use Casebriefs, you can focus solely on the cases covered in your casebook, or you can use the Case Library, which includes briefs of all of the major cases from every major casebook. The Case Library is ideal for researching cases for writing assignments, moot court briefs, law review and other periodicals.

With Casebriefs, searching for cases is a breeze. You can search by topic. You can search alphabetically. You can search the cases in the order in which they appear in your casebook. You can even enter the date you'll cover different cases in class, and sort them by those dates. No matter how you want to look for a case, Casebriefs will help you find it instantly!

For each brief, you can add your own notes, or leave it "as is." Whether you customize the briefs or not, you can print them out and take them to class with you. You can even configure Casebriefs to access Lexis/Nexis and Westlaw directly from the Casebriefs screen (with Lexis/Nexis or Westlaw software and account). Whether you want to compare your own briefs to expert briefs, fill in gaps in your class notes, or research cases for your legal writing class, moot court, law review or other periodicals— Casebriefs is the source you'll turn to, over and over again!

Administrative Law
Includes briefs of all of the major cases from the Breyer, Gellhorn and Schwartz casebooks, many of the major cases from the Bonfield and Mashaw casebooks, plus a Case Library.
ISBN# 0-15-900190-0 $27.95

Antitrust
Includes briefs of all of the major cases from the Areeda and Handler casebooks, many of the major cases from the Sullivan casebook, plus a Case Library.
ISBN# 0-15-900400-4 $27.95

Civil Procedure
Includes briefs of all of the major cases from the Cound, Field, Hazard, Rosenberg and Yeazell casebooks, many of the major cases from the Marcus and Levin casebooks, plus a Case Library.
ISBN# 0-15-900191-9 $27.95

Commercial Law
Includes briefs of all of the major cases from the Farnsworth casebook, plus a Case Library.
ISBN# 0-15-900407-1 $27.95

Conflict Of Laws
Includes briefs of all of the major cases from the Cramton and Reese casebooks, many of the major cases from the Brilmayer casebook, plus a Case Library.
ISBN# 0-15-900192-7 $27.95

Constitutional Law
Includes briefs of all of the major cases from the Brest, Cohen, Gunther, Lockhart, Rotunda and Stone casebooks, plus a Case Library.
ISBN# 0-15-900193-5 $27.95

Contracts
Includes briefs of all of the major cases from the Calamari, Dawson, Farnsworth, Fuller, Kessler and Murphy casebooks, many of the major cases from the Burton, Crandall, Hamilton, Knapp, and Rosett casebooks, plus a Case Library.
ISBN# 0-15-900194-3 $27.95

Corporations
Includes briefs of all of the major cases from the Cary, Choper, Hamilton and Vagts casebooks, many of the major cases from the O'Kelley and Solomon casebooks, plus a Case Library.
ISBN# 0-15-900195-1 $27.95

Criminal Law
Includes briefs of all of the major cases from the Boyce, Dix, Johnson, Kadish and La Fave casebooks, many of the major cases from the Dressler, Johnson, Kaplan, Moenssens and Weinreb casebooks, plus a Case Library.
ISBN# 0-15-900196-X $27.95

Criminal Procedure
Includes briefs of all of the major cases from the Kamisar casebook, many of the major cases from the Allen, Haddad and Saltzburg casebooks, plus a Case Library.
ISBN# 0-15-900197-8 $27.95

Domestic Relations
Includes briefs of all of the major cases from the Clark and Wadlington casebooks, plus a Case Library.
ISBN# 0-15-900408-X $27.95

Estate & Gift Taxes
Includes briefs of all of the major cases from the Surrey casebook, plus a Case Library.
ISBN# 0-15-900396-2 $27.95

Evidence
Includes briefs of all of the major cases from the Sutton, Waltz, and Weinstein casebooks, many of the major cases from the Strong and Mueller casebooks, plus a Case Library.
ISBN# 0-15-900198-6 $27.95

Family Law
Includes briefs of all of the major cases from the Areen casebook, many of the major cases from the Clark, Ellman, Krause and Wadlington casebooks, plus a Case Library.
ISBN# 0-15-900199-4 $27.95

Federal Courts
Includes briefs of all of the major cases from the McCormick casebook, many of the major cases from the Bator, Currie, Low and Redish casebooks, plus a Case Library.
ISBN# 0-15-900409-8 $27.95

Income Tax
Includes briefs of all of the major cases from the Freeland and Klein casebooks, many of the major cases from the Burke and Graetz casebooks, plus a Case Library.
ISBN# 0-15-900200-1 $27.95

Labor Law
Includes briefs of all of the major cases from the Cox and Merrifield casebooks, many of the major cases from the Harper, Leslie and Meltzer casebooks, plus a Case Library.
ISBN# 0-15-900410-1 $27.95

Property
Includes briefs of all of the major cases from the Casner, Cribbet, Dukeminier and Rabin casebooks, many of the major cases from the Donahue, Johnson, Kurtz, and Singer casebooks, plus a Case Library.
ISBN# 0-15-900201-X $27.95

Remedies
Includes briefs of all of the major cases from the Re and York casebooks, many of the major cases from the Leavell and Shoben casebooks, plus a Case Library.
ISBN# 0-15-900202-8 $27.95

Securities Regulation
Includes briefs of all of the major cases from the Jennings casebook, many of the major cases from the Cox casebook, plus a Case Library.
ISBN# 0-15-900411-X $27.95

Torts
Includes briefs of all of the major cases from the Epstein, Franklin, Henderson, Keeton and Prosser casebooks, many of the major cases from the Christie, Dobbs and Shulman casebooks, plus a Case Library.
ISBN# 0-15-900203-6 $27.95

Wills, Trusts & Estates
Includes briefs of all of the major cases from the Dukeminier casebook, many of the major cases from the Wagoner casebook, plus a Case Library.
ISBN# 0-15-900204-4 $27.95

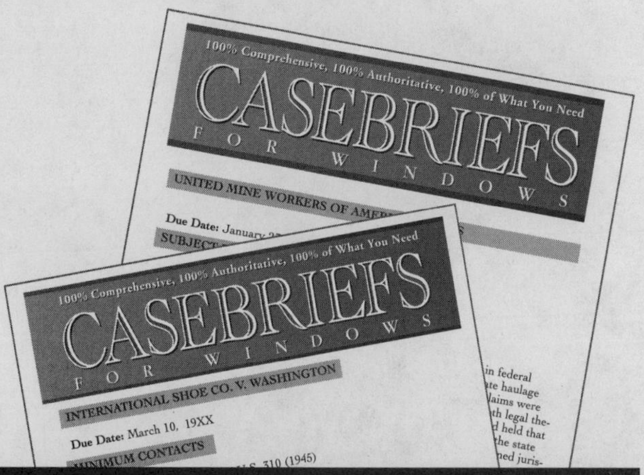

Call To Order: 1-800-787-8717 or Order On-Line at http://www.gilbertlaw.com

Check us out

www.gilbertlaw.com

**America's Best-Selling
Legal Employment Guides!**

gilbert LAW SUMMARIES

**Gilbert, Legalines, Casebriefs,
Law School Legends plus Much More!**

CASEBRIEFS FOR WINDOWS

**Detailed Briefs of Every Major
Case — Easy to Customize,
Print and Take to Class!**

**E-mail the Job Goddess with Your
Job Search Questions!**

BuckABrief.com

**Expert briefs at your fingertips.
All for only a buck a brief!**

Call To Order: 1-800-787-8717 or Order On-Line at http://www.gilbertlaw.com

on the Internet!

Order On-Line!

www.gilbertlaw.com

Pre-Law Center
Learn what law school is really like including what to expect on exams. Order your free 32-page color catalog and a free 88-page sample of Gilbert Law Summaries for Civil Procedure — the most feared first year course!

Bookstore
Review detailed information on over 200 of America's most popular legal study aids — Gilbert Law Summaries, Legalines, Casebriefs, Law School Legends audio tapes and much more. Order on-line!

gilbert LAW SUMMARIES

BuckABrief.com
As a law student, you have every minute of your day scheduled for maximum efficiency. But, somehow, you still find yourself up late at night, sitting in front of your computer, trying to prepare for class. That's why you'll love BuckABrief.com.

BuckABrief.com

With BuckABrief.com you simply click on the name of the case you're looking for, and you instantly have an expert brief of it at your fingertips! You'll find the facts, the issue, the holding, and the rationale, plus expert commentary for each and every case. And all for only a buck a brief! Buy a brief and instantly print it out at your computer. It's just that easy. You'll get everything you need, any time, day or night!

Links to Law Sites
Links to hundreds of law-related sites on the web, including:

- Legal Publications
- Legal Research
- Legal Employment
- International Law
- Department of Justice
- Legal Associations

Employment Center
E-mail the Job Goddess with your job search questions, and download a free copy of *The Myths of Legal Job Searches: The 9 Biggest Mistakes Law Students Make.* View content from some of America's best selling legal employment guides, including *Guerrilla Tactics For Getting The Legal Job Of Your Dreams* and *The National Directory of Legal Employers.*

Wanted! Student Marketing Reps
Become a campus representative and earn hundreds of dollars of free product from Gilbert Law Summaries, Legalines, Casebriefs and more! Join our national marketing program and help promote America's most popular legal study aids at your law school!

1st Year Survival Manual
A must-read for 1L's! Learn how to prepare for class, how to handle class discussions, and the keys to successful exam performance — plus much more!

Taking the Bar Exam?
Learn how to make the transition from law school exams to the bar exam — including what to expect on the MBE, MPT, MPRE, MEE and state essay exams.

Welcome Center
Whether you're about to enter law school or you're already under way, we've created this site to help you succeed!

Order Products On-line!
Fast, easy and secure on-line ordering is now available 24 hours per day, 7 days per week!

Call To Order: 1-800-787-8717 or Order On-Line at http://www.gilbertlaw.com

Employment Guides

A collection of best selling titles that help you identify and reach your career goals.

Guerrilla Tactics for Getting the Legal Job of Your Dreams

Kimm Alayne Walton, J.D.

Whether you're looking for a summer clerkship or your first permanent job after school, this revolutionary book is the key to getting the job of your dreams!

Guerrilla Tactics for Getting the Legal Job of Your Dreams leads you step-by-step through everything you need to do to nail down that perfect job! You'll learn hundreds of simple-to-use strategies that will get you exactly where you want to go. You'll Learn:

- The seven magic opening words in cover letters that ensure you'll get a response.
- The secret to successful interviews every time.
- Killer answers to the toughest interview questions they'll ever ask you.
- Plus Much More!

Guerrilla Tactics features the best strategies from the country's most innovative law school career advisors. The strategies in *Guerrilla Tactics* are so powerful that it even comes with a guarantee: Follow the advice in the book, and within one year of graduation you'll have the job of your dreams … or your money back!

Pick up a copy of *Guerrilla Tactics* today … you'll be on your way to the job of your dreams!

ISBN: 0-15-900317-2 $24.95

Proceed With Caution: A Diary Of The First Year At One Of America's Largest, Most Prestigious Law Firms

William R. Keates

Prestige. Famous clients. High-profile cases. Not to mention a starting salary approaching six figures.

In *Proceed With Caution*, the author takes you behind the scenes, to show you what it's really like to be a junior associate at a huge law firm. After graduating from an Ivy League law school, he took a job as an associate with one of New York's blue-chip law firms.

He also did something not many people do. He kept a diary, where he spelled out his day-to-day life at the firm in graphic detail.

Proceed With Caution excerpts the diary, from his first day at the firm to the day he quit. From the splashy benefits, to the nitty-gritty on the work junior associates do, to the grind of long and unpredictable hours, to the stress that eventually made him leave the firm — he tells story after story that will make you feel as though you're living the life of a new associate.

Whether you're considering a career with a large firm, or you're just curious about what life at the top firms is all about — *Proceed With Caution* is a must read!

ISBN: 0-15-900181-1 $17.95

The Official Guide To Legal Specialties

National Association for Law Placement

With *The Official Guide To Legal Specialties* you'll get a behind the scenes glimpse at dozens of legal specialties. Not just lists of what to expect, real life stories from top practitioners in each field. You'll learn exactly what it's like to be in some of America's most desirable professions. You'll get expert advice on what it takes to get a job in each field. How much you'll earn and what the day-to-day life is really like, the challenges you'll face, and the benefits you'll enjoy. With *The Official Guide To Legal Specialties* you'll have a wealth of information at your fingertips!

Includes the following specialties:

Banking	Intellectual Property
Communications	International
Corporate	Labor/Employment
Criminal	Litigation
Entertainment	Public Interest
Environmental	Securities
Government Practice	Sports
Health Care	Tax
Immigration	Trusts & Estates

ISBN: 0-15-900391-1 $19.95

Beyond L.A. Law: Inspiring Stories of People Who've Done Fascinating Things With A Law Degree

National Association for Law Placement

Anyone who watches television knows that being a lawyer means working your way up through a law firm — right?

Wrong!

Beyond L.A. Law gives you a fascinating glimpse into the lives of people who've broken the "lawyer" mold. They come from a variety of backgrounds — some had prior careers, others went straight through college and law school, and yet others have overcome poverty and physical handicaps. They got their degrees from all different kinds of law schools, all over the country. But they have one thing in common: they've all pursued their own, unique vision.

As you read their stories, you'll see how they beat the odds to succeed. You'll learn career tips and strategies that work, from people who've put them to the test. And you'll find fascinating insights that you can apply to your own dream, whether it's a career in law or anything else!

From Representing Baseball In Australia. To International Finance. To Children's Advocacy. To Directing a Nonprofit Organization. To Entrepreneur.

If You Think Getting A Law Degree Means Joining A Traditional Law Firm — Think Again!

ISBN: 0-15-900182-X $17.95

America's Greatest Places To Work With A Law Degree

Kimm Alayne Walton, J.D.

"Where do your happiest graduates work?" That's the question that author Kimm Alayne Walton asked of law school administrators around the country. Their responses revealed the hundreds of wonderful employers profiled in *America's Greatest Places To Work With A Law Degree.*

In this remarkable book, you'll get to know an incredible variety of great places to work, including:

- Glamorous sports and entertainment employers — the jobs that sound as though they would be great, and they are!
- The 250 best law firms to work for between 20 and 600 attorneys.
- Companies where law school graduates love to work and not just as in-house counsel.
- Wonderful public interest employers – the "white knight" jobs that are so incredibly satisfying.
- Court-related positions, where lawyers entertain fascinating issues, tremendous variety, and an enjoyable lifestyle.
- Outstanding government jobs, at the federal, state, and local level.

Beyond learning about incredible employers, you'll discover:

- The ten traits that define a wonderful place to work … the sometimes surprising qualities that outstanding employers share.
- How to handle law school debt, when your dream job pays less than you think you need to make.
- How to find — and get! — great jobs at firms with fewer than 20 attorneys.

And no matter where you work, you'll learn expert tips for making the most of your job. You'll learn the specific strategies that distinguish people headed for the top … how to position yourself for the most interesting, high-profile work … how to handle difficult personalities … how to negotiate for more money … and what to do now to help you get your next great job!

ISBN: 0-15-900180-3 $24.95

About The Author

Kimm Alayne Walton is the author of numerous books and articles including two national best seller's — *America's Greatest Places To Work With A Law Degree* and *Guerrilla Tactics For Getting The Legal Job Of Your Dreams.* She is a renowned motivational speaker, lecturing at law schools and bar associations nationwide, and in her spare time, she has taken up travel writing, which has taken her swimming with crocodiles in Kakadu, and scuba diving with sharks on the Great Barrier Reef.

E-mail the Job Goddess with your own legal job search questions!

Visit www.gilbertlaw.com for details.

Call To Order: 1-800-787-8717 or Order On-Line at http://www.gilbertlaw.com

Employment Guides

A collection of best selling titles that help you identify and reach your career goals.

The National Directory Of Legal Employers

National Association for Law Placement

The National Directory of Legal Employers brings you a universe of vital information about 1,000 of the nation's top legal employers— *in one convenient volume!*

It includes:

- Over 22,000 job openings.
- The names, addresses and phone numbers of hiring partners.
- Listings of firms by state, size, kind and practice area.
- What starting salaries are for full time, part time, and summer associates, plus a detailed description of firm benefits.
- The number of employees by gender and race, as well as the number of employees with disabilities.
- A detailed narrative of each firm, plus much more!

The National Directory Of Legal Employers has been the best kept secret of top legal career search professionals for over a decade. Now, for the first time, it is available in a format specifically designed for law students and new graduates.

Pick up your copy of the Directory today!

ISBN: 0-15-900434-9 $39.95

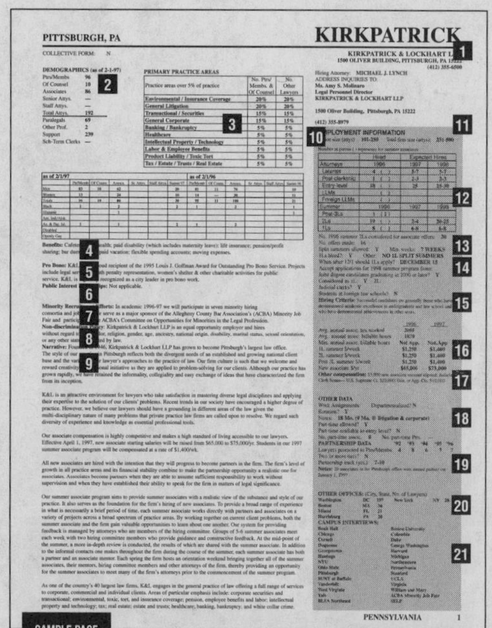

SAMPLE PAGE

Everything You Need To Know About 1,000 Of the Nation's Top Legal Employers— Fully Indexed For Quick Reference!

Including:

Law Firms and Corporations
Listed Alphabetically

Law Firms and Corporations
Listed by State

Public Interest Organizations and Government Agencies
Listed Alphabetically

Public Interest Organizations and Government Agencies
Listed by State

All Employers
Listed By Practice Area

All Employers
Listed By Office Size

Company Information

1. *Name, Address, and Phone Number Of Hiring Partner*
2. *Demographics*
3. *Primary Practice Areas*
4. *Benefits*
5. *Pro Bono*
6. *Public Interest Fellowships*
7. *Minority Recruitment Efforts*
8. *Non-Discrimination Policy*
9. *Narrative*

Employment Information

10. *Office Size*
11. *Total Firm Size*
12. *Job Opportunities*
13. *Summer Associate Information*
14. *Application Timeline For Summer Associates*
15. *Hiring Criteria For All Job Openings*
16. *Salary Information*
17. *Other Compensation*
18. *Other Data*
19. *Partnership Data*
20. *Other Offices*
21. *Campus Interviews*

The Best Of The Job Goddess

Kimm Alayne Walton, J.D.

In her popular **Dear Job Goddess** column, legal job-search expert Kimm Alayne Walton provides the answers to even the most difficult job search dilemmas facing law students and law school graduates. Relying on career experts from around the country, the Job Goddess provides wise and witty advice for every obstacle that stands between you and your dream job!

ISBN: 0-15-900393-8 $14.95

SAMPLE COLUMN

Business Card Resumes: Good Idea, Or Not?

Dear Job Goddess,

One of my friends showed me something called a "business card resume." What he did was to have these business cards printed up, with his name and phone number on one side, and highlights from his resume on the other side. He said a bunch of people are doing this, so that when they meet potential employers they hand over these cards. Should I bother getting some for myself?

Curious in Chicago

Dear Curious,

Sigh, You know, Curious, that the Job Goddess takes a fairly dim view of resumes as a job-finding tool, even in their full-blown bond-papered, engraved 8-1/2x11" incarnation. And here you ask about a business card resume, two steps further down the resume food chain. So, no, you *shouldn't* bother with business card resumes. Here's why.

Think for a moment, Curious, about the kind of circumstance in which you'd be tempted to whip out one of these incredible shrinking resumes. You're at a social gathering. You happen to meet Will Winken, of the law firm Winken, Blinken, and Nod, and it becomes clear fairly quickly that Will is a) friendly, and b) a potential employer. The surest way to turn this chance encounter into a job is to use it as the basis for future contact. As Carolyn Bregman, Career Services Director at Emory Law School, points out, "Follow up with a phone call or note, mentioning something Winken said to you." You can say that you'd like to follow up on whatever it is he said, or that you've since read more about him and found that he's an expert on phlegm reclamation law and how that's a topic that's always fascinated you, and invite him for coffee at his convenience so you can learn more about it. What have you done? *You've taken a social encounter and turned it into a potential job opportunity.* And that makes the Job Goddess very proud.

But what happens if you, instead, whip out your business card resume, and say, "Gee, Mr. Winken, nice meeting you. Here's my business card resume, in case you ever need anybody like me." *Now* what have you done? You have, with one simple gesture, wiped out any excuse to follow up! Instead of having a phone call or a note from you that is personalized to Winken, you've got a piddling little standardized card with your vital statistics on it. Ugh. I know you're much more memorable, Curious, than anything you could possibly fit on the back of a business card.

So there you have it, Curious. Save the money you'll spend on a business card resume, and spend it later, when you have a *real* business card to print, reading, "Curious, Esq. Winken, Blinken, and Nod, Attorneys at Law."

Yours Eternally,

The Job Goddess

Call To Order: 1-800-787-8717 or Order On-Line at http://www.gilbertlaw.com

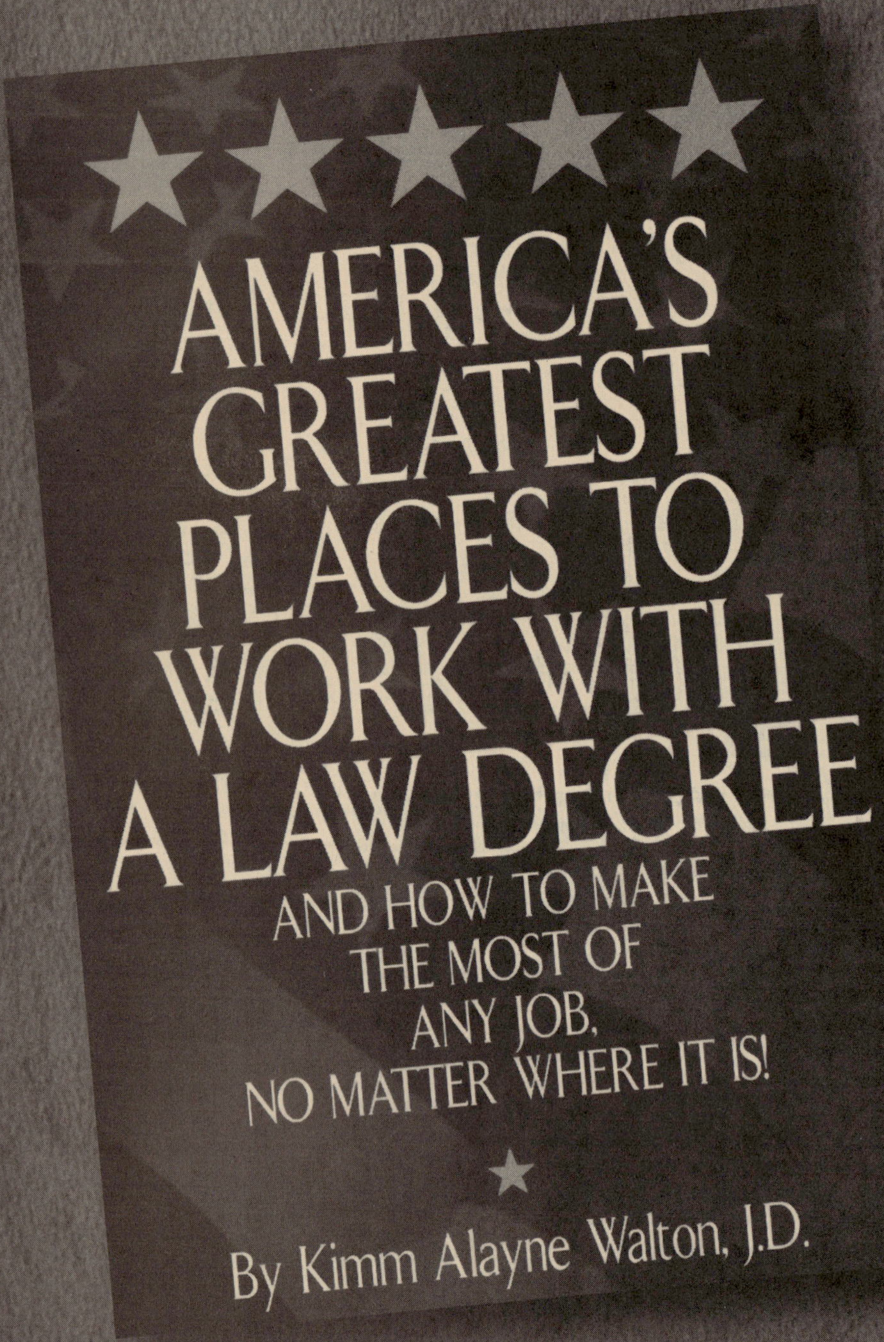

Features Hundreds Of Traditional and Non-Traditional Employers

Discover The Places Where Law School Graduates Love To Work!

Available At Your Law School Bookstore
Order Toll-Free: 1-800-787-8717
Order Online: www.gilbertlaw.com